Praise for *The Browser's Book of Beginnings*

"A mighty oak of a book . . . sparkling essays. Mr. Panati is fearless, far-reaching, formidable, and, when it pleases him, frivolous."
    —*The New Yorker*

"I came away from the book bubbling with new information . . . intoxicated by the influx of so much information. You'll find charming its graceful little essays on everything from the origin of the universe to the invention of the rubber eraser."
    —Christopher Lehmann-Haupt, *The New York Times*

"Entertains, startles and without question will enlighten you. A treasure-house for browsers. . . . It is hard to believe that any one man can explain the beginning of everything, but Panati makes a praiseworthy stab at it."
    —*John Barkham Review*

"An imaginative reference book . . . hundreds of nicely written paragraphs about the origins of everything from the abacus (sixth century B.C. China) to the YMCA (London, 1885)."
    —*People* magazine

"The thing is fun . . . a weapon for stumping supercilious experts."
    —*The Boston Globe*

"An intriguing and informative delight."
    —*Booklist*

"Anyone who doesn't object to being called a 'know-it-all' will thoroughly love this book. Panati provides information with brevity and style. . . . A superb source book."
    —*Eagle Times*

"Everything you ever wanted to know and more."
    —Robin Leach, producer, *The Lifestyles of the Rich & Famous*

"The last word on the first of everything."
    —*Newsday*

"It's the book you would do well to give to any youngster or oldster—it's THE book for everyone. The book is one you have to guard because it seems worth stealing—someone stole my copy."
    —*Sid Archer's World, Chicago*

PENGUIN BOOKS

THE BROWSER'S BOOK OF BEGINNINGS

Charles Panati, a former physicist and for six years a science editor for *Newsweek*, is the author of many nonfiction and fiction books, including three previous works about origins: *Sacred Origins of Profound Things* (1996), *Extraordinary Origins of Everyday Things* (1987), and *Sexy Origins and Intimate Things* (1998). He has made a career out of exploring the origins of things. Researching his own family, he learned that he is not a "Panati" by blood, but through his father's adoption. His obsession with getting to the roots of things gave him a second family: the Hudsons of Kilbaha, County Kerry, Ireland.

The Browser's Book of Beginnings

Origins of Everything
Under, and Including, the Sun

Charles Panati

PENGUIN BOOKS

PENGUIN BOOKS
Published by the Penguin Group
Penguin Putnam Inc., 375 Hudson Street,
New York, New York 10014, U.S.A.
Penguin Books Ltd, 27 Wrights Lane,
London W8 5TZ, England
Penguin Books Australia Ltd, Ringwood,
Victoria, Australia
Penguin Books Canada Ltd, 10 Alcorn Avenue,
Toronto, Ontario, Canada M4V 3B2
Penguin Books (N.Z.) Ltd, 182–190 Wairau Road,
Auckland 10, New Zealand
Penguin India, 210 Chiranjiv Tower, 43 Nehru Place,
New Delhi 11009, India

Penguin Books Ltd, Registered Offices:
Harmondsworth, Middlesex, England

First published in the United States of America
by Houghton Mifflin Company 1984
Published in Penguin Books 1998

1 2 3 4 5 6 7 8 9 10

THE LIBRARY OF CONGRESS HAS CATALOGUED
THE HOUGHTON MIFFLIN EDITION AS FOLLOWS:
Panati, Charles. date
The browser's book of beginnings.
Includes bibliographical references and index.
1. Encyclopedias and dictionaries.   I. Title.
II. Title: Origins of almost everything under, and including, the sun.
ISBN 0 14 02.7694 7 (Penguin)
AG6.P36   1984
031   83–26384

Printed in the United States of America

With love to
Janet, Donna, and Karen,
who survived, unscathed,
"Murder in the Dark"
And for Chris and Sam
— and Buddy

Acknowledgments

I wish to thank Michael Globetti for months of diligent editorial work. Often handling primary source material of a technical nature, he performed each assigned task quickly and efficiently. Without his help, this book would have taken an additional year to complete.

I also wish to thank D. Stuart Conger, Director of Saskatchewan NewStart, Canada, for permission to use material from his monograph, "Social Inventions," published by Saskatchewan NewStart, Prince Albert, Canada. It is a large, scholarly report that examines the origins of numerous educational, governmental, social, and economic organizations and practices.

CONTENTS

CONTENTS

The Origin of This Book

One winter morning several years back, across a table in a café in downtown Manhattan, a woman friend suddenly dropped off in the middle of criticizing a play she had seen the night before and, peering quizzically at me above a golden crescent-shaped roll, said, "Do you know where this comes from?"

"Back there," I answered sleepily, pointing to the bakery at the rear of the eatery. "*Wrong?* Oh, I see. Where does it *come* from? Why, France." Of course I knew, since *croissant* was the French word for "crescent." Her negative nod and gleefully triumphant smile told me, compulsive compiler of facts, that I'd missed this bit of trivia.

"From Austria," she informed me.

It seems the tasty treats were designed by a Viennese baker in 1863 to commemorate the city's victorious stand against the Turks, whose national flag bears a crescent; for decades the proud inhabitants of Vienna took sweet delight in symbolically devouring their vanquished enemy.

Later that day my turn came.

As my friend reached into a gold paper bag for a piece of chocolate, *I* popped a question on the origin of that particular confection, a consuming passion of hers. She knew of course that I was looking for an answer that went beyond Brazil and cocoa beans, and she hadn't the foggiest.

The Aztecs, I informed her, concocted a ceremonial chocolate brew named "bitter water," and Columbus introduced the drink, adding copious amounts of sugar, to the Spanish court, where it was an immediate sensation. Having recently read an article on the subject, I decided to impress her with the entire story. King Ferdinand quickly became a chocolate addict and zealously guarded his secret drink for a full century, before word of it reached Italy and France. So prized, in fact, was the cocoa powder–water–sugar concoction that it was part of the dowry for the marriage of the Spanish princess Maria Theresa to King Louis XIV in 1660.

"And these?" She'd bitten into another butter cream.

Solid chocolate was a serendiptous discovery, I told her, not made until the mid-19th century.

Throughout the remainder of that winter day, as we browsed through shops and, later, had dinner, we continued to play the "origins" game, more often than not with no idea of where most of the objects we encountered came from. Such simple (and un-answered) inquiries that night bounced around in my head, and as I drifted to sleep, I promised myself that I'd research some of the topics that week.

Compulsive about any task I start, over the next year or so I collected the origins of things as diverse as soap (600 B.C.; Phoen-icia), loaded dice (3500 B.C.; Egypt) and the materials of my trade: typewriter, paper, pens, and pencils. (The last appeared in the 16th century; the eraser tip was the invention in 1858 of a Philadel-phian named Hyman Lipman.) There was no pattern to my re-search then.

The eventual realization that I had growing before me the origins of almost everything under, and including, the sun sparked the idea for a book, and the result is before you.

This vast body of material excited me, and I found that, to my good fortune, it also excited my publisher. So, with another year's full-time work, researching things more systematically — like the origins of some languages, like English and Yiddish, as well as the origins of such ethnic slurs as "wop," "spick," and "gringo" — my collecting passion turned into a publishing event.

A few words about the structure of the book and its contents.

The book attempts (immodestly perhaps) to cover a broad range of subjects, and in chronological order whenever possible. It seemed fitting to begin at the beginning, 14.5 billion years ago, with the origin of the universe, and progress through the evolution of galaxies and our solar system, to the emergence of various species of life on the planet, from bacteria to bony fish to bees.

In the discussion of the appearance of the first true human being (*Homo habilis,* 2 million years ago in Africa and Asia), the text focuses on such things as the discovery of fire (*Homo erectus,* 1.5 million years ago), the first intimations of spirituality (Neanderthals, 50,000 years ago), and the origin of "continuous sexuality" in women — for at one time all female primates, including humans, had very well-defined, and limited, periods of heat, or estrus, during which they would allow males to have sex with them.

Commencing with the dawn of cuneiform script, the book progresses through the Phoenicians' development of the alphabet to the origin of shorthand (pre–400 B.C.; Greece. Pitman and Gregg shorthand were developed in England in 1837 and 1885 respectively) through the birth of books, the invention of printing, movable type and the printing press, and the appearance of newspapers, comic strips, and magazines, including a British publisher's bold step in issuing the first woman's magazine, *Ladies' Mercury,* devoted exclusively to "the fairer sex" — a move that soon spawned an entire new industry.

Several chapters cover the human fascination for foods and beverages. Beginning with an early dietary staple, milk (6000 B.C., first regularly drunk by nomads who traveled with herds of milk-giving animals), the origins progress from the first ice cream (a frozen mixture of milk and soft rice paste, concocted in China in 2000 B.C.) to the serendiptous discoveries of wine and beer, and of coffee in A.D. 850 by an observant Ethiopian goatherder who noticed the excessively frolicsome nature of his flock after the goats had nibbled on the red berries of a leafy green plant.

The book continues with separate chapters on the origins of the world's favorite pets, of the oldest religions, of various forms of music — from opera (1597; Florence) to electronic synthesizers (1895; United States) — and of numerous communications and entertainment devices, from FM radio to colored television, from stereo sound to movies.

The origins of transportation vehicles alone occupy three separate chapters: Land, Sea, and Air.

Considering the inexhaustible nature of the subject (virtually everything in creation), I had to make many decisions about what to include and what to omit. Often the choices were hard, for the origins of most things are truly fascinating. The first bagpipes, for example (1st century A.D.; Asia), were made from the gutted and scraped body of sheep. The bag was the entire hide, with the pipes fitted into a wooden plug in the animal's neck, and the drones emerging from plugs in the forelegs. The finished product was not all that dissimilar to the animal whose body was the bag.

In setting my criteria, I attempted to keep the scope of the book as broad as possible, opting for many different subjects described briefly (without being trivial, I hope), rather than fewer subjects treated in greater depth.

Other categories held personal fascination for me, such as music long a passion of mine. Still other categories entered the text because friends, who knew I was researching the book, asked me to include topics of interest to them. My sister, a painter and college art teacher, felt the book would be incomplete without the origin of painting, so I included it, along with the origins of varnish, enamel, lacquer, and the first colored crayons.

A psychiatrist I know requested that I include the origin of his medical specialty. I did gladly, since it enabled me to write about the horrific practice of trephining, the hammering of a hole in an insane person's skull — supposedly to vent the evil spirits causing the madness — a practice that continued, shockingly, into the 1950s in almost as crude a form as when it began.

A fellow writer, an expert on weapons, felt the book must contain at least one chapter on firearms and warfare; a former college classmate, now a chemist, argued that the origins of chemistry, from the days of alchemy to the heyday-discoveries of wonder drugs, would make fascinating reading; a model couldn't see how I could overlook the origins of her profession; my editor thought the section on fruits should be expanded to include vegetables and nuts. And why, asked a cheese-addicted friend, wasn't I writing a chapter on the colorful histories of Brie, Camembert, Doux de Montagne, and the world's many other cheeses? The fact is that every person who knew I was writing the book, or who later saw the manuscript, had his or her favorite topic that I had — woefully, they felt — omitted.

Well, despite the book's subtitle, not everything under the sun, of course, could be included. While reading these 600 pages you will not, for instance, find the origins of the toothbrush (1489; China), Band-Aids (1920; Johnson & Johnson), or Teflon (1938; Du Pont). On the other hand, you will find the origins of many wonder drugs, as well as the origins of firearms and explosives and the mention of vegetables. I tried to be as accommodating as possible to friends.

I hope that there are, in all, enough curious and informative origins here to edify, to entertain, and perhaps to enable you to recoup the cost of this book by winning bets with friends on, say, the name of the French king who, when presented by his royal gardener with the first pineapple grown in his country, snatched up, with characteristic greed and impatience, the yet unpeeled fruit and bit vigorously into it, severely lacerating his lips on its prickly eyes.

Or the name of the American inventor who, but for a few hours, almost beat the Scots Alexander Graham Bell to the invention of the telephone.

Or the popular modern sport that the Cherokee Indians named "little brother of war," because its bloody ferocity was considered excellent preparation for battle.

Just one more; an easy one: the thoroughly American sport that was invented on December 1, 1891, by the physical education instructor at the International Young Men's Christian Association Training School, now Springfield College, in Springfield, Massachusetts.

Or, if you prefer, who was man's first "best friend," the dog or cat, and why?

Or what country developed the first antibiotic in 500 B.C., made from moldy curd of soy beans and used for treating carbuncles, boils, and infections?

Or the civilization that established the first school 5000 years ago, which was surprisingly like those of today, with a "professor," his assistants, called "big brothers," and a disciplinarian known as "man in charge of whip," who beat children who did not turn in homework.

Or the sex fiend who . . . perhaps I should let you read the book.

Happy Browsing,
Charles Panati
New York City

Panati's
Browser's Book
of Beginnings

1

Creation: Stars to Shining Sea

The Universe, 14.5 Billion Years Ago

The universe — the only one we have evidence of, though it may have existed in previous incarnations and may one day die and be reborn — was created 14.5 billion years ago, when a superdense ball of primordial matter, drifting through a black, formless void, suddenly exploded. This was the "big bang."

The scientific reason for that shattering cataclysm remains a mystery. The searing heat of those first few moments of creation forever evaporated the fingerprints of the Prime Mover — whether they were the familiar forces of physics or a spiritual force in the form of a personal God.

We do know that in the ensuing chaos matter vigorously fought antimatter for eternal dominance. When particles of opposite dispositions approached each other too closely, both were instantaneously annihilated, producing radiant bursts of pure energy. The battle for what would become the essence of galaxies, stars, and of life itself raged on for millions of years.

The victor, of course, was matter. The legions of antimatter, what few survived, were banished to remote islands in space, and others were imprisoned, it's believed, in gravitational traps at the centers of numerous present-day galaxies, including our Milky Way.

As the universe expanded, rushing outward to fill the void, it also began to cool. By the time of its one-billionth birthday, it was sufficiently cool to start condensing into **galaxies,** swirling masses of primal mist.

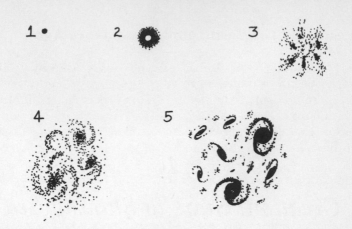

Creation. The universe begins with the "big bang," the explosion that created the particles from which everything would form (1). The universe, 10^{-35} of a second later, has grown to the size of a baseball (2). Ten thousand years later the universe becomes cool enough for stable atoms to form (3). A hundred million years later the universe is a sea of hydrogen and helium gas from which the protogalaxies begin to emerge (4). One billion years later galaxies are taking shape (5).

Matter, now having few foes, was under rule of the god gravity, which gathered together inside each galaxy gases and dust, and fashioned **stars.** Some blazed in isolation, others in great constellations that human beings eons later on a planet that had yet to be formed would imagine resembled dippers, bears, horses, and crabs.

Stars continued to form as the universe aged, cooled, and further expanded. Gravity, in its all-pervasive reach, eventually served as a brake to slow the expansion, limiting physical reality to a bubblelike shell whose dimensions one day would be daringly estimated by a great physicist, Albert Einstein.

Populated now with clusters of matter, the universe was a few billion years old. There were countless galaxies, but only an amorphous hint of our own Milky Way; numerous stars, but not our sun; many planets, but not the Earth.

At a later point in cosmological time, either accident or the hand of God, depending on one's personal belief, began to erect a state of high order at one infinitesimally small place in the swirling Milky Way. It was to become our **solar system.**

The Sun and the Earth, 4.6 Billion Years Ago

Out of the Milky Way's primal mist, hot gases and tiny particles of matter began to coalesce in a remote region of one of the galaxy's two spiral arms. Why the Earth, the other planets of our solar system, and the sun should form in that particular region has no simple explanation, but the area certainly was at a safe distance from the madhouse of antimatter that seethed at the Milky Way's center.

One ball of gases, mainly hydrogen and helium, contracted to form a new, medium-sized star, our sun. Temperatures climbed to millions of degrees, igniting a series of thermonuclear reactions, similar to those which occur in a hydrogen bomb. This fireball would burn under its own power for billions of years.

One day 6 billion years from now the sun, in a state of old age and exhaustion, will swell to what is called a red giant; the expansion will vaporize the Earth and whatever may exist on it at that time. Presumably, human civilization long before then will have escaped to a safer, cooler planet in another region of the Milky Way.

While the sun blazed at the center of the newly forming solar system, 93 million miles away, a gentler, cooler process was occurring.

Tiny particles of matter from the primal mist collided. Some stuck together, and their larger mass, under the lure of gravity, attracted additional matter, until finally a rock existed. In the same way, neighboring rocks formed, and some of those collided and combined. Over millions of years this painstaking process of accretion formed the nucleus of the planet Earth.

At some point the gravitational forces of the nucleus were rapacious enough to gather up all sorts of circling matter and gases. The gases were mainly hydrogen, helium, oxygen, and nitrogen, and the other particles were iron, aluminum, gold, uranium, and many rare elements, all of which would eventually play a role in the diverse forms of life to emerge on the planet.

The neighboring planets in the solar system formed in a similar way, though each was unique in its proportions of various gases and elements. Those mixtures, though, did not favor the complex formation of specific organic molecules that would evolve into animal and plant life as we know it.

*

The Earth came into existence as a barren sphere, lacking all the surface features we recognize today: boulders, mountains, waterfalls, oceans. What forces sculpted it?

The initial credit goes to radioactive elements, like uranium, that were created with the birth of the universe and became trapped inside the Earth. They decayed spontaneously, emitting energy and subatomic particles, and became transformed into new and stable elements.

Radioactive disintegration raised the temperature of the planet, especially at its center. Rocks at the center, and at various pockets near the surface, became molten. Where the surface crust was thinnest, molten rocks erupted through, producing **volcanoes,** smearing lava over featureless terrain, raining down hills of hot ash. The lava contained numerous gases that would be essential for life, and also such noxious ones as sulfur dioxide and hydrochloric acid, which would play their own corrosive roles in etching the planet.

But the lava's most vital ingredient by far was water vapor. It was this precious vapor which cooled to create the Earth's **oceans.**

For millions of years volcanic activity was almost incessant. It produced inland mountains, islands amid vast expanses of water, and the seeds of the continents. The Earth was now rich in complex gases, elements, and minerals, and was awash in water.

It was a planet waiting for life to begin.

2

Sea Life: Sponges to Sharks

Primordial Soup, 4000 Million Years Ago

The Earth, at the relatively young age of only 1600 million years, was a boisterous, bubbling planet. Volcanoes all over the globe erupted continually. Raging storms of noxious winds and acid rain besieged the surface, and the fiery sun's ultraviolet rays constantly bathed the planet, which had yet to develop a protective atmospheric blanket, one that would permit life, once it emerged in the oceans, to evolve onto land. For now, the only refuge for potential life was deep in the sea.

Although the Earth's initial climate was inhospitable to life, it also was the precursor of life's raw ingredients. Hydrogen, methane, ammonia, and carbon monoxide covered the land in a deadly vapor. To verify the existence of this early atmosphere, and the role it played in yielding organic molecules, in the 1950s two American scientists, Stanley Miller and Harold Urey, blended these gases in a sealed laboratory flask and passed electric sparks through it, simulating the fierce lightning storms that once raged on earth. A dark slimy mold formed at the bottom of the flask, and analysis of it revealed all the ingredients necessary for life: amino acids, fats, sugars, and urea.

In this way the first organic molecules came into existence. They fell from the sky into the hot acid ocean, forming a sort of primordial soup. Many were destroyed immediately; the hardier ones survived, many linked together, and some soon learned how to make identical copies of themselves and were organized into genes.

Genes, 3900 Million Years Ago

Charles Darwin proposed that complexity evolves from simplicity through natural selection. This is true for plants, animals, and humans, and it is equally valid for the large DNA molecule, which makes up our genes and transmits all hereditary traits, for single cells and for human beings.

In the Earth's rich primordial soup, simple molecules continually collided to form more complex ones. Some ripped apart; others resisted cleavage by the many reactive chemicals in the ocean and picked up additional molecules, thus forming longer and longer sequences called nucleotides. These molecules were survivors; they contained information that had a future; their structure was worth replicating. In this way, they were primitive **DNA** molecules, simultaneously the source of all hereditary information existing at the time and the very objects to be synthesized according to that information.

Here, at the molecular level, are the roots of the ancient conundrum: Which came first, the chicken or the egg? Function or the information on how to function? As biologists believe today, neither could entirely precede the other; function and information evolved together, each aiding the evolution of the other.

These first self-replicating molecules or genes were only about 100 units long, so they displayed little diversity in shape and information content. By contrast, human gene lengths today extend to millions of units, permitting the rich variety of outward physical appearances and internal bodily functions.

How did genes a mere hundred units long evolve into complex strings of millions of molecules?

Extension of gene length was possible only with the appearance of a mechanism for detecting and correcting random errors that occurred in the process of self-replication. Life, if it was to have a future, had to have a high degree of consistency from one generation to the next. The distinction between a "right" or "wrong" segment in a gene — on a human scale between a normal infant and one suffering genetic malformation — also was a process mastered through natural selection: daughter molecules of "wrong" genes soon died in the primordial soup.

The complex molecule that eventually learned the vital functions of proofreading and error-suppression was **RNA.** It ran up the DNA segment of a gene, searching for errors and, finding one, sliced out the faulty information, replacing it with "right" molecules floating in the soup. The original RNA molecule, originating some 3900 million years ago, allowed genes to increase rapidly in length to produce a multiplicity of new and wondrous organisms in the Earth's oceans.

These early genes, however, were long, gangly, free-floating molecules not contained within the protective walls of cells. Hence, even with their error-detection and correction schemes, they were endlessly plagued with errors. Quite simply, to cut down on the number of mistakes from one generation of primitive organisms to the next, to ensure faithful self-replication — and, later, sexual reproduction — an entirely new biological component was needed: the cell.

Cells, 3800 Million Years Ago

The cell, a complex and harmonious conglomerate enclosed in a plasma membrane, came into existence in part to protect fledgling genes from their hostile, reactive environment. Shielded in the heart of a cell, a gene now had to handle only those occasional random errors of its own which arose in self-replication.

The advantages of a gene living in a cell are as obvious as those of a person spending a harsh winter inside a well-insulated, well-stocked house. Each enclosure offers protection. But the need for protection alone cannot account for the high degree of organization that developed in early cells and exists today. The origin of cellular organization arose as a clever response to an additional need of genes: simplicity.

Imagine, for example, ten large families all living and working in a single room. Regardless of the size of this space, life would be hectic and cluttered, and the potential for infighting high. To simplify things, the space might be divided into ten separate apartments, one for each family. Each apartment might then be further subdivided into rooms for special family members and specific functions, such as working, cooking, recreation, and sleep. This kind of subdividing is precisely what nature did, again through natural selection. To cope with the immense problem of evaluating the quality of information in genes, the cell, in the process of evolution, compartmentalized itself.

*

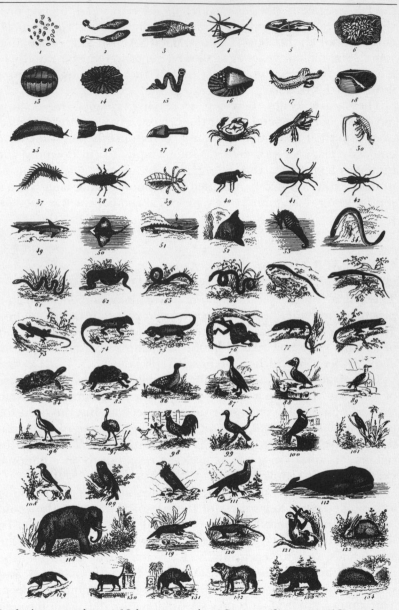

Evolution at a glance, 19th-century view: Sponge (3), oyster (12), crab (28), spider (35), dragon fly (44), shark (49), frog (60), iguana (75), croc-

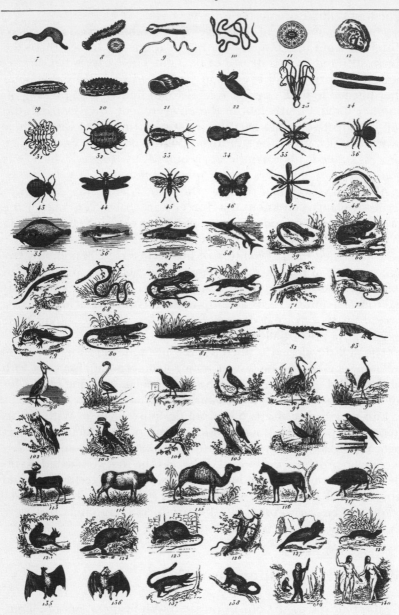

odile (81), crane (95), owl (109), deer (113), horse (116), squirrel (123), cat (130), dog (132), monkey (139), human beings (140).

The first cellular organisms were **bacteria.**

The original bacterial that developed 3.8 billion years ago were different from the oxygen-breathing varieties of today; then, the Earth suffered from a dearth of oxygen. The bacteria fed on carbon in the primordial soup, and multiplied so rapidly that soon they needed to find a new source of food. Rather than preying on another limited ingredient in the environment, they evolved into self-sufficient cells that lived by manufacturing food within their own cell walls, using the sun to supply the necessary energy. The process, called photosynthesis, required hydrogen, which was abundant during the era of volcanic eruptions.

Although we think of photosynthesis today almost exclusively in terms of plants, conditions that forced early bacteria to master the process are still found in such volcanic areas as Yellowstone in Wyoming.

A watershed in the evolution of life occurred 3200 million years ago with the appearance of **blue-green algae.** They produced an oxygen-rich atmosphere that fostered an entirely new kind of organism. The blue-greens accomplished this feat by being the first organisms to extract hydrogen from water, leaving behind pure oxygen, the staff of all later forms of life.

The cell developed a **nucleus,** the headquarters for life, 1400 million years ago. This was a major achievement, for cells with nuclei, called eukaryotes, were the fundamental building blocks for all later plants and animals, including man.

Life now had a means of becoming more diverse. With events in one compartment of a cell independent of those in another, genetic information in each compartment became more complex. New metabolic processes developed. Whereas the first cells could do little more than merely exist in a hostile environment, cells now could enjoy a meal, engage in a self-propelled swim through the oceanic soup, and be fairly confident of reproducing daughters that were faithful copies of the parents.

Viruses, 1300 Million Years Ago

By this time the earth's oceans pulsated with living organisms. Thus, it is not surprising that the next creatures to emerge were pure parasites, incapable of living on their own.

Viruses came into the world as pariahs. They could not feed, breathe, grow, or reproduce without inhabiting a host cell. They therefore invaded all forms of cellular life that came before them, and their structure and behavior 1300 million years ago was virtually identical with that of viruses today.

Viruses are not true cells. In fact, they have been described as "living chemicals," fragments of the hereditary material DNA, surrounded by an envelope of protein. Once a virus invades a cell (of a plant, animal, or human), it commands the cell to produce countless copies of viral material.

The virus's simplicity has been the root of heated controversy. Some members of the scientific community once claimed that the viruses actually were relics of a precellular stage of evolution, predating bacteria. Others, however, argued that viral life was incapable of free existence without a host cell. The prevailing view of virologists today is that viruses originated in a process of degenerate evolution from portions of DNA of bacteria or protozoa.

Protozoa, 1200 Million Years Ago

Protozoa were the precursors of sea sponges, jellyfish, and flatworms. They were the first life form to develop locomotion, propelling themselves through water by the coordinated beat of flailing threads or cilia.

Protozoa resemble other lower life forms in their use of chloroplasts, packets of chlorophyll, for converting sunlight into complex molecules of food. But how they began is an enigma — scientists suspect that each of these organisms (10,000 species exist today) was a committee of smaller ones. They think that a cell which fed by flowing around other particles inadvertently took in some bacteria and blue-green algae that, instead of being digested, survived in a new communal form of life.

Like bacteria, protozoa reproduce by splitting in two, but cell division can be complicated. Two cells, for example, may join together and exchange genes, then later undergo cell division. Was this the origin of sex?

Sex, Pre–1000 Million Years Ago

The origin of sex is ancient, somewhat ambiguous, and decidedly unerotic. If sex is defined as the union of opposites in order to reproduce a new organism, its origin goes back almost to the beginning of life on Earth, for even one-cell organisms sometimes engaged in sexual behavior.

Among the earliest forms of life, reproduction was accomplished by fission: a single cell spontaneously divided to produce two daughter cells. As long as food was plentiful and the cell population not too crowded, this process was the norm. But when temperatures became inhospitable, food scarce, and the population crowded, and many single cells fused to form new organisms — as if instinct told them that reducing numbers increased the chances of survival for their offspring. The offspring in this case was a genetic combination of the parents themselves.

From external appearances these early "mothers" and "fathers" seemed indistinguishable. But they weren't. A cell preferred a mate that was different from itself. In the paramecium, for example, two separate cell populations, or "families," if left alone, will reproduce by cell division or fission. But mix the two families, and each group somehow senses the presence of strangers and mates with them by fusion.

Even the most primitive single-cell organisms hoped to find different mates. The differences initially were extremely slight: a small cell sought out a larger one; a cell with little food in its body preferred a mate with a nutritional bonanza; a cell lacking locomotion chose a mate with whiplike flagella. In fact, all kinds of sexual unions between one-cell organisms were, and still are, possible: a small, stationary, starving cell will still choose a larger, motile one rich in nutrients.

So sex as we know it today evolved out of a basic and vital quest for complementarity — really, of course, a means of producing a greater variety of offspring with a better chance of survival. As evolution advanced, cells increased in complexity and differences between cells became more pronounced. To size, motility, and food supply were added countless other survival attributes. Finally this polarization of opposites resulted in "male" and "female" cells, culminating in the development of the sperm and egg.

Sponges, Jellyfish, and Worms, 700 Million Years Ago

Creatures without backbones, or invertebrates, were the first animals in existence, and the important role they established in the food chains of other animals continues today. An example is a tiny marine worm less than a millimeter long: it's eaten by shrimp, the shrimp by fish, and fish by man. Some invertebrates, too, developed a form of sex that's handy in the absence of mates. The arrow worm, for example, which can run from 1 to 4 inches, has both ovaries and testes and fertilizes itself.

Sponges were the first prominent example of coordination between colonized cells. They eat by drawing water through tiny pores that cover the surface of their bodies, filtering out food particles, then expelling the water through larger vents. The sponge's cellular interdependency is very informal. Individual cells crawl across the sponge's surface like amoebae; and if two sponges grow on the ocean floor near one another, their length, which ranges up to 6 feet, allows them to come in contact and merge into one large organism. Yet despite their complexity, sponges are a poor example of an integrated intercellular animal, for they have no nervous system or muscle fibers.

The **jellyfish,** the best-known of which is the fierce Portuguese man-of-war, was the first free-swimming animal and the first to develop its own defense system to deter predators. A jellyfish is still identifiable by its umbrella form and a digestive cavity that occupies the center of its bulky body.

Sex became more complex with the jellyfish. Its reproduction entails time and energy unknown to lower creatures. Eggs and sperm are released into the sea, and the fertilized egg becomes an embryonic, free-swimming animal different in shape from its parents. Eventually it settles down on the bottom of the sea and grows into a tiny flowerlike organism called a polyp. Later, the polyp buds and produces miniature jellyfish, which detach themselves and swim back into the ocean current.

A major step in the progression of life came with **worms.**

Originally flat, leaf-shaped creatures, they breathed directly through their skin, instead of through gills. But even more important, they were the first animals to have the beginnings of a head, with a mouth in the front end and a few light-sensitive spots above it. They surpassed previous life forms by developing muscle tissue and nerve fibers — the forerunners of musculature and brain.

Flatworms today hardly can be described as possessing true brains, but they do display amazing traits. One freshwater species has demonstrated the ability to learn by negotiating mazes and making decisions based on color codes. More surprisingly, its memory has been shown to exist in a cellular substance, for if a worm that learned the maze is killed and fed to another worm, the second one will correctly wiggle through the maze without training.

Clams and Scallops, 650 Million Years Ago

Many worms, seeking protection from predators and a hostile ocean environment, developed shells. They lived in the muddy sea bottom or attached to rocks and fed through a tentaclelike organ that protruded from the shell.

These shelled worms, or brachiopods, looked deceptively simple but weren't. Each had a digestive tract that ended in an anus and a group of tentacles, covered with cilia, to stir up the water current and attract food around its mouth. Clams and scallops evolved from this line, which today contains about 60,000 species.

The most successful of these creatures was the mollusk, which introduced the concept of a "foot" to the animal kingdom. Possessed of a commuter's need to travel, the mollusk extended a tough fleshy foot from the shell and propelled itself by wagging the appendage. Many species developed a small disc that slipped into place and tightly closed the entrance once the foot was retracted.

Transportation made possible by the foot was enhanced at a later stage in one branch of mollusks that developed gas-filled flotation tanks inside their shells. As the animal grew, enlarging its shell, additional chambers filled with gas, providing buoyancy for its increased weight.

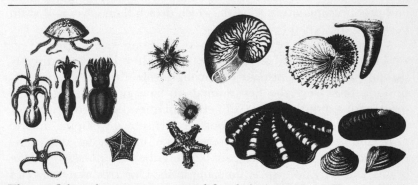

The starfish and octopus are named for their appearance. Transportation of the nautilus (left, middle), after which a submarine was named, was enhanced by gas-filled flotation chambers within the shell.

A living relic of this system is the **nautilus.** A tube extends from the back of its body chamber into the flotation tanks, which the animal can fill with gas when it needs to search for food or flee from a predator. Movement is by jet propulsion; the nautilus squirts water through a siphon, the way animals have done for hundreds of millions of years. Small stalked eyes that are keen, and tentacles that are sensitive to taste, aid in the gathering of food. The nautilus's foot, now elaborated into ninety long, grasping tentacles, grapples with prey, pulling it to a horny, parrotlike beak strong enough to crack shells. Defense, food acquisition, and canniness in travel have given the nautilus the means for withstanding extinction.

Water Insects, 600 Million Years Ago

The first sea animals to exhibit legs were the arthropods, and their creation was a vital link in the evolution of the animal kingdom.

Today their sea-living and air-breathing descendants are the most numerous and most diversified animals alive. They are characterized by paired jointed legs attached to each body segment, an exoskeleton, feelers at the front of the head, and muscle fibers along the back that allow arthropods to roll themselves into balls. Their group includes insects, spiders, centipedes, crustaceans, and scorpions, as well as parasitic ticks and mites — in all, about 80 percent of the entire animal world.

Significant among the arthropods were the **trilobites,** the first creatures that developed well-defined eyes. A single eye might contain as many as 15,000 elements, each with its own lens placed in a precise position that enabled it to transmit light efficiently. The trilobites' eyes gave them a nearly hemispherical field of vision. As the species evolved, the eye became even more complex; its sharpness and sophistication have never been rivaled by another animal — probably because the species lived in a muddy ocean environment, where little light penetrated, and needed a precise optical instrument to collect what food was available.

Trilobites began to span the world's oceans soon after their creation. But once more sophisticated creatures came to populate the seas, the trilobites' supremacy came to an end, about 250 million years ago.

One relative survives, the **horseshoe crab.** A living fossil in the modern world, its armor has been stripped of segmentation over the millennia. It is now covered by a huge domed shield, containing two bean-shaped compound eyes. But beneath its shell remain trilobite characteristics: the segmented body, several pairs of jointed legs bearing pincers at the end, and platelike gills.

Horseshoe crabs live at considerable depths off the Asiatic coast and America's eastern seaboard. Every spring, they migrate to the coast. On three successive nights, when the moon is full and the tides high, hundreds of thousands make their way to the water's edge to mate. The female lays eggs in the sand, and the male coats the eggs with sperm.

Crabs, Shrimp, and Lobsters, 550 Million Years Ago

So vast is the kingdom of arthropods that more than 30,000 species are *not* insects, spiders, or scorpions; they are crabs, shrimp, and lobsters. Like trilobites, all of these armored creatures developed from segmented worms. The crustacean varied slightly from the trilobite in that its nervous system contained not one pair but two pairs of antennae on its head. Yet when the trilobite dynasty

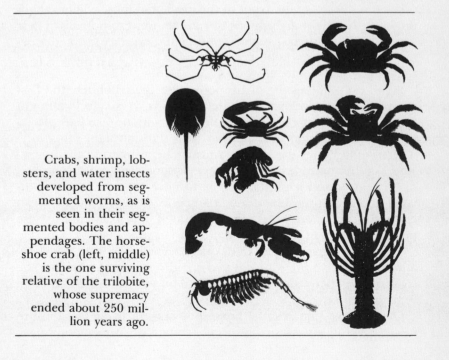

Crabs, shrimp, lobsters, and water insects developed from segmented worms, as is seen in their segmented bodies and appendages. The horseshoe crab (left, middle) is the one surviving relative of the trilobite, whose supremacy ended about 250 million years ago.

ended, it was the crustacean that continued the line — right into the present.

The crustacean's greatest limitation is one that plagued the tribolite: a rigid shell that the animal must periodically shed in order to grow. As molting time nears, the animal absorbs much of the calcium carbonate from its shell into its blood and secretes a soft, wrinkled skin beneath the old shell, and this skin later grows into the new shell. While it is without a shell, the crustacean must show cunning to compensate for its defenselessness. Gradually, the new carapace hardens, and the animal can once again resume its normal life pattern.

Octopus and Squid, 550 Million Years Ago

For reasons that are still unexplained, wormlike creatures with shells began to disappear in great numbers about 550 million years ago. The nautilus was one exception. Another was a group that survived by permanently shedding their shells. From this line descended the two most sophisticated and intelligent of all mollusks, the octopus and the squid.

When they emerged is uncertain. (It may have been as early as 550 million years ago or as late as 200 million.) But the squid's ancestral shell still exists as a remnant deep within the creature, a chunk of powdery chalk called a cuttle bone, which often washes up on beaches.

Since the squid and octopus weren't hampered in growth by a rigid shell, they evolved to immense size. Squids as long as 30 feet and weighing a ton are commonly hauled in by commercial fishermen; in 1933, off the coast of New Zealand, a huge squid was caught, measuring more than 22 yards in length and with eyes 18 inches across, the largest eyes known in the animal kingdom. Larger specimens probably are yet to be found, since squids are intelligent and swift enough to elude man's deep-sea snares. Sperm whales diving to great depths have returned to the surface with scars on their snouts indicating that they had encountered squids with suckers more than 4 inches across. This lends credence to stories of legendary sea monsters that are said to be able to grapple a ship in their tentacles.

Whereas the squid has ten tentacles, the octopus has only eight, which is the origin of its name: *okto,* Greek for "eight," and *pous,* meaning "foot."

Fish were the first creatures to develop backbones, thus beginning the long line of vertebrates.

Fish, 500 Million Years Ago

Fish bear the evolutionary distinction of being the first creatures to possess backbones, and thus were the beginning of the vertebrate lineage that led to amphibians, reptiles, mammals, marsupials, apes, and man.

The earliest skeletal features of the first vertebrates were a simple backbone and a boxed bony enclosure surrounding the brain, the skull. The most primitive fish was the jawless agnathan (which was really a protofish), of which the sea lamprey is a present-day survivor. The agnathan's mouth was merely a sucking organ, and for 100 million years it continued unchanged.

Then the protofish gradually grew streamlined. The slits in the sides of its throat that had originated as filtering vents became walled with blood vessels so that they also served as gills for breathing. The strips of flesh between the gills stiffened with calcium, and the first pair of bones developed. With time, the bones acquired muscle around them and could be opened and closed; fish now had jaws. When bony scales in the skin that covered the jaws grew larger and sharper, the jaws held teeth. Flaps of skin sprouted from both sides of the lower part of the body to toughen into fins. Now fish could swim. For the first time vertebrate hunters could seek food by propelling themselves through the seas with skill and accuracy; after they caught their prey, they had jaws and teeth to tear it apart.

Enter the **shark,** a hardy, fearless creature that first appeared about 375 million years ago.

It was close to this time that the numerous varieties of fish that drove the protofish into extinction branched off to form a new species, one that lost nearly all of the hard bone in its skeleton, replacing it with a softer, more elastic, lighter material, called cartilage. Sharks were the predominant members of this group. Though sharks were now lighter than their primitive ancestors, their bulk of flesh and cartilage was still heavier than water, and to keep from plummeting to the sea floor, they had to swim constantly.

Some sharks then actually lived in fresh water, but the vast majority inhabited the seas. They continued to advance in shape and sophistication until about 90 million years ago, when shark evolution came to a halt. Modern sharks, as well as **skates** and **rays,** are virtually exact copies of their ancestors from that era.

Lichen, Moss, and Fern, 430 Million Years Ago

Life's earliest traces on land were not animals but plants, one-cell organisms that washed ashore and very gradually adapted to the planet's changing atmosphere. Their situation was the same as that of seaweed which washes up on beaches today: it quickly dried out. The problem was elegantly solved about 430 million years ago, when several species of algae developed waxy coatings, or cuticles, that prevented desiccation.

But perhaps the single most important physiological adaption that occurred in early plants was the development of a vascular system; it carried water up from the plant's base (which was not yet as elaborate as roots) to the region that synthesized nutrients. This marked the development of light-loving sensory cells that encouraged plants to reach toward the sun. The blistering enemy had become the guiding light, shining the way toward the future development of an entirely new kingdom of land plants and flowers.

After the algae came **lichens,** the hardy offspring of a symbiotic marriage between algae and fungi.

Lichens soon thrived in regions of the earth where other vegetation was easily strangulated. Today they are found farther north and farther south than any other kind of plant, and at altitudes of almost 20,000 feet. They grow in the desert, on the backs of insects, and in the skulls of dead animals. Some of the 15,000 species of lichens grow 9 feet tall; others are smaller than a pinhead.

Mosses and **ferns** next rooted themselves to land, the former more dependent on water than the latter.

Mosses, in fact, have never become entirely emancipated from water. They were forced to practice two methods of reproduction, sexual and asexual, in alternate generations. The mosses without roots produce sex cells, and each egg remains attached to the stem at the top of the plant while smaller microscopic sperms are released into water and wriggle their way toward fertilization. The egg then germinates while still bound to the parent plant and produces the next asexual generation — a thin stem with a hollow capsule in which great numbers of grainlike spores are produced. When the capsule wall expands to the breaking point, the spores are distributed by wind. Those lucky enough to land on a moist habitat develop into new plants.

Ferns solved the problem that befuddled mosses. Appearing about 345 million years ago, they were the first plants to root deep into the earth for water. This gave them an independence unknown to previous life forms on land, because they could thrive away from ponds and streams, in rain forests and jungles. In fact, they helped pave the way for these two new ecological terrains.

Today there are about 1500 species of ferns. Most of them are still jungle-bound and have changed little over the millennia. By the beginning of the Mesozoic era, about 225 million years ago, all the modern fern families we know today were well established. A few species, however, still hark back to the primordial origins, because they can exist solely in water.

Beans, peanuts, and **peas,** as well as **alfalfa** and **clover,** also developed in the early Mesozoic times. Each underwent a series of evolutionary changes, but during the Cretaceous period, about 136 million years ago, all these plants, which provided a wealth of food for primitive man, were flourishing in almost the very forms we know today.

3

Land Life: Millipedes to Monkeys

Millipedes, 420 Million Years Ago

While algae, lichens, and mosses were adapting to life on land, the first animals emerged from the seas to stake a claim for themselves and their descendants. They were millipedes, segmented creatures resembling their ocean ancestors, crustaceans. Despite their name, millipedes had not a thousand legs but at most two hundred, with some species possessing as few as eight. Certain species were up to 6 feet in length.

Millipedes greatly enhanced their chances for survival on land by adopting a new method of breathing. It called for a series of internal tubes, the tracheae, which replaced the feathery gill attached to each leg. The tracheae were fine networks that delivered oxygen to all body organs and tissues.

Another obstacle to be overcome was reproduction out of water, and the millipedes moved quickly to a novel solution. Since male and female could get about independently, they were able to meet, and the male transferred sperm directly to the female. The reproductive cells of each sex developed in glands close to the second pair of legs, and during mating season the two animals intertwined. The male reached forward with his seventh leg, collected a bundle of sperm from his sex gland, and wriggled alongside the female until he was close enough to her sexual pouch to deposit the sperm.

Three groups have survived into modern times; of them, the

centipedes are closest kin, segmented like the millipedes; the **scorpion** shows divisions only along its tail; and **spiders,** except for a few species in Southeast Asia, have lost all traces of their segmented past.

Amphibians, 390 Million Years Ago

Whereas the millipede lineage led to many of today's insects, modern mammals, including the apes and man, descended from another creature that emerged from the sea 30 million years later.

It came out of swampy rain forests with fishlike bones and tail, but with a new feature geared for traversing the terrain: an early limb, built of two main sections and ending in several digits. It breathed through a mouth and nostrils, taking air into its lungs.

These amphibians did not detach themselves entirely from the sea. Their eggs were shell-less, and the young went through an aquatic larval stage. The earliest forms had a remarkable resemblance to present-day salamanders. At first clumsy and slow, amphibians developed strong muscles and interlocking backbones that enabled them to lift their bodies off the ground and thrust themselves overland with swiftness.

Why the amphibians, with a relatively comfortable life at sea, hauled themselves ashore remains unclear. Perhaps they lived in pools that were seasonal and used lungs and legs to seek other environments when their habitats dried up. It also has been suggested that amphibians were descendants of small fish that, in order to escape becoming prey to larger fish, ventured onto land at night when the humidity was high and returned to the water by day, thus gradually supplementing their diet with terrestrial arthropods while adapting to land for longer periods of time before they eventually found land preferable to the sea.

Whatever the reasons, for 100 million years they thrived on dry land, until reptiles overshadowed them and greatly diminished their numbers. Today, out of the myriad amphibians that once traveled the earth, only a handful of species remains: **newts** and **salamanders,** the smallest in size as well as number; **caecilians,** blind, legless, burrowing creatures; and **frogs** and **toads,** which come in more than 2000 varieties and exist with great diversity in wetlands, tropical forests, and even the world's deserts.

Insects, 350 Million Years Ago

The most primitive insects known were found as fossils in rocks dating back 350 million years. Their bodies were divided into a head with one pair of antennae, a thorax equipped with three pairs of legs, and a segmented abdomen, the basic structure of present-day insects. They were the aggressive pioneers of the terrestrial branch of the arthropods, descendants of millipedes, crustaceans, and segmented worms.

Winged insects appeared 50 million years later.

Primitive, wingless insects found their food by scaling tree ferns in search of spores and vegetable debris. The ascent was easy, but getting down proved more difficult, involving detours over fingered leaf formations and shoots. At some point they started to leap to the ground, extending their "arms" or flapping in order to glide downward. This is one hypothesis for the development of wings.

Another clue to the origin of insect flight is provided by the silverfish. On its back are two flaplike extensions of a chitinous shell that appear to be the rudiments of wings. One theory is that early wings, rather than serving as a means for flight, absorbed the sun's rays like solar panels to help keep the insect's body temperature constant. The warmer the insects, the quicker were the chemical

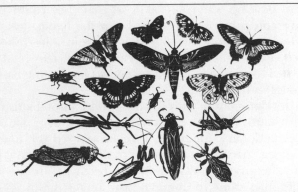

Winged insects began appearing 300 million years ago, followed soon by many of today's pests: beetles, weevils, roaches, and termites. The final major group to evolve was the stinging species, including bees, wasps, and mosquitoes.

reactions in their bodies, building energy that made them more active. If these flaps, or primitive wings, had muscles at their base, they probably were tilted to face squarely into the sun's rays, especially if the blood was circulated through the flaps.

Many of the insects that today we regard as pests began appearing almost as soon as insects evolved wings. First on the scene, about 280 million years ago, were **beetles** and **weevils,** which began the practice of living under the bark of trees. They were followed 50 million years later by **roaches** and **termites,** the latter having the distinction of being the first insect to develop a complex society. (**Ants** would not achieve this sophistication for another 130 million years.)

Also swarming through the skies at this period in evolutionary history were the first **butterflies, moths,** and **flies.** These creatures are believed to be descendants of the so-called Eumecoptera, ancestors of the modern scorpion fly, and the earliest insect to undergo complete metamorphosis.

The final major group of insects to evolve, and the one most dreaded today, was the stinging species. The first to appear were **bees,** 225 million years ago, followed by **wasps** and **mosquitoes.**

Reptiles, 345 Million Years Ago

As amphibians ventured inland, away from sources of water, they began to develop watertight skin so that they could retain body moisture and protect themselves from the harsh rays of the sun. Since they could no longer lay their eggs in water, they began to produce eggs in shells, which were self-sufficient fetal chambers. These shell-covered eggs could be laid to hatch under rocks or logs or in holes in the ground.

The development of lungs had allowed amphibians to abandon water for land; now the birth of the shelled egg, nature's second major evolutionary milestone, forever severed the umbilical cord with the sea. An egg enclosed in a shell also made copulation a necessity, because fertilization had to occur before the shell developed. Reptiles came to dominate the terrestrial life of the world about 280 million years ago, successfully adapting to deserts, swamps, forests, grasslands, rivers, lakes, and even, in the form of flying lizards, to air.

*

During the height of the age of reptiles, **dinosaurs** roamed the landscapes of the major continents, eating plants, animals, and even other dinosaurs, such as the herbivorous brontosaurus. Their fossil remains have been found in North America, Europe, Africa, and Australia. Medium-sized dinosaurs were protected by heavy plates of armor and large spines, but the largest needed no intimidating mantle. Their name, "dinosaur," derives from the Greek words for "terrible lizard," and although a considerable number of dinosaurs were meat-eating giants, many were quite small and ate only plants.

Although some reptiles flourished and then vanished, like the dinosaurs (whose sudden demise is still one of the greatest un-

Lords of the land, dinosaurs reigned unchallenged for 100 million years before their mysterious extinction.

solved mysteries of all times), others, like the **turtle,** plodded stolidly and steadily into modern times with little change. Still others, like the **crocodile,** originated about 200 million years ago with very short muzzles and nostrils near the tip, and only gradually, over 40 million years, developed their present elongated muzzle, with the nostrils back near the base.

Today there are 6000 species of reptiles, including turtles and tortoises, alligators and crocodiles, snakes and lizards — and all lay eggs on land, even the many marine varieties, which spend most of their lives in the home of their ancestors, the world's seas. Among all the living reptiles, **snakes** are amazing in that they survived the loss of limbs, a fate that usually is an evolutionary dead end.

Mammals, 225 Million Years Ago

Mammals evolved from a certain order of reptiles, but what environmental or evolutionary conditions allowed this astonishing transformation?

Mammals belong to the class *Mammalia,* a group of backboned animals in which the young are nourished with milk from special secreting glands of the mother. Mammals are four-limbed (except for certain aquatic groups, like the **whale,** which originated only 70 million years ago), hairy, and warm-blooded. It is the last characteristic that provides the clue to the origin of the new species.

To be warm-blooded is to be endothermic; that is, able to control one's own body temperature. Reptiles, cold-blooded creatures that they were, did not process this highly advantageous capability; to warm themselves they had to bask in the sun, as do their descendants today. A certain group of carnivorous reptiles called *Therapsida* — small, hairy, and shrewlike — made the transition from cool-blooded creatures to warm-blooded about 225 million years ago. Most likely this happened because they were forced to hunt for food during cool nights, when dinosaurs slept to preserve what little heat they could.

Before mammals came into real prominence, though, they were relegated to a secondary role in the animal kingdom because of the spectacular reign of the dinosaurs, which lasted for almost 100 million years. But as the climate of the earth cooled, the cold-blooded dinosaurs, probably unable to cope with the changing temperatures, disappeared, and the smaller creatures that could generate their own body heat, as a result of millions of years of nocturnal foraging, began to flourish. Even today some mammals, such as the opossum, display the nocturnal behavior that originated millions of years ago.

Mammals also introduced a new way of reproducing. The female retained the fertilized egg in her body and supported its growth by the placenta, a lifeline to her circulatory system. Babies of many placental mammals, like the rabbit, fox, and elephant, actually stay in the uterus until they are so developed that they are fully mobile the minute they are born. They remain, however, dependent on the mother's milk until their foraging and hunting skills mature.

Marsupials, a suborder of mammals, evolved the unique process of premature birth of their young. Born immature and virtually helpless, the offspring must find their way into the mother's external pouch, where they suckle and complete their development. The most widely known marsupials today are the **kangaroo** and its close relatives, but when this species first developed, 136 million years ago, the members were much larger than their present-day descendants.

The **koala,** a small marsupial with a short tail and stocky body, originated in southern Australia only about 28 million years ago.

In many ways the placental process has great advantages over marsupial birth, since the young are protected from the hazards of the environment while receiving nutrients from the mother during gestation. Not surprisingly, then, it was placental reproduction that paved the way for the development of apes and man.

Elephants originated about 100 million years ago, evolving from creatures not much larger than a pig. The species was already

Marsupials developed external pouches to house their virtually helpless premature offspring.

flourishing in Africa and Asia about 35 million years later.

The elephant underwent an interesting transformation to develop its trunk. During the course of the animal's evolution, the lower jaw stretched beyond the upper one, and the tusk projected even farther forward. At this stage the elephant's nose and upper lip developed into an elongated fleshy cover that projected over the long lower jaw. Fossil evidence suggests that at this time the elephant's nostrils were well above the start of this flap, back near its eyes.

But the long lower jaw proved less useful than a shorter one, so the upper flap was converted into a tubular proboscis, the trunk, which aided in gathering food. The nostrils gradually had shifted to the tip of the proboscis, so elephants now were able to breathe while submerged in water, bathing and cooling their massive bodies.

Rats, mice, and **squirrels** — mammals and members of the rodent family — appeared 60 million years ago, and fossil evidence suggests that they originated mainly in North America. Gnawing animals, they proved to be particularly hardy and prolific, and their populations quickly burgeoned in whatever new region they invaded. This resulted in their rapid spread into most of the major available ecological niches in an astonishingly brief span of at most 2 million years.

The family of **rabbits** and **hares** (called *Leporidae*) originated about 55 million years ago, and from fossil records (the earliest discovered in northern Asia), they seem to have remained almost unchanged throughout time. From Asia they apparently migrated west to Europe and east across the mass of ice and land that formed a bridge with North America.

Birds, 195 Million Years Ago

Birds became birds to escape their previously imperiled existence on the ground and to partake of the feast of swarming insects that blackened the skies.

In constant danger from carnivorous hunters, the ancestors of birds — slender, sleek-bodied reptiles — first became tree-climbers. Adaptation started. Swaying branches favored the evolution of the grasping foot; the action of climbing from branch to branch favored the enlargement of the claw and elongation of the forelimb, which had been short in their bipedal ancestors; larger eyes provided better vision.

The origin of **feathers,** a novelty in the animal kingdom at the time, was reptiles' scales.

The fact that birds' feathers evolved directly from reptilian scales can be seen in microscopic examinations of the two body coverings, and in chemical composition they are very nearly identical. Feathers initially developed only to provide insulation, but as plumage grew, spreading over the birds' bodies, it eventually enabled them to glide from branch to branch, like today's "flying" lizards.

For flight, weight posed the greatest problem. At first birds' bones were solid, like their reptilian ancestors', but they gradually lightened into paper-thin, almost hollow skeletons, internally supported with cross-struts resembling the jointed underpinning that bolsters the wings of airplanes. Birds' lungs also helped to lighten ballast by expanding into air sacs that bulged into the body cavity and occupied space in an almost weightless manner. A heavy jaw, a requisite of many reptiles and a great handicap for any animal trying to fly, became transformed into a beak constructed of lightweight keratin, eliminating the threat of a bird's becoming top-heavy and plummeting to the ground in a nose dive.

Cranes, which once stood 7 feet tall, with massive heads and bills, have the best fossil record of any avian order, dating back 100 million years. Their descendants are modern cranes, rails, and plovers. **Cuckoos** originated about 60 million years ago, followed 10 million years later by the giant **albatross;** one fossil found in Nigeria has a wing span of 20 feet.

Parrots and **pigeons** are more recent; they originated about 20 million years ago, before the rise of the perching birds, which are the forerunners to most of today's species.

Eagles, falcons, and **buzzards** remain an evolutionary mystery. They have no obvious link with other birds, and for convenience they currently are categorized between ducks and game birds, though they bear no close resemblance to either. If they display anatomical similarities to any bird, it is to owls. Avian experts believe that all falconlike birds originated from an ancestral species about 20 million years ago and that the line of descent has since become obscured.

The fossil record is incomplete for many species of birds because of their delicate bone structures. This is particularly true of

Feathers evolved from the scales of reptiles, birds' ancestors, which became birds to escape the dangerous existence on the ground. *Top:* vulture and buzzard; *bottom:* long-eared owl, grand duke, and short-eared owl.

swifts and hummingbirds; the traces of the latter are only about 2 million years old. Although the fossils of many ancestral birds remain to be discovered, from the current evidence some other species of modern birds appeared in this order:

Herons, storks, and **flamingos** originated about 60 million years ago. The oldest heron fossils were unearthed in England and North America; England and France were the burial grounds of the oldest storks. Both species may have been preceded by 5 million years by the flamingo, whose remains first appeared in Sweden.

Doves, sand grouse, and **turkeys** took wing 40 million years ago. The oldest sand grouse remains were discovered in France, also the site of the earliest dodo fossil. Modern dodos became extinct in the late 17th century, when they fell prey to marauding sailors. They had evolved into pigeonlike birds that had lost the power of flight during their existence in the safety of their predator-free environment and had become as large as turkeys — and, from the sailors' viewpoint, probably as tasty.

Chickens also appeared about this time, but the domestic chicken obviously has a more recent origin. The major ancestor of the several domestic varieties that grace today's tables is the red jungle fowl *Gallus gallus*, whose original home is chiefly India. It's believed that at an early stage of domestication *Gallus gallus* mated with a kindred species, probably *Gallus sonnerati*, and that their offspring gave rise to the breeds we feast on today.

Flowers, 100 Million Years Ago

An extravagantly clever ploy helped saturate the world with flowering species, as colorful plants lured flying insects to aid them in pollination.

The earliest and simplest strategy used by plants to bring insects to their service was the one used by the **magnolia,** which surrounded its pollen-producing stamens with alluringly bright-colored petals. Beetles' diets at the time consisted of the pollen of cycads, and naturally the rich sweetness of the early magnolias easily captured their attention. They fed on pollen but paid for their meals by delivering to their next dining stop the excess pollen that had clung to them while they ate.

At first, the insect needed no specialized organ to reach the center of a flower, nor a particular skill for gathering pollen from loaded stamens. But insects that were indiscriminate about which plants they visited did not always help propagation, because pollen of one species deposited in flowers of another was wasted. In time, particular flowers and particular insects developed together, each catering to the other's requirements and tastes.

Nectar was the flowers' next bribe. Its only purpose was to ingratiate feasting insects so that they became addicted to the sweet liquid and devoted boundless energy during the flowering season to collecting it. The power of nectar enlisted a new throng of "delivery boys," including bees, flies, and butterflies.

Further enticement came when the colors of petals turned iridescent, intensifying toward the center, where the pollen lay, or took on blazing new hues. Making the insects' job as easy as possible, the flowers even evolved markings on their petals that indicated the exact placement of pollen — lines and spots like an airport runway that guided the insects in for a landing. This symbiosis between flower and insect is so complex that botanists are certain that many flowers contain colors visible only to polarized insect eyes, but invisible to our own. As richly colored as a flower garden may be to us, nature has made it a veritable psychedelic experience for insects.

Apes and Monkeys, 65 Million Years Ago

At the crux of the theory of evolution is man's descent from primates. How the earliest mammal — an insect-eating relative of the shrew that was the ancestor of animals as diverse as birds, whales, and rats — could give rise to man has aroused great curiosity, controversy, and concern. Some see the issue as the denigration of religion, a refutation of the Bible; others consider man's origin from apes the supreme insult.

But the implications of kinship are clear. A number of primitive skeletal features (such as the collarbone, long ago discarded by most mammals, but retained by both man and monkey), anatomically relate the two groups. And recent studies of the similarities in the gene-bearing chromosomes of modern chimpanzees and human beings provide the strongest evidence yet, leaving little ground for doubt or rational debate. (See *The Family of Man*, page 35.)

The first true monkey differed significantly from its immediate forerunners, the prosimians, in that sight, not smell, dominated its world. That represented an auspicious transformation. These tree-dwelling animals, swinging from vine to vine high above the ground, needed precise vision to maneuver without injury. They also developed acute color perception to judge the ripeness of fruit and the freshness of leaves and to detect the presence in trees of

The monkey's great visual acuity and finger dexterity necessitated development of a sophisticated brain. Thus began the vast expansion of the cerebral cortex, or "reasoning" portion of the brain. *From left:* Maki family, gibbon, and mandrill.

camouflaged enemies. Ultimately, because their color spectrum was so broad and so integral to their communications and social behavior, monkeys themselves became the most colorful of all mammals.

The origin of the human brain begins here with the monkey. (See *The Modern Brain,* page 47.) Monkeys acquired an enlarged and complex brain that vastly distanced them from their jungle relatives. It was necessary for accommodating not only their new visual acuity, but their finger dexterity as well. The coordination between eyes and hands was advanced and sprang from sophisticated neural engineering. Elaborate connections developed in the brain between areas that governed vision and hand manipulation, allowing monkeys to grasp, finger, and scrutinize an object. They now saw with binocular vision, which gave them a continuous stereoscopic view of the landscape, instead of seeing a separate field with each eye, as their ancestors had done.

With the refinement of these areas of the brain, monkeys became less dependent on smell, so the olfactory portion of the brain diminished in size. In its place there was a huge expansion of the most important part of the brain to evolve thus far, the cerebral cortex. At first this new bundle of gray matter aided monkeys only in coordinating their new visual and manual skills; gradually it increased their ability to learn. It was, of course, the outer layer of the brain that eventually would usher monkeys up the evolutionary ladder to thinking, self-aware hominids and to reasoning, rational *Homo sapiens*.

4

Human Life: Primates to Pundits

The Family of Man, 20 Million Years Ago; Africa

A small, hairy, tree-climbing primate called *Dryopithecus* roamed the earth about 36 million years ago, serving as ancestral stock for such modern primates as chimpanzees, gorillas, orangutans, and man.

Dryopithecus was a herbivore that walked on all fours and had a brain less than one-eighth the size of our own. Its genes are, of course, unavailable, but studies of the genes of modern apes and man indicate that we all evolved from the same origins. The molecular structure of many of our proteins — hemoglobin, for example — is more than 99 percent identical with that of proteins found in chimpanzees. Interestingly, this is the same ratio as in the molecular structure of chimps and gorillas, but smaller than the difference between chimps and such apes as gibbons or orangutans. Thus, not only are humans and chimps distinct evolutionary groups, but so too are chimps and gorillas. This means that genetically we are as much like chimps as they are like gorillas.

The origin of our family tree is under study today. The most recent evidence suggests that eighteen of our twenty-three pairs of chromosomes are in varying degrees identical with those of the three other primates: orangutan, gorilla, and chimpanzee. This broaches the possibility of a new treelike evolutionary scheme. From the common ancestral stock, *Dryopithecus*, the first primate to split off and form a separate species was the orangutan; next was the gorilla. Soon three distinct species roamed the African plains —

orangutan, gorilla, and a combination chimpanzee-humanlike creature.

This last primate differed from the gorilla only in very minor chromosomal alterations, and about 20 million years ago split into two modern lines: chimpanzee and hominid, or the "family of man" lineage, which includes all successors. Thus, of all animals on earth today we are most closely related to the chimpanzee. Consequently, it is not surprising that this primate among all other apes displays the greatest facility for acquiring sign language and using it to communicate abstract ideas. Anatomically, in fact, a baby chimpanzee is so similar to a human of the same age that many anthropologists speculate that if a chimpanzee's aging process could be slowed down, the adult would bear an eerily striking resemblance to a human.

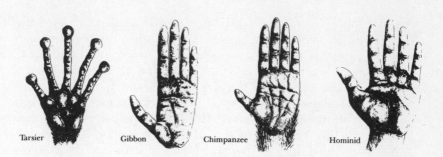

Tarsier   Gibbon   Chimpanzee   Hominid

These hands reflect locomotion and survival strategies of four modern primates. The tarsier, a leaper and clinger, has large finger pads; the gibbon has long, strong fingers for swinging; the chimp can manipulate crude tools with its stubby thumb; the hominid thumb faces the forefinger, an adaptation to bipedalism that increases dexterity. (Drawings by Luba Dmytryk Gudz, from *Lucy: The Beginnings of Humankind,* © 1981 by Donald C. Johanson and Maitland A. Edey.)

Ramapithecus, 15 Million Years Ago; Africa and Asia

Archeologists have determined *Ramapithecus* to be the oldest of the hominids. Its fossils were first found in India and include remains only of jaws and teeth. Although it is uncertain what its head looked like, it is believed to have had a brain capacity of 350 cubic centimeters (as compared to 1400 cc for the human brain). *Ramapithecus* most likely walked on its feet with assistance from its knuckles, a mode of locomotion that enabled it to move about while holding objects in its hands. This led to the further assumption that even the earliest hominids had greater dexterity than modern chimpanzees in handling sticks and other objects.

Ramapithecus takes its name from Rama, a Hindu hero-deity, and *pithecus,* the Latin word for ape. The hominid's existence lasted from about 7 million years, more than twice as long as any other known hominid. The jaws and teeth found in Africa and Asia are powerful and show wear marks indicating that they were used to masticate a coarse diet. From this knowledge we can assume that *Ramapithecus* fed on nuts and tough roots, in addition to softer fruits and shoots of the wet forests — a diet common to modern apes. The hominid may even have moved out into the drier grasslands, where most human evolution took place.

(Many anthropologists believe that *Ramapithecus* belongs in our family tree. But others recently have argued that the hominid was not an ancestor of either modern humans or modern apes, and instead represents a third line that has no living descendants. The issue remains unsettled.)

Australopithecus, 4 Million Years Ago; Africa and Asia

Australopithecus was among the later subhuman species as evolution made its way toward man. The full-grown adult stood about 4 feet tall and had a pelvis that allowed it to assume an upright posture. Its brain size was about 450 cubic centimeters, roughly that of today's chimpanzee. Recent fossils of *Australopithecus afarensis* (from the Latin *australis,* for southern, and the Afar region of Ethiopia, where the first specimens were found), clearly show hips and knees built for walking erect.

The habitats of *Australopithecus* probably were open grasslands dotted with trees and near rivers or lakes that supplied both water and richer vegetation. The hominids probably did not possess sufficient intelligence to make stone tools, but recent evidence suggests that they may have collected stones that had been shaped by forces of nature and resembled themselves, for such icons have been found among their fossil remains.

About 2.5 million years ago, *Australopithecus afarensis* split into two lines — one producing several later forms of *Australopithecus* that died out, and another continuing the hominid lineage that led to man.

Australopithecus, like its human successors, was both a hunter and a gatherer. Its various hominid groups most likely lived in families on the African plains, staying near water sources, where a wide variety of plant foods was apt to grow, scavenging lion kills for meat, and probably catching and eating small game, like hares and turtles. By 1.5 million years ago, *Australopithecus* had wandered into Southeast Asia and begun killing to procure its food — probably because leftovers from meals of other animals no longer could sustain its growing numbers.

Walking Erect, 8 Million to 4 Million Years Ago

The act of walking erect, or bipedalism, seems to have originated gradually from a combination of increased manual dexterity, the use of tools, and brain development. All three factors forced apes up on their hind legs, and a growing reliance on manipulation of objects encouraged them to remain erect in order to carry food and weapons around with them.

The indicator of the type of stance assumed by a creature is the point of entry for the spinal cord into the skull. In the gorilla, for example, the opening for the spinal cord is toward the rear of the skull, indicating a four-legged posture. In modern man, the opening is much farther forward, the head being balanced on the top of the spinal column. By comparison, the ape-man of 4 million years ago had an opening located between these two points, indicating the transition to bipedalism.

The change toward a vertical torso had already appeared among the tree-living primates that used their hands for picking fruit and leaves, and many of these had acquired the ability to stand on their hind legs for short periods when they descended to the ground. For life on the plains, upright posture must have been essential. The ape-men were small, defenseless, and slow in comparison with predators of the plains, and the ability to stand upright and look off into the distance could make the difference between life and death. Upright posture also enhanced hunting ability, since life in the trees had greatly weakened the ape-man's sense of smell, replacing it with sharp vision, which, when coupled with bipedalism, made the ape-man a formidable hunter and tracker.

Bipedalism originated because of another far-reaching factor: the ape-men had hands with precise and powerful grips, developed by their ancestors in response to the demands of life in the trees. When the ape-man stood upright, these hands were ready at all times to compensate for the lack of sharp teeth and claws. Threatened by enemies, the ape-man could defend himself by hurling stones and wielding sticks.

"Bread-Winner" and "Home-Maker," 6 Million Years Ago

Walking erect, according to the latest theory, encouraged development of the family, with its highly efficient divisions of labor, and established the traditional male and female roles of "bread-winner" and "home-maker." This contention is based on the belief that the earliest protohumans, like apes, reproduced very slowly. For example, the period of time required for a female chimpanzee to reach sexual maturity and rear two offspring (replacements for herself and a mate) is twenty-one years; each chimpanzee needs five to six years of nurturing, which the female chimpanzee provides without assistance from the male.

This system made sense in a food-rich tropical forest. But such environments began dwindling many millions of years ago, as global climates turned more sharply seasonal. One species' hardship, however, became another's evolutionary opportunity. The way was opened for a new ape-man that could evolve some means of reproducing faster or surviving longer. According to recent theory, the crucial event was monogamous pair bonding, in which the male helped gather food for his family. Since the newly seasonal environment put food sources farther apart, the best foraging method logically would have been to split up: the female remained close to the home base, giving birth to more offspring and providing them with better care, and the male ventured across the plains to gather food.

Continuous Sex, 8 Million to 4 Million Years Ago

The human female is capable of constant sexual arousal and is physically capable of making love every day of her adult life —

even during pregnancy and shortly afterward. This is most unusual among members of the animal kingdom. No females of any other sexually reproducing species make love with such propensity. All other females have a period of heat, or estrus, during which they copulate, and sex at any other time is highly unusual.

What, then, is the origin of continuous estrus in human females?

According to one modern theory, it harks back to changes that occurred in the female when protohominids began walking erect. Upright posture brought about a narrowing of the pelvic canal, resulting in difficult and often fatal pregnancies. Natural selection favored those females with a proclivity for giving premature birth — to babies small enough to negotiate the narrowed cervical canal. These premature babies required more postnatal care than full-term ones and kept their mothers busier. Thus, these females became more dependent on males for food and protection.

Continuous periods of heat soon became a great advantage for the female, because by maintaining her "sex appeal," she acquired more meat and more protection than did her counterparts who could offer sex less frequently. The females who flaunted their sexiness were better fed, died more rarely of disease or predation, and naturally produced more young, since they were more likely to become pregnant. In time, succeeding generations had disproportionately high numbers of individuals who carried the gene for longer monthly periods of heat, and this led to the evolution of the gene for continuous female sexual accessibility.

Anthropologists also believe that because the largest males probably brought back the greatest amounts of food and offered better shelter and protection from predators, they became the preferred mates of females, and thus fathered larger male offspring. Natural selection, then, favored the genes for large males. This would account for the present difference in size between males and females.

Homo Habilis and Culture, 2 Million Years Ago; Africa, Asia

The name given the first true human being is *Homo habilis,* or "handy man," so called because of his dexterity in fashioning stone tools.

Homo habilis stood slightly under 5 feet tall as an adult and still possessed the apelike jaw and skull shape of his ancestors. More important as an evolutionary trait, however, was his brain capacity, which ranged from 500 to 750 cubic centimeters, about half the size of our own brain. The large numbers of animal bones at *Homo habilis* sites in Africa suggest that he was the first aggressive and skillful hunter in the hominid lineage, instead of merely a meat scavenger, like his ancestors. Plants, roots, eggs, and insects, however, remained staples of his diet, and since there is no evidence that *Homo habilis* discovered fire, he ate meat raw.

While the females and young remained close to campsites, treating hides and occupying their time with other domestic duties, male hunters ventured great distances in search of food. This pursuit, which kept them away from home for days at a time, required the invention of the first vessels for carrying food — which were hollowed gourds — and the first vine-woven baskets used by females for collecting plants and eggs while the males hunted game.

Primitive culture, slight though it was, also originated with *Homo habilis*. One of the oldest pieces of evidence of purely cultural — as opposed to utilitarian — activity lies in the discovery of red ocher paint with the skeletons of *Homo habilis*. Ochers are brightly colored earth minerals of iron long used for pigments. Although the "golden age" of prehistoric cave paintings did not arrive until the advent in Europe of modern man — *Homo sapiens* — the discovery of red ocher paint indicates that rituals may have originated with *Homo habilis*, the first hominid to be bound toward culture.

Homo Erectus and Fire, 1.5 Million Years Ago; Africa, Asia, and Europe

By now man's jaw had receded, giving him a flatter facial profile, and his brain capacity had grown from 750 cubic centimeters to 1100 cc, just short of our own. This hominid brain, however, did not grow uniformly. The greatest expansion was in the parietal and frontal lobes, which in humans today allow for muscle coordination and the ability to concentrate on complex, multifaceted tasks and to plan ahead and contemplate the future. These profound changes in the hominid lineage marked the origin of *Homo erectus*, so named because when the first fossil was discovered it represented the earliest known upright primate.

Homo erectus had obviously greater dexterity than his predecessors. He constructed the first standardized tools for hunting and butchering. His sophisticated brain allowed him to fashion an extraordinary stone implement, a large teardrop-shaped hand ax, whose design and symmetry reveal a keen sense of esthetics. Such detailing, coupled with the ax's utilitarian value, strongly suggest that *Homo erectus* was the first hominid with the ability to conceive a design and then labor over a piece of stone until the plan was executed to his specifications.

With his improved talents, *Homo erectus* became the most successful hominid to that time, and his numbers increased as he began to migrate and adapt easily to other terrains and climates. From Southeast Asia he moved into the Nile Valley and then northward to the eastern shores of the Mediterranean. Hominid remains also have been found farther east, in Java (Java man) and in China (Peking man).

Some African groups reached Europe, and a few crossed over a land bridge that once connected Tunisia, Sicily, and Italy. Others traveled eastward, circumnavigating the Mediterranean, and up north into the Balkans. The proliferation of *Homo erectus* into widely varied environments affected the rest of human evolution, for when modern man appeared more than a million years later, local climates produced the changes that gave rise to the different races of man.

Homo erectus was also the first hominid to discover fire, a breakthrough that enticed him to eat meat, which he could flavor, and keep from spoiling, by flame, and that may have given him a new disease. Some fossil bones of *Homo erectus* are grossly deformed, covered by sheaths of bony tissue up to a quarter of an inch thick. Long thought to be the result of a bacterial disease, the condition, paleontologists now believe, is similar to that found in people today who have been exposed to chronic overdoses of Vitamin A. Apparently *Homo erectus* first contracted this disease by eating animal liver. *Homo erectus* was the first hominid, and the only primate, to make meat a major part of his diet.

Homo Sapiens, 100,000 Years Ago; Africa, Asia, Europe

The stage was set for the entrance of *Homo sapiens* by several drastic events. The world's climate began to grow cold about 75,000 years ago. The shift was gradual and fluctuant, but the trend was clearly toward an Ice Age. So much water eventually became locked up in ice caps that the sea level plummeted and land bridges protruded, emerging onto continental shelves and becoming isthmuses. In search of food, man soon spread into the Americas across the Bering Strait and down the island chains of Indonesia toward New Guinea and Australia.

Dexterous of hand and imaginative of mind, the early woman skinned furry animals and fashioned heavy coats to ward off the cold, and the man constructed huge huts, some nearly 50 feet long, by stretching animal hides over wooden stakes driven into the ground. When the climate became harsh, he moved his family and his precious fire inside to the sanctuary of caves, which offered protection from predators, too.

By 100,000 years ago, man's face already had flattened so that he was recognizably like us, although his eyes were crowned with a bulging brow. His brain had grown to the size of contemporary man's, about 1400 cubic centimeters, permitting him to develop the rudiments of language. (See *Language,* page 49.) These anatomical changes, along with his new behavioral patterns, marked the dawn of a new hominid species, *Homo sapiens,* or "wise man," who was the immediate progenitor of modern man. The earth's population at the time was about 2 million people, spread through disparate locales in Europe, Asia, and Africa and poised soon to enter the Americas and Australia.

Neanderthals and Spirituality, 50,000 Years Ago; Western Asia, Europe

Neanderthal man camped practically on the doorstep of modernity. He lived throughout Europe and western Asia, and with a brain capacity equivalent to our own, possessed tool-making skills that enabled him to fashion long flint knives. Caricatures often show him as a primitive creature with a heavy brow, thick, large nose, and brutish expression, but actually many Neanderthals possessed classic European features and fair, hairless skin.

The origin of Neanderthals is important because of its correlation to the dawning of spirituality in the hominid lineage. This is most graphically shown by the Neanderthals' practice of burying their dead with ritual funerals, rather than abandoning them. They interred the deceased's body, along with food, hunting weapons, and fire charcoals, and strewed the corpse with an assortment of flowers. A Neanderthal grave discovered in Shanidar, Iraq, contained the pollen of eight different flowers. This primal ceremony revealed man's first inclination toward spirituality and a belief in an afterlife.

About 40,000 years ago Neanderthals disappeared rapidly from the face of the earth, a mystifying occurrence. Paleontologists today continue to debate the causes of this abrupt fate: Neanderthals were driven into extinction by invasions of modern man, and many of their traits have been assimilated into our own gene pool; or they evolved into modern man, though this transformation would have to have been carried out at an amazing pace. At least one anthropologist has recently presented evidence that the man-like apes spotted occasionally high in the Himalayas are actually Neanderthals who were forced from their homelands by engulfing masses of modern man.

Homo Sapiens Sapiens, 40,000 Years Ago; Africa, Asia, Europe, America, Australia

True modern man, *Homo sapiens sapiens*, was our immediate progenitor. He emerged throughout Africa, Europe, and Asia, and soon spread to North America and later to Australia. His traits symbolized the vast strides he had made since the hominid stage: he possessed a high native intelligence; he wrought flint knives and piercingly sharp objects, like spear points and arrowheads; and for killing dangerous prey at a distance he invented the bow and arrow and the spear-thrower, an apparatus for launching a spear on a slight trajectory.

"Wise, wise man," as his name translates, was the starting point for the various races of humans, and he was responsible for originating many practices that, in other forms, are with us today. About 30,000 years ago modern man began sketching primitive, colorful paintings on the walls of caves, which culminated in the magnificently detailed and realistic frescoes found by archeologists in caves in France and Spain. Superb renderings of bison, reindeer, ibexes, and other animals are portrayed in vivid detail, grazing or in startled poses as they tried to evade hunters. So skilled in style and technique is one painting that dates to 13,000 B.C. that the cave containing it has been called the Sistine Chapel of prehistory. (See *Art,* page 270.)

Early man's art extended beyond painting to the sculpting of figurines; a favorite model was the buxom female, presumably a "Venus" fertility symbol.

By 18,000 years ago, man reduced his reliance on hunting by domesticating animals for food. About 8000 years later, he came on a discovery even more momentous, one that in fact changed the course of history: he learned that searching for grains, vegetables, and fruit was unnecessary if he settled in one place, planted seeds, and then gathered the harvest. The propitious factor that made the discovery possible was the receding of the last great Ice Age, which had chilled the earth for 60,000 years before letting man return to life on the plains. The transition from wandering hunter to settled farmer provided a stability in the life of *Homo sapiens sapiens,* which culminated about 9000 years ago in the first settlements, and 4000 years later in the establishment of the first cities and the dawn of civilization.

American Indian, 35,000 Years Ago; North and South America

The first humans entering North America constituted the earliest mass exodus in history. As long as 25,000, perhaps even 35,000, years ago they began a steady stream of migration across a broad land mass linking Siberia to Alaska, and through that journey of about 55 miles, they became the first Americans. Authorities are almost certain that the New World was merely a residence of early man, not a breeding ground, because no fossil progenitors have been discovered there.

Descendants of Asian *Homo sapiens,* the American settlers were hunters who quickly scoured the continent in search of game. Over the course of only three to four millennia, they hunted all the great mammals of North America to extinction and were forced to begin a predominantly vegetarian existence. As befitted their Asian descent, these people had dark eyes above wide cheekbones, with copper skin and straight black hair.

Later known as Amerinds, they spread from Alaska all the way to the tip of South America and from California clear across to Maine. As recently as 11,000 years ago, their cultures already had taken on the diverse characteristics that came to represent various Amerind tribes. One practice that gained widespread acceptance was the use of a burial ground, first observed by Neanderthals;

The first settlers of the Americas were Asians who traversed the 55-mile land mass then linking Siberia to Alaska.

relics and icons were placed next to human remains in hopes of helping the deceased achieve eternal life. An offshoot of the burial grounds, "woodhenges" made of posts arranged in circular order, served as astronomical observatories, revealing a sophistication previously thought lacking in early North Americans.

Three important civilizations flourished among American Indians.

The **Incas** of Peru ruled a vast empire in the Andes of perhaps 7 million people. Sophisticated architects, potters, and metal workers, they established a well-organized government and constructed a network of superb roads. The Spanish conquistadors who arrived in the 15th century battled for more than thirty years to subdue the Incas.

The **Aztecs** of Mexico founded their capital, Tenochtitlán, in 1325 in the region that today is Mexico City. They too were fine architects and built elaborate temples for a religion that required numerous human sacrifices. Some victims came from within their own tribes, but others offered to Aztec deities were prisoners of wars that were fought with neighboring tribes specifically to obtain the annual quota of sacrificial victims.

The **Mayas** of Central America established one of the oldest Indian civilizations. Originating about 1000 B.C. in the dense lowland jungles of Central America, the Mayan civilization was characterized by great complexes of pyramidal temples and palaces, which were the focuses of religious and political life. The country was divided into four regions, each ruled from a central towering temple. The people developed a system of picture writing and kept accurate calendars that enabled Mayan astronomers to predict solar eclipses. Wars among the four political centers began to weaken the Mayan civilization about A.D. 900, and in a short time their once-great empire was in shambles. The Spaniards arriving in the late 1500s found the natives living in such primitive fashion that there was sincere doubt as to whether they were actually human.

The Modern Brain, 100,000 Years Ago

The small, hairy primate *Dryopithecus,* which served as ancestral stock for modern apes and man, lived about 36 million years ago and was controlled by a brain with a capacity of only 150 cubic centimeters, or the equivalent of about 9 heaping tablespoons of gray matter. By the time of the arrival of the family of man, or the hominid lineage, in the form of *Ramapithecus* 15 million years ago, brain size had doubled, but its growth was very slight over the next 10 million years. Once the ape-man began to make greater use of his hands to brandish weapons and fashion simple tools, however, the brain's expansion was rapid.

This seemingly sudden growth, after thousands of years of inertia, began about 4 million years ago with the dawn of *Australopithecus,* a short, largely defenseless ape-man who lived on the ground but possessed the ingenuity to break antelope thighbones to lengths that made convenient clubs. In a "mere" 2 million years, from *Australopithecus* to *Homo habilis,* the first true man, brain capacity jumped from 450 cc to 750 cc. The tool-making industry of *Homo habilis,* or handy man, further stimulated brain development, so that by the time *Homo erectus* appeared, about 1.5 million years ago, the human brain had begun enlarging at the phenomenal rate of 20-odd centimeters, or 1 heaping tablespoon of gray matter, every hundred thousand years.

The evolution of speech also must have had a profound effect on the human brain. About 500,000 years ago the rate of growth peaked when the brain expanded at an astonishing rate of more than 200 cubic centimeters every hundred thousand years. No other organ in the history of life is known to have grown as fast. When

Homo sapiens emerged about 100,000 years ago, the brain already had reached its present size of 1400 cc, and changes since then have been insignificant.

The tapering off of growth, or stability of size, can be accounted for in two ways. One is that all the resources of the brain as it now exists have yet to be tapped, so no additional size is required. Second, from an anatomical standpoint, the fetal brain cannot be larger because of the narrow width of the female birth canal, itself a result of humans' erect posture.

5

Language: Sanskrit to Surnames

Language, 1.5 Million Years Ago

Apart from the rote miming of parrots and myna birds, no animal can speak a humanlike language. Many animals make complex sounds, of course, among them dolphins and chimpanzees, but only in humans do these sounds represent objects and events in an arbitrary yet symbolic way. Though the words vary from dialect to dialect, they have specific meanings in each case and are solely the inventions of the human mind.

Since preserving the human voice was an innovation of modern times, the sounds voiced by our distant ancestors left no tangible trace. But by studying the size and shape of fossil hominid brains scientists can obtain a clue to the neural machinery that is necessary for the development and organization of language.

The development of language was a slow and laborious process that seems to have begun with the forerunners of modern man, *Homo erectus,* some 1.5 million years ago. Studies of the cranial capacity of early man indicate that his brain possessed a left hemisphere (which in modern man is the seat of language) slightly larger than the right hemisphere. *Homo erectus* also had a well-developed frontal section of the brain, now known as Broca's area, which coordinates the muscles of the mouth and throat that we use when we speak. Thus, early man was not hampered by a lack of speech apparatus; in fact, he possessed an anatomical structure capable of producing the entire spectrum of vocal effects available to us today. Whether or not he actually used it is unknown.

*

In the total absence of any clue to the speech patterns of prehistoric man, scholars can offer only speculation about how language originated. Several theories have been in and out of vogue.

The Bow-Wow Theory, as named and proposed by the German-born British philologist Friedrich Max Müller in the 19th century, posits that language grew out of man's attempts to imitate natural sounds, as an infant calls a locomotive a *choo-choo* or a cow a *moo.* According to this suggestion, man's first utterances were onomatopoeic or echoic words that emulated the sounds of what was happening around him — for example, *thunder, bump, sneeze, splash, slosh, sizzle, moan,* and *mumble.*

The Pooh-Pooh Theory holds that speech originated from the spontaneous exclamations and interjections of early humans: cries of fear, surprise, anger, pain, disgust, despair, and joy.

The Yo-He-Ho Theory suggests that language evolved from reflex utterances — grunts, gasps, glottal contractions — evoked by strenuous physical exertion, such as hacking up a carcass after a successful hunt or dragging a heavy log through underbrush.

The Sing-Song Theory contends that human speech arose from primitive rhythmic chants associated with ritualistic dance.

Standing alone, each of these theories has flaws, and even combined, their composite effect cannot account for the full complexity of human language. This is particularly true because language as we know it is more the product of the human mind than it is the product of the human vocal cords.

At one time linguists believed that language originated merely to facilitate communication so that one individual could relate to another what he or she should be doing next in the practical matters of daily life. Today, however, it is widely thought that language originated so that early man could **think** more effectively. For without the acquisition of words, and the structure of language to string them together in logical and meaningful order, there can be no such thing as complex human thought. This is evident in human language's most supreme attribute: its limitless creativity. Even today language grows at a rapid pace with the use of new words coined from technology or derivatives of old words attached to trends.

Alone of all the creatures on earth, humans can say things that have never been said — and still be understood. Animals can only repeat the same limited utterances over and over again, as their progenitors have done for millions of years. Man's accomplishment has bestowed on him the capacity to create something new every time he speaks.

Indo-European Language, Pre-5000 B.C.; Russia

Indo-European is the name given to the family of languages to which English belongs. Indo-European is thought to have originated on the Russian steppes near the Black Sea, or slightly north in Lithuania, and to have spread through Europe, Russia, Iran, and India.

The name Indo-European indicates that this family of languages today is spoken throughout most of Europe and as far eastward as northern India.

In most Indo-European languages, the numerals from 1 to 10 and the words of close family relationships, such as father, mother, sister, and brother, are clearly recognizable as coming from the same roots. The English "mother," for example, is easily discernible in Sanskrit *(mata)*, Greek *(mēter)*, Latin *(mater)*, Italian *(madre)*, French *(mère)*, German *(Mutter)*, and Russian *(mat')*.

(In Western Europe today, only one regional tongue, Basque, is not descended from early Indo-European origins; it may be a remnant of a cave language spoken before the last Ice Age. The idea is reinforced by the meanings of many Basque words: "knife" translates as "the stone that cuts," and "ceiling" means "roof of the cave.")

The oldest tongues of the Indo-European family of which clear records exist are **Sanskrit** (2000 B.C.) and ancient **Greek** (1400 B.C.). In Sanskrit, the oldest records are a series of religious poems known as the Vedic hymns; the oldest Greek texts are the Minoan Linear B tablets, containing sparse writing, difficult to interpret, that was not identified as Greek until 1952.

As the Indo-European people migrated throughout Europe, or were conquered and assimilated into other groups, the language developed into numerous subgroups. One was English, which belongs to the Germanic branch; the other comprised French, Spanish, and Italian, which belong to the Latin-Romance branch. The name of the latter, incidentally, has nothing to do with a passion for *amour,* but stems from the Latin word for Roman, which was, not surprisingly, *romanus.*

Many linguists favor Lithuania on the Baltic Sea as the homeland for Indo-European. First, the spoken modern language closest to original Indo-European is Lithuanian. Second, the parent Indo-European tongue contained words for three objects — "turtle," "salmon," and "beech tree" — whose living forms were simultaneously indigenous to that region near the Baltic Sea.

Origin of Indo-European Languages

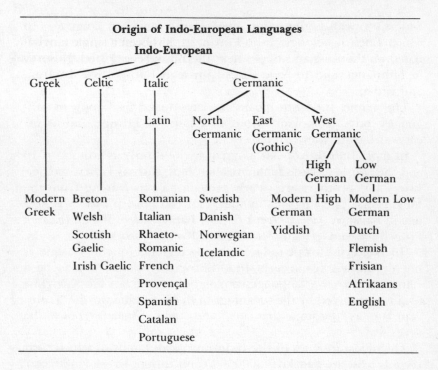

Indo-European

Greek — Modern Greek

Celtic — Breton, Welsh, Scottish Gaelic, Irish Gaelic

Italic — Latin — Romanian, Italian, Rhaeto-Romanic, French, Provençal, Spanish, Catalan, Portuguese

Germanic:

North Germanic — Swedish, Danish, Norwegian, Icelandic

East Germanic (Gothic)

West Germanic — High German — Modern High German, Yiddish

West Germanic — Low German — Modern Low German, Dutch, Flemish, Frisian, Afrikaans, English

Greek, 1600 B.C.

Greek is an ancient Indo-European language that originated around 1600 B.C. Linguists know that around 1400 B.C. several tribes, already speaking a form of Greek, migrated to the Greek peninsula, to most of the islands of the Aegean, and to the west coast of Anatolia, where they established colonies and where their languages underwent refinement. With few exceptions these areas are occupied by Greek-speaking people today.

About 750 B.C. a second vast colonization movement occurred, resulting in the birth of Greek cities all around the Mediterranean and the Black Sea, especially in southern Italy and Sicily. During the following centuries, including the brief span when Alexander the Great made his vast conquests, it seemed that Greek was destined to become the dominant language of the world. Even when Greece was later conquered by the Romans, Greek was still considered the language of culture and was taught to young Romans by their Greek slave-tutors, though it eventually was superseded by the Latin of the Roman conquerors.

Greek, despite its numerous dialects, has been a single language throughout its long history. But it has progressed through several distinct phases. The ancient phase lasted from 1800–1600 B.C., giving way to the archaic and then the classical period, which flourished for four centuries and witnessed the adoption of the Greek alphabet and the creation of the great Homeric epics, the *Iliad* and the *Odyssey*. This was followed by the Hellenistic and Roman phase from 300 B.C. to A.D. 400.

The Greek that is spoken today arose slowly during the Byzantine period, beginning in the 4th century A.D. It derived directly from the Koinē (which means "new"), a fairly uniform variety of spoken Greek that gradually replaced the numerous local dialects after the breakdown of old political barriers and the establishment of Alexander's empire in the 4th century B.C.

There has been strong continuity throughout the many phases of the Greek language. So much so, in fact, that modern Greek resembles ancient Greek more than the Romance languages of French, Spanish, and Italian resemble their progenitor, Latin. Whereas a literate modern Frenchman cannot read and understand classical Latin without special study, an average well-educated Greek can decipher the inscriptions cut in stone by his ancestors twenty-four centuries ago.

Latin, 600 B.C.; Italy

Latin first appeared as the tongue spoken by a small settlement of people around the mouth of the Tiber River in west central Italy. A lack of written records obscures its history up to about 600 B.C., the date of the earliest Latin inscriptions.

The Latin language as it first emerged was a rough, elemental style of speech, severely tailored to a military-agricultural civilization. It lacked most of the refinements of syntax and vocabulary that later distinguished it. Though archaic Latin made scant use of prepositions or rigidly fixed word order, its basic sounds differed surprisingly little from its later classical counterpart: vowels, for example, were distinguished by long and short sounds, and consonants displayed the same dearth of certain phonemes that characterized classical Latin. The sounds represented in modern English by *ch* of "church," *sh* of "she," *j* of "joke," and *th* of "thing" all were absent from Latin.

Latin literature, as far as the written records reveals, began in the third century B.C., and it had a great influence on imposing a structure on the language that in two centuries would evolve into classical Latin.

Today, about half of our English words derive from classical Latin (the other half being Germanic in origin), and many reflect the Roman way of life. Our "mile" stems from the Latin *mille,* meaning "one thousand" and often used to refer to a unit of a thousand formal steps, each about 5 feet, by which Roman cartographers measured the distance between settlements.

Classical Latin, 100 B.C.; Italy

Classical Latin, characterized by complicated syntax, finally emerged five hundred years after the birth of archaic Latin and reigned supreme for more than a third of a millennium. Classical Latin was the language of Caesar, Cicero, and Virgil, a polished tongue capable of expressing the most complex notions, the loftiest of poetic and philosophical thought, and the keenest of legal and judicial expression.

The Roman conquests over much of Europe helped to assimilate it with the languages of other regions, thus forming numerous dialects. Like Greek in its halcyon era, Latin was on its way to becoming a world language when its path was halted by the great barbarian invasions beginning in the 5th century A.D. As the Roman Empire fell to the Germanic marauders from the north, the Latin language was forced to accept and enjoin countless new Germanic words. In fact, there is a huge lexicon of words that were unfamiliar in classical Latin but are found in medieval Latin writings.

The new hybrid Latin continued to evolve during the Middle

Ages, giving birth to various dialects throughout Europe. Disturbed that spoken Latin was falling short of classical standards, Charlemagne, emperor of the Holy Roman Empire, in A.D. 782 invited the scholar and grammarian Alcuin of York to his court at Aix-la-Chapelle to make a study of pure classical Latin so that its use could be reinstated throughout the empire. It soon became obvious, however, that the vernacular of the day was a tongue vastly different from classical Latin.

Realizing the impossibility of returning to classical standards, Charlemagne, in 813, shortly before his death, ordered the Council of Tours to decree that sermons no longer be delivered in *lingua latina* but the new *lingua roman rustica* ("in the rustic Roman language") to make them intelligible to the congregations. Latin remained the official language of the Roman Catholic Church, but the new *lingua romana rustica* gradually evolved throughout Europe into the five primary Romance languages: Portuguese, Romanian, French, Italian, and Spanish.

French, 842; Spanish, 950; Italian, 960

A period of about three hundred years passed before French language evolved from the hybrid form of classical Latin, and another hundred years lapsed before French sprang into full bloom in the middle of the 9th century.

The first document to appear in the new French (today called Old French) was the A.D. 842 Oath of Strasbourg, a treaty of alliance sworn by two of Charlemagne's descendants in the presence of their troops, who, as witnesses to the accord, had to be addressed in their own spoken tongue, which was not yet the new French language. By the late 11th century French had flourished to the point of producing its first truly epic poem, the *Chanson de Roland.*

Old French of this era was primarily the language of a race of hardy warriors and farmers, uncouth and ill-mannered. The tongue was full of strong stresses, hard and full-mouthed sounds, and comparatively little phonetic grace. To a contemporary student of French who recognizes the language for its milk and honey articulation, this probably would have been a roguish speech. Its tones were more similar in rhythm to present-day English than to the softer cadences of modern French.

French achieved prominence as a world language during the golden age of Louis XIV. Gradually it became the intellectual, diplomatic, and literary language of most of Europe. Voltaire, writing to the Prussian king Frederick the Great, commented that everyone at court spoke French and that German was used only to address soldiers and horses.

Also beginning as dialects of classical Latin and gradually evolving into tongues in their own right, Spanish and Italian emerged more than a century after French, in 950 and 960 respectively. Unlike French, both languages retained Latin's soft vowel sounds, but from their inception they merged the many Latin cases into one form.

The derivation of French, Spanish, and Italian from Latin is apparent in numerous modern words. Though the classical Latin for "horse" was *equus*, the slang of the day was *cavallus*. In French it became *cheval*, in Spanish *caballo*, and in Italian *cavallo*.

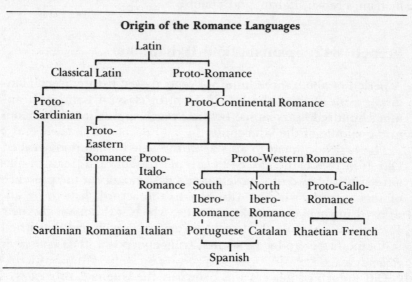

Origin of the Romance Languages

German, A.D. 500

German is a branch of the Indo-European language family that also includes such tongues as English, Swedish, Danish, and Icelandic. Unlike the Romance languages, which are direct variants of Latin, in the case of Germanic languages there are no written records of the parent tongue.

Archeological evidence suggests that as early as 750 B.C. Germanic tribes inhabited southern Scandinavia and northern Germany. These early Germans spoke in numerous dialects, and over the next five hundred years they spread out and split into three general groups: West Germanic, North Germanic, and East Germanic.

The latter group, in the 4th century A.D., lived along the western shore of the Black Sea (modern Romania and Bulgaria) and spoke a tongue called **Gothic,** the oldest Germanic language of which records exist. Our knowledge of Gothic comes primarily from the remains of a 4th-century Bible translation made for the Visigoths living along the lower Danube by a Visigothic bishop of the Arian church named Ulfilas.

Over the next hundred years Gothic spread, along with the conquering Goths, over much of Southern Europe, though it never became a predominant tongue. By the 9th century Gothic was used only in some church services near the lower Danube, and thereafter it seems to have survived only among the Goths of the Crimea, who were last mentioned in the middle of the 16th century by a Flemish diplomat named de Busbecq. On a mission to Constantinople in 1560–1562, de Busbecq collected a number of words and phrases indicating that the language spoken there was still essentially a form of Gothic.

Where the East Germanic language became extinct, the North and West tongues flourished, spread, and developed into several languages spoken today. North Germanic evolved into **Icelandic, Norwegian, Danish,** and **Swedish.** West Germanic gave birth to **Netherlandish, English,** and around the 6th century, to **modern German.**

Prior to this time the West Germanic tongue had the voiceless stops *p, t,* and *k* in much the same distribution as in modern English. Then, during the 6th century, there occurred a change customarily called the "High German consonant shift." After a vowel, the letters *p, t,* and *k* came to be pronounced as long fricatives, *ff, ss,* and *ch.* The word *maken* ("to make"), for example, became *machen; hopen* ("hope") became *hoffen.* (Fricatives are sounds pronounced by forcing the breath, either voiced or voiceless, through a narrow slit formed at some point in the mouth, as in *f, v,* and *z.*) At the beginning of words, and when doubled, *p, t,* and *k* came to be pronounced as affricates: the word *ten* ("ten") became *zehn* (pronounced "tzehn") and *sitten* ("to sit") became *sitzen.* Linguists

Germanic Peoples. The original German language split into three branches. One became extinct, another evolved into Danish and Swedish, and the third gave rise to English and modern German.

argue that only after this consonant shift is there justification in speaking of a German (that is, a High German) language distinct from the other Germanic tongues.

Yiddish, 10th Century; Germany

Yiddish is a true Germanic language featuring elements of German, Hebrew, Aramaic, and the Slavic and Romance tongues. It is the main colloquial language of the majority of Central and Eastern European Jews and, along with Hebrew, is one of their two languages.

Yiddish originated in the 10th century from the needs of Jews from northern France who, driven into exile by the Crusades and later persecuted following the devastating Black Plague, moved throughout the Slavic lands, modifying their native Hebrew tongue. Within several generations most Jews in the region had such little knowledge of pure Hebrew, the language of prayer and liturgy, that they clearly needed a formal language all their own.

For two centuries, Yiddish was considered a vulgar language, suitable for conversation but not for writing. Even when the first Yiddish books were written in the 12th century, they were meant to be read only by women and children.

Over the next hundred years Yiddish translations of the Bible and prayer books appeared, along with secular writings adapted from German and Italian literature. The period is called the *Spiel-mann* era, named after the German minstrels of the time. By the middle of the 18th century, Yiddish had become the standard language of Eastern European Jews. Despite its hybrid nature, Yiddish is so strongly rooted in medieval German that today both Yiddish and German are often comprehensible to those who know only one of the languages.

English, A.D. 700

The English language is a complex hybrid. It originated from three Teutonic, or Germanic, dialects, which themselves decended from the original Indo-European about 3000 B.C.

The first of the German tongues, Jutish, was brought into England about A.D. 449 from Jutland. It was followed forty years later by the introduction of Saxon, which came from Holstein, and then by Anglian, which came from lower Denmark. These three dialects soon superimposed themselves on the thousand-year-old indigenous Celtic, which itself had been modified by scattered remains of classical Latin.

Although Celtic remained the language of some areas of Wales, Scotland, Cornwall, and Ireland (and survives there today), by the 8th century most of the people in the region were speaking the Germanic Anglo-Saxon language, which is considered the oldest form of English.

The next crucial stage in the development of English was the first of many Viking invasions, which began in A.D. 793 from Denmark and Norway. Although the Norse language of the invaders failed to survive in England as a separate tongue beyond 1035, except for many of the pronouns, it effected so many permanent changes in the language that today the tongue most nearly cognate to modern English is Frisian, spoken by the inhabitants of the New Dutch province of Friesland and the islands off the west coast of Schleswig.

(Icelandic, which has changed little over the last thousand years, is the living language most nearly resembling Old English in grammatical structure.)

With the conquest of England in 1066 by William of Normandy, Anglo-Saxon received a near-fatal blow. The French-speaking

Normans established themselves as the ruling caste and treated the native Saxons as inferiors. Although the mother tongue of the first twelve kings and queens, from William I (who ruled from 1066 to 1087) to Richard II (from 1377 to 1399), was French, for three hundred years England remained a land of two languages, French and Anglo-Saxon. As a consequence, modern English has one of the world's largest vocabularies, composed of many synonyms from both French (via Latin) and Anglo-Saxon (via German) origin: "perspiration" (French origin), "sweat" (Anglo-Saxon origin), "dine" (French), "eat" (Anglo-Saxon); "desire," "want"; "deceased," "dead"; and for the bodily wastes of "urine" and "excrement" (both French), the Anglo-Saxon words are impolite in conversation or print.

The two tongues blended into a new language, Middle English, which became the official language of the court in 1362, during the reign of King Edward III, and in 1380 became the language for teaching in the universities at Oxford and Cambridge. Geoffrey Chaucer (1340–1400), greatly helped to nurture the new language. The tongue flowered into Elizabethan English, best known through the writings of William Shakespeare. Shakespeare died in 1616, just four years before the sailing of the *Mayflower*, which brought the Pilgrims, and the new English, to American shores.

The tongue we speak today is approximately half Germanic and half Romance (rooted in French and Latin), with copious additions from Greek in the vocabulary of science and technology. The French influence is strongly felt in words relating to foods and their preparation. *Sauce, soup, fry, toast, roast, boil,* and *jelly, condiments,* and *pastry* may not look French, but they are of French origin.

State and City Names

The study of the origins of place names is known as toponymy, a colorful and sometimes confusing science. Though a "ville" or "town" suffixing a dot on a map sounds simple enough, the influences from so many diverse sources has given toponymy high rank among etymological studies. At least half of America's fifty states, for instance, bear names derived from Indian words:

Dakota	Allied (since the state was the home of the confederated Sioux tribe)
Oklahoma	The Red people

Tennessee	The vines of the Big Bend
Iowa	The sleepy ones
Kansas	A breeze near the ground
Michigan	A great water
Kentucky	The dark and bloody ground
Illinois	The tribe of perfect men
Texas	Friends!
Idaho	Good morning!
Mississippi	Father of waters

Other states' names are of European origin. Some bear the names of queens or virgin queens: Maryland and Virginia; others are derived from the names of kings, like the Carolinas and Georgia, from Charles and George of England, and Louisiana from Louis of France.

California's name was bestowed by the Spanish settlers of the area, who knew of the imaginary land, Californe, mentioned in Ordoñey de Montaldo's 1510 romance, *Las Sergas Esplandian.* He, in turn, had taken the name from the 11th-century French epic, the *Chanson de Roland.* A name of more recent vintage is that of California's largest city, Los Angeles. It is a shortened form of the name bestowed on an area that in 1781 was given the longest name of any American city: El Pueblo de Nuestra Senõra la Reini de los Angeles de Porciúncula, Spanish for "The Village of Our Lady the Queen of the Angels of Little Portion."

New York City has had several names, not all of them flattering. In 1807, Washington Irving nicknamed its original borough Gotham, meaning "the hamlet of the Goths." Gotham was a village in England during the days of King John. As the story goes, the king's subjects, having learned that he was planning to establish a hunting lodge near their Nottinghamshire site, and fearing high taxes and other stringent measures, all acted by preconceived plan as if possessed by lunacy, and the king's messengers reported the spot unsuitable for sane people to inhabit. Gotham since then has assumed the meaning of a town with a "method to its madness."

The borough's actual name, Manhattan, is said to mean in the language of the Delaware Indians "the place where we all got drunk." This apparently refers to a drinking bout in which the natives polished off a barrel of Henry Hudson's favorite and most expensive rum.

First Names, 1.5 Million Years Ago

The story of the use of personal names is sketchy, like many things associated with the early linguistic capabilities of man.

The origin of language itself, about 1.5 million years ago, also is believed to mark the use of first names to distinguish one man from his neighbor, though experts are uncertain what these first names may have sounded like. They are sure only that man already had formed the most basic social group — the family — and required some verbal means of identifying every member to distinguish each one or to summon him or her.

The oldest surviving personal name is believed by archeologists to be En-lil-ti, a word that appears on a Sumerian tablet dating from about 3300 B.C. that was discovered outside Baghdad in 1936. But some feel strongly that En-lil-ti was probably the name of a Sumerian deity. If they are correct, the honor of receiving the first personal name falls on N'armer, the Father of Men, Egypt's first pharoah, who dates back before 3000 B.C.

Among various linguistic theories about the origins of names, the most valid states that people were named for physical characteristics. Put simply, a small man might be called "the Short One," a light-complexioned woman "the White One," and so on. From the early ritual of bestowing names in this manner followed a belief that powers and traits — even physical attributes like size and strength — could be invested in an individual because of the name given him or her. Naming an infant boy "the Strong One," for example, was supposed to ensure his military success when he reached adulthood.

The descriptive quality of names became more specific as civilization advanced. The Romans alone gave such graphic names as Agrippa, "born feet-first"; Dexter, "right-handed"; Seneca, "old"; Cecil, "dimwitted"; Lucius, "light"; and Livy, "bluish."

Names also began to exceed the limitations of physical attributes. These names, many of them connoting intangible qualities, flourished in many civilizations. The Hebrews, for example, used Beulah, "married"; Solomon, "peaceable"; Isaac, "laughter"; Ann, "gracious"; and David, "beloved."

The next kind of nomenclature was that which formed the basis for surnames, those giving an indication of an individual's occupation or location. George is Greek for "farmer," Angelo for "messenger," and Philip for "lover of horses"; Morgan is Welsh for "dweller by the sea."

Surnames, 11th Century

The custom of family names did not really arise in Europe until patrician Venetian families began to hand down a second name from father to son in the 11th century. Burgeoning populations, increased travel by people of various nations and tribes, and improved communications had by then outstripped the supply of available first, or Christian, names.

Prior to the 11th century a surname, if it was used at all, usually represented the name of a primitive clan or tribe. But even this infrequent use of surnames fell into disuse after the fall of the Roman Empire — and was not reinstituted for almost a thousand years.

The first three kinds of surnames were patronymics, like "Michael, John's son," which later evolved to Michael Johnson; trade names, like "Thomas the Baker," which ultimately developed into Thomas Baker; and location names, such as Charles-at-the-well," which eventually became Charles Atwell.

Other, more colorful surnames eclipsed these with descriptions of personal traits or the habits of family ancestors. Drinkwater (in French, "Boileau"; in Italian, "Bevilacqua") was designated a teetotaling relative in the family tree. White (in French, "Leblanc"; in Italian, "Bianchi"; in German, "Weiss"; and in Welsh, "Gwynne") usually meant that a family member had an extremely fine complexion or prematurely gray hair.

Despite the pressing need for family names and the increasing use of them the world over, as late as the 15th century many Englishmen — and virtually all Irishmen — were without surnames. In 1465, King Edward IV decreed that every Irishman should "take to him an English surname, of one town as Sutton, Chester, Trym, Skryne, Crok, Kinsale; or color as whyte, black, brown; or art of science, as smith or carpenter; of office, as cook, butler and that he and issue shall use this name."

Each culture had unique ways of dispensing patronymics. In the 15th century, the Irish adopted the prefix *O* to indicate "descendant of;" it was generally used to describe the grandson of the original. Thus, the first O'Dwyer was Dwyer's grandson. And David, son of Patrick, became David Fitzpatrick, *fitz* being the anglicized form of the Old French word for "son," brought to England by the Normans.

The Italians frequently used *di*, as in di Giovanni, the Italian equivalent of Johnson. The Russians used *vich* and *ich* as patronymic suffixes; they also used *ov* or *ev*, so Petrov means "of the Peters," and Ivanov, "of the Johns." Often they would add the secondary patronymic ending of *sky* or *ski* to form Ivanovsky, which means "of the nature of the descendants of John." The name of the great Russian novelist Fyodor Mikhailovich Dostoyevsky means "Fyodor, son of Michael of the nature of the descendants of Dostoy" — and tells much about his ancestry.

Other surnames came about merely by the addition of *s* to the father's name: Abrahams, Clements, Edwards, Franks, Hawkins, Jacobs, Phillips, Roberts, Samuels, and Waters. Still other modern surnames originated as matronymics: Nelson is "Nell's son," Allison is "Alice's son," and Babson is "Barbara's son." Seemingly, when surnames originated, few traces of male chauvinism historically were involved.

Many common Jewish surnames are of more recent origin. A people shuffled about from one nation to another during medieval times, Jews were forced by harsh laws to change their traditional patronyms, and beginning in the 19th century, many Jews adopted or were given the name of their town of birth. But others, according to the onomatologist Elsdon Smith, "living in crowded, airless, and sunless ghettos, frequently adopted names which alluded to green woods and fields." Hence today we have such Jewish names as Greenblatt ("green leaf"), Rosenblum ("rose bloom"), Lilienthal ("lily valley"), and Rosenthal ("rose valley").

Earlier Jewish surnames arose during the Middle Ages, when German kings and dukes forced Jews to adopt Germanic names and to pay highly for them. Silverberg ("mountain of silver") and Morgenstern ("star of the morning") were among the most costly names; Fischer ("fisherman"), Kaufmann ("merchant"), and Schneider ("tailor") were moderately priced. Since the practice was a system of taxation to fatten royal purses, authorities penalized Jewish peasants who could not afford a fancy name: they were forced to purchase inexpensive names that were blatant insults, such as Schmutz ("dirt") and Eselkopf ("ass head") — names that have since been dropped from use but still appear in old German records.

Ethnic Slurs

Wop

When Italian immigrants started arriving in the United States in large numbers, "wop" actually was a manly compliment; it derived from the Neapolitan word *guappo,* meaning "strong." Later it degenerated into a slur, joined by the word "guinea," the old name for the African coast and presumably applied to olive-skinned Italians to lump them in the same category as black slaves.

Coon

This old Southern term for blacks derives from the last syllable of the Portuguese *barracões* (õ has a nasal *n* sound), the name of buildings that once housed African slaves.

Chink

The expression stems from an American mispronunciation of the Chinese word for "China," *chung-kuo.* Chinaman, an equally pejorative word today, is actually a literal translation of the Chinese term for a Chinese, *chung-kuo-ren.*

Spick

This ethnic slur was inadvertently supplied by early Spanish-speaking immigrants to the United States, from the their mispronunciation of "I don't speak English" — "No esspik English."

Gringo

As though to equal the score on ethnic slurs, the Mexicans began using "gringo" to characterize Americans who marched into their country during the 19th-century Mexican-American War. Hearing American troops continually singing a popular song of the day, "Green Grow the Lilacs," Mexicans ran together the first two words as "gringo."

Honky

The black pejorative for a white American seems to have originated in an American slur for a Pole. White Americans called Polish immigrants "honkies," and when Poles and other newcomers to the United States began to compete with blacks earlier this century for industrial jobs, some blacks applied the term to their white competitors.

Krauts

An American slur on Germans, taken from their love of sauerkraut.

Frogs

A British slur on the French, referring to their penchant for the gastronomic delicacy frogs' legs.

Limey

Originally a New World expression for British sailors, who regularly ate limes and other citrus fruits to prevent scurvy on their long ocean voyages.

Goy

A Hebrew expression for any non-Jew, derived from the Hebrew word *goy,* meaning "nation" and denoting anyone not of the Jewish birth.

6

Writing: Scribble to Shorthand

Writing, 3500 B.C.; Sumer

The first system of writing, devised by the Sumerians, consisted of stylized representations of objects, known as pictograms.

The symbols, crude at first, were used primarily to record agricultural transactions and astronomical observations. Consequently, the first written words of which there is evidence were for **nouns** — particularly for stars and animals. Over the next hundred years Sumerian scribes combined noun pictograms with qualifying **adjectives** to arrive at symbols for such words as "small bison," "big reindeer," and "bright star." Clearly enamored of their new invention, scholars continued to modify their writing system, and by about 3200 B.C. it contained symbols for **verbs;** "to sleep" for example, was represented by a recumbent man. These richer characters are called ideograms.

Greater refinement was needed, however, because the range of human communications by this time already encompassed abstract ideas.

These entered the Sumerian writing system about 3100 B.C. through the straightforward use of homonyms. For instance, to use an English example, a scribe might combine the noun symbols for "bee" and "leaf" to arrive at the abstract concept of "belief." But this enrichment of writing made for slower execution, and adherence to the use of pictures limited the number of ideas that could be expressed. These disadvantages the Sumerians overcame by simplifying their written symbols and teaching combined characters to the next generation as single words in their own right, known as phonograms.

A further attempt to facilitate the speed of writing, and to streamline it, eventually gave rise to the use of abstract symbols, each of which represented a unit of sound within a word, or **syllable.** This writing, known as cuneiform, from the Latin *cuneus,* meaning "wedge," was drawn by the scribe with a wedge-shaped stylus on a wet clay tablet. The cuneiform symbols also came to represent objects and concepts.

By the end of the third millennium B.C. the Sumerian writing system had become sufficiently rich and flexible to record the most complex historical events and literary creations. Inscribed on tablets in twelve columns, these literary compositions range from short hymns and longer myths to children's fables and scholarly essays to epic-length poems, some running a thousand lines. Thus, more

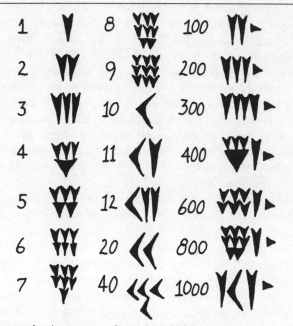

Cuneiform numbering system from 1 to 1000

than a thousand years before the Hebrews had their Bible and the Greeks the *Iliad* and the *Odyssey,* the Sumerians already had created a vast body of written literature.

Numerous Sumerian literary works were excavated around the turn of this century at Nippur, an ancient Sumerian site about a hundred miles from modern Baghdad, and most are housed today in the University Museum of Philadelphia and the Museum of the Ancient Orient at Istanbul.

Hieroglyphics, 3100 B.C.; Egypt

About the time that Sumerian phonograms were undergoing the transformation that would lead to the syllable writing of cuneiform, the Egyptians were devising their unique form of picture writing.

Hieroglyphic writing is found only in Egyptian civilization, and its earliest traces date to the end of the fourth millennium B.C., appearing as annotations to scenes cut in relief on slabs of slate in tombs and chapels. Thus, the earliest hieroglyphics represent lines of hymns and prayers, and the names and titles of individuals and deities.

Hieroglyphics probably originated from the Egyptians' desire to annotate carved pictures of religious offerings, hunts, and fiery battles. Applied to a scene, they lent distinction to people and places, and left an unambiguous record for future generations; a sense of history was important to Egyptians and figured significantly into the development and evolution of their hieroglyphic system of writings. One early inscription accompanying the scene of a pharoah's triumph over his enemies carries the line "the first occasion of the defeat of the Libyans."

Once writing was a flourishing practice, it began to appear without pictures; that is, as pure text on clay tablets and cylindrical stones. This led to the labeling of numerous, everyday items. A jar of wine, for example, might bear the name of the vineyard, of the shipping merchant, of the person who was to receive the merchandise, and of the reigning king.

Hieroglyphic writing vanished after the Muslim conquest of Egypt in A.D. 639 and was not rediscovered until the 19th century. Lapidarian pictures on tombs, temples, and sarcophagi for centuries had been regarded merely as decorations, until Napoleon's army conquered Egypt and a number of French archeologists began wrestling with the problem of deciphering hieroglyphics — with almost no success. All they could determine was that the picture script was related to no other known language.

The decoding breakthrough came with the discovery of the Rosetta stone. A royal proclamation etched on a tablet and dating from the Greek conquest of Egypt in 332 B.C. by Alexander the Great, the densely inscribed stone fortunately contained three scripts: hieroglyphics, a simplified cursive form of the writing, and the same text in Greek — which the French archeologists read fluently. The first two words deciphered by the young French linguist Jean-François Champollion were the names "Cleopatra" and "Ptolemy."

Cartouche of Cleopatra's name from the Rosetta stone

Alphabet, 2000 B.C.; Phoenicia

The Phoenicians were probably the greatest seafarers of the ancient world and inhabited regions that are now Syria, Israel, and Lebanon. Their principal cities were all ports, from which they traded throughout the Mediterranean, as far west as Britain (then known as the "Tin Isles"), and south along the coast of Africa, spreading goods along with Phoenician culture. One of their greatest colonies was Carthage, near modern Tunis, and one of their famous ports, Byblos, is known today as the point of origin where the Phoenician alphabet entered, and profoundly affected, the Greek world.

The Phoenicians' system of writing was unique. Where the Sumerians (in 3500 B.C.) developed pictograms, and the Egyptians (in 3100 B.C.) hieroglyphics — and even the Chinese had devised a pictorial script where images of "eye" and "water" were combined to form "tear"; "woman" plus "child" to give "good" — the Phoenicians, somewhere around 2000 B.C., severed the relationship between pictures and words for all time in all Occidental cultures. By creating symbols with phonetic values for single syllables and consonants, they thus devised the first almost-pure phonetic alphabet. (It still did not recognize vowels.)

The closest system of writing had been Sumerian cuneiform. It is unknown whether the Phoenicians arrived at their largely phonetic alphabet by simplifying Sumerian cuneiform or Egyptian hieroglyphics, or their own form of pictorial script.

The system of using symbols to indicate fundamental word sounds quickly superseded the graphic depiction of objects and ideas, and spread rapidly. Greek legend claims that Cadmus of Thebes first brought the alphabet from Byblos to the Greek mainland about 1500 B.C.

Byblos was also the port from which papyrus traveled to Egypt and Greece, and the city's name has been immortalized in many Greek and Western words: *biblion,* Greek for "rolled paper" or "scroll"; and our words "Bible," "bibliography," and "bibliophile."

The Greeks adopted the Phoenician alphabet (also known as the North Semitic alphabet) of twenty-two to thirty letters and called them by such words as *alpha, beta,* and *gamma,* which are phonetic imitations of important Semitic words, names in most cases: *aleph* (ox), *beth* (house), and *gimel* (camel). To these they added two letters supposedly signifying female and male genitalia — *delta* and *phi.*

In a stroke of genius, the Greeks decided to replace some of the Phoenician syllable letters with vowel signs, thus producing the first purely phonetic, and true, alphabet, composed entirely of vowels and consonants. The Greek alphabet spread throughout the European world, undergoing minor changes, and gave birth to the Etruscan alphabet and then to the Roman.

In giving the letters Latin names, the Romans introduced the alphabet that is in use among Western nations today. The Latin alphabet had only twenty letters, the present English alphabet minus *j, k, v, w, y,* and *z.* The Romans added *k* for use in abbreviations and *y* and *z* to transcribe Greek words, producing a twenty-three letter alphabet.

After being adopted by English-speaking peoples, the alphabet gained its final three letters: *w* arose from a doubling, or formation of a ligature, of *u,* and *j* and *v* as consonant variants of the vowels *i* and *u.*

Paper, Pre—2800 B.C.; Egypt

Paper, in a sense, arose from the banks of the Nile River; its name is derived from papyrus, the reedy plant that flourished in the region and was the first flexible material used by the Egyptians for recording extensive archives.

For a while papyrus was thought not to have existed before the II Dynasty in the Old Kingdom. But the discovery of a blank papyrus scroll in the tomb of a high official who died during the early stages of the I Dynasty has pushed back the origin of paper.

The papyrus plant was converted into paper by a simple process. Fibrous layers within the stem of the plant were removed, placed side by side, and crossed at right angles with another set of layers similarly arranged. The sheet was dampened with water, then pressed tightly. When it dried, its sap acted as an adhesive to cement the two layers together, forming a relatively smooth and — judging from the numerous papyrus records still in existence — extremely durable writing material.

The first paper was made in Egypt from the papyrus plant, which grew along the Nile; rag paper originated centuries later in China. The snow-white paper popular today appeared shortly after the discovery of chlorine, in 1774.

Papyrus was plant paper. The first **rag paper** seems to have originated in one of the early imperial courts of China, when a clerk, Ts'ai Lun, in A.D. 105, concocted a formula out of fishnets, old rags, hemp waste, and parts of the mulberry bush.

Pleased with the relatively smooth, flexible product, the Chinese continued to use the formula, modifying it in time. But paper moved westward at a snail's pace; it reached Central Asia only in 751 and Baghdad in 793.

The arrival of paper in Asia Minor put the brown rag material (for it had yet to be bleached) on Europe's back doorstep, and the Islamic culture eventually introduced paper production techniques to the Europeans by the 14th century. Paper mills soon flourished in Spain, Italy, France, and Germany, and with the invention of printing in the 1450s, the demand for paper skyrocketed.

Until the 18th century paper-making called for boiling and chemically treating rags and linen to break down their fibers, then pressing the viscous material into sheets. But supplies of the ingredients often were scarce, forcing paper manufacturers to advertise and solicit for rags and, in times of extreme dearth, to scour streets and city dumping grounds. With the growing popularity of newspapers throughout the world in the late 18th century, a new procedure for making paper was essential.

Wood pulp came to the fore. A method of using pulp, first outlined in an 1800 book, offered several imaginative suggestions as to how paper could be whipped up from the pulp of trees — and even of vegetables — and soon a major wood-pulping process forever freed the paper industry of its reliance on cotton and linen rags. The birth of modern paper had arrived, and would go unchanged for more than 150 years.

The **bleaching** of paper stock to produce snowy white sheets began shortly after the discovery of the element chlorine, in 1774.

Chlorine bleaching, indispensible to almost all paper-making today, was not successful at first because of a lack of chemical knowledge, which resulted in paper of an inferior quality. Though it was relatively easy to turn paper white, slight incorrect temperatures, chlorine concentrations, and bleaching times could yield a product that crumbled under the pressure of a printing press or tore under the sharp scratch of a metal-tipped pen. Nonetheless, white paper was deemed so esthetically desirable — and so superior in minimizing eyestrain, a serious drawback with gray-brown paper — that chlorine bleaching techniques survived initial skepticism within the paper industry and eventually matured into the science it is today.

Pens, Pre–2800 B.C.; Egypt

With a finger dipped in colored liquid — the juice of a berry and, occasionally, blood — early man was able to stroke symbols on his body and on cave walls. The finely frayed ends of green twigs, meanwhile, accounted for the cave paintings made in France and Spain in 15,000 B.C., depicting herds of reindeer and rapacious hunts.

But the first penlike devices originated concurrently with the dawn of writing, about 3500 B.C., in Sumer. Sumerian scribes used sharp-pointed styli, shaped from twigs, to etch their pictograms, and later their cuneiform script, into wet clay tablets, which then were hardened in ovens. And four centuries later the Egyptians adopted similar devices for recording their hieroglyphics.

The first real pens appeared with the Egyptian invention of papyrus, most likely between 3000 and 2800 B.C. These earliest writing implements were usually reeds and rushes with tubular centers that could suck up a narrow column of colored liquid and, when tilted at an appropriate angle, release it in a slow, coarse stroke. Since these pens grew wild along the Nile River, Egyptian scribes had an inexhaustible supply of writing implements.

The ancient Greeks used needle-pointed styli for writing as early as 1296 B.C., then later adopted reedlike pens and ink; in China, before 1000 B.C., brushes made of camel's and rat's hair were used for painting pictograms.

Quill Pens, 6th Century B.C.

When the feathered quill pens became part of man's stationery implements, writing entered a phase of unprecedented ease of execution and control of characters that exceeded even the Chinese capabilities of calligraphy with fine hair brushes.

For more than a thousand years, the quill reigned as the standard writing instrument for people of many civilizations. Birds, of course, supplied the basic instrument, and man adapted it to his needs. First a freshly plucked (or found) quill was dried, then cleaned of all oily and fatty materials that would interfere with the absorption of ink. To stave off brittleness, the quill was dried by the slow application of gentle heat.

Large wing feathers made the best quill pens, and three fowl offered the finest choices: swans, turkeys, and geese. The feathers of the last were preferred because of their sturdiness (though some of the finest early etchings and writing apparently were done with elegant black crow quills).

Russia and Holland crafted the highest-quality pens. When supplies began to dwindle early in the 19th century, an Englishman, Joseph Bramah, invented a device that cut quills into 3 or 4 lengths with a point on each to make nibs for writing that could be fitted into a prepared holder.

England, at this time in a paroxysm of quill mania, was importing more than 30 million quill feathers a year. But the quill's inherent brittleness, despite ingenious attempts to achieve suppleness, led the English to experiment with different writing points during the years 1800 to 1835. Sculpted points from animal horns and tortoise shells were used, along with more costly and ornate versions in gold, studded with tiny rubies. Already on the horizon, however, was a pen point at once simple and sturdy, and soon to be inexpensively mass-produced.

Steel-Point Pens, 1780; England

Steel-point pens, which originated in England, represented a major advance in writing flexibility, and a great saving in cost.

Once the steel point appeared, many English inventors experimented with refining its geometry to achieve maximum ink storage (with minimum spillage) and the smoothest writing style. The man who in the 1780s came closest to these goals with the first machine-made steel pen points was John Mitchell, of Birmingham.

Still, there was considerable room for improvement, and the search for the perfect steel pen point continued. In 1830, another Englishman, James Perry, was granted a patent for a point that wrote with a smoothness superior to all its predecessors, because it had a hole located at the top of the central hairline slit, joined on both sides by one or more additional thin slits, ensuring a slow and steady stream of ink.

Small refinements continued to be made, and the cost of steel-point pens, now mass-produced, was soon within the economic reach of every family, teacher, and student. The first man to build a career solely on the manufacture of new pen points was Thomas Sheldon, an Englishman who opened a machine shop in 1828. (Though the metal-tipped point was hailed as a writing breakthrough, it apparently was not truly a "first," because years later archeologists discovered bronze pen points embedded in solidified ash among the ruins of Pompeii.)

Today, fountain pen points are made from more flexible met-

als, such as plated nickel and ferrous alloys, whose strength is bol-
stered by traces of highly wear-resistant metals, often alloys of
ruthenium, which are welded onto the tip.

Fountain Pens, Early 19th Century; England

By the start of the 19th century, writing implements had come a
great distance from Sumerian pointed styli and Egyptian hollow
reeds, but they still suffered from a major inconvenience: they had
to be continually dipped into inkwells.

The first fountain pens (so named because their ink flowed continuously, like water in a fountain) were a welcome improvement,
but they too suffered drawbacks: a fountain pen's thin cylindrical
ink reservoir had to be carefully hand-filled by an eyedropper; and
the early inks, funneled through the narrow reservoir, often clot-
ted before reaching the pen point, a bane to perfect penmanship.

A significant improvement in fountain pen design appeared in
1884. A New York stationer, L. E. Waterman, devised a practical
ink-filling system that was to dominate the field into the middle of
this century.

Waterman's ink reservoir was a pliant rubber chamber that made
contact with a plungerlike lever on the exterior surface of the pen.
Lifting the lever squeezed air from the chamber and created a
vacuum; releasing the lever then sucked ink into the chamber. The
air-tight chamber, along with improvements in the quality of ink,
reduced the clogging problem to a minimum. So successful was
Waterman's device that his name soon became synonymous with
the fountain pen.

Improvements resumed only in the 1950s. A fountain pen that
did away with the need for a plunger — by absorbing ink strictly
through capillary action in the inner chamber (the action that draws
up mercury in a thermometer) — made its debut in the United
States in 1956 and was hailed as the "pen with no moving parts."
An immediate success, this model was bettered a few years later
by the appearance of a fountain pen that was filled by the injection of an ink capsule, called a cartridge, into its writing chamber.
Cartridge pens are still the most popular fountain pens found in
the United States, though the older practice of hand-filling a rub-
ber-chamber pen from an inkwell remains in vogue among fountain pen aficionados throughout the world.

Ball-Point Pens, 1888; United States

A rotating ball that under externally applied pressure distributed ink evenly to paper was the brainstorm of the American inventor John H. Loud. On October 30, 1888, he was granted the first patent for a ball dispenser pen, though his early and somewhat crude models were designed for writing on rough surfaces such as cardboard, and not for fine handwriting on paper.

Loud's several ball-point pen designs over the years never aspired to the heights of granting the user flawless penmanship, but the basic mechanics of his original ball point were strikingly similar to contemporary models.

The modernization of ball-point pens was the work of Lazlo Biro, a Hungarian living in Argentina during World War II; in fact, the ball-point pen is a spin-off of war technology. By relying on improved methods for grinding ball bearings for machines and weapons, and for fitting them snugly into orifices, Biro produced the first ball-point pen suitable for writing on paper.

By the middle of the 1950s ball-point pens were sweeping the writing-implement market. The pen's forte was its reliability, but also contributing to its success was the fact that its reservoir of specially designed ink lasted through scores of letters, reams of reports, or several handwritten chapters of a book. The ball-point pens of the 1950s operated with a precisely ground ball spinning in a housing that contained four to six shallow grooves adjacent to the ball. The numerous grooves helped distribute the ink uniformly around the ball, allowing for even strokes of the pen, unlike earlier models, which wrote in halting stops and starts. Gravity forced the ink down the shaft, where it escaped around the ball in measured amounts.

Early ball-point pens had smooth stainless steel balls in brass housings and skipped annoyingly over greasy surfaces. Today, specially designed balls with microscopic surface roughness continue, as manufacturers not long ago boasted, "to write through butter."

Ink, 2697 B.C.; Egypt

Ink, not surprisingly, came into existence simultaneously with pens, and its evolution throughout the ages has been every bit as complex and colorful as the implements that contained it.

The ink used with the earliest Egyptian reed pens achieved its jet-black color from carbon black or from finely pulverized pin ash. These ingredients often were mixed together, then added to lamp oil, containing a gelatin derived from boiled donkey skin. This last element, which gave the ink its viscosity, had a decidedly unpleasant odor, so the ink had to be perfumed by the addition of musk oil. The oldest extant report on the preparation of this fragrant and primitive writing concoction dates to 2697 B.C., during the late II Dynasty of the Old Kingdom, though historians disagree as to precisely when the ink came into general use.

Carbon black remained the predominant ingredient in all inks throughout the Middle Ages, though various civilizations experimented by adding gums, glues, and resins. When the ingredients were evenly dispersed throughout the ink, the final product permitted its user to write with excellent penmanship, but for writers who had to mix their own batches, ink became a great hindrance to their profession.

A new writing fluid was discovered about A.D. 1100, and for a while it seemed to be a major advance. It was a solution of an iron salt (ferrous sulfate), gum, and a liquid extract of nutgalls, outgrowths found on certain varieties of oak trees that contain tannic acid, a staining agent. Ink made with tannic acid had many desirable textural advantages, and the acid was abundant not only in oak trees but also chestnut wood and bark and sumac leaves.

However, ink made by the new formula proved unstable; over a matter of weeks or months clear black script faded to muddy brown. This might not have been too disastrous had paper in those days been pure white, but typically it was gray-brown, and made faded ink illegible.

Many of the problems associated with ink, especially the tendency for its microscopic particles to clog fountain pen points, were niftily solved by the invention of synthetic dyes, which, in aqueous solution, became modern ink. It achieved a tenacious permanence — outlasting, in theory, the paper pages it covered — by the addition of various salts and metals, much like a paint base.

Technology invariably is challenged by new problems, and just when fountain pen ink had reached a high degree of perfection, a new type of pen emerged with its own specific ink needs.

Ball-point pen ink initially was based on a solution of dye in oleic acid, with special oils and resins added to enhance smooth flow. But because of their inherent oiliness, the first inks took a long time to dry, and they smudged with irritating frequency. Furthermore, when sheets of writing matter were stacked atop others, the inks transferred from one page to another in ghostly images.

The modern solution to these and other problems was the synthesis of new organic oil-free dyes and fast-drying solvents to contain them. Ball-point pen ink today — a chemist's pastiche of organic dyes, glycols, aromatic alcohols, and polyhydric ethers — is about 10,000 times as viscous as water, dries rapidly (if not instantly), and resists fading even when directly exposed to bright light. And though the paper it is on may yellow, then brown, and then crack, the ink, in blue, black, brown, red, or green, will not appreciably lose its own vividness.

Pencils, 16th Century; England

Long before Columbus set foot in the New World, the Aztecs in North America used graphite, a soft, black, lustrous form of carbon found in nature, to scratch ceremonial marks on slate and stone.

But the first people to conceive of writing with long thin graphite sticks encapsulated in wooden shafts and ground at the tip to a point were the Germans in the 16th century. Since that time pencils have become the single most common writing implement in the world.

Before the modern pencil surfaced in Germany, it had incarnations in other countries. Graphite pencils (commonly referred to as lead pencils) originally were made in a crude form in England shortly after the discovery, in 1564, of the world's purest graphite deposit at a mine near Borrowdale, Cumberland. The mine was worked for almost three hundred years, and portions of its yield went into making pencils, called marking stones. These early pencils actually were chunks of graphite pared into small square-cornered sticks that left as much of a mark on the user's hand as on the paper. In England and Germany marking sticks later were wrapped tightly with string to fashion pencils (the string could be slowly unwound to expose more stick), and finally were inserted into grooves cut in narrow outlays of wood.

As other uses for graphite were discovered in industry, supplies dwindled rapidly, since most of the substance came from the Borrowdale mine. By the late 1700s the mine was nearing depletion, and little of the precious graphite was going into making pencils, which became scarce as writing instruments. Chemists seeking a way to reduce the graphite content in pencils experimented with many materials. The first that proved satisfactory was a blend of refined graphite powder and muddy clay that was fired in a kiln. Discovered by the Frenchman Nicolas-Jacques Conté in 1795, the process, with only limited refinements, is still the basis of pencil-making today.

America's first pencil-maker was William Monroe, who in 1812 opened a business that soon broke the United States of its dependence on German pencils, which at the time dominated the world market. In 1858, Hyman Lipman, a Philadelphia inventor, was granted a patent for a minor refinement, and a major convenience, that gave pencils their distinctively modern appearance: a small metal band at the upper end of a pencil that held a **rubber eraser.** Lipman sold his pencil-cum-eraser patent in 1872 to Joseph Rechendorfer of New York.

Mechanical Pencils, 1822; England

The mechanical pencil was a welcome innovation because its lead point could be extended easily by the flick of a wrist, thus eliminating the dependence on pencil sharpeners. Conceived by two British inventors, S. Mordan and J. I. Hawkins, the first mechanical pencils were produced in 1822 and underwent few modifications until 1877, when lead was loaded and advanced through a spring mechanism. At this time, leads were still fairly large in diameter, far from ideal for fine handwriting. A thin-diameter lead, fitted in a mechanical holder that was twisted to achieve forward extension, first appeared in 1895 and proved an immediate success.

For a number of years various thicknesses of lead were tried, and a diameter of 0.046 inches became the generally accepted standard soon after the turn of the century. Sufficiently thin to permit handsome penmanship, it was also thick enough to prevent frequent breakage. As leads were made harder, their diameters were reduced, and in 1938 the preferred standard was 0.036

inches. Today, the thinnest leads, pushing the limits of practicality, are 0.012 inches and are most popular in Japan.

Shorthand, Pre–400 B.C.; Greece

Shorthand, a method of writing rapidly by substituting characters, abbreviations, or symbols for letters, words, or phrases, can be traced to ancient Greece. The historian Xenophon used a crude shorthand system to write the life and teachings of Socrates, and a form of abbreviated writing also was used by Roman legal scribes.

The first extensive Latin shorthand system was developed by Marcus Tullius Tiro, a former slave and member of Cicero's household. His **notae Tironianae** ("Tironian notes"), devised in 63 B.C., remained in use for more than a thousand years, and was complemented by his shorthand dictionary.

In the Tironian alphabet, devised to record speeches in the Roman Senate, each letter was abbreviated into a stroke, which could later be joined to other strokes.

Both Julius Caesar and the emperor Titus were among many Romans who favored the use of shorthand. But during the Middle Ages — perhaps because scholarship in general fell into disrepute — shorthand became associated with evil spirits and witchcraft, and a person employing it was believed to be possessed by the devil. Not until the late 12th century, after considerable prodding from Thomas Becket, archbishop of Canterbury, did King

Henry II revive the use of Tiro's shorthand system. A scholarly interest in the practice peaked in the 15th century, when Benedictine monks found a lexicon of Ciceronian notes and a psalter written in Tironian shorthand.

It seems that many famous writers throughout history preferred shorthand. Cicero's orations, the sermons of Martin Luther, and the plays of Shakespeare and George Bernard Shaw were all written in abbreviated script, which had various names: stenography (literally, "narrow writing"), tachygraphy ("swift writing"), and brachygraphy ("short writing"). Perhaps the most effective shorthand system arose late in the 19th century, when the British stenographer Samuel Taylor introduced an abbreviated style of writing, a hybrid of its many predecessors, which later spawned the modern Pitman and Gregg shorthand methods.

Pitman Shorthand, 1837; England

Invented by Sir Isaac Pitman, the shorthand method of writing that bears his name gained almost universal acceptance within a half-century of its debut, in 1837. A spelling reformer, Pitman published his system as *Stenographic Sound-Hand,* for its salient feature was writing by sound, a technique that quickly surpassed the more cumbersome Taylor method already in use, and won Pitman knighthood from Queen Victoria.

Pitman based his system on twenty-five single consonants, twenty-four double consonants, and sixteen vowels. The method allowed related sounds to be represented by similar signs, with shading used to eliminate strokes; the shortest signs represented the shortest sounds, and single strokes stood for single consonants.

Pitman's brother, Benn, introduced the method to the United States in 1852, and after slight modifications it swept stenography schools throughout the States and Canada. In fact, a survey taken in 1889 revealed that 97 percent of all shorthand users in America preferred Sir Isaac Pitman's method over competing systems. Translated into every major and many minor languages, it reigned supreme until a system developed by another Englishman, John Robert Gregg, gained popular acceptance.

Gregg Shorthand, 1885; England

A young London stenographer (born in Ireland), John Robert Gregg studied both Taylor and Pitman shorthand for inspiration and developed a unique shorthand style in 1855 that became known as the Gregg System.

Gregg was only a boy of ten living in Ireland when he taught himself a version of Taylor shorthand. Finding it easy to master, he then tackled Pitman shorthand, but instinctively felt that the angles, shading, and positioning of its symbols left much to be desired. In search of a way to improve it, he studied a history of shorthand by Thomas Anderson, a member of the Shorthand Society of London. Selecting pieces from Pitman, bits from Taylor, and hints from his historical sources, Gregg fashioned his own system. It used independent characters for vowels and consonants, with all characters written on a single line, and was ruled by a few abbreviation principles.

By 1885 Gregg had completed work on his system, and three years later, at the age of twenty-one, he published *Light-Line Phonography*, the first pamphlet setting forth Gregg shorthand. It contained numerous examples of Gregg's reliance on curve-motion shorthand, featuring circles, hooks, and loops. In fact, its primary motion was curvilinear, based on the geometrical figure of the ellipse and on the oval slope of longhand writing.

The natural fluidity of his system, as well as its immediate popularity in England, augured success abroad. In America, shorthand had flourished only along the East Coast, but when Gregg brought his system to the States in 1893 he personally introduced it to the entire country. Traveling through the Midwest, the West, and the South, he gave demonstrations to large audiences of secretaries, most of them women, who knew that stenography skills would bolster their chances of employment. His system received a major boost when secondary schools throughout the country adopted it as part of their curricula. Today, in schools around the world where shorthand is taught, the Gregg system is the dominant method.

Machine Shorthand, 1906; United States

An American, Ward Stone Ireland, invented the Stenotype machine and opened a new era in the manual recording of speech.

A court reporter and stenographer, Ireland devised his machine with a compact keyboard of twenty-two keys that were small, light to touch, and silent. The operator could use all eight fingers and both thumbs in "dictating" to the machine, and several keys could be struck simultaneously, further accelerating word recording.

The Stenotype later was joined by the Stenograph, a similar machine used primarily, as was the older model, in conference rooms and in court reporting. Both machines print roman letters on a strip of paper that folds automatically into the back of the machine. Adept with either keyboard, a stenographer can operate a machine while maintaining eye contact with the speaker.

Machine shorthand in recent years has succumbed to the ease, inexpensiveness, and compact size, not to mention utter infallibility, of voice tape recorders. On the horizon is the futuristic voice-operated typewriter, which, when perfected, will be able to type verbal dictation either directly from a person or from a prerecorded tape.

Braille, 1824; France

Braille, the universally used system of writing and reading by the blind, is based on a code of sixty-three characters, each made up of one to six raised dots arranged in a six-position matrix. It was invented in 1824 by a fifteen-year-old French boy, Louis Braille, who had been blind himself since the age of three.

Various special alphabets had been devised for the blind prior to Braille's invention. They included letters engraved in wood, cast in lead, and cut in cardboard. Most were awkward and difficult to learn. One of the few that had any real effectiveness was a system by another Frenchman, Valentin Haüy (1745–1822), who was the first to emboss paper to help the blind read. Haüy's letters in relief were actually a punched alphabet, and imitators immediately began to copy and improve on his system. Composed entirely of letters, it could be mastered quickly by a person already familiar with the alphabet, and consequently one early system, called Moon Type, invented by William Moon in 1845 in Brighton, England, is still used in Great Britain for people who lose their sight late in life.

Young Louis Braille dedicated himself to developing a practical alphabet for the blind shortly after he had started school for the blind in Paris and found that the library had only fourteen books in embossed characters. The few students who did check out the books continually complained of the cumbersome alphabet they contained and soon gave up reading, in frustration and disgust. An even more glaring weakness of that embossed letter was that students were unable to write in it.

To solve the problems, Braille began experimenting with a communication method called night-writing, which the French army used for nighttime battlefield missives. With assistance from an army officer, Captain Charles Barbier, Braille pared the method's twelve-dot configurations to six and published his results in 1829.

Although Braille's classmates quickly gravitated to his system, it was not widely accepted for several years; even Braille's own Paris school did not adopt the system until 1854, two years after his death.

In the United States, the Braille method underwent modifications during the 1870s by a blind Boston teacher, Joel W. Smith, who changed its name to American Braille. Though other methods of enabling the blind to read were attempted, particularly the so-called New York Point System, developed in the 1860s by William B. Wait, Braille won out. In 1916, the United States sanctioned Louis Braille's original system of raised dots, and in 1932 representatives from agencies for the blind in England and the United States met in London and arrived at a modification they called Standard English Braille, Grade 2, which soon was adopted throughout the English-speaking world.

7

Beverages: Tea to Tab

Milk, 6000 B.C.; Eurasia

Man's discovery of milk must remain a conjectural fantasy: we can envision an early herder slaughtering a cow or reindeer and timorously sticking a finger into the white, creamy substance in the belly of the beast, withdrawing it, inserting it into his mouth, and emitting a guttural grunt. Once man tasted milk, his appetite for it as a major staple of survival became insatiable.

The first milking undoubtedly came in the enlightened Neolithic era, begun by nomads who traveled with herds of milk-giving animals whose meat supplied most of their food. In fact, the Aryans who reached India by 1750 B.C. brought with them eating habits so dependent on milk and milk products that the cow became a sacred animal in that country and retains that status today.

The first pictorial evidence of milking is contained in a frieze dating from 2900 B.C. at Ur, the ancient Sumerian city on the Euphrates River, in what is now southern Iraq.

Almost every ancient civilization prized milk. The early Greeks drank primarily goat's milk and used sheep's milk for making cheeses; the Romans drank milk only when it was mixed with wine, though, like the Greeks, they relished cheese; and the biblical references to Canaan as a "land of milk and honey" indicate that the Hebrews prized milk and drank it whenever possible, though its consumption was considered an extravagance.

The milking of farm animals began in China about 2000 B.C., and drinking milk was considered a symbol of wealth. A favorite dish of an early emperor, and of later Chinese nobility, was a soft paste of rice and milk that was frozen in platters — a predecessor of **ice cream,** which, interestingly, is the only form of milk that many Chinese show a predilection for even today.

Milk was never very popular among the American Indians, who for centuries had no domesticated milk-bearing animals. When the Spaniards introduced milk to the New World in the 15th century, the Indians found the drink disgusting; they viewed it as an animal's excretory waste.

A wide range of female animals give milk, including yaks, buffalo, pigs, and, of course, humans. But the composition of milks varies greatly. Goat's milk, which is 4.3 percent butterfat, is richer than cow's milk, with 3.9 percent butterfat, and the animal product that most closely resembles human milk in many properties is ass's milk, though it contains only a third of the calories a baby needs.

The richest milk of any domesticated animal is that of reindeer; it has a high butterfat content of 22.3 percent; 10.3 percent protein (about three times that of cow's milk), and only 2.5 percent sugar (half as sweet as human milk). These figures account in part for the long lives of the healthy Laplanders, who coexist with reindeer in Arctic regions and drink the milk as often as they can get it — which is not all that often, since at the height of milking season female reindeer give only a cup a day.

The richest milk on the face of the earth will not be found in supermarkets, however; it is the milk of the female killer whale, which has a whopping butterfat content of 35 percent.

Reindeer milk, a rarity even among reindeer, is the richest milk from any domesticated animal. It contains three times as much protein as cow's milk and about half as much sugar.

Alcoholic Beverages, Pre–9000 B.C.

Since fermentation can occur in any organic potpourri containing sugar, alcoholic beverages probably were discovered by accident, before man abandoned his food-gathering methods and settled into a farming life.

Quite likely, fallen grapes or other fruits, perhaps even pure honey, were exposed to warm sunlight, which accelerated fermentation, and man stumbled on this aromatic concoction. He must have sampled it with curiosity and caution, and if the taste did not immediately suit him, the euphoric feeling he soon experienced was enough to send him back to the brew again and again.

By trial and error he discovered the chief ingredients of fermentation — fruit or grain, sugar, heat, and aging. During seasons when fruit was not available, he learned the trick of substituting starchy vegetables: first chewing the vegetable to mix it with an enzyme (zycase) in human saliva that triggered fermentation. Although several hundred groups of preliterate societies are believed to have come up with some kind of alcoholic drink, thousands of years passed before man began cultivating crops suited specifically for the production of alcohol.

Cultivation actually began about 4000 B.C., and the process of fermentation spread quickly through early civilizations. Alcoholic beverages played key roles in religious and social ceremonies, particularly births, feasts, marriages, coronations, funerals, and declarations of war and peace. Through its consumption at these events, alcohol firmly established its niche as one of the oldest and most ubiquitous drugs. According to clay tablets dating to 2100 B.C., beer was a common prescription of Sumerian physicians for a myriad of illnesses, and among Egyptian doctors in the next millennia alcoholic potions accounted for more than 15 percent of their prescriptions.

Laws governing the imbibing of alcohol were imperative almost from the outset. The first two major civilizations, the Egyptian and the Sumerian, both eventually restricted the manufacture and sale of alcohol, and by 1770 B.C., Hammurabi, king of Babylonia, troubled by the excessive intoxication and rowdiness of his subjects, mandated that drinking houses be regulated. Exempt from early drinking laws, priests eventually replaced water in worship rites with alcohol, claiming it was essential if they were to reach

Drunkenness is as old as alcohol itself, and laws governing drinking were a necessity among even the oldest civilizations. Priests, however, to reach transcendent states during rituals, were allowed to get soused.

the transcendent states in which they foretold the fortunes of kings and the futures of societies.

Wine, 4000 B.C.; Near East

Egyptian records first mention wine-making only as late as 2500 B.C., but archeologists have discovered that the best grape species for producing wine, *Vitis vinifera,* was being cultivated in the Near East by 4000 B.C.

At an even earlier date, inhabitants of the Nile Valley domesticated the wild grape species *Vitis sylvestris,* which grew from the Nile to Gibraltar on the far side of the Mediterranean, and was the progenitor of *Vitis vinifera.* Thus it is likely that by 4000 B.C. Egyptians, and possibly Sumerians, were experienced drinkers, if not already connoisseurs, of wine.

Wine-making originated as major commerce in the Near East and spread to the Minoan and Greek civilizations. The Greeks built a thriving wine trade throughout their colonies; they planted grapes from the Black Sea to Spain. It was the Greeks, in the millennium before Christ, who introduced wine to Western civilization, favoring the *Vitis vinifera* grape. Shortly afterward the vine began to flourish in the terrains for which wine has become legendary: lower Europe, particularly Italy and France. These areas possessed ideal climates and topography; as the Roman poet Virgil observed, "Vines love an open hill."

The Romans were chiefly responsible for the migratory routes of various vintages of wine. Along with the spread of the Holy Roman Empire went cultivation of the grape, and by the 5th century almost all the great vineyards of the modern European world were thriving. Among them: **Bordeaux, Burgundy, Rhine, Moselle,** and **Danube.**

During the period of the Roman Catholic Church's vast hegemony in Europe, many of the great vineyards were owned by the church; wine, of course, was used during Mass. It was also regarded as a restorative, medicine, and disinfectant.

Throughout history, wine was largely the product of the *Vitis vinifera* species. But fermentation of other grapes — for example, *Vitis labrusa,* a native American variety — has become popular. So too has the fermentation of other fruits that lend their names to such drinks as peach wine, blackberry wine, and banana wine. Today, in fact, there are more than 5000 varieties of grapes, about two hundred of which are fermented for wine. Most wines worldwide have an alcohol content of 10 to 12 percent.

Beer, 4000 B.C.; Near East

Beer is the product of a relatively simple process called brewing, which begins with the preparation of malted barley. Barley grains are first soaked, then allowed to germinate, during which time enzymes convert the grain's starches into sugars that can be fermented into alcohol. The germinated grain is called malt, which, when mixed with hops, gives beer the tangy taste that has made the drink one of the most popular alcoholic beverages in the world.

According to ancient legend, Osiris, the Egyptian god of agriculture and of life, taught his people to brew beer about 4000 years ago.

The practice eventually spread to the Sumerians, Babylonians, and Assyrians. Originally the soaked barley was buried in clay pots to hasten germination, and the resulting malt was mixed with water and allowed to ferment by exposure to airborne yeasts. Flavoring beer with **hops** began in Egypt about 1000 B.C.

The Greeks introduced beer to Western culture. Pliny the Elder mentions the practice of flavoring with hops, and implies that beer may have been known in Mediterranean countries even before wine. Brewing beer took hold with the most success in Northern Europe, where grapes for wine-making fared poorly. Early societies brewed beer not only from barley, but from wheat, millet, corn and rice — practically any cereal. The ancient Japanese and Chinese favored millet and rice beers. By the beginning of the Christian era beer was a popular drink among Germanic and Nordic tribes, and the Celts and Saxons even established beer taverns. Our modern words "malt," "ale," and "beer" are all of Anglo-Saxon origin.

During the Middle Ages monks improved brewing techniques, and by the 13th century A.D. many towns in Great Britain had breweries that sold beer directly to local citizens. With the growth of transportation and commerce, breweries began to distribute their products through local merchants, but even the biggest breweries were hard pressed to fill orders in the face of overwhelming demands for the beverage. Only with the Industrial Revolution was it possible for brewers to produce beer commercially in great quantity.

The two major kinds of beer today are lagers and ales; lagers, the more popular, require up to six times as long a fermentation period as ales. Various manufacturing practices cause the color, flavor, sweetness, and alcoholic content of beer to vary greatly, but in America, at least, there is no mistaking the favorite dispersal vehicle: the six-pack.

The first beer sold in cans in the United States was Kreuger Beer, brewed in Newton, New Jersey, in 1935.

Liquor, 800 B.C.; China

The Chinese were the first people to encounter liquor; they discovered that distilling beer yielded an alcoholic drink with considerably greater punch.

Arrack, their potent drink dating from 800 B.C., was made by collecting and condensing vapors of boiled rice beer and then adding the liquid back to the original brew. Repeated enough times, the process could transform 10 percent alcoholic beer to 40 percent alcoholic arrack.

Distillation was so simple, in fact, that production of the proverbial "hard stuff" seems to have begun about the same time in two other areas, the East Indies and Asia Minor. The Arabs, who gave us the word "alcohol," perfected an intoxicating liquor from their favorite wine, and though both the early Greeks and Romans were acquainted with distillation — and may have concocted various liquors — oddly there is no record of liquor in either culture before A.D. 1000.

Production of distilled spirits in Western Europe began only after trade lanes opened with the Arabs in the 8th century A.D. Once the Romans began making liquor, however, they did much to refine the technique by using metal drums and stills. When they conquered the British Isles, the Romans found that their new subjects already had mastered a brewing technique that gave them mead, one of the most popular early liquors in Western Europe.

Natural sugar was the key ingredient in all early distilled spirits, the two most visible examples being grapes for brandy production and honey for making mead. During the early Middle Ages, sugar gave way to starchy grains, the basis of today's most popular whiskies. Grain liquor was so potent, and so popular, that by the 17th century governments for the first time placed restrictions on distilling.

Among the most widely consumed liquors today are blended Scotch whiskey, a mixture of malt whiskey and Scotch whiskey, and grain whiskey, made from a mash of wheat, rye, or corn and barley malt. Bourbon whiskey, which takes its name from Bourbon County, Kentucky, where it was first made, is distilled from a grain mash that is at least 51 percent corn. Irish whiskey is made from unmalted cereals (barley, wheat, or rye) mashed with malted barley. Canadian whiskey comes from a strong blend of flavored rye whiskey and a lighter corn-based whiskey. Other distillates are brandy, made from wine or the fermented juice of fruits, and rum, from fermented molasses, a by-product of the crystallization of cane sugar. The addition of sugars to liquors produces a smooth, rich distillate called liqueur, which seldom needs aging.

Tea, Pre–2737 B.C.; China

Perhaps a great deal of tea's appeal lies in its mystical origins, since the beverage is shrouded by the arcane and engulfed in Oriental lore.

The first tea was said to have been concocted by the legendary Chinese emperor Shen Nung, who, the tale goes, was boiling water when leaves from a nearby bush floated down into the pot. An

Clockwise: Plants that give us chocolate, wine, and tea: Theobroma cacao, Vitis vinifera (the best grape for producing wine, already cultivated by 4000 B.C.), and Thea chinensis.

entry in Shen's medical diary, dated 2737 B.C., presages what later tea lovers would come to declare about the drink: "It quenches thirst. It lessens the desire to sleep. It gladdens and cheers the heart."

Japanese lore goes the Chinese one better: the bush so fortuitously pleasant to Shen was created out of "nothingness" by the Buddhist monk, Bodhidharma.

Whatever tea's true origin, its popularity in China reached the point that in A.D. 780 merchants commissioned a book to delineate tea's rise as the national beverage and extol the pleasure of drinking it. The tea plant, whose leaves are still plucked by hand, as they have been for more than four millennia, has been an economic boon for many exporting countries, since it can be harvested year round.

Tea's arrival in the West came much later. Only when trade routes to the Orient became commonplace in the 16th century did the beverage emerge in Europe. Its reception there was, to say the least, unusual. A Venetian merchant hailed the drink as "much esteemed" and cited its medicinal influence for curing fever, stomachaches, and arthritis. A Dutch doctor concurred. Tea, he said, was an elixir that made its drinkers "exempt from all maladies and [enabled them to] reach an extreme old age."

There were doubters, however, who assailed tea and sparked heated debated about its consumption. "The impertinent novelty of the century," scolded a French physician, and a German doctor, in a more dire appraisal, warned that tea "hastens the death of those who drink it, especially if they have passed the age of 40 years."

Not everyone cited tea as a cause of physical infirmities; some blamed it for other seemingly unrelated circumstances. After tea became the vogue in England in the next century, a women's magazine said tea caused housewives to develop a phlegmatic disposition, and an important political economist lambasted tea for paralyzing the English economy, because time previously used for work was spent in drinking tea. Today tea has won favor over coffee among many people because of its lower caffeine content.

The monsoon areas of Asia — China, India, Sri Lanka — are principal producers of the three major kinds of tea: black tea, which makes up 90 percent of the tea trade; oolong tea, a mildly fermented variety; and green tea, made by steaming green leaves, then rolling and roasting them until they acquire a blue-green tint. Tea, like coffee, thrives in high elevations, making much of the Asian continent favorable to its growth.

Coffee, A.D. 850; Ethiopia

Coffee is almost as much a part of modern man's daily existence as sleep. Consumption is prodigious, and no other beverage comes even close to rivaling it as the most widely drunk refreshment in the world.

While many legends surround the discovery of coffee, perhaps the most valid involves a 9th-century Arab goatherder named Kaldi. As the story goes, Kaldi, noticing the frolicsome spirit of his goats after they had eaten the red berries of a leafy bush, tossed down a handful himself and, experiencing a pronounced friskiness, proclaimed to his fellow tribesmen the wonders of coffee.

For the next four hundred years coffee berries were only chewed for their stimulating effect. The Arabs first brewed the mellow roast, which since has been like nectar to coffee lovers everywhere, in the middle of the 13th century. About a hundred years later wild coffee plants, which resemble evergreen bushes, were transported from Kefa, Ethiopia, and cultivated throughout southern Arabia.

The Muslims of this region quickly developed an addiction to coffee, employing its energizing effects to prolong religious services. A quandary arose when an orthodox priest proclaimed the drink an intoxicant and therefore prohibited by the Koran. But even the threat of severe penalties did not inhibit consumption by zealous Arabs and the rapid spread of the beverage to neighboring countries.

Coffee's introduction into Europe in the 16th century caused a similar saturation of societies as one country after another relished the drink. London coffee houses, first established around 1650, soon built a thriving business exporting coffee, and they became political, social, and literary bastions through the patronage of fashionable coffee drinkers. The custom of drinking coffee reached the American colonies in 1689, and coffee houses flourished in New York, Boston, and Philadelphia. By this time, coffee plantations had spread to Central and South America, where the tropical temperatures and mountainous topography were ideal.

The coffee plant itself is believed to be of African origin; genus *Coffea*, family *Rubiaceae*. Its stimulating qualities, which affect the central nervous system, come from the caffeine in the ripe bean. Caffeine is present in amounts between 0.8 percent and 1.5 percent for the *arabica* species, and 1.6 percent to 2.5 percent for the *robusta* species that grows in South America.

Carbonated Soda, 1785; Europe

Today's carbonated water and other beverages stem from a European attempt to duplicate the effervescence of the continent's pure and popular springs, which were treasured for their reputed health benefits.

Jan Baptista van Helmont (1577–1644), a Flemish chemist, first used the term "gas" to refer to the natural water's carbon dioxide content. A Frenchman, Gabriel Venel (1723–1775), mistakenly called the liquid "aerated water," and another scientist labeled its contents "fixed air."

Many chemists were fascinated by the effervescence, and scores of studies were conducted in the late 18th century. Among the experimenters were members of the prestigious Royal Society of London, including such reknowned scientists as Henry Cavendish and Joseph Priestley, the discoverer of oxygen. The most famous spa at the time was Bad Pyrmont, near the German city of Hameln, whose water contained a mixture of minerals and attracted much attention.

Priestly, experimenting in a brewery near his house, published *Directions for Impregnating Water with Fixed Air,* a treatise of dubious worth that nonetheless won him the Copley Medal from the Royal Society. In his report, he also elaborated on the alleged medicinal value of artificially carbonated water.

The first to identify correctly Priestley's "fixed air" as a combi-

Chemists were bedeviled in their early attempts to duplicate nature's bubbly beverage, which was simply carbon dioxide, first identified by Antoine Lavoisier.

nation of oxygen and carbon was the French chemist Antoine Lavoisier, who called it *gaz acide carbonique*. In 1775, John Mervin Nooth perfected laboratory equipment in England that let him prepare small amounts of effervescent water, and seven years later the English chemist Thomas Henry described how carbonated waters could be made commercially. Shortly afterward, factories and bottling plants began operating in London, Paris, Geneva, and Dublin.

America's initial experiments with artificially carbonated water began before the start of the 19th century. In 1807, at Yale University, Benjamin Stillman opened a public establishment for dispensing the "soda water" he had begun bottling. Joseph Hawkins, a Philadelphian, bottled and sold artificially carbonated waters at about the same time, and in 1809 received the first U.S. patent for the preparation of "imitation mineral waters." Later in the century, some popular carbonated sodas appeared, and new products continue to challenge the taste and marketing ingenuity of manufacturers.

1. Dr. Pepper, 1886
2. Coca-Cola, 1886
3. Hires Root Beer, 1886
4. Pepsi-Cola, 1898
5. Canada Dry Ginger Ale, 1904
6. 7-Up, 1933
7. Diet-Rite, 1962
8. Tab, 1963
9. Diet Pepsi, 1965

Carbonated sodas were packaged almost exclusively in glass bottles until the **aluminum can** was introduced in 1960.

The American invention that did away with the need for a can opener or "church key," Alcoa's **tab-top can,** made its debut in 1963.

Fruits: Apples to Oranges

Fruit

The story of Adam and Eve and their expulsion from the Garden of Eden always includes mention of the apple as the forbidden fruit, though, in fact, the fruit is not identified in the first book of the Bible. But no one seems to know what kind of tree the serpent hid in until Satan felt assured enough to make his pitch to Eve. The Koran, however, says the forbidden fruit was the banana. As if all this uncertainty weren't enough, scientists do not know the origins of most fruits.

Many fruits can be traced only to their discovery by explorers. The lime, for instance, wasn't known until the 17th century, when sailors traveling to the New World drank its juice to prevent scurvy, a malady caused by vitamin C deficiency. Since then, citrus fruits have attracted a large following as wellsprings of vitality and good health. Among them are oranges, grapefruits, and tangerines.

The apple is just one of many fruit varieties that originated with the common blooming rose. Others include the pear, peach, plum, apricot, and cherry. Less numerous, but indispensable to world commerce, are vine fruits, of which the grape is unequaled in universal importance for its wine yield. Vine family members are the watermelon, the canteloupe, which is one of the least caloric and most nutritious of all fruits, and the honeydew, whose storied past has it adorning the tables of pharoahs.

Though gourmands in many lands prefer kiwis, kumquats, and

mangoes for exotic fare, the coconut is unbeatable as a source of many useful items. Edible pulp, refreshingly sweet milk, and valuable oil are all coconut products. The oil is ideal for making margarine, soap, and suntan lotion. The fibers from the coconut's husk itself are used in fashioning rope, and the tree's trunk often is cut into wood for building huts and fences.

More myth than fact surrounds the fig, which also is rooted in the lore of Eden, where its leaves supposedly clothed Adam and Eve after their fateful meal. Figs and dates provided sustenance for the early Greeks, and the trees of both remain heavily cultivated today along the eastern Mediterranean.

Accounts of the origins of several popular fruits follow.

Apple, Pre–1200 B.C.; Asia Minor

Rock-hard, soot-black, and resembling hunks of coal rather than sumptuous red fruit, carbonized apples dating to 6500 B.C. have been discovered in Asia Minor. But it is not known whether they grew wild or were cultivated in orchards. Either way, they represent the oldest evidence in a postagricultural land of this king of fruits, belonging to the family *Rosaceae,* which, appropriately, includes the queen of flowers, the rose.

Ramses II of Egypt was the first known cultivator of apples; he ordered orchards planted along the delta of the Nile in the 13th century B.C. The Egyptians dug up young trees with the dirt still surrounding their roots and placed them in holes circled by tiny irrigation canals. This way the soil from which the trees originally obtained nutrients was undisturbed, and Egypt's arid land was made amenable for growing apples.

Greek cultivation of the "golden fruit" — which was given to Hera from the Garden of the Hesperides as a wedding present when she married Zeus — began in Attica at least by the 7th century B.C.

The Romans proved to have greener thumbs than the Greeks (who found cultivation a delicate process in their harshly dry climate) and grew at least seven different varieties, according to Cato the Elder in the 2nd century B.C. A later Roman naturalist, Pliny, boasted of eating thirty-six different kinds of apples popular during the 1st century A.D.; he distinguished between perishable varieties and hardier winter apples that would keep in storage.

The most famous variety — the Api, named for an Etruscan

horticulturist who cross-bred it — outdates almost all known modern apples and has been a popular fruit over the centuries. Louis XIV of France deemed it one of only seven varieties of apples he saw fit to plant; it can still be purchased in France under its early name, *pomme d'Api,* and occasionally in the United States as the Lady Apple.

Interestingly, the apocryphal episode most widely associated with the apple — its tempting presence in the Garden of Eden — is an arbitrary attribution. Though the apple is cited in various parts of the Bible, there is no mention of it in Genesis. Scripture claimed only that Adam and Eve ate the forbidden fruit of the tree of the knowledge of good and evil. Only much later, when artists and sculptors began dealing with the story in a graphic way, did they give the fruit an identity, and according to one historian, they chose, "naturally, the fruit which stood for all fruits, the apple."

Other accounts also have absolved the apple of all culpability. Biblical scholars maintain that if the Hebrews had named a specific fruit for damning the inhabitants of Eden, it would have been the pomegranate, and when Christianity reached India, story had it that the forbidden fruit was the banana.

That Isaac Newton, witnessing the fall of an apple from a tree in his orchard at Woolsthorpe in 1666, was prompted to speculate about gravity is not hearsay, since Newton told the story himself. In fact, one tree in his orchard was coddled into old age, and when it died its remains were preserved. Though the species was never recorded, horticulturists believe it was a costard.

Olive, 3500 B.C.; Crete and Syria

Used as a body cleanser, an all-round medicine, a lubricant to aid in moving obelisks and pyramid blocks, and often as a main dish to a meal, the olive — Plato's favorite food and the backbone of early Mediterranean commerce — has proven to be one of the most durable, delectable, and desirable of ancient fruits.

Yes, fruits. Though few people think of the olive (or the tomato) as a member of the fruit family, its proper botanical niche is alongside the fig, date, and apple.

Although olives were depicted in ancient Egyptian paintings, these are believed to have been wild fruit, since it is thought that the early Egyptians did not eat olives but only used their oil as a lubricant and as a fuel for lamps. Cultivation probably began in Syria and on the island of Crete about 3500 B.C.; and less than a thousand years later olive oil was Crete's major export, shipped to Egypt and throughout Asia Minor.

Except for the grape, wrote Pliny the Elder, "there is no plant which bears a fruit of as great importance as the olive." This was especially true in the dry, rocky soil of Greece. The adaptable olive tree flourished in soil that strangled and starved other plants and crops, and its oil enriched a land poor in animal fats. Greek olive oil soon became renowned for its superior quality and was frequently traded for grain and other staples. So essential was it to the Greek economy that when the Spartans assaulted Athens, their first move was to destroy the olive groves of Attica to undermine the Athenians' economy.

Olive cultivation spread through Western Eruope, but not at first in contiguous countries. From Greece, the olive tree was transplanted to the faraway country of Spain in the 4th century B.C., arriving via Carthaginian traders. In the 5th century B.C. olives were planted in the Roman territory of Latium, and around 640 B.C. Greeks from Asia Minor migrating to Marseille brought the olive to France.

The olive and its rich oil entered Italian cooking immediately. The Romans ate olives at the beginning of meals as appetizers and at the end to freshen their mouths, and special dishes of olives and bread sometimes constituted the entrée. As part of their allocation, even slaves received olives, along with rations of salt and wine, but they were of inferior quality, deficient in oil.

Olives first reached the United States via Mexico, when Franciscan priests transplanted trees in California in the mid-1790s. Unimpressed with the fruit, Californians virtually ignored the olive and its light amber-colored oil for more than a hundred years. It was only late in the last century that olive cultivation began to acquire the aspects of a thriving business.

Pear, 3000 B.C.; Sumer

Early evidence for pears in the Orient comes from seeds found in a Chinese tomb dating from 2100 B.C., but little else is known about the fruit's use in China.

Many historians think the pear actually originated earlier as a

Peach: A Chinese symbol of immortality. Pear: 17th-century Italians knew of 209 varieties, not all of them tasty. Grapefruit: Less than 300 years old. Pineapple: King Louis XIV attempted to eat one unpeeled and cut his royal lips. Figs: According to Matthew 21:18–19, Jesus was hungry when he entered Jerusalem and found a fig tree bearing leaves but no fruit. He said it would never again grow fruit, and the tree withered away.

food in Sumer, where healers used it as an ingredient in many of their medicines, and later prescribed it in its natural form. A pear a day, so to speak, kept the doctor away, and not surprisingly the fruit began to be eaten at mealtime.

Though the pear supposedly was known to other early civilizations, such as the Hittites, the Hebrews, and Phoenicians, reliable documentation begins with the Greek writer Homer, who provided instruction on how to grow pear orchards. The Greeks passed this information on to the Egyptians, then to the Romans, where Pliny claimed to have tasted thirty-eight different varieties. (Remember, he also boasted of tasting thirty-six different kinds of apples.) A later writer declared that there were too many varieties to list, and a 17th-century Italian book listed 209 different kinds of pears.

Pears increased in variety — to four hundred — when they reached France. Only twenty-five, however, were deemed suitable for the palates of connoisseurs. By the late 19th century, England claimed to have 850 kinds of pears.

Not all of these had a sweet taste and smooth texture. One problem with excessive cross-breeding is that it can emphasize the grittiness of pears, which is caused by stone cells that accumulate and become harder the longer the fruit remains on the tree. That is why pears are picked early and permitted to ripen in warehouses or at home.

The pear reached America from several geographic points. Jesuit missionaries from France brought it to the Iroquois of the St. Lawrence Valley in the 17th century, and a pear tree was planted in Eastham in 1640 by Thomas Prence, governor of Plymouth Colony in Massachusetts. Nieuw Amsterdam, later New York, received its first pear sapling from Holland in 1647.

Pears moved westward along with the missionaries, and Spanish friars in the 18th century planted seeds in California, where the fruit flourished, eventually yielding more than a thousand varieties.

An astronomical number — nearly 5000 — different pears have been recognized in Europe in the past century, all the offspring of about twenty species. This has led botanists to conclude that variety, though it may well be the spice of life, has become the curse of the pear. For quantity alone has not improved the quality of the fruit. The most savored pear of the world's multifarious varieties probably is the Comice, the "queen of pears," which is also one of the most commercially successful and widespread pear.

Orange, 2200 B.C.; China

The orange, a berry in the botanical classification of fruits, originated in southern China but was not as sweet as today's varieties, which have been bred for higher sugar content.

Its place of origin has been fairly well established from the numerous wild varieties of oranges found in the Orient, from the prevalence there of pests and diseases that plague the fruit, and from the fact that Chinese cultivation of orange groves is documented in texts dating from 2200 B.C.

The orange did not enter the Western world for many centuries. Alexander the Great's troops, marching through the Orient in the 4th century B.C., discovered the banana but seem to have overlooked the orange entirely. The West first tasted the fruit when it was introduced to the Romans in the 1st century A.D.

Its route to Rome was circuitous; it traveled through Arab lands to the Red Sea coast of Egypt, then by camel caravan up the Nile, by boat to Alexandria, and finally by Mediterranean vessel to Ostia, the port of Rome. The journey took several months, and though the condition of the highly perishable fruit is unknown, it understandably was regarded as a rare luxury and was very expensive.

At some stage of this exhausting journey, traders saw the chance to plant saplings closer to home, in North Africa; here the Moors coveted the fruit and carried it to Spain following their 8th-century conquest. By the 12th century the region from Granada to Seville had become one of the world's outstanding citrus-growing areas.

France began cultivation about a hundred years later, and Italy followed in the 13th century, when St. Dominic planted oranges in the garden of Rome's Santa Sabina convent. So popular were oranges in Italy that food authorities believe the five golden balls on the heraldry of the Medici family, which dates from the 14th century, may represent oranges.

Christopher Columbus brought oranges to their well-suited New World home in the late 15th century, planting on Hispaniola seeds he had collected in the Canary Islands in 1493. The first continental region to produce oranges probably was Panama, where they were grown by 1516.

The introduction of the orange to the famed citrus country of Florida came in 1539, when Hernando de Soto planted seedlings south of St. Augustine. The chief custodians of the fruit were the Seminole Indians, who treasured its taste and were particularly smitten with orange slices marinated for several days in honey.

Moving westward, oranges were planted in Arizona between 1707 and 1710, after having been imported from Mexico. The natural progression led them to California, where the orange industry had taken root by 1769. It did not begin to thrive, however, until two navel orange trees from Baía, Brazil, by way of Washington, D.C. — hence **Washington Navel** — were planted there in 1873. It's believed that these two trees were the ancestors of all California navel oranges.

Banana, 2000 B.C.; Indus Valley

The banana has proven a conundrum for historians. One early European discoverer of the fruit mistook it for a giant fig. Actually, the banana isn't even a fruit; it's an herb.

Botanists think the banana made its appearance 4000 years ago in the Indus Valley, but they are uncertain whether at the time it grew wild or was cultivated. Cultivation, nevertheless, must have occurred early in the banana's history, since wild varieties, sometimes described as jungle weeds, are leathery, unappetizing, and full of bothersome seeds. When man brought the plant under his control, he cross-bred species to enhance the flavor and rid it of seeds, but the second "improvement" made future crops sterile, unable to produce without human intervention.

Delicate and perishable, the banana was confined to its native region for hundreds of years. Though Alexander the Great and his soldiers discovered the plant as they marched through India, apparently they did not return with samples, for bananas seem never to have reached classical Greece or Rome. Their export is thought to have occurred first with the Arabs, master traders of the Far East, who took bananas throughout the Near East and into northern Egypt in the 7th century A.D.; and it was during this period that the Koran was written, identifying the banana as the forbidden fruit of the Old Testament.

Bananas reached America in 1516 when they were planted by Friar Tomás de Berlanga on the island of Hispaniola. The first bananas imported into the United States came to the Centennial Exposition in Philadelphia in 1876, where, great curiosity items, they were wrapped in tin foil and sold for a dime apiece.

Surprisingly, however, the banana, which today is one of the most widely consumed fruit-related foods, was not regularly available in North America until after World War I, when refrigeration was installed on oceangoing vessels.

Peach, 2000 B.C.; China

For centuries botanists traced the peach's origin to Persia. Its scientific name, *Prunus persica* ("Persian plum tree"), reflects this belief.

But its true birthplace is ancient China, where eating peaches was thought to preserve the body in perpetuity. Indeed, to poets who elegized it, to sculptors who carved it, and to painters who captured its image in water colors during the Ch'in Dynasty, the peach was the paramount symbol of immortality. Called *tao* in Chinese, the peach was exchanged among friends and lovers as a token of affection, and was immortalized in the writings of Confucius in the 5th century B.C.

From the Far East the peach spread west, reaching Persia some time in the 3rd century B.C., and from there the Romans began importing it, in the 1st century A.D. They considered it a tasty, gratifying food whose trees mysteriously would not reproduce after their first yield. The Romans had not yet discovered that the peach is a temperate-climate fruit and requires a cool, dormant period of at least two winter months to rejuvenate for the task of yielding fruit in the spring.

During the Middle Ages, Europe imported peach trees from Persia, but in their new home the trees yielded small, tasteless fruit so dry that when they were cut open, the pit fell away from the pulp. Cross-breeding improved the stock, and the Spaniards brought the tastier varieties to the New World, where the American Indians developed a truly insatiable craving for them. The Natchez tribe went so far as to name one of their thirteen months for the fruit.

In the hospitable American soil, peach cultivation spread from tribe to tribe so quickly that in 1663 William Penn wrote that "not an Indian plantation [is] without them." And when Thomas Jefferson, a peach addict to the core, became President, he had the fruit trees planted at Monticello.

Plum, 1800 B.C.; Babylon

Trees bearing hard, dark purple plums grew in the Hanging Gardens of Babylon, yet it seems that these wild fruits were not eaten for pleasure, but were used as an ingredient in many herbal medications.

In the following centuries there is little mention of plums (genus *Prunus*). The Roman naturalist Pliny in the 1st century A.D. commented that the *Prunus damascena*, one of the earliest domesticated plums, migrated from Syria to Greece and then to Italy. But Pliny's tart, watery plum differed from the hard, acidic wild plums that earlier had been eaten by the Greeks. Thus, it appears that the 1st-century Romans ate the first plums, fresh from the tree, similar to those we enjoy today.

Plums were not peculiar to Europe, however. Bernal Díaz, chronicler of the Cortez conquest of Mexico, reported that on Easter Sunday, 1519, local Indians fed the conquistadors a meal that included plums, and that a few days later high-ranking Aztecs arrived with baskets brimming with plums. Though no description was given to identify the species, they most likely were hard wild plums with pits similar to those found by archeologists in Peru, where the Incas had cultivated the fruit from the 1st century B.C.

Spaniards had been accustomed to the softer, sweeter *Prunus domestica.* The Indians had served them the tougher, tarter *Prunus americana,* at that time still a wild fruit.

Plums were still wild in November 1621. Undoubtedly, this is the reason they were not a great success when served at the first Thanksgiving dinner that year. Americans continued to complain about the inferior quality of their own plums, compared with European varieties, which, of course, had been domesticated and selectively bred for more than 1500 years.

Pilgrims in the Massachusetts Bay Colony eventually imported European plum trees. They also continued to improve American plums until the fruit was competitive with its continental cousins. So much so that around the mid-19th century one American variety, the **Jefferson plum** — developed in 1825 in Albany, New York, and named after the third President — was planted in England, where it still is widely grown and popular today.

Strawberry, 1st Century A.D.; Italy

"Doubtless God could have made a better berry, but doubtless God never did," wrote an admirer in 1600. That concisely defines the strawberry's popularity throughout the ages.

Countless civilizations apparently recognized strawberries and picked them in the wild, those species being so tasty that for centuries no one thought to domesticate the plant. Yet where many other fruits became major sources of early commerce, the strawberry, because of its high perishability, did not become a commercial commodity until the dawn of refrigerated transportation, about a hundred years ago.

Strawberry seeds have been found at 7000-year-old sites in

Denmark, Switzerland, and England, but in scant quantities. Archeologists believe that early man, surrounded by forests rich in larger fruits (and numerous vegetables), probably shunned the small, harder-to-locate, and harder-to-pick strawberries. And since early man's main concern was quantity, not quality, more strawberries were required to fill his belly than he could readily find.

Strawberries are not mentioned by the writers of early civilizations. Even the ancient Greeks had not discovered strawberries, though they did eat the berries from the "strawberry tree," which bears fruit resembling strawberries but of an inferior taste.

The Romans were among the first people to recognize the vine-growing strawberries, though for years they confused them with fruit from the strawberry tree. Pliny, in fact, called the vine "the only plant which crawls among the ground whose fruit resembles that of bushes." While the Romans thought the ground and tree berries to be the same, they did distinguish between the superior-tasting vine berry and the bland tree berry, which Pliny called "a fruit little esteemed."

Throughout the Middle Ages there was little mention of strawberries, and certainly no concern with domesticating wild species. The fruit surfaced in France when strawberry-loving Charles V in 1368 had vines planted in the royal gardens of the Louvre, and when the Duchess of Burgundy, who liked her berries with cream, had them planted in her gardens. At this time strawberries were being used in Germany as a medicine, and shortly afterward in England men ate for dessert strawberries covered with wine; women preferred theirs with cream. Still, these were small, wild berries.

The cultivated strawberry, which yielded a larger, sweeter, lusher fruit, was first written about in 1608, when Sir Hugh Plat published a book in which he explained how to improve the quality of strawberries. Whereas tart wild berries had been popular, the new sweeter strains of fruit were a smash, eaten raw, topped with milk or cream or liqueur, or tucked into pastries.

Since then, plants have been cross-breed to increase hardiness, taste, and yield, and to minimize maturation time. These experiments have been vastly successful, for modern strawberry varieties, grown around the globe, produce more food per acre per period of time than any other fruit in the world.

Pineapple, 1493; Guadeloupe

Named by its dicoverers for its resemblance to a large pine cone and its taste like that of sweet apples, the pineapple received more paeans of praise than any other fruit. "The princess of fruits," extolled Sir Walter Raleigh. "The gods might luxuriate upon it and it should only be gathered by the hand of a Venus," exclaimed its alleged Brazilian discoverer, Jean de Lery, in 1555; another early writer found the fruit so regal that "the King of Kings has put a crown upon its head, which is like the essential mark of its royalty."

Although credit for the pineapple had gone to de Lery, the fruit actually was discovered in 1493 by Spanish explorers on the Caribbean isle of Guadeloupe. They also found the pineapple, a member of the *Bromelia* family, which includes forty-five genera and more than sixteen hundred species, thriving on other tropical islands, as well as on the South American mainland.

The fruit enjoyed a healthy reputation among islanders. They hung crowns sculpted from pineapples above their huts as a welcome to visitors; they planted thick hedges of pineapple plants around their villages so that the spiky-edged leaves would discourage intruders. In fact, a common rite of passage for Carib boys was to race pell-mell down rows of pineapple bushes, silently enduring the leaves' bloody lacerations.

The Spaniards were first to record the existence of the pineapple, but the fruit probably had been cultivated a thousand years earlier by the American Indians. Not only is there evidence that the fruit was known to the Indians, but the species discovered by the Spaniards throughout the Caribbean were all seedless, a clear indication that the plant had been dependent on man for its reproduction for such a long time that it had abandoned the function itself.

Europeans were immediately enamored of the strange new fruit Columbus's men had brought back to the continent. One aficionado reported that it "had a delicious taste which combined the flavors of melons, strawberries, and pippins" and was "one of the best fruits in the world," easily arousing the appetite of a fussy eater.

Pineapples spread in 1616 to Italy, where the Italians made the first attempt (unsuccessful) to grow the fruit in hothouses, then to Holland and England.

One of the first pineapples grown in France was offered to King Louis XIV, who, with characteristic greed and impatience, snatched the yet unpeeled fruit from the royal gardener's hand and bit vigorously into it, severely lacerating his royal lips on the pineapple's prickly eyes. Under royal fiat, the cultivation of pineapples in France came to an abrupt halt and did not resume until Louis's successor ascended the throne.

The pineapple's route in commerce was the reverse of most foods. It went from the Americas to Europe, and later from Peru to China; from there it reached the Philippines, and in 1777, through the

Strawberry: It produced more food per acre per period of time than any other fruit in the world. Banana: It is said that the serpent in the Garden of Eden hid in the leaves of the banana tree. Cherry: A descendant of the rose. Grapes: Of the approximately 8000 varieties, natural and man-made hybrids, all those of the Old World have developed from a single species, *Vitis vinifera*. Watermelons: Halved, hollowed out, and dried, they are said to have served early Greeks and Romans as helmets.

efforts of English explorer Captain Cook, it arrived on the Hawaiian Islands, today one of its principal homes.

Grapefruit, 18th Century; Jamaica

The grapefruit is a species related to a group of citrus fruits brought to the New World by European settlers. Amazingly, it is less than three hundred years old. Even as a new species, though, the grapefruit has been phenomenally popular, particularly in this health-conscious country, where the fruit is cherished for its few calories and high-energy boost.

Though the grapefruit entered the civilized world under the noses of accomplished botanists during an era when plant science already was well established, its origin remains largely a mystery. Known at various times as the pomelo and shaddock, the grapefruit was christened with its current name when John Lunan, in his botanical report, *Hortus Jamaicensis,* wrote that he had discovered a new fruit in Jamaica that, to his tongue at least, tasted exactly like a grape, though it was considerably larger, possessing a thicker, pithy, and inedible skin. Since no other botanists who later tasted the fruit were reminded of grapes, one of them proposed retaining the name grapefruit because the fruit grew in grapelike clusters.

Although botanists over the years have searched such disparate regions as Indochina and the Pacific Islands, they have been forced to concur with Lunan that the fruit originated solely in Jamaica. This presented them with a puzzle: How did the grapefruit suddenly appear on the isolated island?

Two theories are popular: the natural cross-breeding of two citrus species that had been brought to the New World, or the possibility of a natural mutation occurring in a single citrus species. The first possibility assumes that one of the grapefruit's parents was a fruit native to Malaysia as early as 1500 B.C. and known as the "lemon-melon" or "pumelo" (anglicized to pomelo). Its other parent is unknown.

The second theory also credits the pomelo, but as the sole parent of the grapefruit. Pomelo seeds were brought to Barbados in 1696 by an East Indian trader, a Captain Shaddock, and it is possible that birds carried the seeds to Jamaica, where, in their new environment, they underwent a mutation into a new fruit.

After considerable professional debate, botanists recognized the grapefruit in 1830 as a genuinely new species and named it *Citrus paradisi.*

The origins of ten other popular fruits:

1. Figs, 4000 B.C.; Syria
2. Grapes, 4000 B.C.; Caspian and Black seas coastal regions
3. Rhubarb, 2700 B.C.; eastern Mediterranean lands and Asia Minor
4. Cantaloupe, 2400 B.C.; Iran
5. Watermelon, 2000 B.C.; Central Africa
6. Mandarin Orange, 220 B.C.; China
7. Lemon, 11th century; northern Burma
8. Papaya, 14th century; West Indies
9. Mango, 16th century; Southeast Asia
10. Lime, 17th century; Americas

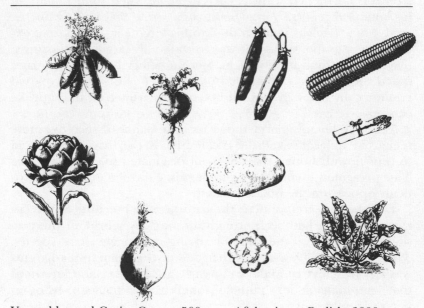

Vegetables and Grain. Carrot, 500 B.C.; Afghanistan. Radish, 3000 B.C.; China. Peas, 3000 B.C.; Near East. Corn, Pre–7000 B.C.; Near East. Potato, 3000 B.C.; Peru. Onion, 3200 B.C.; Egypt. Squash, 9000 B.C.; Mexico. Asparagus, 200 B.C.; eastern Mediterranean. Artichoke, 500 B.C.; central Mediterranean. Spinach, A.D. 647; Iran. The dates represent the oldest seeds found, and are the first food mentioned in the historical record.

9

Cereals: Corn to Croissants

Cereal, Pre–7000 B.C.; Near East

The cultivation of a tall wild grass that still grows on the sandy hills and fertile river deltas of the Near East sparked the birth of civilization.

Early man always had gathered wild wheat, which bears nutritious seeds that are easily plucked and winnowed from their husks. But somewhere around 9000 B.C. he experienced a change in fortune when he realized that he need not rely on chance encounters with the plant. If he forwent eating all the seeds he gathered in favor of planting some of them, he could settle down beside his plots and wait for grain to sprout.

As a hunter-gatherer, early man required 10 to 15 square miles of land to feed himself. But as a farmer, now he could cultivate the same space to yield food for 5000 people.

The domestication of **wheat** probably was a serendipitous discovery. Some clever man or woman must have made the crucial observation that one season's sprouts of wheat were growing in exactly the same place where seeds had been spilled, or hidden, during the previous year. This awareness must have been followed by centuries of experimentation while man learned the best methods of planting and the peak seasons and soils.

Today archeologists are confident that by 7000 B.C. domesticated wheat was growing in the Tigris-Euphrates Valley. They have matched ancient wheat seeds found during an excavation in the region with those of a related wild wheat that still grows there, and found striking genetic similarities.

Success with wheat must have encouraged early people to attempt cultivating numerous other crops. Though they doubtless met many failures, they experienced a second great accomplishment around 6000 B.C. in domesticating **barley.**

Unlike today's grain, which bears six vertical ranks as a result of genetic mutations, their barley bore only two ranks, but was equally nutritious. Then, barley was grown exclusively for human consumption and eaten raw; today, barley is fed primarily to livestock and is used in making whiskey and beer.

Wheat, on the other hand, is still used primarily for human consumption, mainly in cereals, crackers, and breads.

Cultivation of crops and the domestication of animals enabled peoples to abandon their nomadic hunter-gatherer life and settle down; it marked the birth of civilization.

While people in the Near East were cultivating wheat, barley, and later **oats,** two important crops appeared in China, one a grain and a nutritious complex carbohydrate, and the other the first domesticated legume, which is still one of the single best vegetable sources of protein.

Rice was first cultivated in the ideal wetlands of China before 5000 B.C. About 3000 years later Chinese mixed a soft rice paste with milk, froze the mixture, and produced the first ice cream.

Rice, unlike wheat and barley, thrives in wet soil, so the monsoon lands of China were ideal for cultivating the crop. By 5000 B.C. the Chinese had mastered the relatively difficult science of raising rice.

Rice is unique among grains in that each sprout, after reaching a certain height, must be transplanted by hand into a muddy paddy that cannot be permitted to dry out. Today scientists in the United States, a newcomer among rice-cultivating countries, are trying to prove that such individual care of each plant is unnecessary and only impedes the speed with which the crop can be grown. If successful, their new techniques will drastically reduce the cost of rice, but also may result in the disappearance of a custom that has become synonymous with China.

About 3000 B.C. the Chinese domesticated the **soy bean.** Not until the 19th century did the cultivated form reach Japan and then Korea and other Asian and European countries, where it was used primarily for livestock. With more than forty species existing today, the soy bean finally is experiencing a rediscovery of its earliest purpose: to serve as an inexpensive substitution for meat. Only recently has the attitude in the United States toward soy bean consumption become similar to that in the Far East, where it remains the chief source of protein. Today more than half the world's annual yield of 50 million tons of soy beans is grown in America.

Despite the many advances of modern science, all the major cereals had been domesticated by about 3000 B.C., and not a single new major crop has been introduced since.

Corn, Pre–3000 B.C.; South America

The only native American grain, corn, was known to the American Indians long before Columbus discovered the New World; it constituted as much as 80 percent of their diet. Called "maize" by inhabitants of Central America (and by Britons, who use the word "corn" for wheat), corn has proved the most versatile of all grains and is second only to wheat as the main ingredient of breakfast cereals.

Surprising new evidence about maize reveals that the American Indians were far more advanced in agronomy, the study of crops, than historians were willing to give them credit for. Archeological findings in what is now Venezuela confirm that maize did not evolve naturally, as was presumed, but was a hybrid devised by the American Indians through the cross-breeding of numerous generations of native American grasses. In fact, the immediate progenitor of corn, identified today by chromosome tests, was a grass called "teosinte," known to later Mexican Indians as **madre de maize,** or "mother of corn."

Once perfected, maize's bountiful yields and high resistance to disease were responsible for a population boom. In a period of several hundred years the populations of tiny villages along the Orinoco River, which had been more or less stable in size for centuries, suddenly grew fifteenfold. Corn later spread into Mexico, and it reached Europe through Spain after Columbus's second voyage, in 1496.

Bread, 2600 B.C.; Egypt

Bread as we know it today took thousands of years to evolve.

The ancient Eygptians first roasted wheat and barley over open fires. They later learned that the flavor, texture, and digestibility of whole or cracked grain could be improved by the addition of water, which produced gruel.

Flat, or sheet, bread evolved when layers of the rich, viscous gruel were placed on hot stones over a fire.

This progression from roasted seeds to sheets of bread is believed to have begun about 6000 B.C. and ended in 2600 B.C., when Egyptian bakers made a momentous discovery. If the mixture of cracked grain and water was not baked immediately, fermentation occurred, resulting in a zesty dough. When baked, the dough expanded to yield a softer and lighter bread.

With the discovery of **leavening,** the Egyptians greatly expanded their baking skills to include more than fifty different varieties of loaves. Wheat was the main staple, but they also used barley, which has a higher gluten content and thus produces a heavier bread. The standard leavening agent, a sour dough, was prepared in large quantities and kept in constant stock to inoculate fresh dough. This meant bread could be baked as it was needed.

Such culinary skills almost demanded that flat baking stones be replaced with a more versatile cooking device, and the Egyptians invented the **oven.** Many examples remain today. They are made of Nile clay, tapered at the top into an open cone and divided inside by horizontal shelves. Through the hole in the top of the oven the baker could, when necessary, poke the expanding dough.

Baking went unchanged for centuries. Though the Romans baked bread, early writers make no mention of bakers until the 2nd century B.C. When bakers are described, it is clear that they were mostly freed slaves who removed the cooking burden from women who wanted nothing to do with hot ovens.

A typical Roman loaf weighed 1 pound, similar to a modern loaf, and was molded by hand into a mound shape. One variety, *panis artopicius,* was cooked on a spit; a second blend, *panis testuatis,* was baked in an earthen vessel.

Croissants, 1863; Austria

The shape of the croissant is distinctive, and the origins of that pastry are just as clear at its shape.

Bakers in Vienna created the crescent-shaped treats to commemorate the barricaded city's successful stand against a besieging army of Ottoman Turks in 1863. The shape of the croissant came about specifically to embolden the Austrians after their redoubt repelled a Turkish invasion. The croissant derived from the crescent emblem on the Turkish flag, and when the pastry was lustily devoured by the Viennese, it symbolized Austria "swallowing up" the invading Ottoman army.

The discovery of leavening by the Egyptians led them to produce more than fifty different varieties of bread. *Bottom:* The national flag of Turkey inspired an internationally popular food.

Croissants spread westward and soon became a staple of the French breakfast cuisine. From Paris during the Roaring Twenties, the sumptuous bread made its way to America, where it was sold in bakery shops and, in time, during the 1970s, began to be distributed by commercial bakers.

10

Spices: Sugar to Salt

Sugar, 3000 B.C.; India

According to a popular South Pacific legend, the human race did not evolve from the ape but from a sugar cane stalk. One bud suddenly sprouted, blossomed, and materialized into a man, and another was transformed into a woman.

Considering the climate, soil, and abundance of sugar cane that thrived in the region, the legend is understandable; and it is quite likely that sugar was first extracted from cane in the Solomon Islands, although the evidence is circumstantial.

Sugar's first recorded consumption seems to have occurred in India, where cane grew earlier than 3000 B.C. A royal crown, fashioned entirely from sugar crystals, is described in the sacred Hindu text the *Atharvaveda,* written about 800 B.C. Likewise, the old Indian word for sugar, *gaura,* probably came from the name Gur, an ancient monarchy in Bengal and the current term for a kind of impure industrial sugar.

At a much later date sugar was known in the West. In the 4th century B.C. one of Alexander the Great's Greek generals, Nearchus, returning from a campaign in India, recounted seeing a "miraculous reed," able to produce honey without the intervention of bees.

Sugar cane handling, and methods of making sugar, spread from India east to Indochina and west to Arabia and then to Europe. The name of sugar bespeaks its travels: in Sanskrit, India's ancient language, it is called *sarkara,* or *sakara* (originally "sand" or "gravel"), which became *sukkar* in Arabic, *sakharon* in Greek, *zucchero* in Italian, *sucre* in French, and sugar in English.

Candy, 1000 B.C.; Egypt

Man's "sweet tooth," present at birth, was satisfied by candy for the first time in Egypt's New Kingdom during the XX Dynasty. A hieroglyphic of the period depicts a "confectioner" tasting his product. Without sugar — it would not arrive in the region for many centuries — Egyptian candy-makers began with honey, endlessly altering its flavor with dashes of herbs, nuts, spices, and the juices of fruits. (In fact, many modern Italian confection recipes that date to Roman times do not call for sugar.)

Sweets were a prized commodity, and a talented confectioner was an important man in the community. Much thought, experimentation, and sampling by family and friends went into the production of each new candy. The Romans went so far as to revere their confectioners as highly skilled craftsmen, equals to their master road-builders and architects. Pots, pans, strainers, and measuring cups belonging to one Roman candy-maker were unearthed at an archeological dig at the city of Herculaneum, destroyed by the eruption of Vesuvius on August 24, A.D. 79.

The cultivation of sugar cane — one of two major sugar sources today, the other being sugar beets — began in Persia during the Middle Ages. For a long while a Persian with a sweet tooth would cut a piece of the cane and chew it. Only when sugar-refining methods were introduced a few centuries later did Persian candy become a reality.

The first sugar exports to Europe began during this period and almost immediately incited overwhelming demands for candy. Only limited quantities were exported, and sugar was turned by apothecaries into hard candies and taffy and sold at a tidy profit. Since sugar was not yet a common household item, homemade candies were concocted in the kitchens of only the wealthiest families.

The Venetians, among Europe's cagiest merchants, developed the first large-scale sugar import trade, bartering with the Arabs in the 14th century. They advanced candy-manufacturing on the continent, producing a wide variety of shapes, sizes, and flavors. Two hundred years later sugar was in widespread use throughout Europe, and candy was a mainstay in every apothecary shop.

Ridley & Co., a candy factory on Hudson Street, New York City. Before the discovery of sugar in 3000 B.C., candy was made from honey, flavored with herbs and spices.

Chocolate, 1000 B.C.; South America

Civilization tasted chocolate first as a bitter drink and only thousands of years later as a sweet solid confection, the form in which it is best loved and most consumed today.

A product of the cocoa bean from the cocoa plant, indigenous to South America, chocolate was a ceremonial brew of three Indian civilizations, the Mayas, the Toltecs, and the Aztecs. So prized, in fact, was chocolate that for some time the cocoa bean was used as currency.

The Aztecs allowed the beans to ferment in the pod before they were roasted. Broken kernels were roasted in earthenware vessels, then ground into paste in a heated concave stone. The naturally bitter flavor was sweetened somewhat by the addition of vanilla, as well as various spices and herbs. The paste then was molded into small cakes and put out to dry on shiny leaves beneath a tree. When the time came to brew the drink, the cakes were crumbled, mixed with hot water, and stirred with a wooden beater, called a **molinet,** until the desired consistency was attained. The Aztecs called their chocolate drink *xocoatl,* meaning "bitter water."

Chocolate reached Europe early in the 16th century, when Columbus brought it back from the New World. The beverage, known as "cocoa," was mixed with generous amounts of sugar and became such a sensation in the royal court of Spain that King Ferdinand swiftly issued a gag order: absolutely no one was to disclose knowledge of the new drink, under penalty of death. Apparently, the subjects of the king were quite impressed by his edict and took him at his word, for the Spaniards zealously guarded their secret for a full century before its disclosure reached other lands. This covetousness was not unlike the modern-day safeguarding by, say, Coca-Cola of its secret formula.

But when chocolate found its way into Italy in 1606 the Spaniards lost their monopoly, and soon Italians set out in search of their own sources of cocoa. Chocolate reached France as part of the dowry for the marriage of the Spanish princess Maria Theresa to King Louis XIV in 1660. On sampling the drink the French royalty, it was reported, swooned over its rich taste.

England got a chocolate craving when a Frenchman opened a London shop in 1657, selling chocolate blocks that could be made into beverages; soon these chocolateries flourished throughout Europe. Chocolate reached North America when the English opened a chocolate factory in the Massachusetts Bay Colony in 1765, using beans from the West Indies. Europeans, recognizing Africa's ideal climate, began cultivating the cocoa plant there, and today Africa is the world's largest cocoa producer.

Until the 19th century, chocolate remained only a beverage, but it was destined soon to become a candy. In 1828, in the process of perfecting a finer "chocolate powder" from the cocoa bean, C. J. van Houten of the Netherlands isolated for the first time the cocoa bean's creamy butter. A curiosity for a while, the butter was mixed in 1847 with a chocolate liqueur by the English firm of Fry and Sons, and the result was the first **solid eating chocolate,** sweet-tasting and very dark in color.

Two years later Daniel Peter of Switzerland experimented with adding dry milk powder to chocolate, and produced the first light **milk chocolate,** the kind that now dominates the world confectionery market.

Today most milk chocolate is formed by using more whole milk solids than chocolate liqueur. Ordinary commercial milk chocolate usually contains 10 percent chocolate liqueur and 12 percent whole milk solids. Many manufacturers, especially those who export fine chocolates, increase chocolate liqueur as high as 15 percent, and whole milk solids up to 20 percent.

Chocolate remained a drink until the mid-19th century, when the cocoa bean's creamy butter was discovered and mixed with a liqueur by an English firm to produce the first solid eating chocolate, an immediate sensation.

Candy Bars, 19th Century; United States

Candy arrived in the New World with the early colonists; as one legend has it, hard candies, along with bangles and a small amount of money, helped persuade the Indians to sell Manhattan Island to the Dutch for the equivalent of $24. But the tremendous success of the candy business in its early days — both in the United States and around the globe — was minor compared to the surge in sales once the American candy bar entered the scene. Perhaps no other single foodstuff has enjoyed such a sweet success story.

The year 1894 saw the first **Hershey Bar,** concocted by a confectioner in Lancaster, Pennsylvania: Milton Hershey. Made of the simplest and purest ingredients — sugar, cocoa, chocolate, and milk — Hershey's bar, which sold for a few pennies, was a resounding hit. Two years later, Leonard Hirschfield, a candy-maker in his twenties with a young daughter nicknamed Tootsie, introduced the first paper-wrapped candy, the chewy **Tootsie Roll.** Carried in a pocket or purse with no mess, it too was immensely popular and encouraged competitors.

One confection pioneer who accepted the challenge was Peter Paul Halijian of New Haven, Connecticut. In 1921 Peter Paul manufactured a delectable nickel bar of bittersweet chocolate and

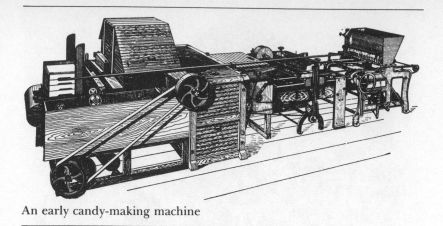
An early candy-making machine

coconut called **Mounds.** In 1947 he topped his Mounds success with a new bar, **Almond Joy.**

By this time annual global candy production was well into the millions of pounds, and the craving of the average person for a candy bar had a long way to go before peaking. Both baseball and World War II boosted candy sales immensely. With Babe Ruth's soaring popularity in the 1920s, the **Baby Ruth** bar — though not named for the feared slugger — was introduced in 1921 and sold briskly throughout the decade. Contrary to popular belief, Otto Schnering, who dreamed up the nickel fudge-peanut-caramel-chocolate confection, did not name the bar for Ruth, but in honor of President Grover Cleveland's daughter, Baby Ruth Cleveland. Two years later Schnering turned another of his sweet dreams into reality: the **Butterfinger** bar.

But if one man dominated the commercial candy bar phenomenon, it was a forty-year-old Minnesota confectioner, Franklin Mars. His first creation was nothing less than a **Milky Way** of delights, blending together sweet milk chocolate, corn syrup, milk, sugar, cocoa, malt, butter, and frothy egg whites. Milky Way sales after only two years produced an astronomical (at the time) $800,000. Undaunted by the millions of cavities he was encouraging, Mars launched a second candy bar in 1930, one whose immediate success must have sent him to the bank in **Snickers.**

Two years later came his third nickel bar, **3 Musketeers,** followed in 1940 by a gem of a publicity ploy that showed true marketing ingenuity. Mars, Inc., Franklin's company, created the colorful little candy that "melts in your mouth, not in your hand," designed specifically with war-bound GIs in mind so that, as the company claimed, soldiers could get a quick energy boost from a candy that would not gum up their trigger fingers: **M & M's,** of course. The candy craze continued to climb for two more decades; then the sweet taste of success soured somewhat in the 1970s, with a public concerned about cavities, health, and, not least of all, expanding waistlines.

Salt, 6500 B.C.; Europe

Man's eating changed drastically once he discovered seasoning; only the invention of cooking had a more profound gastronomic effect on him.

The practice of seasoning food did not arise accidentally. Man actively sought a way to spice up his bland diet after he changed from hunter-gatherer to farmer and began eating predominantly vegetarian fare. Salt, he found, imparted a savory flavor to just about every crop he was cultivating at that time: wheat, barley, potatoes, and assorted vegetable greens. He may well have been a salt addict.

The first salt for seasoning was obtained by burning naturally salty plants and extracting white salt crystals from the charred debris. Unfortunately, it took many plants to make just a pinch of precious salt; the process of extraction must have been tedious.

An even greater demand arose for salt once man started to prefer his meat cooked. Eaten raw, animal flesh contained natural salts that sated his hunger for seasoning, but when the meat was boiled in large pots the salt was quickly leached out. So man began to search for other sources of salt.

At some point during the early Neolithic age he discovered salt mines. It was an inevitable discovery, since salt mines are located throughout the world, without discrimination to terrain or climate. They are found in rocks of all geological ages, buried deep in damp areas because of the solubility of salt in water, and close to the surface in arid regions, where moisture is scarce and cannot wash away the salt.

Archeologists know that by 6500 B.C., people living in Europe were actively mining what are thought to be the first salt mines discovered on the continent, the Hallstein and Hallstatt deposits in Austria. Today these caverns are tourist attractions; they are situated near the town of Salzburg, which of course means "City of Salt."

In addition to the Austrian deposits, Neolithic man appears to have mined salt in at least twelve other places in Europe, and by modern historical times he was mining salt throughout Asia and Africa. When Alexander the Great made his conquering jaunt into India in 328 B.C., he found five kinds of salt being mined there: sea salt, rock salt, red salt, black salt, and earth salt.

Salt had been used in China since at least 2000 B.C., and Marco Polo discovered salt mines during his first trip to the Orient.

In Italy the early Roman architects built roads from Rome to the Adriatic to mine sea salt, naming the route Via Salaria, literally "Salt Way." And it was the Roman writer Petronius, in the *Satyricon,* who gave us the expression "not worth his salt," for Roman soldiers were given special allowances for salt rations, called *salarium,* for "salt money," which is the origin of our word "salary."

Consumed for millennia in increasing amounts, salt in modern times has found its way into almost all canned, frozen, and processed foods. In the United States today the average adult consumes 2.5 teaspoons a day, more than twenty times what the body needs. Dill pickles, for example, contain 928 milligrams of salt; a frozen meat loaf dinner, 1,304 mg; and a fast-food chicken dinner, 2,243 mg. Many doctors believe that the link between salt and high blood pressure has been well established and that salt is largely responsible for the hypertension that affects 35 million Americans.

11

Books: Dictionary to Dickens

Books, 2800 B.C., Egypt

When we use the word "book" today, we mean a bound text, but in ancient times books, or pages of related text, came in cumbersome packages that could not be carried under an arm or read on the way to work. In Babylonia and Assyria a book consisted of a numbered collection of rectangular clay tablets, inscribed with cuneiform and packaged in a labeled container. A scholar needed several library scribes to help him cart a book from its shelf to a reading table.

Lighter books, though still large and awkward to handle, appeared in Egypt shortly after the discovery of papyrus, about 3000 B.C. They took the form of sheets of papyrus, inscribed with hieroglyphics, rolled around cylindrical shafts of wood; several such scrolls, lying flat in a box or standing upright in an earthenware pot, constituted a book. To make written texts easier to handle and more portable, the Egyptians constructed smaller "rolls" of papyrus that could be unwound and read.

The Greeks, whose papyrus came from the Phoenician port of Byblos, adopted the idea of rolls and took it one step further by developing leaflets of folded papyrus, which they bound together by hand to make the first modern-looking book — the Greek Bible. They named it after the city, Byblos, that provided them with paper. The Romans, too, used papyrus rolls and called the book *volumen*, a word that also has entered our language.

Other civilizations had their own versions of books. The inhabitants of northern India wrote on birch bark and collected manuscript pages in wooden birch boxes; writing in the south was done on palm leaves strung together by thread. In the Orient, until about 200 B.C., the Chinese wrote their ideograms with animal-hair brushes on numbered collections of bamboo tablets, then switched to scrolls made from the waste products of silk manufacturing. (They had domesticated the silkworm about 3000 B.C., and a thousand years later the production of fine silk was already a high art.)

Middle Easterners, on the other hand, scrawled on leather (preferably the skin of calves and lambs), from which **parchment** or **vellum** was said to have been invented about 165 B.C., by Eumenes II of Pergamum, when a rival book collector in Egypt suddenly halted supplies of papyrus.

With the production of vellum, books entered a new era. The codex, in which sheets of vellum were folded vertically to form leaves, gave books an evolutionary boost toward their present form. Although the Greeks had used papyrus codeices for their Bibles, and the 2nd-century Romans employed them for the Gospels and Epistles, the vellum codex, more pliant and less brittle, became the predominant text form after the 4th century. A Roman book at this time consisted of a vellum codex bound by string between thin waxed wooden (often beech) sheets. This may be the root of our word "book," derived from the German *boc*, meaning "beech."

The content of early books was religious. Almost all of them contained prayers, hymns, or rituals concerned with man's immortality, or myths, legends, and epics that provided accounts of his origins. These books were later spiced with semisacred codes of law, collections of proverbs and precepts, and priestly discourses on divinity, medicine and magic, history, astronomy and astrology.

Books may have been traded, or loaned, during the early eras, since the Egyptian **Book of the Dead** was required reading fare for mourners at every funeral. But mainly, books were produced and preserved in palaces and temples, and they contributed greatly to the concept of compulsory education for freemen.

Dictionary, 600 B.C.; Mesopotamia

For centuries after writing developed, people continued to speak without recourse to any authoritative reference books that explained what a word meant or how it was to be used. Considering the poor communications among cities within the same empire, the lack of references caused considerable confusion, because various groups used the same word to express different ideas. It was out of this linguistic turmoil — which worsened as people spread across Asia and Europe, falling victim to numerous conquering tribes that had their own words and meanings — that the need for dictionaries arose.

The earliest preserved dictionary is an Akkadian word list from central Mesopotamia dating from 600 B.C. About this time the Western-style dictionary was emerging from the labors of Greek philosophers, who had begun to analyze speech patterns and language, establishing the roots of grammar and syntax. The Greek language already was in transition from its archaic origins to its classical beginnings, and over the next several centuries it continued to evolve to such an extent that by the 1st century A.D. commentaries on words and their usage were an absolute necessity. After a lengthy 1st-century lexicon by Pamphilus of Alexandria, the Greeks became skilled compilers of dictionaries, which they revised frequently.

Bilingual Dictionary, Middle Ages; Europe

So numerous were the languages and dialects spoken in Europe during the Middle Ages that bilingual dictionaries offered the only solution to a frustrating continental logomachy.

While classical Latin was still regarded as the universal language throughout much of Europe, since the fall of the Roman Empire in A.D. 476 the language's purity had eroded into pidgin speech or had been supplanted by regional dialects. Thus, the first bilingual dictionaries were compiled to help people ignorant of the dialects of affluent groups who controlled commerce and ruled society. One early bilingual dictionary clearly explains that the book was intended for foreigners, artisans, farmers, and others of the "bourgeoisie," since fashionable folk were well acquainted with the prevailing dialect.

The first printed bilingual dictionary was an English-French vocabulary designed for travelers, compiled by William Caxton and published in England in 1480. English and French words, along with their meanings, appeared in parallel columns and occupied twenty-six pages. This was followed in 1496 by a scholarly Latin-English dictionary by the noted grammarian John Stanbridge; and three years later came publication of a hefty English-Latin work by a Dominican friar of Norfolk, Geoffrey the Grammarian (Galfridus Grammaticus, as his name appeared on the cover), titled *Storehouse for Children of Clerics.*

The first completely English dictionary was published in London in 1604. Compiled by Robert Cawdrey, a schoolmaster, it contained only 3000 words and possessed a title almost as long: *A Table Alphabeticall, conteyning and teaching the true writing and understanding of hard usuall English wordes, borrowed from the Hebrew, Greeke, Latine, or French &c.*

Early dictionaries were devoted primarily to "hard words" or meanings assumed to be rare, but by today's standards the dictionaries were not very helpful. As late as 1676, in *An English Dictionary Explaining Difficult Terms,* the best text of the day, the lexicographer Elisha Coles defined "horse" only as "a rope fasten'd to the foremast shrouds, to keep the sprit-sail sheats clear of the anchor-flukes." If that encapsulation had none of the properties of a Kentucky Derby winner, Nathaniel Bailey, the father of English lexicography, did little to clairfy the multiple meanings of the word. He dismissed the English equine with the epithet "a beast well known," elaborating only that the word could be used both for the male and the female of the species.

Nor did the most renowned English lexicographer, Samuel Johnson, strain to be impartial (or specific) when he defined "oats" as "a grain which in England is generally given to horses, but in Scotland supports the people." From Johnson's definition, a Spaniard fluent in English, but unfamiliar with oats, would have had no way of recognizing the grain even if it had turned up as his breakfast cereal.

American Dictionary, 1828; Noah Webster

Noah Webster's *An American Dictionary of the English Language,* first published in 1828, was such a remarkable tome that it has never gone out of print; it has been only amended over the years to assure its accuracy. Less well read than Samuel Johnson, but possessing a true genius for definitions, Webster produced a dictionary that was far superior to British compilations of the day, and replaced their parochial, often useless, definitions with ones precise and well honed.

Webster often boasted that he could "single-handedly standardize American speech" and that his dictionary was a major step in that direction. But as he grew older, and saw repeated need to revise his dictionary, he found himself concurring with Johnson that language can be described and, to a certain extent, influenced, but it cannot be controlled.

Webster, in fact, must share credit for the advancement of American lexicography with his one-time employee, Joseph E. Worcester. Between successors of Webster's volume and Worcester's *A Dictionary of the English Language* (1860), a spirited competition entered lexicography that shaped and amplified the English language; it generated a host of general, specialized, and technical dictionaries, and provided a wealth of information for later historians and linguists.

Encyclopedia, 4th Century B.C.; Greece

The word "encyclopedia," from the Greek *enkyklopaidea*, originally meant a complete system of learning that was intended to provide a student with an all-round education in mathematics, science, philosophy, and literature. Today we regard an encyclopedia as any large or multivolume reference work, complete with maps, illustrations, and diagrams; a book more often consulted than studied.

Unfortunately, the earliest extant encyclopedia survives only in fragments. It represents the long and loving labors of Plato's nephew, Speusippus, who codified the ideas on natural history, mathematics, and philosophy of Pythagorus in a series of articles. It was not the first Greek encyclopedia, however, for many of Aristotle's lectures at the Lyceum provided students with a comprehensive cultural background; later they were collected into volumes that, because of the breadth of subjects they covered, also fulfill the modern definition of encyclopedia.

The Romans had a penchant for comprehensive books of knowledge. Their greatest encyclopedia was the *Historia naturalis,* written in A.D. 59 by the naturalist Pliny the Elder, a round-up of every fact, myth, and fancy of the day. Though it was undiscriminating in distinguishing truth from fantasy (or perhaps because it was), Pliny's encyclopedia gained immense popularity and had widespread influence throughout the Roman Empire. All later Roman works borrowed heavily from it; as much as 90 percent of the 3rd-century text *Collectanea rerum memorabilium (Collection of Memorable Things),* by the Latin grammarian Gaius Julius Solinus, was lifted from Pliny's work. *Historia naturalis,* despite its faults, served as a standard source for European encyclopedias for more than 1500 years, and it remains to this day an important chronicle for students of Roman sculpture and painting, areas it handled with accuracy.

The first encyclopedia compiled entirely by a woman was the 12th-century *Hortus delicarum (Garden of Delights)* by the abbess Herrad, who died in 1195. Handwritten, the manuscript is beautifully illustrated with 636 miniature drawings that were added especially to edify the nuns in her charge.

Perhaps the greatest of all encyclopedias of the Western world has been the *Encyclopaedia Britannica.* Three Scots, Andrew Bell, Colin Macfarquhar and William Smellie, were responsible for the first edition, which appeared in England between 1768 and 1771. It has been revised frequently since then; the last edition appeared in the mid 1970s, with a staggering nineteen volumes of text (the *Macropaedia*), six of detailed outlines (the *Micropaedia*), and one (the *Propaedia*) that is an abbreviated survey of the knowledge covered in the entire series.

Since the appearance of the first Greek encyclopedia, more than 2000 encyclopedias have been issued throughout the world; many now are lost or out of print, but many others have been periodically updated and are still available. If they all could be gathered and arranged on a library shelf, they would stretch a distance of about 2 miles.

Library, 5th Century B.C.; Greece

An argument can be made that libraries came into existence along with clay tablets about 3500 B.C., for early civilizations recognized no distinction between a record room or archive and a library. And since the earliest texts dealt largely with religious matters, it is not surprising to find these libraries in houses of worship.

One archeological example was a temple from the 3rd millennium B.C. in the Babylonian town of Nippur whose anterooms were stocked with clay tablets containing prayers, hymns, and rituals. But a collection of religious books for the exclusive use of priests constitutes a library only in a very restricted sense of the word, perhaps the way an individual's books are his personal library.

True public libraries, which stocked books on many subjects for the benefit of scholars and students, had to await two developments: the writing of scholarly texts on history, science, and philosophy; and the notion of books as a means of conveying knowledge from one generation to the next. Both of these ideas fully flowered for the first time in the 5th century B.C., owing to the Greeks' interest in education for freemen. Institutional libraries sprang up in Athens at this time, devoted to all areas of learning, but with a strong emphasis on the hottest topic of the day, philosophy, which then and for centuries to follow was inextricably linked with science under the rubric "natural philosophy."

Most Greek schools of thought had their own libraries. The most notable exception was the Stoics, who did not believe in private property, but the Epicureans and students of Plato cherished libraries, and many of their early works exist today because of meticulous preservation.

The Peripatetics, Aristotle and his disciples, established the most thorough and famous collection of books in all of Greece. The geographer and historian Strabo (63 B.C.–A.D. 24) cited Aristotle's library as the model for the later institutions at Alexandria, which rank as the greatest libraries in antiquity. The judicious acquisition of papyrus books by Ptolemy I Soter and his son, Ptolemy II Philadelphus, with the wise assistance of their adviser Demetrius of Phalerum, gave these libraries by the middle of the 3rd century B.C. an abundance of books that surpassed anything throughout the civilized world.

The ambitious aim of the founders of the Alexandria libraries was to collect the entire body of Greek literature, in the best-preserved copies and arranged in systematic order. Staffed over the years by the most famous Greek writers and scholars, and housed in a temple to Zeus and a temple to the Muses, the libraries had collections of papyrus and vellum scrolls that numbered in the thousands.

Literature, 3000 B.C.; Sumer

The Sumerians created the first major literary work, an epic poem, during the so-called Heroic Age, named for an era in which Sumer, the cradle of writing, was faced with several struggles to maintain possession of its fertile Mesopotamian land.

The first of several epic poems embodied the adventures of early Sumerian kings, Enmerkar, Lualbada, and Gilgamesh. The popularity of the last of these is permanently ensconced in history by a five-cycle tale, the *Epic of Gilgamesh,* the single most important development in Mesopotamian literature and the first masterful piece of human writing.

King Gilgamesh — part human, part deity — is in search of immortality. His efforts are temporarily thwarted by a hostile god, who persuades a ruffian, Enkidu, reared among wild animals, to challenge Gilgamesh in battle. Vanquished by the king, Enkidu eventually befriends Gilgamesh, and they embark on colorful adventures, among them a major escapade in which the two men kill a wild bull that had been sent by the goddess of love to destroy Gilgamesh because he had shunned her marriage proposal. Enkidu, after dreaming that he will be punished by death for slaughtering the bull, awakens ill and soon dies, but Gilgamesh discovers a magical plant that, if eaten, will restore youth and ensure immortality. A serpent snatches the plant from Gilgamesh, who, dejected and anxious, returns to his capital to await whatever fate the goddess has in store for him.

The epic was adopted by the Babylonians, who, endowing it with more fluid prose style, turned it into one of the earliest masterpieces.

The greatest of their own epics, from the 3rd millennium B.C., was *Enuma elish (The Epic of Creation),* which told how Marduk, the city deity of Babylon, slew the female monster Tiamat and created the world from her body, a deed for which the other gods rewarded him by granting him universal rule.

The origins of our Western literature begin with the Greeks of the 4th century B.C. and the writings of the conquering Romans, which were translated into vernacular languages and spread throughout Europe by Christianity. Though the ancient period of Western literature ends with the fall of the divided Roman Empire in A.D. 476, by that time civilization had created all the major genres: epic, tragedy, comedy, satire, history, biography, and prose narrative. One of the most popular forms of present-day literature, the novel, would not appear for many centuries.

Novel, 1740; *Pamela*, Samuel Richardson

The origin of the English novel stems from a social circle of young Englishwomen and their spiritual mentor, Samuel Richardson.

The group gathered in Richardson's home in a London suburb, and discussion often centered on "advice for the lovelorn," with Richardson playing the role of a wise and shrewd surrogate father. When love affairs became entangled, Richardson offered to help straighten them out by writing conciliatory letters in the women's names to suitors in a style superior to anything the women could manage on their own.

Richardson's letters patched up many a troubled affair, and soon he enlarged his letter-writing with ambitious resolve. He composed a book of letters for all occasions, such as the avuncular reprimand "From an Uncle to a Nephew, on his keeping bad Company, bad Hours, etc., in his Apprenticeship." With profit in mind, Richardson felt certain that the letter-writing public would stampede booksellers for his volume, since they would be required only to copy the letters and fill in the appropriate names. And he was right. The book made money and presumably solved the problems of many families and lovers.

Letter Number 138, "A Father to a Daughter in Service on hearing of her Master's attempting her Virtue," sparked the idea for a book. As Richardson was drafting this letter, based on an actual occurrence he had come across years earlier, in which a servant girl had to rebuff the aggressive and persistent advances of her young master in such a way as not to lose her job, he suddenly realized that the story contained enough drama for a book, probably a series of letters between the bewildered girl and her fretful parents, in some distant place. The book would entertain and instruct, thought Richardson, and young people everywhere could glean valuable lessons for coping with problems of love and morality.

Again, he was right. After three months work, the book, *Pa-*

mela, or Virtue Rewarded, was finished, and Richardson became the witting father of the English novel. He knew to a degree that he had shaped a new style of literature, because immediately after the book's publication he wrote to a friend that he hoped the novel "might introduce a new species of writing." It did — one that dominates the world's bookshelves today.

Gothic Novel, 1764; *The Castle of Oranto*, Horace Walpole

Like so many pioneers in other fields, Horace Walpole merely introduced, but did not perfect, his contribution to literature. Nonetheless, *The Castle of Oranto*, Walpole's only work of fiction, was the true precursor of the genre that many early authors, at one time or other, tried their hand at — the Gothic novel.

Walpole, the son of Sir Robert Walpole, an 18th-century English prime minister who had fallen from grace, was an effeminate dilettante and gossip-monger, whose collected letters could easily fill fifty volumes. The often libelous tenor of his correspondence is to be found in *The Castle of Oranto,* an amateurish text that somehow managed to hit on the themes, atmosphere, mood, and even props that characterize all later Gothic fiction.

The novel captivated audiences through its picaresque plot, which dealt with a beautiful Protestant virgin who is the prisoner of a lecherous and satanic Catholic hero-villain, darkly handsome and menacing, who resided in northern Italy. The poor heroine endures countless supernatural incidents in the hero's castle that jostle her mind to the point of madness: trap doors mysteriously open to dungeons, family portraits weep, and caskets open in the dead of night.

Historical Novel, 1814; *Waverley,* Sir Walter Scott

The historical novel owes its popularity to Sir Walter Scott's dramatization and glamorization of history, bound by high moral precepts. Scott was not the first to write historical novels, but though his characters were shallow, his dialogue stilted, and his style often slapdash, he was the true father of the genre. His books were successful because the protagonists were champions of valor and principle.

Poetry was Scott's first love, but his verse was eclipsed when Lord Byron's became popular in 1812. Outrivaled, he turned to fiction, first publishing anonymously because fiction was considered tawdry stuff. In fact, he referred to himself as "the Great Unknown," for though his novels sold briskly, not until much later in his career did they bear his name.

As in his poems and earlier ballads, Scottish history permeated Scott's fiction, particularly themes from the 17th and 18th centuries.

When the publishing concern of Ballantyne, in which Scott had an interest, collapsed in the financial panic of 1826, he felt partly responsible, and poured every ounce of energy into his writing, hoping that sales from his novels could help recover investors' money. Consequently, his later fiction suffered as commercial priority superseded artistic design, and the backbreaking toil eventually killed him.

American Novel, 1823; *The Pioneers*, James Fenimore Cooper

The American novel was galvanized by the emergence of an archetypal hero who endures and triumphs, the quintessential underdog overcoming all obstacles strewn in his path. James Fenimore Cooper was his principal creator, launching Natty Bumppo into the wild in the Leatherstocking Tales — *The Pioneers, The Last of the Mohicans, The Prairie, The Pathfinder,* and *The Deerslayer* — to battle evil and fight for justice.

Cooper became the first American novelist to enjoy widespread success in Europe, largely because the continent considered the "red man" a great curiosity, and Cooper's Indian tales had a vibrant frontier air to them. So avid were Europeans for Cooper's works that the last deathbed message of the great Austrian composer Franz Schubert was a note asking for the latest Cooper novel.

Cooper's discovery of the classic American hero won him a treasured role in literature. For this distinction, he has to thank the indomitable Natty Bumppo, hardy woodsman, skillful hunter, Indian ally, and nemesis of man's wastefulness. Cooper was the first to capture successfully the resilient, restless, and self-reliant American pioneer.

Serial Novel, 1840; England

Almost 150 years ago a literary form evolved in England that radio and then that television later would imitate as the "soap opera."

The serial novel was a flexible publication that appeared in monthly installments over a period of a year to eighteen months. Each installment, or serial, carried three or four chapters and sold for a shilling. Unlike magazine serializations today, which are extracted from already completed novels, the serial novel's installments were written as the author composed the story.

The serial novel's most important advantage was the time it allowed the novelist to chart public reaction, much as a soap opera does today, allowing him either to pander to it or jar it with rash developments. Sales for each installment predicated a serial's popularity, gauging the characters' appeal while letting the author know if his twists and turns of plot were delighting the public.

Serials gave many of the best English writers their first taste of fame: Dickens, Thackeray, George Eliot, and Trollope all flourished in this form. But the burden to produce imaginative material monthly stymied many other authors. Dickens, his fecund mind never suffering from a dearth of characters or plights, soared into prominence with a harshly realistic style and prodigious output.

Much of his reputation stems from a shrewd perspicacity for analyzing readers' tastes, as seen in *The Old Curiosity Shop*. As the novel drew to a close, the heroine's straits clearly foreshadowed her death, and an outpouring of readers' sympathy beseeched Dickens to spare Little Nell. But Dickens was impervious to their pleas, understanding only too well the subconscious Victorian delight at the death of fictional children.

Still, Dickens was not entirely unaffected by readers' requests. He polished off *Great Expectations* with an ending that boded more happiness for Pip than he had originally intended. So great was Dickens's popularity in the United States that thousands lined the docks at Boston Harbor to await the British vessel carrying the latest installment of his most recent serial.

Courtyard of Harper & Brothers, publishers, New York City

Modern American Novel, November 8, 1900; *Sister Carrie*, Theodore Dreiser

Since a storm of controversy coincided with the publication of the first modern American novel, its origin is known precisely. *Sister Carrie* was Theodore Dreiser's first novel, and it broke completely with British novelistic traditions and with all previous post–Civil War fiction.

In this and later novels, Dreiser showed his disdain for the genteel fiction of the past, exposing the squalor, the pity, and the deception inherent in the American success ethic; the optimistic rags-to-riches myth was to Dreiser a nightmare of delusions, an invitation to immorality and corruption. Reviewed favorably enough, the book sold only five hundred copies before the publisher's wife insisted it be withdrawn on moral grounds.

Censorship defeated Dreiser for a while. But the embattled author, who had been supporting himself as a journalist and editor of women's magazines, recovered his self-confidence in the 1920s and penned a masterpiece, *An American Tragedy*.

Modern British Novel, 1900; *Lord Jim*, Joseph Conrad

Coincidentally, one of the first modern British novels appeared the same year as *Sister Carrie*, and though *Lord Jim* was more subtle than Dreiser's condemnations of society, Conrad's book had an equally alarming effect.

As was true of his American counterpart, Conrad had known little of lavish living. In fact, this British soothsayer was a Polish expatriate (born Teodor Józef Konrad Korceniowski), whose father, a writer, had been exiled to Russia for his activity in Polish revolutionary groups.

Writing of man's alienation in a hostile universe, Conrad, once a merchant marine, used the sea as his allegorical vehicle for calling attention to "the true horror behind the appalling face of things." His favorite narrator, the old salt Marlow, told of the necessity of steadfastness and solidarity if the human community — symbolized by a marginally seaworthy vessel buffeted by raging tidal waves — was to survive.

12

Printing: Pulitzer to Popeye

Printing, 2nd Century A.D.; China

The reputation of Chinese as craftsmen perhaps has no sounder basis than their devising of the first method of printing.

By the 2nd century they already had the necessary tools for putting together printed material: paper, which they recently had discovered through experimentation with wood products; ink, which they had used for more than twenty-five centuries; and the final piece of the printing puzzle, surfaces bearing texts carved in relief, or outlined against a two-dimensional background.

Some of these texts were sculpted into pillars of marble; they usually were Buddhist precepts. Pilgrims wanting to copy their wisdom merely applied wet sheets of paper, daubing the pillar's surface with ink to make the relief characters stand out on their crude copies. Other relief carvings were religious seals. Their use, which became extremely popular, led the Chinese to experiment with inks, and a high-quality, fast-drying product was in use by the 4th century.

Over the next 150 years marble pillars and seals gave way to **wooden blocks.** Easier to carve and more manageable to handle, wooden blocks could accommodate type of almost any height and width, and the wood's natural porosity was superior for absorbing and transferring ink to paper.

The entire printing process involved five steps. First, a text was handwritten on paper (a positive) and applied face down to a flat wooden block that had been freshly coated with a rice paste to absorb the ink's impression. The negative, or mirror image, then was chiseled by an engraver to produce the letters in relief. A positive print was made when the wooden block was inked over with a paintbrush, then pressed against a sheet of paper. To enhance clarity the back side of the paper was brushed completely with ink, limiting the text to only one side of a page.

The oldest existing works printed by this method include many Buddhist incantations that had been ordered by the Japanese empress Shotoku between 764 and 770, and the first known book, *The Diamond Sutra,* a collection of Buddhist maxims and scriptural narratives, printed in China in 868. Surviving from an order placed in 932 by a minister, Fong Tao, is an extensive collection of Chinese classics, covering more than 130 volumes.

Movable Type, 11th Century; China

Individual printing characters originated some time between 1041 and 1048 through the industriousness of a Chinese alchemist, Pi Sheng, who mixed clay and glue to form the movable type, then hardened each character by baking it.

Text was set by arranging the letters side by side upon an iron plate that had been coated with a resin, wax, and paper ash to grip the type. When the set plate was heated and then cooled, the type solidified in place and could be used to print multiple copies. To free the type for use in other texts, the entire block was heated until the gummy paste softened and the letters could be lifted out.

Pi Sheng had devised the first individual and reusable type, but the first printing press that could efficiently accommodate movable type was not invented for another three centuries.

Pi's process was a boon to the book business, and thousands of texts appeared throughout China. Clay type eventually gave way to carved wooden letters, and in 1313 the printer Wang Chen undertook the most massive printing project the country, and indeed the world, had ever witnessed. He instructed his craftsmen to carve more than 60,000 characters of movable wooden blocks in order to publish a treatise on the history of technological innovation. Chen also dispensed with Pi's cumbersome and time-consuming method of immobilizing type and instead devised compartmental wooden cases of various fixed dimensions.

Movable-type printing was introduced to Korea in the 13th century and later flourished there under King Htai Tjong. In 1403 he ordered a text printed from 100,000 pieces of type made of cast bronze, thus popularizing metal type in the Orient.

Printing Press, 1450; Germany

Johannes Gutenberg, a German, generally is hailed as the inventor of the printing press, as well as of the refinements in typography that permitted its development: adjustable, compartmental type-setting matrices, and the use of lead to produce durable typefaces in great numbers and with identical appearances among the same letters. But since the late 15th century, skepticism has continued to mar the validity of Gutenberg's claim.

The evidence in favor of Gutenberg is largely circumstantial. The two most famous pieces of printing attributed to him, the forty-two-line Bible of 1455 and the "Astronomic Calendar" of 1447–1448, clearly do not bear his imprint. That he was the publisher is solely a deduction based on historical evidence.

Gutenberg was by trade a silversmith and presumably capable of originating the inventions attributed to him. But his role in the printing partnership established in Mainz, Germany, with the businessman Johann Fust and Fust's future son-in-law, a calligra-

Franklin Printing Press and Bible. The first Bible printed by Johannes Gutenberg in 1455 was forty-two lines long.

pher named Peter Schoeffer, is assumed to have been chiefly as a designer; this is based on the interpretation of a lawsuit that Fust and Schoeffer won against Gutenberg in 1455.

Ironically, the most convincing evidence on Gutenberg's behalf emerged from Schoeffer's son, Johann Schoeffer, grandson of Fust. The younger Shoeffer prefaced a literary publication in 1505 by praising the man sued by his forebears, writing that the "admirable art of typography was invented by the ingenious John Gutenberg at Mainz in 1450." Four years later, however, Schoeffer experienced a change of heart and became Gutenberg's most bitter detractor, claiming that the idea for the printing press originated only with his father and grandfather.

But the younger Schoeffer's earlier statement has proven to be more historically certifiable, and probably more accurate as well. Authorities believe that Schoeffer's about-face could have resulted from little new evidence, since John Fust had died in 1466 and Peter Schoeffer in 1502. Unless some cogent evidence surfaces, the credit for inventing the printing press will remain a testimony to the creative genius of Johannes Gutenberg.

Gutenberg's printing press, which was based on the winepress of the time, could print about three hundred sheets a day, a prodigious accomplishment then, and one that let books be produced more quickly, cheaply, and accurately than ever before, thus boosting the spread of knowledge and accelerating the rise of the Renaissance.

Stereotyping, a process of duplicating printing plates made from set type, was introduced in France about 1790; **lithography,** the process of reproducing graphics on a flat stone and transferring it to paper, evolved six years later.

The all-metal printing press originated in England about 1795, and innovations and improvements continued over the years on the continent and in the United States. By the early 19th century printers could turn out about three hundred pages an hour — the output of an entire day's work in Gutenberg's time.

Newspapers, 59 B.C.; Rome

The first regular organ for spreading the news dates to the Roman gazette *Acta Diurna (Action Journal),* which began daily publication in 59 B.C.

Posted throughout the city in places where the population congregated, the paper was begun by Julius Caesar and was not all that different from today's daily tabloids; it printed social and political news, details of criminal trials and executions, announcements of births, marriages, and deaths, and even highlights of sporting and theatrical events at the Circus Maximus and Colosseum. However, like later state news organs, such as the Soviet *Pravda,* the *Acta Diurna* was controlled by the government and had its news coverage strictly censored.

The only other early newspaper existed in the Orient. The Chinese *pao* ("report") was a government-controlled, long-lived court circular whose distribution began with the 7th century T'ang Dynasty and ran continuously until the end of the Ch'ing Dynasty in 1911. Hand-printed in its early days, and later printed with wooden blocks, the *pao* featured social and political news, palace intrigues (the equivalent of today's White House gossip), and any astronomical event (such as a falling meteor) that might portend a period of feast or famine. Written primarily for Chinese officials under such names as *Ti-pao (Palace Report)* and, later, *Ti-chan (Court Reading Matter),* the paper also chronicled the views and events of the mandarins, or high public officials.

By the early 17th century newspapers had evolved to the stage where they would be recognizable today.

Perhaps the earliest "true newspaper," which originated from a commercial bulletin that was circulated among merchants in Antwerp and Venice, was the Dutch *Nieuwe Tijdinghen,* published in 1605. Emphasizing trade news, it also contained social and political commentary, and what must have been the first international news, since the Dutch merchants who traveled extensively served as sort of "foreign correspondents," gathering a wealth of news from remote lands.

Other Dutch papers soon began appearing in Amsterdam. Called *corantos* ("currents of news"), they issued daily and weekly news exclusively in Dutch until 1620, when several *corantos* were translated into English and French. A year later an English one was printed in London by a stationer, Thomas Archer, who was arrested for not having a license to disseminate the news.

A colleague of Archer's, Nathaniel Butter, did obtain a license and thus became the "father of English journalism." On September 24, 1621, he printed the English translation of a Dutch paper as "Corante, or newes from Italy, Germany, Hungarie, Spaine and

France." It was the century for the birth of newspapers in many countries: the first tabloids appeared in Austria (1620), Denmark (1634), Italy (1636), Sweden (1645), and Poland (1661).

Newspapers, as they came to exemplify freedom of the press, were most evident in the United States. The first publication cited as a landmark of modern journalism was the 1835 *New York Herald,* which operated independently, without government strictures and outside pressures. Its credo was to record the news "with comments suitable, just, independent, fearless, and good-tempered," and in little more than a year after its initiation, the *Herald's* circulation was a healthy 40,000 daily. Its publisher, James Gordon Bennett, had founded the newspaper largely out of dissatisfaction with a partisan press that allowed President Andrew Jackson to keep sixty full-time journalists on the government payroll.

Another New York publisher, Horace Greeley, founded the *New-York Tribune* in 1841 to trumpet ideals he believed needed public hearing. Among them were opposition to slavery and encouragement of westward expansion; it was the latter that led Greeley to say "Go West, young man!"

A third New York newspaper, the one that became arguably the most influential publication in the world, was the *New York Times,* which began in 1851 under the editorship of cofounder Henry Jarvis Raymond and soon outstripped its competitors for credibility in the realm of print journalism.

Magazines, 1663; Germany

The magazine as a multipage publication had its origins in the West following the invention of the printing press. Whereas newspapers early in their development were designed to appeal to the general public, magazines were intended to deliver specific material to special interest groups. Their evolution in Europe was straightforward — from printed leaflets to pamphlets to almanacs — and they filled the middle ground between newspapers and books.

The first magazine is taken to be the 1663 German publication *Erbauliche Monaths-Unterredungen* (Edifying Monthly Discussions). Started by Johann Rist, a poet and theologian from Hamburg, it strongly reflected his two vocations and appeared more or less monthly for five years. Other magazines with a religious or philosophical bent soon followed, including the 1665 *Journal des scavans,* the earliest French magazine, and the Royal Society of London's *Philosophical Transactions,* begun the same year. Philosophy, religion, and literature merged in the first Italian magazine, the *Giornale de'letterati,* which originated in 1668 under the editorship of the scholar-clergyman Francesco Nazzari.

Today, we might call these early publications "journals," and reserve the term "magazines" for lighter, more entertaining fare — which also appeared in the 17th century.

Since the birth of the printing press had resulted in a book boom, it was only natural for the early magazines to comment regularly on newly published works, both fiction and nonfiction, a trend that soon gave rise to formal **book reviews.** Recognizing a new and potentially profitable marketplace for promoting their wares, publishers by the late 17th century had begun to advertise their books in magazines. (They had been advertising in newspapers for more than a hundred years.)

Magazines for light reading, or pure diversion, were now beginning to appear and were selling out quickly. The first of this sort was the 1672 French publication *Mercure Galant,* founded by the writer Donneau de Vise and featuring poems, colorful anecdotes, feature articles, and gossip on the nobles at court — in all, a formula that was to be widely copied by many future magazines.

*

Editors of an early women's magazine putting together their publication.

The lighter literature attracted a growing female readership, and soon publishers throughout Europe realized they could sell more magazines if they included features of interest to women.

The first to do so successfully was a German jurist, Christian Thomasius, who in 1688 published an amusing magazine bearing the cumbersome title *Entertaining and Serious, Rational and Unsophisticated Ideas on All Kinds of Agreeable and Useful Books and Subjects.* It could contain anything, and did, and its success spawned a string of similar magazines, each trying to increase the number of female readers by offering what it thought women wanted: articles of high moral tone but low intellectual content.

Then, in 1693, after testing several experimental issues, a British publisher took the bold step and introduced the first **Women's Magazine** devoted exclusively to "the fairer sex." *Ladies' Mercury,* as it was called, offered advice on etiquette, courtship, child-rearing, and female health and beauty, along with dollops of light verse and heavy doses of gossip.

Soon, several women's "penny weeklies" began appearing, and during the next century scores of Georgian and Regency magazines contained fashion tips, embroidery patterns, and even sheet music of popular songs. *La Belle Assemblée* was among the first periodicals that encouraged women to unburden their woes in its letters column, and *The Female's Friend* was an early advocate of women's rights. Unpopular with men, and with many women as well, it did not last long.

Comic Strips, 19th Century; United States

The modern comic strip started out as ammunition in a newspaper war between giants of the American press during the late 19th century.

The first full-color comic strip appeared in January 1894 in the *New York World,* owned by Joseph Pulitzer. The first regular weekly full-color comic supplement, similar to today's Sunday funnies, appeared two years later, in William Randolph Hearst's rival New York paper, the *Morning Journal.*

Both were immensely popular, and publishers realized that supplementing the news with comic relief boosted the sale of papers. The *Morning Journal* started another feature, the "Yellow Kid," the first continuous comic character in the United States, whose

Early British *(left)* and German "comics." Before the birth of the "strip," comics were single-frame images.

creator, Richard Outcault, had been lured away from the *World* by the ambitious Hearst. The "Yellow Kid" was in many ways a pioneer. Its comic dialogue was the strictly urban farce that came to characterize later strips, and it introduced the speech balloon inside the strip, usually placed above the characters' heads.

The first strip to incorporate all the elements of later comics — one that we would readily recognize as modern — was Rudolph Dirks's "Katzenjammer Kids," based on Wilhelm Busch's "Max and Moritz," a European satire of the 19th century. The "Kids" strip served as the prototype for future American strips. It contained not only speech balloons, but a continuous cast of characters, and was divided into small regular panels that did away with the larger panoramic scenes of most earlier comics.

Newspaper syndication played a major role in spreading the popularity of comic strips throughout the country. One comic to benefit from early syndication was "Little Nemo in Slumberland," created in 1906 by Winson McCay and illustrated in a fairy-tale style, evoking dream-world images both exciting and humorous.

Though weekly colored comics came first, daily black-and-white strips were not far behind. The first appeared in the *Chicago American* in 1904, drawn and written by Claire Briggs and titled "A. Piker Clerk." It was followed by many imitators, and in 1907 Harry C. Fisher's "Mr. A. Mutt" appeared, the forerunner of the immensely popular "Mutt and Jeff." Starting in 1915 black-and-white comic strips became a staple of daily newspapers around the country.

The Origins of Other Famous Comic Strips:

Comic	Date	Creator
"Krazy Kat" (first strip aimed at intellectual adults)	1911	George Herriman
"Bringing Up Father" (a gag strip, first to achieve international fame)	1917	George McManus
"Gasoline Alley" (realism in comics, with characters actually aging)	1919	Frank King
"Popeye" (seafaring caricature of a sailor gaining superhuman strength by eating spinach)	1919	Elzie Crisler Segar
"Winnie Winkle" (first career-girl comic strip)	1920	Martin Branner
"Tillie the Toiler" (emphasized fashion among young men and women)	1921	Russ Westover
"Tarzan" (earliest adventure strip; abandoned caricature style for documentary realism and adopted cinematic techniques)	1929	Harold Foster
"Blondie" (a domestic comedy that achieved international fame)	1930	Chic Young
"Dick Tracy" (a detective seeking justice, introduced, appropriately, during the days of mob violence)	1931	Chester Gould
"Flash Gordon" (first space-age strip with exotic uniforms and weapons)	1933	Alex Raymond
"Li'l Abner" (backwoods humor with a voluptuous heroine and he-man protagonist)	1934	Al Capp
"Superman" (the first "superhero," with superpowers, who crusaded against villains on earth and in space)	1937	Jerry Siegel and Joe Shuster

13

Civilization & Education: Sumerians to Jesuits

Civilization, 4000 B.C.; Nile Valley and Mesopotamia

If civilization is depicted best by the rise of cities and governments, by people who can support themselves through the cultivation of crops and the domestication of animals, then the first civilizations on earth arose in two regions near one another. The great and long-lasting Egyptian civilization dawned on the banks of the lower Nile; the highly literate and shorter-lived Sumerian civilization emerged between the Tigris and Euphrates rivers in the region that today is the lower half of Iraq. Centuries later the Greeks labeled this region Mesopotamia, from *meso* ("between") and *potamos* ("river").

The location of the Sumerian civilization within a valley made it vulnerable to invasions. It flourished for only eighteen centuries before its extinction, but left an indelible mark on culture and humankind. In that relatively brief period, the Sumerians gave the world writing, schools, the two-party legislature, the pharmacopoeia, epic poetry, and literary debates, to name just a few of their innovations.

The geography of Egypt, on the other hand, largely precluded outside invasions. The result was a coherent, conservative civilization that continued nearly unchanged for at least 4000 years. When the last Egyptian kingdom finally fell apart, it was not an enemy that ransacked it, but the ravages of internal weakness, bickering, and overindulgence.

From the dawn of these two civilizations to the present, historians recognize the origins of twenty-six civilizations, of which only six still survive.

Civilization	Dawn	Origin	Cradle
Far Eastern (Japan and Korea)	A.D. 645	Related to Chinese	Japan via Korea
Western	A.D. 675	Related to Greek	Ireland
Orthodox Christian (main)	A.D. 680	Related to Greek and Western	Anatolia, Turkey
Hindu	A.D. 810	Related to Indic	Kanauj, Jumna-Ganges, Daub
Orthodox Christian (Russian)	A.D. 950	Related to Greek	Upper Dnieper Basin
Iranic (now Islamic)	A.D. 1320	Related to Aramaic	Oxus-Jaxartes Basin

Schools, 3000 B.C.; Sumer

The first schools were a logical outgrowth of the cuneiform system of writing devised by the Sumerians about 3500 B.C., and the earliest textbooks, found in the Sumerian city of Erech, consisted of several hundred rectangular clay tablets, many containing word lists meant for study and memorization.

Although most of the tablets were inscribed with financial and administrative memoranda, the "study sheets" clearly indicate that not long after the invention of writing, scholars already had begun to think in terms of formal teaching, and of a rigorous nature at that. By the middle of the 3rd millennium several schools catering to children and adolescents were flourishing in Sumer, where pictogram writing was the skill first learned by every student. Scores of clay tablets, the equivalent of today's student notebooks or worksheets for homework, recovered from the Sumerian city of Shuruppak and dating from 2500 B.C., range from the crude scrawls of first-graders struggling to perfect their pictograms, to the expert penmanship of advanced students composing essays and poetry. The thousands of tablets that have been translated so far yield a rather comprehensive picture of just how sophisticated the Sumerian school system was.

The head of a Sumerian school was the *ummia* ("expert" or

"professor"), though he was also known as the "school father"; a student was called "school son." The *ummia*'s assistants were "big brothers," and their duties included composing new tablet texts for pupils to copy, examining their worksheets, and listening to them recite studies from memory. Every faculty of the early schools had several "men in charge of drawing," either the equivalent of today's art teachers or perhaps architects, and at least one disciplinarian, or "man in charge of the whip," who kept track of attendance and maintained classroom order. Punishment was summarily administered for the slightest infraction of school rules.

Sumerian education was grueling work. Students attended classes daily from sunrise to sunset, and vacations at a particular school were left to the headmaster's discretion. Some schools, in fact, never awarded a respite. Education usually began in childhood, ran into early adulthood, encompassed a variety of religious, economic, administrative, and literary subjects, and concluded only when a student was deemed an "educated man." Women did not attend school.

One of the most fascinating documents to be translated to date is an essay on the daily life of one Sumerian schoolboy.

The student, according to the essay, dreads punishment for being late for school "lest his teacher cane him" and pleads with his mother hurriedly to prepare lunch. She packs him "two rolls" to eat on the way; he runs, but still arrives late. "Afraid and with pounding heart, I entered before my teacher and made a respectful curtsy." Despite the gesture of deference, he is caned by the "man in charge of the whip."

Later in the day he is caned again by other teachers for talking in class, for interrupting, and for wandering off the school grounds. When a teacher canes him for poor penmanship, the most unforgivable of offenses, he conceives a plan that Dr. Samuel Kramer, a Sumerian authority, believes is the first case of student "apple polishing." The boy's parents invited the teacher to their home, lavished on him their best food and wine, then "dressed him in a new garment, gave him a gift, put a ring on his hand."

Seduced by all these blandishments, the teacher not only gave the boy passing grades, but showered him with praise: "Of your brothers may you be their leader, of your friends may you be their chief, may you rank the highest of the schoolboys . . . You have carried out well the school's activities, you have become a man of learning." As indeed he had.

Educational Innovations, 3000 B.C., Sumer, to 1969, U.S.

From the early Sumerian schools of 3000 B.C. sprang the concepts of tuition and of separate elementary schools and universities. In other civilizations arose a myriad of educational firsts: the Greek system of public education, teachers' contracts, and licenses, Roman bilingual education, the awarding of diplomas, schools for girls and for the deaf and blind, compulsory attendance, and the very modern concepts of computer teaching and television classes in the home. What follows are the origins of some of the highlights of educational innovations.

Tuition, 3000 B.C.; Sumer

From the first, schools cost money, and only those who could pay received an education. A teacher's salary was the money he received from his students for each class, which constituted tuition. Perhaps this explains why students were so severely whipped for cutting classes.

Elementary Schools, 2500 B.C.; Sumer

Priests established the first true elementary schools to train scribes in economic and administrative subjects, especially in regard to temple and palace bookkeeping.

Universities, 2500 B.C.; Sumer

The Sumerians crowned their innovative education system with universities, which they called "houses of wisdom." Among the studies the students were required to master were linguistics, theology, magic arts, medicine, astronomy, and mathematics. The house of wisdom usually was under auspices of the temple.

Public Education, 500 B.C.; Athens

The Athenians believed that good citizenship was based on a proper education, which was made available to the male members of any family who could afford to pay a modest matriculation fee.

Free Education of War Veterans' Male Children, 500 B.C.; Athens

An obligation to soldiers who had been killed in battle was recognized by the Athenian government when it paid education fees for boys who had lost their fathers in war.

Teachers' Contract, 445 B.C.; Athens

For a time teachers could be dismissed at the whim of a school administrator. To ensure a measure of stability to the burgeoning profession, Protagoras introduced contracts that lasted as long as three years and could be renewed.

State-Supported Schools, A.D. 75; Rome

Vespasian opened the doors for state-supported schools with his stipend of 100,000 sesterces — silver coins (later made of brass and copper) — that was an endowment to be paid from the imperial treasury.

Bilingual Education, A.D. 100; Rome

The Romans believed that those who were fluent in both Latin and Greek would be successful in commerce and diplomacy.

State-Supported University, A.D. 410; Constantinople

The emperor Theodosius, seeking to expand the Roman education system, initiated the government-financed university system to broaden the minds of Roman scholars.

Modern University, A.D. 1000; Paris

The French philosopher Abélard organized a body of students in Paris, who had completed the curricula offered at lesser colleges and cathedral centers, and founded the University of Paris, regarded as the first modern university because of its broad system of learning and specialization in various disciplines.

Western Grammar Schools, 1100; Europe

Priests founded these fundamental classes to meet a need for proficiency in Latin, and in time the schools acquired the nature of preparatory schools.

Western High Schools, 1525; Nuremberg, Germany

Secondary schools were divided into two tiers or levels, grammar and high schools, to ensure that students were not passed into a higher realm of education until they were proficient in a variety of subjects.

Pictured Textbooks, 1652; Hungary

John Amos Comenius, the Moravian educational reformer and theologian, conceived this textbook breakthrough to make learning a more enjoyable and informative experience. He may have been the first to profess that a picture was worth a thousand words.

School for Deaf, 1760; Paris

Abbé Charles de l'Epée invented the sign language used by the deaf and made it the teaching tool in a school he founded in Paris.

Sunday School, 1780; Gloucester, England

The first Sunday schools were opened by Robert Raikes to educate children who worked in factories six days a week and could attend class only on Sunday. They originally had no religious theme.

Nursery School, 1781; Scotland

These so-called infant schools originated to accommodate parents who had nowhere to leave their children, aged three to six, while they were at work.

School for Blind, 1784; Paris

The first school for the blind, L'Institution Nationale des Jeunes, was a privately run institution opened by Valentin Haüy, but state aid eventually was given.

Braille was invented in 1824 by a fifteen-year-old French boy, Louis Braille, who had been blind since the age of three. The standard form used today was adopted in 1932.

Teachers' College, 1808; Paris
Napoleon Bonaparte declared that these schools should offer a demanding field of study that would prepare their graduates to fulfill the needs of the secondary school system that his regime established in 1802.

Correspondence Courses, 1871; New York
The Chautauqua Methodist school began mail-course instruction for individuals who lived far from regular schools. So successful proved the endeavor that it was quickly adopted by business and secretarial schools.

I.Q. Tests, 1905; France
Early tests of intelligence, prepared by Alfred Binet and Théodore Simon, were devised primarily for the purpose of selecting mentally retarded students so that they could be given special instruction. In time, they came to be called I.Q. (intelligence quotient) tests.

Junior High School, 1909; Berkeley, California
The aim of junior high schools was to provide vocational options for those who wanted to begin working instead of completing their secondary education.

Junior College, 1910; Fresno, California
Overcrowding in four-year colleges, the need for better instruction in the early years of college, and a demand for education facilities nearer the home prompted the California legislature to enact a law that made possible the first junior colleges.

14

Governments & Organizations: Crowns to Corporations

Kingship, 3000 B.C.; Sumer

Religion was at the fore of Sumerian life for the first five hundred years of its civilization, and because of its central role, the priests of the cities formed society's most influential body.

Their claim to supreme power appeared quite logical to the Sumerians: since the gods owned all the lands of a city-state, and the priests were intermediaries between the gods and men, the priests were put in charge of all lands, which were "rented" from the gods. Through this manipulation, in many Sumerian cities the religious leaders made all major decisions concerning agriculture, trade, and war.

By 3000 B.C. the conditions of peace and war required strict leadership. The cities were often at war with one another, and there was continuous threat of invasion from northern tribes. To help allay fears, the power of the kingship arose in major Sumerian cities. Characteristically, its origin was attributed to the gods, for if a god possessed a city, the deity could pick his own representative to rule it.

The line of demarcation between a priest-ruler and a divinely appointed king-priest was ambiguous and interpreted in many ways over the course of history. As the representative of the gods on earth, the king held the major religious position in the state, and

A Collection of Crowns.

there was always the potential for conflict between him and the priests. The emphasis of the priest's rule, however, was likely to be religious and domestic; the king's was secular, with an emphasis on war.

Thus, the origin of secular leadership was to protect the people and property and to maintain peace. Kingship probably originated as a temporary expedient in times of emergency, with the king elected by assembly, but by 2700 B.C. the role carried a hereditary distinction.

Modern Jury, 1066; England

The jury is a salient feature of the Anglo-American legal system; a man's guilt or innocence is decided by a group of his peers, who weigh evidence in cases brought to trial.

The origin of the jury as a legal institution is sketchy. Many early civilizations had their own forms of juries, and the Athenians by the middle of the 5th century B.C. gave their judicial system a measure of independence by introducing jury pay; this meant that for the first time even the poorest citizens could temporarily abandon work to serve on a jury.

The Western jury system, an integral part of early British society, is thought to have been brought to England by the Norman invaders in 1066.

Although today's juries hand down verdicts, initially that was not their only function. In the earliest times, a jury was composed of witnesses to a crime, who passed judgment based on what they themselves had seen. As medieval society spread and towns grew larger, the jury was called on not to present testimony against, or provide support for, the accused, but only to settle the issue of guilt or innocence in a court of law presided over by a magistrate. The jury made decisions based only on evidence presented in court. In cases lacking ample evidence or witnesses, the accused often was subjected to trial by ordeal. If he survived any of several forms of torture, his survival was taken as proof of his innocence, and he was freed. This barbaric practice ended in most countries in the 15th century.

Modern Postal System, 18th Century; England

Most early societies had systems for transmitting messages. As civilization expanded, communication became an essential element in the ancient world. The earliest postal system originated about 2000 B.C. in Egypt as a means of prompt conveyance of orders from the pharoahs to their lieutenants in regions throughout the empire.

Although the Persians and the Greeks also developed communication systems, the Romans, with their well-unified empire and superb roads, conceived the most elaborate mail delivery scheme, composed of numerous relays stations. Some historians contend that in a single day a Roman dispatch could cover 170 miles — a feat not equaled again in Europe until the 19th century.

The modern postal system dates almost 150 years to a British treatise, *Post Office Reform: Its Importance and Practicability,* by Rowland Hill, an educator and civil servant. The extensive study examined postal costs and concluded that the single fixed rate for all mail, regardless of weight or destination, did little to cover the costs of delivering a letter. From this idea sprang the practice of pricing a letter by weight and the distance it had to travel.

Hill also introduced the **postage stamp,** an adhesive label that served as a prepayment of postage for uniform rates and could be bought by the sender in advance at any post office. By 1840 stamps could be purchased in books of twenty. Questions have arisen over whether Hill or one of his assistants actually conceived the idea of a postage stamp, but in light of his vast renovations of an almost paralyzed system, the point becomes moot.

Government Innovations, 3100 B.C., Egypt, to 1945, U.S.

The earliest governments in both Sumer and Egypt were inextricably linked with religion. In Sumer, about 3500 B.C., the first rulers were priests who claimed divine right to the land. In the Old Kingdom of Egypt, which began about 3110 B.C., the government also was under the king-god.

But the Egyptians believed that their divine system of government had been created at the beginning of time, along with the seas, mountains, and skies. The great pyramids, which were all erected during the Old Kingdom, were thought to join earth with heaven by their towering height. What follows are the origins of major government innovations from Sumerian and Egyptian times to the present.

Dynasty, 3100 B.C.; Egypt

The Egyptian rulers, or pharoahs, were grouped in families, or dynasties. A dynastic government resolved the instability and conflict that might arise from the question of succession following a pharoah's death. The I Dynasty was that of the Egyptian pharoah Menes.

Interstate Commerce, 1292 B.C.; Egypt

A letter found in Boghazkeui from a Hittite king to Ramses II of the XIX Dynasty discusses selling iron to Egypt. It is the first written record of international trade.

Military Pay, 405 B.C.; Rome

The general Marcus Furius Camillus ordered his troops reimbursed after they were kept in the field all winter one year during the ten-year siege of Veii. Army life became more attractive to men who previously had worried about how to feed their families while they were away at war.

Corporations, 100 B.C.; Roman Empire

Under Roman law the corporation became an entity that could own property, make contracts, litigate, and engage in many activities. Many such bodies came about as group ventures with pooled resources.

Parliament, 991; England

The Anglo-Saxon kings and aristocrats began this body, known as the *witenagemot* ("meeting of the councilors"), in a manner quite different from its current evolution. There was no element of popular representation in the beginning.

House of Lords, 1066; England

The aristocracy established the House of Lords as a lineal descendant of the Great Council or King's Council of the Norman and Plantagenet kings.

Tariffs, 1275; England

Under King Edward I, special fees were levied on imported and exported goods in order to raise money for the government and protect home industries. Such duties were called "poundage," because they were based on weight.

Think Tanks, 1832; Philadelphia

The U.S. secretary of the treasury, confronted by dangerous boilers that kept exploding in American steamboats, contracted the Franklin Institute of Philadelphia to study the problem. Since then the government has had a hand in sponsoring scientific research and development at universities and private think tanks.

United Nations, 1945; San Francisco

The United States, Great Britain, and the Soviet Union were instrumental in establishing the charter for this peacetime body to deal with political, economic, social, legal, and military problems on an international basis.

Social Service Innovations, 2100 B.C., Egypt to 1905, U.S.

There is a tendency to think of social services as a modern-day invention, the largesse of a wealthy, industrialized, humane society. But many charitable organizations, private and governmental, existed in ancient and medieval times. The Sumerians, for example, had both a welfare program for the temporarily unemployed and adoption facilities for childless couples. What follows are the origins of many major social services throughout the ages.

Welfare, 2100 B.C.; Egypt

Like the Sumerians' government, which provided welfare in the form of food to the families of farmers during periods of drought and crop failure, Egyptian rulers gave mandatory allotments of seed to farmers who were experiencing a bad season. The Egyptians also were generous to palace beggars.

Adoption, 1800 B.C.; Sumer

A childless couple in Sumer could adopt a child so that their worldly possessions could be passed to an heir. Legislation for this transfer of property from a barren couple to their adopted child or children, and just how it was to be divided, has been found in ancient Sumerian law codes.

Unemployment Insurance, 1789; Switzerland

The Swiss city of Basel enacted legislation that provided for coverage against the hazards of industrial life with the first unemployment plan; the seriously sick and disabled were eligible if they could prove their impairment was job-related.

Parole, 1837; Australia

The state felt that often a prisoner reached a point in his penal career when further incarceration was useless in rehabilitation. The prisoner was released into the community, but was subject to supervision and restrictions, such as total abstinence from alcohol. If he disregarded the restrictions, he was sent back to prison to finish out his term.

Probation, 1841; Boston

John Augustus, a Boston cobbler, began a self-imposed stint as a probation officer for the rehabilitation of released criminals. The new concept worked with many criminals, and in 1878 the city of Boston began an adult probation program; within two years it was adopted by the state.

YMCA, 1844; London

George Williams began this organization to improve the spiritual condition among young men "in the drapery and other trades." The Y offered a fourfold philosophy: "Companionship, physical exercise, and education and religious activity." The association grew rapidly after the turn of the century as a lay, self-governing voluntary group that sought to provide interesting leisure activities for a small number of the thousands of young men who flocked to England's industrial towns. It began ministering to boys in 1890, and after 1918, its original religious objectives began to switch from the evangelical toward broader ones.

Reform School, 1846; Massachusetts

The Massachusetts legislature deemed that juvenile offenders should be treated differently from adults (although the law was not enacted until 1899) and placed in reform schools rather than prisons. In 1854, girls were also sent to such places of confinement.

YWCA, 1855; London

Emma Roberts established the women's Y as a counterpart to the male institution and as a source of Christian housing and cultural development. Single women moving to London were greeted and given reasonably priced rooms that otherwise were virtually impossible to find.

Red Cross, 1864; Switzerland

Jean-Henri Dunant urged the formation of an international relief agency to provide aid to people in distress, particularly during war, regardless of national origin, color, or creed. The Red Cross was established by the Geneva Convention.

Legal Aid, 1876; New York

Arthur von Briesen established the New York Legal Aid Society to aid immigrants who frequently were the victims of illegal activities, such as extortion and wage violations.

Women's Prison, 1879; Massachusetts

A penal institution for women was necessitated by the rampant abuse of women in prisons where they were not segregated from men. Other states quickly followed.

Sick Pay, 1884; Germany

Bismarck, the German statesman, gave workers sick pay to counter socialist agitation. Two thirds of the insurance was paid by the workers; the remaining third by the employer. The state was excluded from any responsibility.

Juvenile Court, 1899; Chicago

The city government of Chicago began granting authority to noncriminal courts for making neglected children wards of the state, a policy begun to keep minors out of the company of hardened convicts in prisons.

Four-H Club, 1904; Minnesota

The organization as originally started was a corn-, potato-, and tomato-growing contest at school fairs, but emerged as a society for young farmers and homemakers. The four leaf clover was adopted as the national symbol in 1910, but the name Four-H — for "head, heart, hands, and health" — was not used until after 1920.

Rotary, 1905; Chicago

The Rotary began as a fellowship and volunteer community service with the original intention of rotating the place of meetings, the chairmanship, and even membership, which was to last for one year only. Continued membership in the early days was contingent on re-election and was limited to one person from each trade or profession in the community.

Boy Scouts, 1908; England

Sir Robert Baden-Powell started the worldwide organization as the means for training boys "in the essentials of good citizenship." He first wrote a book called *Scouting for Boys*, which lured youths away from gang life by giving them the option of forming Boy Scout patrols. He proposed the patrol system, troups, the scoutmaster, scouts' oath, scouts' law, and a uniform, and instructed boys in skills needed for camping and outdoor life. Boy Scout camps began in 1908, the same year the magazine *The Scout* started publication.

Old Age Pension, 1908; Great Britain

Parliament decided that national funds were to be set aside for the elderly within limitations of age and means, but that individuals would not be subjected to testing to determine whether they were destitute. In Germany, Bismarck had begun pension insurance in 1889, but the cost was divided between workers and employers, with the state making only periodic contributions.

Minimum Wage, 1909; England
The Trade Boards Act affected the "sweat industries" by imposing a floor for wages exactly a hundred years after Samuel Whitebread's call for such legislation had failed to pass Parliament.

N.A.A.C.P., 1909; United States
New York was the first state where Negro community leaders rallied to "combat racism, stamp out lynching and the Lynch Law, to eliminate racial discrimination and segregation and to assure Negroes of their constitutional rights." By 1950, the N.A.A.C.P. boasted more than 400,000 members in 1600 chapters in the fifty states and the District of Columbia.

Girl Guides, 1909; England
Agnes Baden-Powell, sister of the man who started the Boy Scouts, suggested an organization for girls, with the same high ideals of character and good citizenship.

The eight-hour workday first originated in Great Britain in 1908. The law limiting the length of the workday was enacted by Parliament to "curtail the exploitation of labor by management."

Social Security Act, 1935; United States

One of the many pieces of legislation quickly passed by Congress during the early days of Franklin D. Roosevelt's "New Deal" was the Social Security Act. It provided for unemployment insurance and for retirement and death benefits and established a nationwide framework of incentives, support, and standards for financial assistance to people in three groups — the aged, the blind, and dependent children — and was considered anathema by many.

Alcoholics Anonymous, 1934; Ohio

Robert Smith initiated this movement for reforming alcoholics in Akron. He capped it off with the publication, in 1939, of his book, *Alcoholics Anonymous.* The first AA clubhouse opened in New York City the next year, and Al-Anon has been self-sufficient since, charging its members no fees or dues.

Advertisement, 1000 B.C.; Egypt

Criers flaunting their wares constituted the earliest advertisements. Hustling through streets in ancient times, they shouted out the advantages of their pottery, fabrics, cattle, and even their slaves; and they thought nothing of denigrating the goods of competitors. What their pitches lacked in subtlety and subliminal enticements was made up in sheer decibels, and, all things considered, ancient advertising was not that dissimilar to the Madison Avenue approach of today.

The origin of written advertising is thought to be a 3000-year-old "wanted" poster found in Thebes, in Egypt. In large letters it offered a reward of a "whole gold coin" for the capture and return of a runaway slave named Shem. History never recorded whether Shem was recaptured or the reward paid, but poster advertising in marketplaces and temples became a popular means of promoting all sorts of goods, and throughout the Middle Ages it vied with the word-of-mouth technique.

The dawn of the modern era of advertising began about 1450 in Europe, owing almost entirely to the popular use of the printing press and movable type. Fliers could be printed in great numbers and either posted in public places or inserted in printed pamphlets, books, or newspapers — all of which were tested to see which drew the best response.

Hyperbole is not the invention of Madison Avenue; if anything, today's advertising is the most honest in history.

Newspapers, not surprisingly, came out on top. Early newspapers found that they could handsomely augment revenues by accepting advertising, and some of the initial regular accounts in the mid-1600s, which ran in British newspapers, were for coffee, chocolate, and tea. In the 1670s the *London Gazette* was the first paper to designate a separate section as an "advertising supplement," the forerunner of the copious colorful inserts that fatten our Sunday newspapers today.

To manage the growing business of newspaper advertising, new agencies came into being. They boasted of their sure-fire sales techniques of combining catchy copy with pictures (not necessarily pictures of the products being promoted, but merely photographs and drawings to catch the reader's eye).

Advertising spread throughout the print media, often commanding more space than the news. By the middle of the 18th century, advertising had so proliferated throughout society that Samuel Jonson wrote in *The Idler:* "Advertisements are now so numerous that they are very negligently perused, and it is therefore become necessary to gain attention by magnificence of promise and by eloquence sometimes sublime and sometimes pathetick."

Coins, 640 B.C.; Anatolia

From the earliest agricultural times some 9000 years ago people used cattle for currency, a practice that has carried into the present in our word "pecuniary," from the Latin *pecus*, meaning "cattle."

Metallic money appeared considerably later, about 2000 B.C., in the form of bronze ingots, often shaped like cattle and traded on the open market according to their weight. Not only were amulets of cattle infinitely more convenient to exchange than the real thing, but the intrinsic brilliance of the metallic pieces heightened their esthetic appeal. Exchanging money then, however, always required the presence of an honest balance-beam scale and often was accompanied by a fiery dispute when the honesty of one of the parties was impugned.

By about 1000 B.C. bronze had been superseded by the purer, rarer metals, silver and gold, and cattle shapes had given way to heads of cats (particularly in Egypt, where cat worship reached obsessional heights), statuettes of rulers, deities, or merely ornamental medallions. These pieces, too, derived their worth from weight, a troublesome standard that would survive only a few hundred years longer.

The first protocoins were produced by the Lydians of Anatolia about 800 B.C. Made of electrum, a natural alloy of gold containing as much as 35 percent silver, these pieces were crude, bean-shaped ingots that bore a punchmark signifying their worth; thus obviating the need for a scale.

Around 640 B.C. the Lydians began producing the first true coins (the word "coin" is a Latin derivative from **cuneus,** or "wedge"). They were made by a smith hammering a punch through a sheet of electrum as it lay on his anvil. Being a malleable alloy, electrum made possible the imprinting of a figure of a man or an animal on the coin's face; a particular relief signified a coin's value, which almost immediately led to cheating on the ratio of gold to silver in the currency.

Coins, of course, allowed payment for goods to be made by count instead of weight, a great boon to commerce and convenience, but one that opened the possibility of counterfeiting. Facsimiles of coins were fashioned of cheaper metals; precious gold and silver were shaved off the edges of real coins; and bunches of coins were

Eight coins, front and back, and their values as of the mid-19th century. Persian gold piece (1), $7.35. East India rupee (2), $6.20. Belgian lion (3), $9.00. Gold sovereign of Brabant (4), $6.50. East India gold piece (5), $4.90. Dutch East India piece (6), $4.90. Danish ducat (7), $2.35. Danish Frederic d'or (8), $7.90.

shaken for hours in leather bags so that the cheater could collect the dust produced by friction — a tedious procedure to be sure, but one that yielded more dust than we might imagine, since coins then were made of purer, and hence softer, metals. The introduction in the late 17th century of milling, or serrating the edge of a coin, finally put an end to the profitable practice of coin shaving. And today's more solid coins shaken for hours in a bag might leave a wisp of dust, but it would be more copper and nickel than silver, and definitely not worth the time and energy.

U.S. Coin Images, 1890

A long-standing reticence, perhaps born of American's abhorrence of monarchies and kings, kept faces and portraits off United States coins as a regular practice until 1909, the centennial of Abraham Lincoln's birth.

The **Lincoln penny** was the first coin to carry a portrait. Congress passed the enabling act, but at the same time stood by an earlier law, stipulating that every American coin must bear a symbol of liberty. With the issue of the Lincoln penny, Congress and the federal mint realized that great men like Lincoln and George Washington would not be treated as deities but as paragons of freedom and liberty.

Washington was not honored with a coin until the bicentennial of his birth, when his portrait was put on the quarter. Others' roles in representing American virtues were more quickly acknowledged: the **Roosevelt dime** was issued in 1946, a year after the death of four-term President Franklin D. Roosevelt, and the **Kennedy half-dollar** was minted in 1964, less than a year after the youngest President in American history was assassinated. The **Eisenhower silver dollar** arrived in 1970, exactly a decade after the former supreme Allied commander and President left office.

Paper Money, 18th Century; France

Although several early societies experimented with paper currency — most notably the Chinese during the 1st millennium B.C. — coins of silver and gold predominated as the major form of exchange. The reasons were understandable enough: coins were far more durable than paper and less likely to be destroyed by fire, and coins contained the very precious metals that made money worth its salt. It required a leap of both imagination and of courage to establish a form of currency that was only backed by a precious metal but of itself was intrinsically worthless.

The real origin of paper money in the Western world as a medium of exchange that eclipsed the use of coins began in France in the early 18th century. Over a span of many decades most of the money in circulation gradually had come to consist not of actual gold or silver but of fiduciary notes — promises to pay up a debt in specified amounts of the precious metals. Both private citizens and banks issued such fiduciary money, either in the form of paper bank notes, or merely as transferrable book entries that came to be called deposits. Over a period of time the state acquired control of this fiduciary system.

In addition to the French government, the American colonies under the Continental Congress printed their own paper money, called "fiats," which were really promises to pay. As can happen with any fiduciary money, fiats initially were overissued, diluting their worth. Soon their exchange could be redeemed only for a small fraction of the denoted value in metallic money. When the public refused to accept fiats, reins were tightened and paper money returned eventually to a vogue it has enjoyed — despite periodic overissuing and the departure from the gold standard — to the present day.

Paper Money Images, 1861; United States

The first portraits to appear on paper money were rather randomly selected. Among the first was Secretary of the Treasury Salmon P. Chase, whose likeness adorned $1.00 bills from 1861 to 1864; in 1886, silver certificates were issued with Martha Washington's portrait on the front; and, even later, images like that of the Washington Monument and names of famous Americans surrounded by wreaths were imprinted on paper currency. All these appeared without any real uniform direction from Congress, which in 1962 finally gave the secretary of the treasury responsibility to determine whose image will appear on our paper money.

Bills already in circulation carried portraits chosen by a special panel appointed in 1925 by Secretary of the Treasury Andrew W. Mellon. The secretary, however, overruled a committee vote that only presidential portraits should grace the notes because they had a "more permanent familiarity in the minds of the public than any other." Mellon was sure that such figures as our first secretary of the treasury, Alexander Hamilton, and our quintessential American and statesman, Benjamin Franklin, also would be immediately recognizable to people in this country, and he gave them a place on our currency.

The most widely distributed note, the $1.00 bill, naturally carries the likeness of George Washington, but the rationale for other bills' images and proposed likenesses was never as sound. In 1928, for example, the Mellon committee recommended President James A. Garfield for the $2.00 bill "because of the sentiment attached to our martyred Presidents and because his flowing beard would offer a marked contrast to the clean-shaven features of Washington." Mellon, however, rejected the committee's recommendation and selected instead the image of Thomas Jefferson.

Insurance, 3000 B.C.; Babylon

Insurance, a service for handling risk, has existed in some form almost since man began to record his history. The earliest insurance policies were the so-called bottomry contracts, a form of marine protection favored by merchants of Babylon about 3000 B.C.

The contracts, often only oral, granted loans to merchants with the proviso that if a particular shipment of goods was lost at sea, the loan did not have to be repaid. Interest on such loans varied with the risk of transportation, as did the cost of a policy; both peaked during period of heavy piracy on the seas. The availability of insurance played a large role in spurring international trade, tempting otherwise timid merchants to risk sending their wares over what then were great distances, in minimally sophisticated ships, often under hazardous weather conditions.

Marine insurance also was practiced by Hindu society by 600 B.C. and was commonplace by the 4th century in the Greek shipping empire. It was the Greeks, in fact, who initiated mandatory written contracts, tightening many of the legal loopholes of the earlier policies, oral or written. Virtually every nation that had commercial contact with the Greeks through maritime lanes adopted the Greek bottomry insurance contracts.

Insurance policies of all sorts had evolved to their present basic form quite early in history, certainly before the Middle Ages. Four points that were salient then remain paramount in all policies to this day: (1) the objects insured must be sufficiently numerous and similar to allow a reasonable calculation of the probable frequency and severity of their loss, (2) all the insured items — goods on a ship or buildings on a block — cannot be insured by one broker, (3) any loss must be accidental and probably beyond the control of the insured party, and (4) there must be some way to determine if a loss has actually occurred and how great it was.

Fire Insurance, 1666; England

Ironically fire insurance, something no modern homeowner would be without, did not become a reality until 4600 years after the introduction of marine coverage. In fact, had it not been for the tremendous wave of public sentiment and the toll of poverty in the wake of the Great Fire of London in 1666, fire insurance might not have been thought of for many more years.

Shortly after the great conflagration several fire insurance agencies opened their doors. Londoners, however, barely recovered from the shock of the vast destruction, made prime targets for insurance fraud. Get-rich-quick companies collected sizable premiums from unsuspecting businesses and homeowners, then vanished in the night; if fire did strike, there was no one to make good on the policy.

Some sectors of the public were not without their own unscrupulousness. Merchants on the verge of bankruptcy suddenly saw a new route to solvency through heavily insuring their businesses, then surreptitiously burning them to the ground.

Two legitimate and respected British insurance companies managed to remain impervious to the high sham of this period, infamously known as the "bubble era," the London Assurance Corporation and the Royal Exchange Assurance Corporation. Our modern property and liability policies stem from their innovations.

Lloyd's of London, 17th Century; England

The most famous insurance concern in the world, Lloyd's of London, which insured Jimmy Durante's nose, Liberace's fingers, and Elizabeth Taylor's large diamonds, actually began not as an insurer but as a coffee house, and its role today is misunderstood by many people.

Lloyd's is an international insurance *market*. The company does not itself transact insurance business, but encourages competitive policy bidding among member underwriters, who accept insurance on their own account and bear the full risk.

Lloyd's opened its doors in the 17th century as a coffee house, a social gathering place, and almost immediately was frequented by merchants, bankers, and insurance underwriters. Soon anyone seeking an underwriter for maritime insurance knew he was more likely to find a policy broker sipping imported coffee at Lloyd's than in the company's office.

Edward Lloyd, the proprietor, began to supply his customers with shipping information gathered along the docks from sailors, which meant the underwriters had more leisure time for imbibing Lloyd's coffee. He eventually oversaw policy bidding in his establishment, and the next logical step seemed to be the formation of a group of underwriters for marine insurance. As British sea power increased, Lloyd's of London became a dominant concern in maritime insurance and a symbol of national stability. The company later added fire insurance and other property risks.

The term "underwriter" is thought to have originated from the practice of having each risk-taker write his name under the total amount of risk he was willing to accept at a specified premium.

15

Religion: Bible to Buddhism

Judaism, 18th Century B.C.E. (Before the Common Era); Israel

The forebears of Abraham, the founder of the Hebrew people, lived in Chaldea, in southern Babylonia. It was from there that Abraham moved to the land of Canaan, comprising what we know today as parts of Israel and Lebanon. There his son Isaac was born, and Isaac's son Jacob. These three — Abraham, Isaac, and Jacob — are known as the patriarchs of Judaism.

The religion takes its name from Jacob's fourth son, Judah. (The name "Jew" evolved from the Latin Judaeus, which, in turn, came from the Hebrew Yehudi.)

Tradition identified the God of Israel, Jehovah, with the creator of the world, who had been worshiped by man since the beginning of time. (The Jews wrote his name as YHWH, the Tetragrammaton. Scholars believe it was pronounced Yahweh, hence Jehovah. Because Jews believe it a sin to pronounce the name of God, they use other terms for him, like Elohim.) God is supposed to have promised Abraham peace and prosperity in Canaan, and bountiful progeny. These promises were fulfilled in the 13th century B.C. through the actions of the Hebrew leader Moses. He liberated the people of Israel from Egypt, brought down the Covenant obligations on them from Mount Sinai, and led them close to the Promised Land.

Throughout history, Jews have been subjected to mistreatment and persecution in whatever countries they settled in because of their religious beliefs. From 311 to 1790 they faced severe discrimination in both Christian and Muslim regions. Jewish emancipation began in 1791 in France, but a new period of pogroms during the 19th century led to the creation of Zionism, or the movement for a Jewish homeland, to avoid prevalent anti-Semitism. The first Zionist Congress was held in Basel, Switzerland, in August 1897, but not until May 14, 1948, was Israel recognized as an independent state.

The awarding of self-determination to Jews was spurred by the genocidal policies of Adolf Hitler of Germany in World War II. Hitler's Nazi party, founded largely on an anti-Semitic platform, made scapegoats of Jews for Germany's failure in World War I and the country's depressed economy during the 1920s, culminating with the "final solution," which called for the extermination of all people of Jewish ancestry.

The revealed laws of Judaism are embodied in the **Torah,** written down by Israeli scribes in the seventh century B.C. It includes the first five books of the **Old Testament,** known as the Pentateuch handed down by Moses to Jews after he had received them on Mount Sinai, probably around 1250 B.C. Today, followers of Judaism, most numerous in the United States and Israel, exceed 15 million people.

Hinduism, 1500 B.C.; India

Hinduism, perhaps more than any other faith, is a collection of religious beliefs. The spiritual ideas of nomadic Aryan tribes who invaded the Indian subcontinent blended with tenets prevalent in the Indus Valley and forged a religion unique in that, unlike others, it has no individual founder, but instead is based on a loose confederation of personal and local deities.

Hinduism was established during the 2nd millennium B.C., probably about 1500 B.C. It was implemented by the Brahman caste, consisting of priests. According to Hindu belief, caste is an innate attribute, without which man has no place in society and cannot marry. Even today, the Brahmans are the only Hindus permitted to read from the **Vedas,** the hymns, verses, incantations, and treatises that date to the Aryan invasions and are the basis of Hindu learning. The **Upanishads,** which elaborated on the earlier Vedas, were a compendium of metaphysical and philosophical speculations first circulated about 900 B.C.

Contained within these texts are instructions on how a Hindu must live. According to the Vedas, a Hindu's destiny is determined by all his actions, and their consequences, during the successive phases of his life. The sum of this is his *karma*. A good life in the present will bring him to a higher life later. A debauched life might result in his being reincarnated as a lowly animal. The process of continual birth and death comes to an end only when the soul reaches a state of perfection through an ideal life.

Hinduism is one of the few religions that worships animals, although animal homage is secondary to the adoration paid the deity who rides on the animal. The killing of cattle and peacocks is strictly prohibited by orthodox Hindus. The religion has been largely refined over the last century, tinged with some Christian elements. It is estimated at present to have almost 450 million followers.

Shintoism, 600 B.C.; Japan

Shintoism, once the state religion of Japan whose foundation lies in the forces and forms of nature, arose about 660 B.C. It was said that the first Japanese emperor, Jimmu Tenno, and his successors were descendants of the ruler of heaven, the sun goddess. For more than two millennia Shintoism remained the state religion, until in 1946 Emperor Hirohito formally renounced his divinity as part of a peace pact with the conquering Allied forces at the end of World War II.

Shintoism, however, remains entrenched in Japanese worship, with an estimated 60 million followers. They abide by an oral tradition first set down by imperial order in two books, the **Kojiki** (records of ancient matters) in A.D. 712 and the **Nihongi** (chronicles of Japan) in A.D. 720. The **Yengishiki,** compiled in the 10th century, records rituals and prayers, including ancient ones. The religion was first practiced formally during the preceding century to distinguish Shintoism from Buddhism, which had made inroads to Japan by way of the Asian mainland.

Shintoism ("the teaching" or "the way of the gods") was a welcome alternative for individuals who abhorred complicated religious ceremony. Its simplicity and the embracing of nature made it an iconoclastic ideology, with deities beseeched only to fulfill the physical and spiritual needs of its followers. Adoration was not only of renowned figures but of natural wonders as well.

The teaching of Shintoism carries strains of Confucianism, Taoism, and Buddhism, despite an attempt in the mid-19th century to expurgate all Buddhist principles.

Confucianism, 551 B.C.; China

The Far Eastern beliefs known as Confucianism is named for its chief proponent, the Chinese philosopher Confucius, although other didacts called **Ju,** or meek ones, contributed significantly to its principles.

Confucius, or K'ung Fu-tzu, to give him his Chinese name, was an accountant in the province of Lu. Later, he became the first Oriental to teach all ranks of people the six arts of Chinese culture: history, numbers, ceremonies, music, archery, and charioteering. Among his teachings was the imperative ideal of *jen,* or benevolence, which formed the main ethic of Confucianism. He also pointed out that truth could be discovered only by acknowledging one's faults, and he strongly stressed altruism and the obeisance of children to parents.

Confucianism as taught by the master himself dwelled on a belief that people could best be led by example, and Confucius when lecturing pointed to a previous period of history, attributing the prosperity of the people to the leadership of the emperors. He did not believe in prayer, but taught that man directs his own destiny.

Many theologians tend to recognize Confucianism more as a philosophy than as a formal religion, because it has no church, clergy, or institutions in which to conduct worship.

The greatest spreading of Confucianism for many years came from students, who, embracing the **Wu Ching** (Five Classics) compiled by Confucius, used it to emphasize the development of human nature and the person as an individual.

Confucianism was made the state religion of China during the T'ang Dynasty, A.D. 618–906, but a recent push to restore its former status was rebuffed, although Confucianism still claims more than 300 million practicioners today.

Buddhism, 534 B.C.; India

Buddhism began with an Indian prince, Siddhartha (563–483 B.C.), whose self-scrutiny and introspective ideas formulated the basis of a religion that relies heavily on meditation. Buddhism at one time was the fourth largest religion in the world, and today its followers are among the most disciplined of any religious group, living ascetic, passive lives.

The religion developed in the first half of the 6th century B.C. Siddhartha, a member of the Gautama family of the Sakya clan, wandered for six years, formulating his beliefs; he then meditated forty-nine days until he achieved enlightenment, or **Nirvana.** Later, Siddhartha was known as the Enlightened One, or Gautama Buddha, or simply Gautama.

Siddhartha taught salvation in Bihar, west of Bengal, until he died at the age of eighty. Buddhism embodies four Noble Truths. The first is that man suffers from one life to the next. The second states that the origin of suffering is craving, whether for pleasure, possessions, or the cessation of pain. The third truth holds that craving can be cured by detaching oneself of all things, including the self. The fourth truth delineates the detachment, enjoining an eight-pronged path of righteous conduct, effort, intentions, livelihood, meditations, mindfulness, speech, and views.

The Buddhist canon was orally transmitted for several centuries. It was first collected in three main books, named the **Vinaya,** the **Sutra,** and the **Abhidharma** — all written in the Pali language — between 29 to 17 B.C. They pointed out that Buddhism has no place for God and does not hinge on divine judgment or the promise of messianic redemption. Its most potent tenet is an inexorable law of cause and effect, which makes an individual's fate ineluctable. Zen Buddhism, one school of the religion, says that enlightenment can be attained only by prolonged meditation and deprivation.

Buddhist monks are celibate and adhere to vows of nonviolence, poverty, and vegetarianism. In Indian Buddhist tradition, only the clergy have hope of attaining Nirvana, whereas the Mahayana, Buddhists in Indochina, China, and Japan, acknowledge that laymen may also achieve the highest level of enlightenment.

Buddhism spread rapidly into Asia after it was sanctioned by the Indian emperor Asoka in the 3rd century B.C., but later was displaced in its native region by Hinduism.

Buddhism. Buddha means "the enlightened one," and enlightenment, through prolonged meditation and deprivation, is the goal of the religion that has 160 million followers.

Taoism, 6th Century B.C.; China

The second and more obscure of Chinese religions is Taoism, which originated with the philosopher Lao-tzu, thought to have lived between 604 and 531 B.C. His ideology was based on a belief that Tao (Tao was the Way — to the Ultimate and Unconditioned Being) was right conduct and the virtuous practice of thrift, humility, and compassion. Form and ceremony held no place in the religion.

Among the tenets of Taoism is polytheism — worship of more than one god — although this was not originally ascribed to by Lao-tzu. Taoism as early as the 5th century A.D. was ministered by monastic orders and lay followers, and in the 8th century, the master of heaven transcended the pantheon of gods to become secular leader of Taoist worshipers.

Other characteristics of Taoism are certain moral principles and two declining schools — the 13th-century Northern school, which emphasized man's life, and the Southern school, which arose probably in the 10th century and stressed the nature of man. Charity and moral culture later were added to Taoist regimen. Among the principles are simplicity, patience, contentment, and harmony, which led some scholars to look at Taoism with skepticism and to refer to it as the religion of the semiliterate.

Taoism began its decline about A.D. 906, after the T'ang Dynasty, and today its followers number fewer than 52 million. Many abandoned it in favor of Buddhism.

Christianity, A.D. 26; Palestine

Jesus Christ gave rise to the Christian religion, its name taken, of course, from its founder. Some scholars date Christianity from Jesus' birth, which modern historians believe occurred in 4 B.C.; most associate its origin with the inception of Jesus' preaching, which began in A.D. 26, when he was thirty years old.

The principles of Christianity are elucidated in the religion's definitive text, the Bible, particularly in the New Testament. Jesus ordered his disciples to spread his teachings, and four of them — the apostles Matthew, Mark, Luke, and John — composed the Gospels of the Bible. The earliest **Gospel,** written by Mark, dates from A.D. 65.

Christianity's most abiding doctrine is belief in and love of God, the first of the Ten Commandments handed down to Moses at Mount Sinai. The second commandment in terms of devotion is to "love thy neighbor," as stated by Mark. Other precepts specifically mentioned by the commandments are the abolition of hatred and fornication, and a mandate against adultery and coveting others' possessions.

The crucifixion of Jesus in A.D. 30 has been the source of endless theological and historical debate. According to the New Testament, Jesus came to Jerusalem knowing it meant certain death. He was tried first by the Jewish high court for blasphemy and then was turned over to the Roman state for a second trial. Although his messianic claims were considered seditious and a threat to the stability of Roman-held Jerusalem, it may have been the demands of the incensed populace that led Pontius Pilate, the Roman procurator, to order his death.

From the Middle East, Christ's teachings were spread by his twelve apostles. One of the most successful was Paul, a man of Jewish birth, Roman citizenship, and Greek culture, who took the Word to Rome in A.D. 42. He was martyred in A.D. 67, but his teachings thrived and in time became the theology of the Holy Roman Empire. Christians were persecuted at various times until A.D. 313, when the Emperor Constantine became enamored of the story of Jesus, embraced Christianity, and proclaimed it the official religion of Rome.

With Roman sanction, the bishop of Rome — the Pope — was given jurisdiction over all Christians and was known as the Holy Father. According to the Bible, Peter was appointed by Christ as first Pope. The present Pope, John Paul II, is his 263rd successor and rules the Roman Catholic Church from the Vatican, which is a sovereignty in its own right.

The Catholic Church, the largest group of Christians, with almost 1 billion devotees, proclaims itself the "true" church, because its beliefs were formulated by men associated directly with Jesus, or else spoken by Jesus himself. It includes both the Roman denomination and the Eastern Orthodox, known as "the Holy Orthodox Catholic Apostolic Eastern Church," and has a universal following. Among its congregations are those of the Byzantine rite, Armenian rite, and Coptic rite — all recognizing the hierarchical supremacy of the Holy See.

Also included in Christian worship are the various Protestant faiths, which grew from Martin Luther's break with Catholicism in the 16th century.

The term "protestant" acquired its present-day meaning in the 17th century, when the Anglican community in North America began calling itself the Protestant Episcopal Church. Later, Luther's severing of ties with the Catholic Church became known as the Protestant Reformation. The origin of the word is taken from the formal *protestatio,* delivered by the rulers of the evangelical states of the Holy Roman Empire in 1529 to the repressive Diet of Speyer, which was opposed to innovations in theology.

Islam, A.D. 622; Saudi Arabia

Islam is one of the few established religions that can be traced to an exact point in time. It was founded on July 16, A.D. 622, by Muhammad, and is often called Muhammadanism in deference to him.

The followers of Islam are called Muslims. They practice strict adherence to the **Koran,** the second most influential tome in the world after the Bible, which calls for prayer five times daily by a worshiper facing in the direction of Mecca, the holy city; fasting in the month of Ramadan; payment of alms; and a pilgrimage to Mecca.

Muhammad was an enigmatic figure. He was a member of the Koreish tribe and at one time a shopkeeper in Mecca. In A.D. 616,

A whirling dervish dances himself into a transcendent state. Today Islam has an estimated 600 million adherents.

he became a public preacher, and later, after Allah, the one almighty deity in Islamic faith, had appeared to him many times at Mecca and Medina, he was able to compile the Koran from that divine association.

The Koran was collected by Muhammad's secretary, Zaid ibn Thabit, and codified almost twenty years after the Prophet's death, in A.D. 651, by Uthman, a caliph who ruled that all other versions of the Koran be destroyed except for Zaid's collection.

Muhammad broke from the Christian world in A.D. 622, a year later referred to in Islamic annals as A.H. 1, for *anno hegirae,* or the year of exile. At this point, Muhammad turned away from sanctioned religion. He prayed at the pagan temple at Mecca, where worship was made to the God Allah. Into his hands was put all that Muslims held sacred. He was made administrator, general, judge, and legislator, and only through him divine revelations made known. The traditions and sayings of his life became the foundations of Islam, and although other religious founders are recognized, Muhammad is proclaimed the last of the prophets. His followers today number more than 600 million.

16

Man's Best Friends:
Afghan to Abyssinian

Domestic Dogs, 12,000 B.C.

A companion to man for more than 14,000 years, the dog eclipses all rivals in its place of prominence in the pet world. The domesticated dog has survived three distinct eras — the first as mascot and scavenger in early camp settlements, the second as hardy working stock diverting predators from sheep and cattle, and finally, in its present niche, almost exclusively as a pet, yet at times still deployed for protection.

Despite the wide variety of sizes and temperaments among the more than a hundred different breeds — from the huge Irish wolfhound to the tiny chihuahua — all dogs belong to a single species, *Canis familiaris,* which evolved less than a million years ago.

Much farther back in time, about 40 million years, there lived a tree-climbing carnivore called *Miacis,* who evolved into a four-legged creature that served as the ancestral stock not only for dogs, but also for cats (which appeared about 7 million years ago, long before dogs), hyenas, raccoons, seals, bears, wolves, and jackals. The last two animals are believed to be the immediate progenitors of the *Canis* lineage, which, throughout Europe, Asia, and North America, developed into different breeds: the African hunting dog, the Indian wild dog, the South American bush dog, and the English dog, which seems to have descended specifically from the gray wolf.

Archeological evidence shows that even before humans began breeding dogs for specific traits and appearances, canines already existed throughout the world in multifarious variety.

The so-called **Southern sight hounds,** among the earliest distinct breeds, were probably derived from the Indian wolf. They were treated with great affection by the flourishing cultures of the Near East about 5000 years ago. Among them was the **saluki,** a favorite hunting dog of the Sumerians; the **greyhound,** which makes numerous appearances in Egyptian tomb carvings of 4000 B.C.; and the long-nosed, shaggy-haired **Afghan hound,** which first appeared in Egypt about a thousand years later.

Throughout Europe even more diverse groups of dogs emerged. A wolflike dog from the north *(Canis inostranzewi)* became the large **spitz dog, mastiffs,** and **St. Bernards,** and a primitive scent hound *(canis intermedius)* evolved into **pointers, setters,** and **beagles.**

The modern **terrier,** and **Doberman pinscher,** and the **schnauzer** all descended from one progenitor, *Canis palustris.*

After dogs became domesticated, they developed certain traits that distinguished them from wild relatives. One such characteristic is the upturned tail, ranging from a sickle shape to a tight curl. This feature probably comes from the original stock of domestic dog, pointing to a common ancestry for all breeds. A further trait that distinguishes the dog from the wolf is its smaller teeth, which suggests that early man may have found the smaller, less toothy animals easier to tame and control. Barking, too, is an exclusive and inherent trait acquired by the domestic dog.

*

Give and Take. Scavenging for food brought the wild dog to the caveman's campfire, but man soon learned he was a better hunter when teamed with a dog. The result: domestication.

There are two popular theories as to how dogs came to be domesticated. The first involves cubs; the second, adult canines.

Homo erectus and early wolflike animals both hunted the same game and preferred caves for shelter. According to the "cub" theory, competition for shelter forced the issue of domestication. A bitch and her mate occupying a cave could have easily been evicted by club-wielding *Homo erectus,* leaving behind a litter of cubs. This novelty posed no threat to the new occupants, and if food was plentiful, the cubs probably were kept for amusement.

The second theory centers on early man's and dog's pursuit of game, for the dog's domestication seems to coincide with the era of man's greatest need for help in hunting and procuring quarry. The dog's native hunting skills — its superior bursts of speed, keen hearing, and canny sense of smell — greatly enhanced man's hunting ability. But experts insist that the dog first approached man, or vice versa, on an even proposition, as companions, before the dog was relegated to working in man's behalf.

Dogs probably made their entrance, authorities think, as scavengers, attracted to the earliest campsites by the scent of food. During bountiful times, man probably began allowing dogs to finish off remains of carcasses, perhaps even welcoming them for this role. At some point man realized that he was a superior hunter when teamed with dogs — and that he was safer from wild animals — and thus began the relationship that has led the dog to the distinction of being regarded as man's best friend.

Afghan

The dog's name stems from its early home, Afghanistan, but actually the Afghan hound's origin was the Sinai Peninsula, between the Gulf of Suez and the Gulf of Aqaba. Later the dog's habitat became the country for which it is named. The Afghan's popularity soared in Europe after World War I because of its elegant bearing and appearance, particularly its aquiline face, crowned with long, silky hair.

Beagle

The ancient Britons, perhaps as early as A.D. 500, already had developed the special attachment to the beagle that modern civilization later renewed. The beagle originated in Great Britain, where its natural hunting instinct and its prowess in trailing hares soon made it legendary. But when fox-hunting supplanted the chase of

Genealogy of the Dog

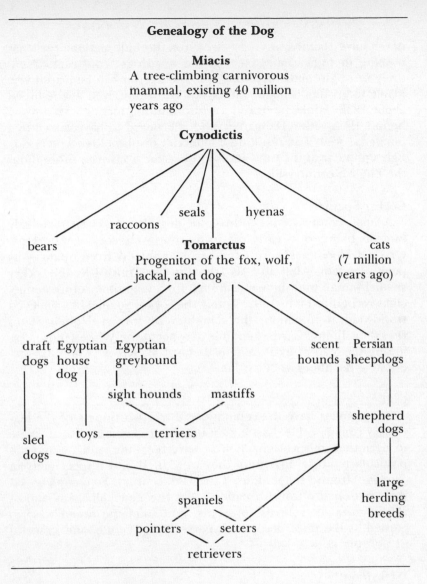

Miacis
A tree-climbing carnivorous
mammal, existing 40 million
years ago

Cynodictis

seals   hyenas

raccoons

bears   cats

Tomarctus   (7 million
Progenitor of the fox, wolf,   years ago)
jackal, and dog

draft   Egyptian Egyptian   scent   Persian
dogs   house   greyhound   hounds sheepdogs
        dog

        sight hounds   mastiffs

                                                     shepherd
                                                     dogs
sled   toys ———— terriers
dogs

                                                     large
                                                     herding
                  spaniels   breeds

          pointers   setters

                retrievers

the rabbit in the 18th century, many beagle packs were evicted from
hunting clubs. Recently, however, they have again achieved prominence, both as hunting hound and pet.

Bull Terrier

The famous American general George S. Patton, Jr., believed in
reincarnation, but the pet bull terrier constantly at his side could

never have claimed any past lives, for the bull terrier breed has nothing to reincarnate. One of the few dogs "constructed" entirely through mixed breeding, the bull terrier can be traced verifiably to an Englishman, James Hinks, who arrived at the breed about 1836. Hinks interbred a white hunting terrier with a greyhound, then with a Dalmatian, and is believed to have mixed in a pointer as well. The resulting bull terrier displayed tenacity in dog fights popular at the time and soon became a favorite throughout the English countryside.

Cocker Spaniel

A small, compact, and enthusiastic dog, the cocker spaniel likely owes its name to its early use in hunting woodcock, a waterfowl. Original bloodlines were exported to England from Spain — its point of origin — but after its arrival in the British Isles the cocker spaniel was an unfashionable animal for a long time before kennel clubs recognized it in 1892. Today the cocker spaniel has achieved worldwide approbation; the daughter of former United States President Jimmy Carter kept one as a pet at the White House, following the lead of ex-President Richard M. Nixon, whose Checkers stole headlines as "First Pet."

Collie

Few animals have the reputation of trustworthiness of the legendary cinema collie, Lassie, so it usually comes as a great surprise to learn that collies originally were carefree, independent, and not particularly noble dogs until they were bred into respectability in England around the middle of the 19th century. So complete was this "personality transformation" that the new collie was almost unrecognizable from its forebears, and soon the breed was regarded as the most decorative, persevering, gentle, and graceful of working dogs.

Dachshund

Characterized by a genetic mutation that causes chondrodystrophy, which stops the growth of its legs during early development, the low-slung dachshund has always been suited for work close to the ground, such as sniffing out ferrets. An early theory traced the dachshund's existence to Egypt, where its likeness is depicted in murals. But since the chondrodystrophy appeared as a mutation only in the 19th century in Germany, the idea has been abandoned. Instead, the dachshund probably originated from the taller German hound, inheriting its attributes of tracking, flushing, and retrieving, both on land and in water.

Doberman

A carefully planned genetic schedule, or "recipe," led to the Doberman, or Doberman pinscher, as it often is called. A German tax collector bred the first Doberman around 1870, probably mixing shepherd dogs and cattle dogs, and later adding genes from the Manchester terrier with greyhound blood. The Doberman's fierceness and streamlined body make the breed a favorite security dog.

German Shepherd

The German shepherd's tenacity and versatile disposition apparently have served the dog well over the centuries. The shepherd belongs to a group of dogs whose present form can be traced farther back in time than any other breed, almost 20,000 years. Originally a hunting and watch dog, the German shepherd (also called the Alsatian) became a cattle dog once farm animals were domesticated. In modern times, the shepherd has reverted to its original function as watch dog; because of its loyalty and size, it has become the preferred guide dog for the blind. Anthropologists believe that during the Bronze Age (3500–1000 B.C.) the shepherd was too small and weak to protect herds from hostile tribes and large carnivorous animals and thus was bred with the wolf to heighten its strength and ferociousness.

Greyhound, badger, and chase dog *(left to right)*. Archeological evidence shows that centuries before humans began breeding dogs for specific traits and appearances canines already existed throughout the world in numerous varieties.

Greyhound

A storied past surrounds the sleek and exquisite greyhound, whose ancestors are depicted as early as 4000 B.C. in Assyrian carvings. The breed surfaced in England in the 9th century, where a painting shows a duke handling a brace of greyhounds. Swift and nimble, the greyhound early became a racing animal, coursing hares for Egyptian audiences as far back as 200 B.C. Modern greyhound racing, in which the dogs pursue a mechanical hare drawn around an oval track, flourishes along parts of the East Coast of the United States. High-strung and ill-tempered, greyhounds generally are bred only for racing, and when their track careers end, because of old age or injury, the animals are destroyed.

Irish Wolfhound

The tallest of all dogs, the Irish wolfhound in an early era proved to be not only man's best friend but his best weapon as well. Accounts of roles played by the wolfhound in war are legendary. Serving as watch dogs and protectors, wolfhounds were part of the Celtic invasion of Greece in 273 B.C. Even earlier the Romans became acquainted with the dog when seven of the animals performed in the Circus Maximus. The Irish wolfhound almost disappeared in modern times, but the dog was revived by a British army captain, who in 1862 penned some of the remaining wolfhounds and began breeding them.

Poodle

Though often depicted as exotically groomed at the end of a bejeweled leash, the poodle has origins that give the dog a sturdier reputation than the posh one the breed has today. Poodles are found in paintings as far back as 1500, but the only certainty about the dog's beginnings was its popularity in Mediterranean countries during the Middle Ages. First used as a retriever of ducks, then as a circus trick dog, and later as a hunter, the poodle eventually became a pet and the national dog of France. The poodle's woolly, curlicued coat allows for elaborate clipping styles that seemingly become trendier the more outlandish they appear.

St. Bernard

Named for the monk who founded a famous monastery in the Alps, the St. Bernard seemed a godsend to early travelers and to skiers stranded on the slopes. With remarkable sense of direction and almost radarlike prescience of snowstorms and avalanches, the St. Bernard rescued the snowbound with amazing proficiency. By 1830, however, inbreeding had weakened the dog and deprived it of many of its natural skills. The breed later was crossed with similarly large Newfoundlands and Great Danes, producing the first long-haired St. Bernard.

Domestic Cats, 3000 B.C.; Egypt

Contrary to popular myth, the domestic cat was not a direct offspring of lions and tigers. Though its actual origin remains shrouded in its 7-million-year past, experts think the modern cat's true ancestor was the caffre cat of Egypt, a breed tamed and then trained for hunting.

Domestic cats do bear similarities to their ancient jungle relatives. But this is because both evolved from the same ancestral stock. The tree-climbing carnivore *Miacis,* existing 40 million years ago, evolved into the small four-legged *Cynodictis,* which was the immediate progenitor of all cats.

The relationship between jungle cats and domestic cats, in fact, is not unlike the evolutionary closeness between modern apes and humans — the latter two are from the same ancestral stock, *Dryopithecus,* who lived some 36 million years ago — but each evolved into different species while retaining numerous similarities in anatomy and behavior. Thus, a small, furry cat — not exceptionally vicious, and exceedingly clever — coexisted with the giant jungle felines and survived many of them.

Unlike the stronger, larger early wolflike dogs, whose hunting skills could assist primitive man in capturing game, the cat, being weaker, was apparently not befriended by man until very recently in history: only 5000 years ago in Egypt. But once the relationship began, cats assumed a unique position. Whereas dogs quickly became man's best friend, cats almost immediately were worshiped as deities.

The cat was held in such high esteem among ancient Egyptians that it was protected by law from injury and death. Idolatry was so strong that a cat's death was mourned by the entire family, and both rich and poor embalmed the bodies of their cats in exquisite fashion, wrapping them in the finest linen and placing them in mummy cases made of precious materials, such as bronze and even wood, which was scarce in timber-poor Egypt.

From many ancient drawings and statuettes, it can be seen that the average Egyptian cat was slimmer and longer than today's Siamese breed, with a mottled coat like today's tabby. The cat existed in two distinct forms: one was sharp-nosed and long-eared; the other, whose descendants are modern long-haired cats, was short-eared and blunt-nosed.

Cats spread quickly through civilization. Sanskrit writings more than 2000 years old speak of cats' roles in Indian society. In China, about 500 B.C., Confucius kept a favorite cat. About A.D. 600 the Prophet Muhammad preached with a cat in his arms, and at approximately the same time the Japanese began to keep cats in their pagodas to protect sacred manuscripts.

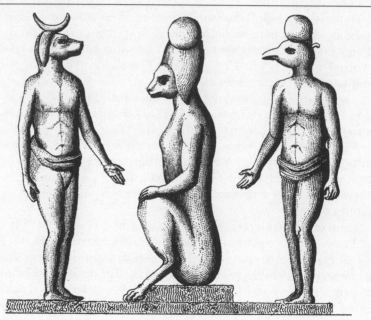

Cat Idolatry. Egyptian cat god, Canop, between gods Anubis (with the head of a jackal) and Horus (with a hawk's head). Egyptians capitalized on the cat's craftiness in protecting the great granaries from rats and mice. Later, in England, where cats quickly ridded the country of rodents, a wealthy landowner imposed a fine of sixty bushels of corn on anyone willfully putting to death one of his beloved "mousers."

Cat remains dating to A.D. 500 were discovered in Etruria, and may have been from the first European cats kept as pets. Cats were so highly prized that a prince decreed in A.D. 948 that a kitten cost the equivalent of a penny before its eyes were opened, and after it caught its first mouse the price doubled. Both sums were a lot of money in those days. Anyone caught stealing or killing a cat from the prince's granaries was fined a sheep and a lamb, or as much wheat as would cover the dead animal when held up by its tail with the nose touching the ground.

All honors slipped away from the cat during the Middle Ages, when some religious fanatics connected it with witches and black magic. The animal once looked on with approbation suddenly became a dreaded and feared creature. Many societies attempted to drive cats into extinction, because witches were supposedly able to disguise themselves as cats, which made every cat untrustworthy. The scare mounted to paranoia, and many innocent women and their harmless pets were burned at the stake. Black cats in particular suffered this ignominious fate, singled out for persecution as agents of the devil. In France, thousands of cats were burned until King Louis XIII halted the shameful practice.

Eventually the witch hunts died out. Black cats still portended bad times, but only to the superstitious. Finally the cat crawled back into the lap of its master in the protective fondness — if not idolatry — of the past. The first **cat show** was staged at Great Britain's renowned Crystal Palace in 1871 and became an annual event. People began to place great emphasis on cat breeding, experimenting to produce elaborate feline bloodlines and introducing the first pedigrees.

Long-Haired Burman

According to an Oriental legend, the first Burman cats were kept as oracles in Burmese temples hundreds of years ago. The cats were sacred and figured in the belief in transmigration of souls.

A Burmese myth claims that many years before the coming of Buddha, in the Temple of Lao-Tsun in the mountains of Lugh in Indochina, lived an old Kittah priest, Mun-Ha, whose oracle was a white cat called Sinh. Day after day they sat together, admiring the golden statue of the goddess Tsun-Kyankse, who presided over lost souls. Worried about a threatened invasion of his country, the old priest eventually keeled over dead in front the goddess. The cat Sinh jumped onto the priest's throne, rested against the silvery head of its departed master — and this contact prompted the miracle of transmigration. The cat's fur suddenly assumed the golden color of the statue, its yellow eyes were transformed to the sapphire blue of the goddess's, and its paws and ears darkened to the brown of the earth, except for the tips of the paws that touched the head of the old priest; they remained snowy white. When other priests entered the chamber, a compelling gaze from the cat instructed them to repel the invaders, which they did successfully.

Burman cats are said to be descendants of this temple-bred lineage. First exhibited in France in 1931, they were imported into England and later, as they gained official recognition, throughout the world.

Russian Blue

Russian sailors are thought to have brought these cats to England aboard the cargo ships that traded between Archangel and London. Many years ago they were known as Archangel cats or the Blue Foreign Type, and only after World War II was the name Russian Blue adopted. Their short-haired, seal-smooth coat is the result of many years' selective breeding, and today the forename "Russian," like "Abyssinian," does not denote country of origin. Russian Blues are among the most attractive of domestic cats, and one of the few breeds that like water.

Abyssinian

Abyssinians were imported to Great Britain in 1869 from Abyssinia, now Ethiopia. First shown at England's Crystal Palace two years later, they were immediately fancied because of their resemblance to cats depicted in ancient Egyptian frescoes and statuettes, suggesting that they might be descendants of this sacred breed. But the cat is more the result of genetic experimentation in Abyssinia than an actual ancient breed. Judicious breeding by British fanciers has improved the intelligence of the Abyssinian, and the cats' distinctive appearance creates an overwhelming demand for them as pets.

Siamese

The Siamese is possibly the most popular pedigreed cat in the world today, earning that distinction in England and the United States. Like the Abyssinian, its body lines resemble those of the ancient Egyptian cats, though the origin of the Siamese cannot be

Is this the cruel origin of catgut?

traced to a definite time in history. The first pair of these exotic animals apparently was brought to England in 1884 by a Mr. Gould, the consul general at the royal palace in Bangkok, Thailand, or, as it was called then, Siam.

Similar cats resided in the royal palaces and temples of Siam for hundreds of years, where they were guarded and treasured to such an extent that only a few ever were given away. The male and female given to Gould were for many years the progenitors of all domestic Western Siamese. Their body contour, coloring, intelligence, and almost mystical cross-eyed stare lend credence to the belief that modern Siamese are descendants of the royal cats of Siam.

Manx

The Manx, often called the "Rumpy" because of its tail-less hindquarters, is somewhat of an enigma among cats. Manx are among the most expensive cats because their litters often fail to reproduce pedigreed offspring. If two of these tail-less cats are mated, they may produce kittens with tails, with only stumps, or totally without tails. Their rarity is compounded by the fact that continual inbreeding to isolate the "tail-less" gene seems to have produced a lethal gene that kills off many kittens before or shortly after birth.

Cats without tails existed in Japan and Malaya before they proliferated in the West. According to one legend, the Manx appeared on the British island after the wreck of a Spanish galleon close to the coast.

A second bit of lore is that warriors fighting the Irish who had invaded the Isle of Man began killing the cats for their beautifully bushy tails, which they used to decorate their helmets, in imitation of the invaders' richly plumed headgear. Observing this slaughter and multilation of her kin, a wise old mother cat is supposed to have climbed to the top of a high mountain to bear her next litter. To ensure the safety of her offspring, she bit off their tails right after they were born. Female Manx of each succeeding generation were imparted this secret, and in time all the cats were born without tails.

Brown Burmese

The Brown Burmese cat is one of few breeds originating in the United States. In 1930, a female brown cat was brought to America from Burma. The cat, of no particular breed, was sleek, intelligent, and attractive. As no brown male was available, the cat was mated to a Siamese, and the offspring later were carefully bred to produce the Burmese, which won speedy recognition in the United States. Burmese, aside from making enchanting pets, possess great stage presence. They are rarely nervous, and their mellow temperament and an innate entertaining quality that attracts judges make them cat-show favorites the world over.

17

More Friends: Bunnies to Broncos

Rabbit

Rabbits have gone virtually unchanged since they first appeared during the Eocene period about 60 million years ago. They originally were classified as rodents, but fossil evidence later showed them to be lagomorphs, which differed from rodents in several respects. Lagomorphs, for example, have long, erect ears, hind legs longer than the front, and cannot effectively hold food with the forelimbs when feeding.

The two orders probably evolved from different ancestors, since the habit of "refection" is common to lagomorphs but not to rodents. In refection — also known as coprophagy — rabbits pass food twice through the stomach for better assimilation. Unlike some other animals, which regurgitate their food, the rabbit and hare achieve refection by swallowing fecal pellets.

The Romans were responsible for domesticating the rabbit, which flourished throughout their empire as a source of meat. Rabbits reached Britain in the 12th century, but four hundred years passed before they were prized for their fur, largely by 16th-century monks. Selective breeding then enhanced the animals' rich coats. In England early domestic rabbits were farmed in enclosed warrens and protected by strict game laws. One 1816 law, exemplifying the severe restraints, imposed a prison sentence of seven years for rabbit theft.

Hamster

The hamster was the first desert rodent to become a popular pet, owing in no small measure to its swift breeding habits: offspring are born only sixteen days after conception — the shortest gestation period for any mammal.

The animal was first recognized as a species in 1839, shortly after British zoologists discovered several in the wilds of Syria. But no specimens were bred in captivity for almost a hundred years, until an expedition of the department of zoology of the Hebrew University at Jerusalem went into the woods near Aleppo in Syria — the same location where the animals first were found — and returned with a burrow of seven hamsters. Of these, four escaped and one female was killed by a male, leaving three specimens, a male and two females.

Inbreeding of hamsters to achieve the kind of genetically pure strain necessary for medical research proved to be easier than with their laboratory predecessors, white mice, and in no time the animals existed in large numbers. All the thousands of research animals in Europe and America for many years were descendants of the original three litter mates. By the 1940s hamsters were being cared for as pets throughout the world. Fondness for the animal developed despite its nocturnal nature, which makes it lethargic during the day.

Hamsters are hardy survivalists. Their habit of hoarding, for example, enables them to withstand food scarcity; it also gives rise to the animal's common name, taken from the German verb meaning "to hoard." The hamster has evolved broad cheek pouches specifically for carrying its food.

Guinea Pig

The guinea pig — or cavy — got its domestic start when a group of sailors brought to Europe several of the animals from the Guiana coast of South America in the 16th century. Today about twenty species survive, all native to South America. The English cherished the animals as pets, and by 1800, guinea pigs abounded in Britain.

There seems to be no clear explanation for the cavy's common name, guinea pig. Some argue that the forename came from an anglicized version of "Guiana," which may well be true. But the reference to "pig" has stymied experts up to the present. A bevy of explanations have been put forward over the years — alluding to the animal's eating habits, voice, and pudginess — but none convincing enough to merit a cachet from animal authorities.

Throughout the United Kingdom "cavy" enjoys widespread use. Thus, it is curious that the highly scientific Germans should have allowed the misnomer "pig" (by way of the word "swine") to creep into their name for the creature, *Meerschweinchen,* meaning "little pig from over the sea." Americans have always preferred "guinea pig" and have used the term as slang for a person willing to try untested products, presumably because the animals frequently were used in laboratory experiments. Yet based solely on that criterion two other terms for a person testing something untried would be "hamster" or "mouse."

The animal is thought to have derived from the frenetic wild cavy of Peru, domesticated by the Incas, long before the Spanish conquest, as one of their few sources of meat. The wild grassland animal sought shelter in rocks, caves, and abandoned burrows of other animals, and its long hair offered natural camouflage in grass. Some species burrowed for protection. The domestic descendant, however, shows no proclivity for burrowing. Another trait distinguishing the domestic guinea pig from subterranean animals is its birth process: females bear surprisingly mature young, which are able to withstand relatively adverse conditions from the moment they leave the womb.

Gerbil

Like the hamsters, today's gerbils — both pets and laboratory animals — are largely the offspring of a small number of animals brought into captivity from the wild. Breeding began in 1935, after Japanese scientists took twenty pairs of Mongolian gerbils from the Amur River on the Russian-Chinese border. In 1954, four pairs were sent to the United States and bred; the first twelve male-female pairs were sent to England, soon followed by another twenty-four.

The appeal of the gerbil is based largely on the animal's friskiness, curiosity, and agility, and on its shiny dense coat, the color of golden sand or ocher.

Armand David, a French missionary and naturalist, is credited with the earliest sighting of the gerbil in 1866. He tentatively named the animal "yellow rat," because of its surroundings in Mongolia, a region covered by the loess of Asia and drained by the Yellow River. When specimens were sent to Paris the following year, they were given their correct zoological status by naturalist Henri Milne-Edwards.

Horse, Pre–1,000,000 B.C.; North America

The first people to domesticate the horse (a mammal of the family *Equidae,* species *Equus caballus*) was probably a tribe of Indo-Europeans that lived in the northern steppes near the mountain chain adjacent to the Black and Caspian seas. They did not ride horses but, as can be seen in numerous cave drawings from around

Horses were ridden bareback for at least the first twelve centuries after domestication. Cushions were later introduced to soften the jolts and jars of journeying, but nothing was done to improve stability until the Han Dynasty of China introduced the rigid saddle in the 3rd century B.C. Stirrups originated in India in the 2nd century A.D. and, uncomfortably, fitted only the big toe. Three hundred years later, seeking additional comfort and the ability to ride while wearing boots, the Chinese molded the stirrup to accommodate footgear. Because stirrups made "shock combat" possible, they were regarded by later military experts as the most significant invention prior to gunpowder in the history of warfare.

5000 B.C., they used horses for meat and hides. About a thousand years later horses were called on to haul firewood, rocks, and building materials, and only beginning in the Bronze Age (about 3500 B.C.) were they ridden, first bareback, then saddled.

The horse was a boon to man in his roles as hunter, herdsman, and warrior. It also added greatly to his mobility and stature; a man on horseback commanded instant respect. So much so, in fact, that centuries later, when the Spanish reintroduced the horse to the New World after it long had become extinct in North America, Indians viewed a conquistador on his horse as a single, albeit bizarre being — a new god to be worshiped.

The horse was not always the large animal it is today. Early traces of the ancestor of the horse have been found in rocks along the Mississippi Valley dating from 50 million years ago. The fossils suggest that the protohorse was a small foxlike animal with a pointed face that walked on four toes but possessed a fifth as a useless appendage.

Eohippus, as the creature is called, fed on swampland vegetation. As the ground hardened, stretching into grasslands and forests, the horse's legs responded by growing longer and the toes contracted. Throughout this transformation *Eohippus* gave rise to three intermediate forms *(Orohippus, Protohippus,* and *Hipparion),* reached the size of a pony, and possessed only three toes. About 1 million years ago, the *Equus* appeared; it was the direct ancestor of the horse, donkey, and zebra, with stronger teeth for feeding on tough grasses and even longer legs for eluding predators. By the time *Equus caballus* emerged, the animal stood on only one toe, and that was enveloped in a protective hoof.

Many early horses must have migrated out of their native North American habitat up through Canada and, aided by the land bridges that existed during the Ice Age, crossed over into Asia. Thus they escaped the mysterious circumstances that were soon to wipe out the entire North American horse population. The Asian horse, a sandy brown animal called *Equus caballus przewalskii,* spread eastward, giving rise to Chinese and Mongolian breeds; farther westward there arose the mouse-colored European *Tarpan.* Wild horses migrated to the southwest, to Asia Minor, and from there to Egypt and the Mediterranean countries, establishing local breeds in those parts of the world.

In 1519 the Spanish explorer Hernando Cortez transported the horse back to the New World. Some of the horses escaped captivity and thrived on the Western plains, where they were called mustangs. Until relatively modern times, man's success at breeding horses was at best sporadic.

Donkey

Geographic factors caused the donkey to develop quite differently from the horse and zebra, though all three share a common ancestor that was no bigger than a dog. A native of East and North Africa, the donkey evolved in mountainous country, where the prevailing high temperatures, great aridity, and sparse vegetation sharply contrasted to the conditions faced by the horse on the Eurasian steppes.

Either the Egyptians or the Libyans around 4000 B.C. first corralled the donkey into the service of man.

Both societies domesticated the animal mainly as a beast of burden for hauling food supplies and construction materials. Although the Egyptians prized the donkey for its energetic toil and for what they saw as its great beauty, somewhere in early history the donkey became scorned for its stolid disposition — largely a product of constant inbreeding — and its very name became synonymous with stupidity and stubbornness.

Its common nickname, "jackass," began as a derogatory human expression, "Jack Ass." Its abbreviated name, "ass" (*ezel* in Dutch, *Esel* in German), is the origin of our word "easel," for it was the patient *ass* who held the artist's canvas while he painted. Not rattled by a child's nervous fidgeting or awkwardness, the donkey makes the perfect mount for the novice rider, who later can graduate to the more temperamental horse.

Parakeet

Parakeets — in turquoise, blue, chartreuse, and white — were one of the great animal novelties of the 19th century. Tens of thousands, perhaps millions, were netted in Australia and imported to England in 1840, where they were first exhibited in public. A half-century later, a caged parakeet in the living room was a sign of British chic, and the trend soon spread to the continent and then to the United States.

Parakeets, or budgerigars, as they are called in Great Britain, are the most common of all pet birds. They are small parrots who use their strong beaks for dehusking seeds and scaling trees. The birds' zygodactyl feet — two toes pointing forward and two backward — also help make climbing effortless.

The parakeet was assigned the Latin name *Melopsittacus undulatus* by ornithologists, which translates as "song of a parrot that is wavelike." The name "budgerigar" (nickname, "budgy") is an English derivation of the Australian aboriginal term for the bird, "betcherrygah."

Canary

Like the parakeet, the canary can credit its popularity as a pet to romantic Britons who espoused it as a "lovebird," although the canary's domestic origin is far more mundane.

The bird had a special reputation in British mining communities, where it accompanied miners underground when there was a risk of exposure to deadly gas. The canary is so quickly asphyxiated by noxious carbon monoxide fumes that it provided a sensitive barometer for the presence of the gas. The practice of taking along a canary occasionally is still used today in mining accident rescues.

Unlike parakeets, which by nature are tree climbers, the canary is strictly a percher, with three toes pointing forward, one backward. The bird is the namesake of the Canary Islands, to whose lush tropical forests they are indigenous, just as they are to the Azores and Madeira. Predating almost all birds introduced into captivity, the canary spread throughout Europe after the Spaniards' 15th-century conquest of the Canary Islands.

The Spanish cleverly controlled the canary's popularity by selling only male birds. As demands for canaries grew, the Spanish hiked prices enormously. Since only they had knowledge of the bird's origins and habits, customers weren't certain whether the birds were being bred in captivity (which should have brought *down* their cost) or were continually being imported from some exotic land. This monopoly lasted for several decades. When a ship carrying a cargo of canaries foundered off the Mediterranean coast in 1622, thousands of male and female birds escaped and were blown by winds to Elba, where they established a flourishing colony. The Spanish exploitation scheme was exposed when French and Italian travelers to Elba recognized the birds and captured many for their own domestic breeding.

Turtle

After surviving in the wild for more than 200 million years, and having undergone surprisingly little change for much of that stretch, turtles in recent times have become pets, though more as curiosities than for any pleasing traits they possess.

Early in their evolution the *Chelonia* — the reptilian group including turtles, tortoises, and terrapins — were soft-bodied creatures. They had a normal vertebrate skeleton and the scaly skin of a reptile, sufficiently thick to protect them from many dangers — but apparently not enough. For the scales eventually gave way to a soft shell, beneath which the flesh receded until the shell fused with the backbone and rib cage.

The tensile shell common to all land tortoises gradually formed at great expense to the animals, which had to sacrifice speed for the added protection provided by the hard shell, and had to modify the mechanics of breathing under the shell's crushing weight. To accomplish this latter feat turtles developed a series of chest contractions that create pressure changes within the rigid body cavity, thus drawing air in and out of the lungs. Any surprise or sudden disturbance causes a turtle involuntarily to force air out of its windpipe, which produces the hissing sound characteristic of many reptiles.

Goldfish

The story of the goldfish is a parable (if not a parody) of supply and demand. About a thousand years ago, the Chinese conceived the idea of aquaculture and decided that the goldfish, a kind of carp, was an ideal candidate to be farmed for food. At the time, the fish was greenish-bronze in color, and its only real distinction was an ability to breed in shallow ponds, which meant it could survive in water poor in oxygen — the reason that the Chinese chose it for their pioneering farming venture.

Through selective breeding the fish's size increased tremendously. But as soon as the first glistening gold mutations appeared, the fish acquired a reputation as an ornament and immediately was stocked in the garden pools of the emperor and wealthy aristocrats.

Breeding goldfish for their esthetic properties became such a lucrative business that their cultivation for food was completely abandoned. All further breeding endeavors focused on making the fish more golden, metallically shimmering, and prolific.

The goldfish was imported to Europe about the turn of the 18th century. Suppliers could not keep up with pleas for more of these novel creatures, and one hatchery opened after another. In time, more than a hundred varieties were bred, until finally there existed such a surfeit of goldfish that it suffered its present ignominy — being sold for pennies in plastic bags at five-and-ten-cent stores. Still, the goldfish is an easy-to-keep pet, remarkably hardy; some species live fourteen years or longer.

Draft Animals, Pre–5000 B.C.; Europe

Early man began domesticating animals about 10,000 years ago for their meat, milk, and hides. He apparently did not immediately exploit them for work. In fact, the notion of using animals to supplement or replace his own muscle power seems not to have arisen for another several thousand years.

Once the "beast of burden" concept developed, the relationship between man and draft animal flourished and has been fruitful ever since — at least as man tells the story. Even with such modern power sources as steam, electricity, and oil, people still till more than 80 percent of the world's arable land with the help of animals.

Archeologists know that before man began keeping written records he had already put draft animals to work. This is clear from the unearthed remains of harnesses, bits, wheels, and wagons and from early chariots used in ceremonies. A wealth of substantiating evidence comes from ancient tomb paintings, temple decorations, statuettes, coins, and seals (such as signet rings) that bear impressions of oxen, mules, and horses in the employ of man.

The very earliest animal corralled into work seems to have been **reindeer.** Numerous snow sleds pulled by reindeer and dating to before 5000 B.C. have been discovered in Northern Europe.

Mules hauling railroad tracks

Land sleds, on the other hand, drawn by oxen, were being used in Mesopotamia by 3500 B.C., and Egyptian art of that period depicts pack asses toiling under heavy loads. A boom in the draft-animal displacement occurred some time before 3000 B.C. with the invention of the plow and wheel. The animal was no longer limited by the load it could carry on its back or drag across the ground, now that it could pull heavier loads on wheeled wagons.

From Mesopotamia, draft animals spread rapidly eastward and westward. Animals were drawing wheeled vehicles in the Indus Valley by 2500 B.C., throughout Europe by 2000 B.C., in Egypt by 1600 B.C., in China by 1300 B.C., and in Britain by about 500 B.C.

Other draft animals that lessened the burdens of early man were:

Cow
Although they were first domesticated during the 6th millennium B.C., cows did not pull plows until about 3500 B.C. For the next 2000 years they were the main animals used for heavy transport, existing as a team of two oxen hitched to a sled, cart, or plow. They remain in use today throughout hilly and poor regions of Europe and Africa.

Onager
An early draft animal first used in Mesopotamia in the 4th millennium B.C., the onager remained in service for only about a thousand years, when it (along with cows and donkeys) was replaced by the horse. At that time, domestication of the onager was abandoned, and most descendants of the beast (including the zebra) today roam free in the jungles of Africa.

Dog

Dogs evolved as draft animals by pulling small carts throughout Western Europe; later they helped propel sleds through frozen regions, bearing up well in icy climates and displaying a degree of determination rare in other animals. Today, dog teams of six to eight animals pull sleds in double file through Arctic regions and upper Russia. Their use for hauling carts was banned in England in 1885 as inhumane, and today a "dog cart" is a vehicle towed by a pony, often, oddly enough, with a box under the carriage seat for carrying dogs. However, the original practice continued up to the end of World War II in countries such as Belgium, the Netherlands, and parts of Germany, France, and Switzerland, where dogs pulled produce carts to market.

Domestication of Other Animals. Cattle, 6000 B.C.; Asia Minor. Sheep, 6000 B.C.; Central Asia. Goat, 5000 B.C.; Asia Minor. Pig, 4000 B.C.; Asia. Chicken, 4000 B.C.; Near East. The Romans bred chickens for the table and are reputed to have imparted a finer flavor to the birds by drowning them in red wine.

Elephant

Bulky and slow, but incredibly strong, elephants were instrumental in the ascent of many early civilizations. Seals from the Indus Valley dating to 2500 B.C. show elephants engaged in arduous work. They have been ridden and serving as beasts of burden ever since. The African elephant is historically associated with conquests of Hannibal of Carthage, who tried to take the huge beasts across the Alps when he invaded Italy in 218 B.C. North African elephants also played a major role in the Ptolemaic Wars, but excessive exploitation and a shrinking environment soon brought them to extinction. Asian elephants are employed today in lumbering — toting or dragging logs through the jungles of Sri Lanka and Burma. They also are sparingly used as baggage carriers, and are able to transport loads of more than 800 pounds.

18

Communications:
Smoke Signals to Stereo

Communications

Like many African tribes today, primitive man communicated in the beginning by beating sticks against resonant logs and tree trunks, then diversified his sounds with drums of stretched animal skin. The precision and versatility of sounds made possible with drums of various shapes and sizes enabled him to conceive elaborate patterns, or codes, for signaling of war and peace, of ideas and emotions.

Drums, in turn, spawned **wind instruments,** such as reed pipes and whistles made from carved bones and rams' horns. All of these artifacts have been found throughout the regions of Africa and Eurasia that served as man's earliest homelands.

Smoke signaling also was a favorite means of early communication. Though we tend to associate messages of puffy white bursts of smoke with the American Indians on the great Western plains, smoke signaling was used by the ancient Chinese, Egyptians, Assyrians, and Greeks.

At night, when smoke was impossible to observe, networks of **fire beacons** were lit. According to legend, Queen Clytemnestra in 1804 B.C. received news of the fall of Troy and word of her husband's homecoming to their palace at Argos by a string of beacon fires covering 500 miles, with nine relay points located on the highest mountains. The relatively rapid communication gave Clytemnestra and her lover, Aegisthus, time to plot the execution of the returning king Agamemnon.

In modern times man has developed numerous sophisticated modes of optical and electromagnetic communications.

Telegraphy, 18th Century; Switzerland

The origin of telegraphy, the first major electrical mode of communication, is marred by litigious claims.

In 1829, Joseph Henry, a prolific and energetic American scientist, constructed the first electric motor and working electromagnet, devices that made possible the invention of telegraphy. Two years later Henry built an electric telegraph, but believing that scientific discoveries were the property of all mankind, he did not patent his invention. In 1844 Samuel F. B. Morse, designer of the code that bears his name, took out a patent on telegraphy, never acknowledging Henry's contributions and, in essence, taking all the credit, and the subsequent financial reward, for the breakthrough.

While history has by now recognized Henry's magnanimity and Morse's duplicity, it turns out that several forms of telegraphy were attempted, and a few actually succeeded, years before Henry beeped his first message over electrical wire.

Almost immediately after the discovery of electricity, scientists attempted to harness it as a communication system. It offered many plusses: theoretically messages could be sent over thin, lightweight wires, with minimal interference from the environment, and at seemingly incomprehensible speeds — in fact, the speed of light.

Many ingenious schemes were tried. A London inventor in 1727 devised a system that transmitted electrical impulses through a thin wire one sixth of a mile long. A colleague soon topped him by sending an impulse over 2 miles of wire, the first wire to be strung through the air. In the air at that time, too, was an intense feeling of competition: Who would send an electrical message the farthest distance?

Perhaps the most outlandish, though entirely workable, scheme was that proposed in 1753 by a Scottish inventor. He envisioned a system of twenty-six separate wires, one for each letter of the alphabet, with a lightweight pith ball suspended from each wire at its receiving end. The slight movement of a ball would signify the arrival of a letter, which then could be written down, re-creating the original message. Of course, the tediousness of compiling the message all but defeated the potential instantaneousness of sending it. Nonetheless, a Swiss inventor built an experimental model, which worked.

All of these systems were forms of telegraphy. But the word "telegraph" was coined only around 1792, by a French physician and inventor, Claude Chappe. He developed an optical, not electrical, communication system and coined its name from the Greek *tele,* "far," and *graphein,* "to write."

As to the true origin of electrical telegraphy, historians believe that the earliest model, which depended on static electricity and used an electroscope as a receiving device, was a system of Swiss design constructed in the early 1700s. By the end of that century Alessandro Volta had devised the **voltaic battery,** which served as a dependable source of steady current and made long-distance telegraphy a reality.

Russian scientists in 1832 set up a successful telegraph circuit between the tsar's winter and summer palaces, transmitting business of state, and in Germany a year later physicists Carl Gauss and Wilhelm Weber constructed an electrical two-wire telegraph line of copper and sent a message for 1.4 miles, over city housetops and offices. The era of modern electrical communication was thus born — a full decade before Morse's claim to discovery.

Morse Code, 1835; United States

The success of any electrical communication system lies in the cleverness of its coding, for it is neither words nor numbers that are transmitted, but a series of electrical impulses that represent these things only by some arbitrary, abstract, prearranged plan.

Early telegraphy had attempted to transmit the alphabet in various direct and coded ways, all clumsy and rather costly in the energy they consumed. But the Morse code, devised in 1835 by American painter-turned-inventor Samuel F. B. Morse and applied three years later, was the single biggest breakthrough to revolutionize the field of telegraphy.

Morse's system was the ultimate in simplicity. It called for the use of an electromagnet, a device that becomes magnetic when activated by a current and raps against a metal contact. Thus, a series of short electrical pulses repeatedly makes and breaks the magnet, and, consequently, taps out the message. The message according to Morse was to be coded in dots and dashes, each group representing letters, numerals, and punctuation. In all, an elegant scheme.

This was not Morse's original conception, though. His first attempt at establishing a telegraphic code depended on rows of markings of different lengths on a moving tape; these denoted the ten numerals. From this elementary scheme he devised more comprehensive alphabetical codes, but abandoned them all when he was a professor of art at New York University in 1832, the year he and an assistant, Alfred Vail, dreamed up the system of dots and dashes. By 1837 Morse had secured a patent for his code and formed a partnership with Vail to establish a communications company.

The inaugural long-distance telegraphy message was dispatched on May 24, 1844, when Morse, at the U.S. Capitol in Washington, sent to Vail, at the Mount Clare station of the Baltimore and Ohio Railroad in Baltimore, the now-famous "What hath God wrought!" — a transmission over a line made of iron wire with glass doorknobs for insulators.

As promising as Morse code telegraphy was, it had some hurdles to overcome. Chief among them was people's fear that electricity passing in lines over their homes and farms would adversely affect their children and crops. One band of farmers in the South demolished an entire telegraphy system through their region, claiming it had caused periods of drought that resulted in a sequence of bad harvests. Nevertheless, telegraph lines soon were stitched across the country; carrying messages in Morse code, they played a major role in opening up the American West.

Telephone, 1876; United States

The word "telephone" originated long before the actual invention of the device in 1876 by Alexander Graham Bell, a Scot living in the United States.

Bell's telephone (from the Greek *tele*, "far," and *phonē*, "sound") was patented only a few hours before another American inventor,

Telegraph operators

Elisha Gray, could gain accreditation for a similar, and in many ways better, device. Had Bell been just a few hours later in getting his designs to the patent office, what we know today as the Bell System worldwide might have been called the Gray System.

The telephone was waiting to be invented. The mechanics of sound vibration were well understood by the beginning of the 19th century, as were the principles of electrical transmission. And in 1831 the great physicist Michael Faraday provided the final ingredient by demonstrating how electrical impulses could be converted from pieces of iron and steel. Thus, all the components for the telephone were available for at least forty years before Bell combined them into a homogeneous technology and spoke the first message over wire at his home at 5 Exeter Place, Boston: "Mr. Watson, come at once. I want you." Thomas Watson, of course, was Bell's twenty-two-year-old assistant; Bell himself on that memorable day, March 10, 1876, was only twenty-nine.

Bell and Gray, working independently, and supposedly without knowledge of one another, undertook a series of experiments between 1872 and 1875 that were strikingly similar. Gray was the first to build a receiver, in 1874. He had realized that if sufficient electrical tones were transmitted simultaneously over a wire, the human voice could be faithfully simulated.

Bell conceived of his own type of receiver several months later, but, like Gray, he lacked a transmitter to complement it. While experimenting with telegraphy the following year, he discovered, he thought, a way to make a crude transmitter that would generate electrical oscillations that his receiver could pick up. His assistant, Watson, built the device, but much to both men's regret, the system as a whole did not work, mainly because of excessive electrical noise in the components; it was as large as the signals being sent. Pressed by financial obligations, Bell had no choice but to abandon temporarily his work on the telephone.

Gray, however, went ahead. He devised a transmitter with a flexible membrane that relied on a solution of water and acid to conduct vibrations, but never tested it. Nonetheless, on February 14, 1876, Gray filed at the patent office a "notice of invention," a step removed from an actual patent application. Bell, meanwhile, had resumed work on the telephone, completed new designs, had them notarized in Boston on January 20, and then made his formal bid for a patent on the same day that Gray filed — but some hours earlier.

Bell, of course, obtained the patent. But he had not yet successfully transmitted speech, and in some ways Gray actually was closer to that goal with his particular invention: a metal diaphragm receiver and variable-resistance transmitter. But it was Bell, whose ideas appeared the less imaginative of the two, who doggedly pursued the telephone. Gray, perhaps demoralized by failure to receive a patent, became stymied and eventually gave up.

Commercial telephones came into operation in the winter of 1878. The first switchboard was installed in the offices of the Holmes Burglar Alarm Company of Boston, who used its network of alarm lines to clients' homes for phone transmission during the day and for security services at night. On April 4, 1877, the first telephone had been installed in a private home — that of Charles Williams of Somerville, Massachusetts, who was then manufacturing Bell's invention. With no one else to call — since phone exchanges had not yet opened — Williams had a line run to his Boston office so that his wife could reach him during the day, a move he did not seem to regret.

The U.S. courts, recognizing the tremendous communications potential of Bell's invention, granted him the broadest possible license in using electricity for the instantaneous transmission of the human voice. The city of New Haven, Connecticut, received the first commercial phone exchange when the District Telephone Company opened its doors for service on January 28, 1878. It had only twenty-one customers, and the one telephone operator, George Coy, greeted callers with a hearty "Ahoy!"

By 1887, only a decade after the phone's debut, there were 743 main exchanges and 444 branch exchanges in the United States. This initial phone network used about 146,000 miles of insulated wire to connect the homes of over 150,000 subscribers.

The origin of the **pay phone** began with an inventor from Hartford, Connecticut, William Gray, not related to Elisha Gray. He installed a nickel-operated coin phone in the Hartford Bank in 1889 and began other installations throughout the area two years later.

The origin of the automatic **direct dial telephone** (in which calls are placed directly, without the assistance of an operator) was patented in March 1889 by Almon Strowger and went into service at La Porte, Indiana, three years later. Strowger, an undertaker by profession, wanted to eliminate reliance on operators for a very personal reason. He was convinced that one of the local operators, the wife of his main rival in the funeral business, was deliberately diverting calls for undertakers to her husband's funeral parlor.

Wireless Telegraphy, 1894; Italy

Like the telephone, wireless (radio) telegraphy was a communication tool that went through frenetic refinement in its early years. In fact many scientists seriously questioned whether such a device could ever be built.

Their doubts are easy to understand. Sending electrical signals over wires, as telegraphy did, made sense physically: wire, after all, was a real physical medium that could carry current. But what about something as insubstantial as air? And even if electromagnetic waves could propagate through air, wouldn't they be at the mercy of unpredictable electrical storms and other atmospheric disturbances?

Three men are prominent in finding the answers to those questions and thus in contributing to the development of wireless telegraphy. James Clerk Maxwell, a professor of experimental physics at Cambridge, England, in 1864 proved mathematically that an electrical wave could produce an effect at a considerable distance from the point at which it occurred (hence electrical signals were not confined to traveling along a wire). Maxwell also predicted that such signals, or electromagnetic waves, traveled at the speed of light (which meant that earthbound communications would essentially be instantaneous).

It was all theory, though, for twenty-two years. Heinrich Hertz, another physicist (whose surname today is the term for cycles per second, a frequency wave motion), in 1888 experimentally demonstrated that Maxwell's predictions were true, at least over short distances. At the center of a parabolic metal mirror, he set up two conductors separated by a short gap, a configuration known as a spark gap. A wire ring connected to another spark gap was placed about 5 feet away, at the focus of another parabolic collector in line with the first. Hertz found that when a spark leaped across the first gap, it caused a smaller spark to jump the gap in the ring 5 feet away.

He had proved that electromagnetic radio waves travel in straight lines and that they can be reflected by a metal sheet, just as light waves are reflected by a mirror, and that wireless telegraphy certainly was a feasible concept.

With the groundwork laid, the Italian physicist Guglielmo Marconi repeated Hertz's experiments at his family's country house, the Villa Grifone, at Pontecchio, near Bologna. He bettered Hertz's efforts by getting secondary sparks (the ones in symphony with the primary sparks) to leap a distance of 30 feet. A major scientific achievement, to be sure, but still an impractically short distance to transmit a message.

Modifying his design several times, Marconi gradually increased the transmission distance to 300 yards, then to 2 miles, and, in 1889, the width of the English Channel. This was more like what the early dreamers of wireless telegraphy had hoped for.

Marconi demonstrated the almost unlimited potential of radio waves in 1901, when he bridged the Atlantic Ocean with a signal — the letter *s* — in Morse code. It traveled from Poldhu, Cornwall, to a wired kite that served as the receiving antenna at St. John's, Newfoundland, a distance of almost 2000 miles. Radio, now, was just waiting to be born.

Radio, 1906; United States

In 1906, Lee De Forest, a thirty-three-year-old American inventor, built the first amplifying **vacuum tube,** which was almost immediately wedded with Marconi's wireless invention to produce radio. An experimental station at Brant Rock, Massachusetts, built by a Canadian, Reginald Aubrey Fessenden, is credited with broadcasting the first radio program — on Christmas Eve, 1906. For this momentous occasion Fessenden arranged a modest program of two short musical selections, followed by the reading of one poem, then a brief holiday greeting by himself. The broadcast was heard, and greatly appreciated, by ship wireless operators within a radius of several hundred miles.

The following year De Forest began regular radio broadcasts from his headquarters in lower Manhattan. The early shows were similar to today's D.J. programs in that De Forest played only phonograph records (provided by Columbia records). Since there still were no home radio receivers, De Forest's audience was ship wireless operators in New York Harbor.

Despite the great novelty that radio undeniably was, it did not become an overnight success for the simple reason that only a few people — in fact, only wireless telegraphy buffs — owned receivers. There was a proliferation of amateur radio stations after restrictions placed on airwaves during World War I were lifted, but even these stations had a broadcast range of only a couple of miles and could be heard only by other amateurs who had adequate receiving apparatus. Thus, for its first several years, radio broadcasting was pursued strictly as a hobby.

The first person to envision the mass appeal of radio was David Sarnoff, a leading radio pioneer of the 1920s. Sarnoff, who later became the head of the Radio Corporation of America and its affiliate, the National Broadcasting Company, had had the prescience as far back as 1916, when he was still a manager at the American Marconi Wireless Company, to predict that one day there would be a radio receiver in every home: "A radio music box can be supplied with amplifying tubes and a loudspeaking telephone, all of which can be neatly mounted in a box."

The first **daily radio broadcasts** began in 1910 from the Charles Herrold School of Radio Broadcasting in San Jose, California, which is still operating today as station KCBS, San Francisco, making it the world's oldest continuously run radio station. Just a year earlier, Marconi shared the Nobel Prize in physics with Karl Braun, who made important modifications that considerably increased the range of the first Marconi transmitters.

The first modern **commercial radio station** was KDKA in Pittsburgh, which began broadcasting with the Harding-Cox presidential election returns on November 2, 1920; it also played music and presented the day's news. Other "ham" operators noted KDKA's

Famous Debuts: "Amos n' Andy," March 19, 1928; "The Ed Sullivan Show," November 20, 1929; "The Jack Benny Program" and "The Burns and Allen Show," 1932; "The Bob Hope Show," 1934.

success, applied for public broadcasting licenses, and joined the embryonic business. By the end of 1921, eight commercial stations were offering news commentary and music over the American airwaves. By the mid-1930s almost every American household had a radio.

FM Radio, 1941; United States

"AM is for Average Music, FM for Fancy Music." Though technically incorrect, of course, that sentiment, spoken by a young man from a coal-mining town in rural Pennsylvania, did accurately characterize for many people the early days of FM radio, when it broadcast only classical music, leaving pop songs to AM stations.

FM, which stands for frequency modulation (AM stands for amplitude modulation), was invented by Edwin Howard Armstrong in an attempt to bring crystal clarity to high frequencies and rich resonance to base notes, all with a minimum of static and distortion.

One might think that FM's inventor would have been greeted by salvoes of praise, and that his invention would have been immediately welcomed into the marketplace. But the development of FM radio, despite its great promise, which was recognized immediately by everyone, was for many years mired hopelessly in red tape and sordid politics. The American solons of progress besmirched Armstrong's reputation, and their hectoring ultimately led to his suicide.

Armstrong had devised one of the first effective AM radio receivers while still a college student in 1912. But as a music lover, he was displeased with the distortion and static produced by his and other early receivers. He realized that the problem was due in large part to the fact that stations broadcast in AM, which, as its name implies, can boost a signal's amplitude (or volume) but is incapable of strengthening its frequency, the more important component of sound, particularly for music, which has a range of frequencies far exceeding that of the human voice.

Armstrong, whose inventive genius is often compared with Edison's, built the first frequency modulating transmitter. His early tests, launched from atop the Empire State Building in an experimental studio loaned to him by the newly formed Radio Corporation of America, proved his point. Music transmitted by FM was virtually free of static and possessed a fidelity hitherto impossible to obtain with AM. Surely, thought a pleased young Armstrong, radio broadcasting was about to be revolutionized.

But he was wrong. Fearful that its vast expenditures in AM broadcasting would be undermined and its prominence in radio severely encroached on, RCA, along with other networks, involved Armstrong in endless litigation, making him an outcast in the industry. Even the Federal Communications Commission, influenced by the networks' hostility toward Armstrong, assigned the entire FM band to an unfavorable broadcasting range and severely restricted the transmission wattage of FM radio stations. Soon the FCC issued further rules that placed other restrictions on FM broadcasting and almost halted its growth.

Armstrong plunged into depression. He had for years fought the broadcasting industry and the FCC, opening a skeleton chain of FM stations throughout New England to give that area the first high-quality radio music; now these stations were in jeopardy. Singlehandedly he had devised almost all the basic circuitry that is used in FM broadcasting today; now there was a chance that under a new FCC ruling all that equipment would become obsolete. In 1954, with his many ingenious patents threatened by corporate lawsuits, Armstrong leaped from his Park Avenue apartment to his death.

Motion Pictures, 1877; United States

The evolution of cinema machines was a gradual process, and the prehistory of motion pictures spans a period almost as long as its present history. It is a story of genius and duplicity, in which one great inventor, Thomas Edison, at first took only modest interest in the medium, then did an about-face and claimed credit for other people's ideas and for inventing the motion picture himself. In short, it's a tale worthy of becoming a movie.

Eadweard Muybridge was the first person to apply the principles of still photography to motion.

An English adventurer who had settled in California after the gold rush of 1849, Muybridge was hired in 1872 by Governor Leland Stanford to help him win a $25,000 bet. Stanford, a horse fancier of both breeding and racing, had wagered with a contemporary that at some point in a horse's gallop, all four of its hooves left the ground. To capture the rapid motion, Muybridge strung twelve still cameras along a racetrack, stretching strings across the track, each attached to the shutter of one camera. As the horse galloped past the cameras, its hooves successively caught the strings and snapped them, releasing the camera shutters and taking a sequence of rapid-fire pictures. Stanford won his bet.

Muybridge, meanwhile, realized he had created something unique. The original galloping of the horse could be resynchronized if the still photographs were mounted on a revolving wheel and projected with an intense lantern. Though what he had was not actually motion pictures, Muybridge captivated crowds with his contraption for more than twenty years.

The first true motion pictures taken with a single camera rolled in 1882.

Etienne-Jules Marey, a Frenchman, constructed a cylindrical photographic plate behind a lens that captured twelve images in one second as the plate executed a full rotation. Marey had produced multiple exposures. But if motion pictures were to become anything more than a mere curiosity, someone would have to develop a photographic-recording medium that could rapidly capture thousands of multiple exposures — **film.**

Enter Thomas Edison, a genius who was not keen on letting rival inventors secure a foothold in the fledgling profession. Edison, already prominent for a number of inventions, in 1888 took out a patent application for what he called an "optical phonograph." Though this may sound like today's new video discs, it was actually a moving film strip, finally developed in 1891 by Edison's employee William Dickson.

Several film strips were run in May of that year before members of the National Federation of Women's Clubs, who often lunched with Edison's wife. Motion was frequently erratic, since the film strips did not have sprockets, an invention that Dickson added the following year and for which Edison took all the credit. (Dickson eventually quarreled with Edison and left the laboratory.) Edison's film strips were not designed for projection onto a screen; they were to be viewed in a box called a Kinetoscope (also an invention of Dickson's for which Edison claimed credit) by one person at a time.

On February 1, 1893, Edison opened the world's first **motion picture studio** at his laboratories in West Orange, New Jersey. After producing numerous film strips to be viewed through the Kinetoscope, Edison opened the first **movie theater** on April 14, 1894, at 1155 Broadway, New York City. For a nickel, a customer could watch a brief film strip of the great body-builder, Eugene Sandow, lifting weights and performing gymnastics; or of Buffalo Bill mounting a horse and shooting his pistols. The "peep-show" theater was a great success.

Film projection onto a screen, however, already was underway in other countries. Which country was first, though, remains open to debate almost a century later. Though the Edison laboratory indisputably built the first motion picture camera, Edison personally opposed projecting pictures on a large screen, believing it had no future. Since this revelation was made known, many countries have claimed the motion picture as their invention, including England (inventor: William Friese-Greene), France (Louis-Jean and August Lumière, brothers who introduced the word "cinema"), and Germany (Max and Emil Skladanowsky). These inventors either patented machines for projecting motion pictures or actually began projecting pictures in public before Edison's name became associated with the discovery.

That occurred in 1896, with the invention of the **Vitascope,** or the Edison Projector, a device that really depended heavily on the work of another American inventor, Thomas Armat. The Vitascope was Edison's entrance into projection; and with a stockpile of films on a variety of subjects, he immediately dominated the market.

The triumphant debut of a projected film to a paying audience in the United States took place on April 23, 1896, at Koster and Bial's Music Hall at 34th Street and Broadway (the present site of Macy's department store). The *Dramatic Mirror* gave it an enthusiastic review:

> The first picture shown was the Leigh Sisters in their umbrella dance. The effect was the same as if the girls were there on stage; all their smiles and kicks and bows were seen. The second picture represented the breaking of waves on the seashore. Wave after wave came tumbling on the sand, and as they struck, broke into tiny floods just like the real thing. Some people in the front rows seemed to be afraid they were going to get wet, and looked about to see where they could run to, in case the waves came too close.

Other film milestones appeared in rapid succession. The origins of such techniques as **slow-motion, dissolve,** and **fade-in, fade-out** were all pioneered by the French experimental cinematographer Georges Méliés in his films *Cinderella* (1900) and *A Trip to the Moon* (1902).

The first **3-D film,** *The Power of Love,* was made in 1922, long before the gimmick reached its peak popularity in the 1950s, when the studios used it as a means to lure audiences back to the theaters.

Edwin S. Porter's *Great Train Robbery* in 1903 heralded the first successful **close-ups,** and also was the first American-made film with a coherent plot. In 1912, to the delight of thousands, the French stage actress Sarah Bernhardt originated the **star system,** appearing in the title role in *Queen Elizabeth,* a French film distributed in the United States by Adolph Zukor. With the major cinematic techniques well established, and the star system underway, the modern motion picture had arrived.

Television, 1926; England

Almost half a century before television became a reality, it had been a feasible invention, with the fundamental principles independently developed to varying degrees in Germany, England, Scotland, France, Russia, and the United States. One reason this apotheosis of communication devices did not come about sooner was that there was poor communication among its many pioneers; another was that the ideas were beyond the state of technology that was available at the time.

The single major principle on which all forms of modern television operate — the rapid scanning of a scene line by line to build up a picture — had been proposed as early as the 1880s by W. E. Sawyer in the United States and Maurice Leblanc in France. A device that could accomplish this feat — a mechanical-to-rotary wheel that broke down and reconstructed an image — was developed in 1884 in Germany by a twenty-four-year-old inventor, Paul Nipkow.

But perhaps the most remarkable contribution to television came in 1908 from the Scottish electrical engineer A. Campbell Swinton, who outlined a method that, in all its essential details, is the basis for modern television. He proposed to use two scanning cathode ray tubes, magnetically deflected at both the camera and the receiving screen. Swinton's brilliant ideas, as well as those of Sawyer, Leblanc, and Nipkow, were left to others to put into practice almost two decades later.

Meanwhile, experimenters in England and the United States were trying something less ambitious. The neon gas discharge lamp, developed in the United States in 1917, made it possible to project various shades of gray on a receiving tube, simply by varying the input current fed to the tube. This was modulated light, and just the thing John Logie Baird in England and Charles Francis Jenkins in the United States had been eagerly awaiting. Working independently, both men by 1923 were combining the modulated light and Nipkow's scanning wheel to reconstruct a scene in line-by-line sweeps.

The British beat the Americans by two years. On October 2, 1925, in the attic of his home, Baird succeeded in transmitting a recognizable image of the head of a discarded ventriloquist's dummy named Bill. He then hurried down to the office on the ground

floor and persuaded a startled office boy to come up to his laboratory. The frightened boy, sitting under bright lamps, became the
first living image to be transmitted by television. Overnight Baird
became famous. In 1927 he made a transmission from London to
Glasgow, and in 1928 from London to New York.

The Americans entered the picture, so to speak, in 1927, and
with a clearer image on their screen. That year Jenkins set up the
first intercity television transmission in the United States; it was
not done over the airwaves but by wire, connecting the secretary
of commerce, Herbert Hoover, in Baltimore, with the New York
office of the president of AT&T, Walter Gifford. The ghostly image appeared on a 2.5-inch screen in Gifford's office, and since
there was no sound transmission, the two men communicated
during the broadcast by telephone.

Television Broadcasting, 1931; United States

Experimental television broadcasts began in the United States in
1928, and in England in 1929. But this was not really television
that anyone would want to watch. Even researchers who had to
watch for long periods of time developed eyestrain and splitting
headaches. The problems were inherent in the use of the neon
light source and Nipkow's rotating wheel — both were crude sub-
stitutions for Swinton's brilliant idea of using a scanning cathode
ray tube.

Just such a tube was patented in 1930 by Philo T. Farnsworth,
a twenty-one-year-old inventor. The same year, Vladimir Zwory-
kin of the Radio Corporation of America devised a superior television camera. So important were these two inventions to the birth
of modern television broadcasting that for the first time RCA was
forced to pay royalties to an outside inventor — Farnsworth. RCA
began its experimental station, W2RBX, in New York on July 30,
1930. One of the first scheduled television shows, broadcast on
Tuesday evening, July 21, 1931, introduced Kate Smith, singing
"When the Moon Comes Over the Mountain."

By the early 1940s there were twenty-three television stations in
operation throughout the United States. World War II precluded
expansion, but when wartime restrictions were lifted in 1946, television mushroomed. By 1949 more than a million sets were in use,
and the number had increased tenfold two years later. By 1959

America had more than 50 million television sets in households across the country.

Phonograph, 1877; United States

A Frenchman almost invented the phonograph. Léon Scott, a French inventor, in 1857 constructed a device he called the phonautograph. The machine traced wavy lines, representing sound, on the smoked surface of a rotating cylinder. Scott never perfected his device. But twenty years later, on November 20, 1877, at his laboratory in Menlo Park, New Jersey, Thomas Edison used the same basic principle to construct the machine into which he shouted, "Mary had a little lamb," and then heard it played back in recognizable fidelity. It was the first time the human voice had been recorded and then reproduced, heralding the birth of a new multimillion-dollar industry.

Edison's phonograph, developed jointly with his assistant John

"Mary had a little lamb" was the first "record."

Kreusi, was elegantly simple. Tin foil wrapped around a rotating cylinder was scratched by the point of a stylus, or vibrating recording needle. Sound waves were recorded as variations in the depth of the grooves, a process later known as hill-and-dale recording. To play back the recorded sound, the grooves were again run under the stylus, and the mechanical vibrations were transformed into electrical signals and then into sound waves.

For the next ten years Edison worked to improve the quality of sound recordings. In 1887 at his newly constructed laboratory at West Orange, he replaced the hand-crank mechanism with an electric motor, and substituted wax for tin foil on the recording cylinder. The same year a German inventor living in the United States, Emile Berliner, produced the first phonograph **disc,** which eventually replaced Edison's cumbersome cylinder, although during the discs' first few years of production, Berliner saw them chiefly as toys for curious children and adults. Berliner's first discs were made of zinc, coated with a thin layer of fatty substance and etched in an acid bath.

Many luminaries of the era, such as Alfred Lord Tennyson, Robert Browning, and Johannes Brahms, were easily cajoled by Edison into making recordings. Brahms played a Hungarian rhapsody for the representatives Edison sent abroad armed with phonograph and cylinders. The first **classical recording,** however, was made at Edison's New Jersey laboratory in 1888 by a Polish pianist and child prodigy, twelve-year-old Josef Hofmann.

That same year Edison persuaded the German pianist and conductor Hans von Bülow to record a Chopin mazurka. Impressed with the results, von Bülow invited Edison to the Metropolitan Opera House in New York City to attempt a symphonic recording of a program he was to conduct. The evening's offerings were Beethoven's Symphony No. 3, the "Eroica"; Wagner's *Die Meistersinger* overture; and one of Haydn's "London" symphonies in B-flat Major. It marked the first recording of **symphonic music.**

*

For many years disc records were 78s, called by the number of revolutions per minute. They were brittle, scratched easily, and had to be turned over frequently, since a side did not play for very long.

The first long-playing **33 1/3 record** was demonstrated by RCA in 1931 and, to prove the point, contained Beethoven's entire Fifth Symphony (with Leopold Stokowski conducting the Philadelphia

Orchestra). RCA knew that LPs would be expensive, but they had not counted on the Depression, which shrank the market for many years. LPs did not begin replacing 78s until after 1948, when inventor Peter Goldmark of the Columbia Broadcasting System made technological improvements in the records that raised their fidelity and lowered their price.

Stereo, 1881; France

Today we think of stereo in terms of records and tapes, but it was originally developed for an entirely unrelated device — the telephone — as part of the 1881 Paris Electrical Exhibition.

About a hundred years ago, Clément Ader, a French engineer who later became known for exploits as an aviation pioneer, was working arduously to improve the telephone, which Alexander Graham Bell had invented only five years earlier. Ader made a crude but elaborate stereo sound system by placing eighty telephone transmitters around the stage of the Paris Opéra. He wired the phones to telephone receivers in a hotel suite of four rooms in the Palais de l'Industrie, several miles away. Visitors at the exhibition sauntered to the hotel phone hook-up and listened with amazement to the quality of sound being broadcast live from the Opéra stage. Actually, Ader's transmission process closely resembled those used today by radio stations and record companies, now called binaural stereo reproduction.

Ader was never quite certain what to do with his invention. The phonograph had only recently been invented, and faithful monaural recording was difficult enough. It was not until the 1930s, after the development of the record disc, that stereo, as well as high fidelity, began to draw the serious attention of researchers.

Many scientists contributed to the invention, and the patent for hi-fi stereo is shared internationally, with the inventor's claim awarded to Bell Laboratories of the United States. They successfully made the first stereo recording at the Academy of Music in Philadelphia on March 12, 1932, when Leopold Stokowski, an avid supporter of stereo sound, conducted the orchestra in a rehearsal of Scriabin's *Poem of Fire*.

The early inventors of stereo were looking for a way to create an illusion for the listener of being present at a live concert. Ader and others had attempted to duplicate orchestral sound with a multiplicity of recording microphones or transmitters. Alan Dower Blumlein, an English inventor included in the stereo patent, discarded this overly ambitious goal and sought instead a technique for fooling the ears and brain into believing that they are experiencing actual orchestral richness. He discovered that music came across in stereo if he recorded two channels of sound in a single disc groove.

The technique works because the human brain and ear localize a sound source by using a consensus of opinion derived from several factors (when sight is excluded): primarily the amplitude of the sound and the phase difference — the difference in arrival time of a signal — between the two ears. Blumlein's contribution involved converting phase differences in the original sound into differences in amplitude that could easily be recorded in a disc's grooves. When signals containing these artificial differences in amplitude are reproduced from a pair of loudspeakers, each loudspeaker communicates with each ear.

Ader filed for and received a patent for his stereo technique. But the number of subsequent stereo innovations was so huge that Ader's technique was forgotten, rediscovered, repatented, forgotten again, then discovered a third time. The latest discovery came in the 1970s, when inventors turned to the binaural technique for its simplicity in producing what appeared for a while to be a new trend in recording listening pleasure, quadraphonic sound.

19

Music: Renaissance to Rock

Music, 3500 B.C.; Mesopotamia

Early men struck sticks together to frighten away beasts. In time these "clappers" came to be used rhythmically to accompany work songs in the fields and thus ease the hardships of labor. The clappers also were used in dance rituals to please the gods and bring good harvests. Hence music was born.

Though such theories must remain speculative, it is clear that the cradle of Western music was the fertile area between the Tigris and the Euphrates rivers, known as Mesopotamia. The Sumerians, the Babylonians, and the Assyrians, who flourished in this region from about 3500 to 500 B.C., left remains of every basic type of musical instrument:

Idiophones, devices like the triangle, which when struck resonate as a whole;

Aerophones, tubular devices that resonate a column of blown air;

Cordophones, with strings to be plucked or struck; and

Membranophones, made of animal skins stretched over a resonating cavity.

A hymn engraved in stone, dating from 800 B.C., is evidence that the Mesopotamians had even developed a primitive system of musical notation.

Playing an ancient drum, or membran-ophone, made of animal skin stretched over a resonating cavity.

Of eastern Mediterranean cultures, it was the Greeks who furnished the most direct link with musical development in Western Europe. Two Greek religious cults — one devoted to Apollo, the other to Dionysus — became the prototypes for the two esthetic poles, Classical and Romantic, that thread throughout Western cultural history.

Chant, 4th Century A.D.; Italy

With the decline of the Roman Empire, the institution destined to perpetuate and expand the musical heritage of antiquity was the Christian Church. By the early 4th century a form of music called plainsong or plainchant had developed. It was monophonic (with only a melody line), normally sung *a cappella* (without instrumental accompaniment), employed no time signatures, and was sung in Latin.

In Milan, the 4th-century bishop Ambrose first codified this growing repertoire of chants, and the body of music became known as **Ambrosian chant.**

The music was reorganized in the 6th century by Pope Gregory I and then became known as **Gregorian chant,** which encompassed a vast body of traditional melodies that was the foundation for the later development of Western music. During this time the church developed strict rules governing how music could be played and sung; for example, melodies could be sung only in unison.

Harmony, Middle Ages; Europe

Music consisting of two or more vocal parts — called polyphony — emerged gradually during the Middle Ages. The lack of definite knowledge regarding its origin has given rise to several plausible theories: it resulted from singers with different natural vocal ranges singing at their most comfortable pitch levels; it was a practice of organists adopted by singers; or it came about when the repetition of a melody at a different pitch level was sung simultaneously with the original statement of the melody.

Whatever motivated this dramatic departure from traditional monophony, it was already established in A.D. 900, when it was described in *Musica enchiriadis,* a manual for singers, and one of the major musical documents of the Middle Ages. Polyphony was a revolutionary concept destined to give an entirely new direction to the art of sound.

Wandering Minstrels, 7th Century; Europe

The earliest accounts of men who made an occupation of traveling from one locale to another, singing songs and performing acrobatics, are from the early Middle Ages. The Goliards were itinerant minor clerics and students who, from the 7th century on, roamed the land, singing and playing topical songs, satirical and often scabrous, dealing with love, war, famine, and other issues of the day. They began a practice that would be popularized by three notable groups: *troubadours, Minnesingers,* and *Meistersingers.*

Troubadours, 12th Century; France

Partially motivated by the code of chivalry spread by the Crusades, many of the noblemen in southern France took up a new life style. Calling themselves troubadours, they circulated among the leading courts of the region, devoting themselves to writing and singing poetry in the vernacular. The movement flourished in Provence during the 12th and 13th centuries. About the middle of the 13th century, some aristocrats in northern France, among them Adam de la Halle, took up the pastime, calling themselves *trouvères.* Approximately 2600 poems and 260 melodies of the troubadours have been preserved, and 1400 of the *trouvères'* melodies.

Minnesingers, 12th Century; Germany

German counterparts of the troubadours, the *Minnesingers* ("love singers") flourished from the 12th to the 14th centuries. They produced a literature of German poetry and song *(Minnelied)* dealing with a variety of subjects, including those of a religious nature. The most typical song was performed in three sections: first the melodic phrase was sung, then it was repeated with a different line of text; and this was followed by a new melodic phrase. Many of the *Minnesingers* hailed from German aristocracy.

Meistersingers, 15th Century; Germany

Where the *Minnesingers* often hailed from aristocracy, their successors, the *Meistersingers* ("master singers") were members of middle-class guilds. They flourished during the 15th and 16th centuries, and their music, called *Meistergesang,* was created and governed by strict rules. The most famous of all *Meistersingers* was Hans Sachs, who was later immortalized in Richard Wagner's opera *Die Meistersinger von Nürnberg.*

Wandering Minstrel

Musical Notation, 9th Century; Italy

Staff notation had its roots in the "neumes" of plainchant and secular song of the 9th to 12th centuries. Neumes were graphic signs indicating the rise and fall of the voice.

Their origin lies probably in signs devised by Greek and Roman grammarians 1100 years earlier to guide declamation, such as ╱, *acutus* (high voice), ╲, *gravis* (low), and ∧, *circumflexus* (falling). The musical adaptations of these signs took many different regional forms.

Unlike the note symbol, which developed later, each neum usually comprised several notes and indicated their approximate relative pitches. The notes signified by a neum belonged to a single syllable of text, though in elaborate chant the notes of a single syllable might be split up into several neumes.

Neumes were intended only as a memory aid to singers who knew words and melody by heart. Between the 10th and 12th centuries, however, there occurred significant developments leading toward a notation that could be sight-read.

The first important step toward indicating exact pitch, initiated near the end of the 10th century, was the introduction of a horizontal line, representing the tone F, above or below which neumes were written. This was the origin of the **staff.**

Soon afterward, two-line staves in color were used to indicate the tones F (upper line in red) and C (lower line in green or yellow). By the 11th century four-line staves were described by the musician Guido d'Arezzo. This is the staff used in Gregorian notation.

Additional lines gradually were added, up to eleven or more, then separated into two staves by the elimination of the middle-C line. Eventually, by about the 13th century, five-line staves, which are used today, came into favor.

Bars entered staff notation in the 17th century, but regularly spaced barring came only in the 18th century. Separate **tempo** indications, arising first in the 17th century, were verbally expressed: for example, *adagio, largo, presto.* The **metronome mark,** an absolute indication of tempo, originated in Beethoven's time.

The indications for loud and soft, **dynamics,** arose early in the 17th century, expressed by words like *forte, mezzoforte, piano;* only later were these abbreviated as *f, mf, p.* Graphic signs for dynamics and attack, such as the **staccato dot** and the **crescendo mark,** appeared in the 18th century.

Fugue, 1330; France

It is often said that the fugue is the most complex and highly developed type of composition in Western music. The term "fugue," from *fuga,* the Latin word for "flight," was first used about 1330 by Jacques de Liège, the author of *Speculum musicae,* an important medieval treatise.

At that time fugue referred to a technique of musical writing based on strict imitation. Later, after its emergence as an independent musical form in the 17th century, the fugue became a composition in counterpoint based on a generating theme, in which different parts, or voices, enter successively in imitation, as if in pursuit of each other. Heir of all compositional techniques that had developed earlier, the fugue differs from its ancestors (the *motet,* the *ricercar,* the *canzona*) in having a more specifically total character, unity of form, and a greater economy.

The fugue reached its peak through the genius of J. S. Bach. Each of his fugues amazes by the freshness of its inspiration, the wonders of its writing, or by its gigantic proportions. These are marvelously represented in the two volumes of *The Well-Tempered Clavier* (1722–1744), two sets of twenty-four preludes and fugues going through the cycle of the twenty-four major and minor keys.

Renaissance Music, 15th Century; Flanders

The first true Renaissance music was largely the work of Flemish composers — some six generations of them in all between 1400 and 1570. They spurred musical development in France, Italy, Germany, Spain, and England.

It is surprising that such a small region as Flanders, in what is now northern Belgium, should have produced such an enormous amount of talent. But at a time when its larger neighbors were engaged in long and disruptive wars, or suffering the effects of plague, Flanders — then part of the French dukedom of Burgundy — had a stable, highly developed, and thriving middle class that was relatively free, fond of the arts, and ready to patronize

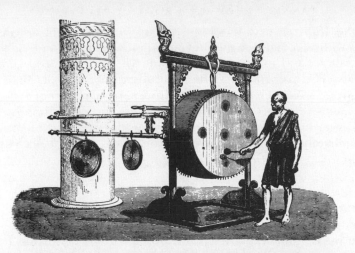

Chinese Gong. Chinese writings claim that Oriental music originated in 2697 B.C. The emperor Huang Ti sent a scholar to the mountains to cut bamboo pipes that could emit sounds matching the call of the phoenix.

its artists. Musical education in the cathedral choir schools of Flanders and northern France was one of the chief factors that contributed to this wealth of talent. Musical composition was taught, as well as singing, and every chorister therefore had the opportunity to emerge as a composer.

Jean d'Okeghem, born in 1430, was one of the most important 15th-century Flemish Renaissance composers, and his 36-part motet was held to be one of the wonders of the world. He was master of the king's chapel in Paris during the reign of Charles VII.

This century also marked the birth of the **madrigal** in Italy.

Chamber Music, 1450; Germany

In its original sense chamber music referred to music composed for the home, as opposed to that written for the theater or church.

Since the "home" could often be as small as a drawing room (or as large as a palace chamber), the music was composed for a small ensemble, dispensed with a conductor, and permitted no more than one player to a part.

This new "home music" sprang up in Germany in the middle

of the 15th century. It was customary to supply folk-song melodies with two or three countermelodies, to expand and elaborate the whole, and to arrange the result for small groups of instruments. The instruments to be used often were not specified; they might be whatever was available in a particular home. When instruments were specified, they usually were strings and winds. Since not every home had instruments, a considerable body of the original chamber music was written for voices without accompaniment.

Sonata, 1561; Italy

The word "sonata" comes from the past participle of the Italian verb *sonare,* "to sound."

"Sonata" originally denoted a composition played on instruments, as opposed to "cantata," sung by voices. Its first such use was in 1561, when it was applied to a suite of dances for lute. The term has since acquired other meanings; most frequently it refers to a composition in two or more movements, played by one or two instruments.

Baroque Era, 17th Century; Italy

Baroque music originated in Italy at the beginning of the 17th century as a new expressive style of singing modeled on natural speech. It is also the music of the first operas.

The genius of Claudio Monteverdi, who was master of music at St. Mark's Church in Venice for thirty years, beginning in 1613, was able to embrace both old and new musical styles. The richness of his sacred and secular music (especially his operas) stems largely from his imaginative synthesis of both traditions. In contrast to older "analytical" or "architectural" music, an urgency to express emotions came to dominate the music of the Baroque age, a trend that sometimes led to excessive ornamentation.

The Baroque era reached its zenith in the work of Johann Sebastian Bach and George Frederic Handel. Both were born in the same year, 1685, in the same part of Germany; both were reared in the Lutheran Church, and both were primarily organists. But because of different environmental circumstances, each became a master of a different musical form.

Handel, because of his conditioning in Italy, was primarily a dramatic composer, writing operas, oratorios, and secular cantatas, mostly after he moved to England. He also wrote extensively for orchestra and instrumental ensemble.

Bach, by contrast, was influenced by his lifelong employment in the church and by his dedication as a teacher. His works therefore include passions, cantatas for church services, liturgical organ pieces, and harpsicord compositions, many of which were intended to be instructional.

Opera, 1597; Florence

Our word "opera" is an abbreviation of the Italian phrase *opera in musica,* "work in music," and today represents a form of theater consisting of a dramatic text or libretto ("little book") combined with singing and instrumental accompaniment. Though works in antiquity had combined poetic drama and music, thus intimating later operatic developments, the earliest universally accepted true operas first appeared in late-16th-century Italy.

The unique literary-musical texture that is opera originated in the city of Florence, among a coterie of intellectuals and artists who gathered regularly at the palazzo of the theatrical impresario Jacopo Corsi during the 1590s. This group included three notables in the history of music: Emilio de' Cavalieri, the composer who was to write what is often called the first **oratorio,** *Rappresentatione di anima et di corpo (The Representation of Body and Soul);* composer-singer Jacopo Peri, who would write the first opera; and the composer Claudio Monteverdi, who later wrote opera's first masterpiece, *La Favola d'Orfeo (The Fable of Orpheus),* which is still staged today.

This talented group, which also included the poet Tasso, devised small theatrical dramas with musical accompaniment and solo vocal lines, with the intent of reviving ancient Greek theater. To them, words were more important than the accompanying music, so they dispensed with the complex polyphony of the day and adopted monophony, that is, the accompaniment of singing or recitation on musical tones of one melody at a time. This new use of monophony was what eventually led, after many false starts, to the emergence not only of opera as it exists today, but also of the cantata and the oratorio.

The distinction of being deemed the "first opera" goes to Peri's

Giuseppe Verdi conducting one of his own operas

Dafne, with text by the Renaissance pastoral poet Ottavio Rinuccini. It was staged in Corsi's palazzo during the pre-Lenten carnival of 1597–1598. The text, divided into a prologue and six scenes, was published in 1600 and survives, but all that remains of Peri's music is the prologue and one aria. The earliest opera to survive in both music and text is also by Peri: a setting of Rinuccini's pastoral *Euridice,* also in a prologue and six scenes, which was staged at the Palazzo Pitti in Florence on October 6, 1600.

Opera soon was imported by France, but because of the popularity of spoken drama there, and the novelty of the new dance form, ballet, opera did not become a French art until the time of Jean-Baptiste Lully in the last half of the 17th century. One Frenchman of letters, Charles de Saint-Evremond, called it "a bizarre thing in which the poet and the composer go to endless trouble to produce a wretched result."

Opera had an equally hard time getting a foothold in England, where it had to compete with the popular court masque, an aristocratic entertainment derived largely from ballet. The English statesman Lord Chesterfield saw operas as theater "too absurd and extravagant to mention. I look upon them as a magic scene contrived to please the eyes and the ears at the expense of the understanding." The first, and perhaps still the finest, English opera was *Dido and Aeneas,* by Henry Purcell, which was first sung in 1689 by the pupils at a girls' school in London.

Classical Era, 18th Century; Austria

The Classical period, which rose on the foundations of the Enlightenment in response to the overdeveloped, ornamental style of High Baroque music, found two masters in Franz Joseph Haydn and Wolfgang Amadeus Mozart. Their Classical style distinguished itself from the many-voiced Baroque and Rococo by its greater clarity and simplicity of thematic treatment and chordal accompaniment.

The prolific Haydn, a short, dark man with a face pitted by smallpox, was born in 1732 and is considered the father of the Classical period. The Classical composer *par excellence,* he was in many ways the typical figure of the Enlightenment: moderately religious, moderately daring, intelligent but not aggressively so, adventurous but not nearly so revolutionary as his contemporary, Mozart. With Haydn, everything was in intellectual and emotional balance.

Mozart, born in Salzburg in 1756, was one of the most exploited child prodigies in the history of music, and he paid the price, growing into an envious, cantankerous adult — who happened to produce sublime music. Drawing on Haydn, the Italian influence, and his own immense genius, he proved a brilliant exponent of every musical form bequeathed by his predecessors. He lived only thirty-five years, but in that short span gave the world a legacy of music equaled only by Beethoven.

Romantic Era, 19th Century; Germany

Ludwig von Beethoven's third symphony, the "Eroica," written in 1803, marked the end of the Classical period and the beginning of the Romantic style in music.

Having absorbed Classical elements from Haydn and Mozart (whose last three symphonies to a degree prefigure Romanticism), Beethoven embarked on a course that in music is parallel to the emergence of the Romantic concept of the liberated individual. The "Eroica" itself is a pivotal work in this respect, revealing a powerful impetus that was to burst forth in his later compositions.

Beethoven was the first composer whose personality and character made a purposeful impact on the types and style of music he composed. Inspired by the revolutionary forces of the times, he declared himself a free artistic agent, with neither allegiance nor responsibility to any patron. He transformed the standard Classical forms of sonata, symphony, concerto, and quartet by infusing them with a powerful emotional intensity.

Subjectivity replaced the formalism of the Classical period, in that impulse and inspiration played a major role in the motivation of both the composer and the performer; and the listener's response was expected to be more sensory than intellectual.

Several new forms of composition originated in the Romantic era, principally the **concert overture,** the **symphonic poem** (later called the tone poem), and the **symphonic suite** and **symphonic variations.** The most popular instrument of the period was the piano, and among the great Romantic composers who wrote for the instrument were Chopin, Schumann, Liszt, and Brahms.

Modern Era, 20th Century; France and Vienna

Striking changes in musical style occurred about 1900, marking a major turning point in the history of Western music. Never before had change been so rapid, and never before had there been such a diversity of styles. Conventions that had governed Western music for centuries were giving way to the intense search for new expression in sound, first in atonal, and then in electronic music.

Harmony in music began to disintegrate in reaction to the lush sounds of the chromatic music cultivated by Richard Wagner from 1865 to the 1880s. French composer Claude Debussy, using a whole-tone scale of five tones, free treatment of rhythms, and subtle dynamics of loudness and softness, turned away from Wagner in 1902 when he composed the atonal and Impressionist opera *Pelleas and Melisande.*

Perhaps the first truly 20th-century composer, Debussy, born in 1862 at St.-Germain-en-Laye just outside Paris, first suggested a dramatic change in musical style with his revolutionary 1894 *Prelude to the Afternoon of a Faun.* He certainly prefigured the developments in atonality that would soon occur in Vienna, led by Arnold Schoenberg.

The first ten years of the new century witnessed convulsive changes in the arts and sciences. Sigmund Freud published *The Interpretation of Dreams* in 1900, the same year Max Planck announced his quantum theory, radically altering the view of energy as a continuous wave, replacing it with discrete particles. Three years later the Wright brothers realized the age-old dream of powered flight. Albert Einstein in 1905 published his special theory of relativity, revamping forever the concepts of space and time. And in 1910 Vassily Kandinsky painted his first full nonrepresentational work, launching a new era in painting. Thus it is not surprising that within that same active, tumultuous decade, in the year 1908, Arnold Schoenberg composed his *Book of the Hanging Gardens,* destroying completely the long-held concept of harmony and tonality, replacing it with dissonance — or as many called it, noise.

Schoenberg, born in Vienna in 1874, liked to say that he was committed to the "emancipation of dissonance." In 1912 he produced the classic *Sprechstimme* ("speech-melody") work, *Pierrot Lunaire,* for five musicians and a reciter who loops and slides through the poems rather than singing them. Stravinsky, himself a modern giant, called *Pierrot Lunaire* "the mind and solar plexus of early twentieth-century music."

Electronic Music, 1895; United States

Following closely on the dissonance of atonal music, electronic music represented a further search for new modes of musical expression, this time through modern scientific technology.

An American, Thaddeus Cahill, made the first attempt to generate musical sounds electronically. At his home in Massachusetts in 1895, he assembled rotary generators and telephone receivers, converting electrical impulses into sound waves. Thaddeus named his device the Telharmonium and worked to perfect it for more than a decade. When it finally debuted at a public demonstration in Holyoke, Massachusetts, it was a complete failure. Beset by engineering complexities, and an inability to project sound more than a few feet from the transmitters (because loudspeakers and amplifiers had yet to be invented), the Telharmonium softly grunted, groaned, and squeaked.

In Italy, the Futurist painter Luigi Russolo also was experimenting with electronic music. His approach was more radical. Russolo proposed in 1913 that all music be destroyed and that new instruments derived solely from electronics technology of the day be fashioned to perform music appropriately expressive of the industrialized age. Russolo's electronic instruments, which really were noise generators, grated, hissed, rumbled, scratched, and shrieked, and understandably never caught on.

Though Cahill's instrument had failed, his views on electronic music generation were sound, putting him at least two decades ahead of his time. By the 1950s electronics technology was sufficiently sophisticated that visionaries like Cahill could convert their ideas into a new form of music.

The earliest and most successful of the modern instruments was the RCA Electronic Music Synthesizer, designed by Harry Olson and Herbert Belar, research scientists at the company's Princeton Laboratories in New Jersey, and unveiled to the public in 1955. It could convert virtually any electrical wave — saw-toothed, squared, sinusoidal — into musical pitches.

Four years later RCA introduced a more advanced model and turned it over for experimentation to the Columbia-Princeton Electronic Music Center. Several composers wrote specifically for the new instruments, most notably Princeton University's Milton Babbitt, who in 1961 created *Composition for Synthesizer* and *Vision and Prayer* and in 1963 *Ensembles for Synthesizer*.

Jazz, Blues, and Rock 'n' Roll, 20th Century; United States

The United States in this century has popularized several forms of music; the unique one is jazz. To some authorities the term means simply any improvised instrumental music; others view it as any form of popularized neo–folk song.

Dixieland jazz, a dance-band style, originated among blacks in New Orleans. Unable to read music, they began improvising — using cornets, trombones, clarinets, banjos, and drums — on such popular tunes as "When the Saints Come Marching In" and "Oh Didn't He Ramble." In the 1920s the jazz beat shifted from the American South to Carl Sandburg's "City of the Big Shoulders," Chicago, where it underwent several changes. The standard jazz combo picked up piano, tuba, and tenor saxophone; guitar replaced banjo; and for the first time white musicians entered the field.

The American South also produced the blues, which grew out of Negro work songs and spirituals during the first three decades of this century. As its name implies, blues dealt with melancholy themes of self-pity, alienation, and lost lovers, and the music had distinctive harmonics, characterized by plaintive third and seventh intervals, and a slurring of melodic line above and below normal pitch. Its dolorous solo songs, popularized to a large extent by women, especially "Ma" Rainey, Bessie Smith, and Ethel Waters, soon permeated jazz.

Many musical styles of this century have come and gone, among them **ragtime** (which ended around the same time as World War I), **boogie-woogie** (popular during the 1930s), and **bop** (the rage in the 1940s). But perhaps the most enduring style, originating in the 1950s and giving birth later to **acid rock, disco, punk,** and **new wave,** is rock 'n' roll.

Although its roots are often disputed, it clearly is a hybrid, owing most, perhaps, to bop and jazz, and borrowing somewhat less from blues, though Elvis Presley, high priest of the form, incorporated blues' plaintive tones into many of his early songs. Around the end of World War II jazz underwent a series of rapid changes, leading it into the realms of "cool jazz" (as opposed to the "hot jazz," or totally improvised melodies of the 1920s), funky hard bop (or rebop), and rock 'n roll. Rock ensembles, or combos, typically contain a greater variety of instruments than those of jazz, and rock music is more diversified in melody, rhythm, and harmony, borrowing techniques at times from Classical music. Though it is a genuine hybrid, it is also a genuinely distinctive breed of music, one that has undergone several transformations in the last two decades, but lately shows signs of returning to its 1950s roots.

20

Instruments: Oboe to Bagpipes

Lyre, 4000 B.C.; Mesopotamia

Greek legend attributes the invention of the lyre, a forerunner of the harp, to the god Apollo. To atone for stealing cows from the chief deity, Zeus, Apollo presented him with a lyre, which he had accidentally discovered by brushing against a turtle shell that lay on the ground; the sinews resonated musically as he struck the carapace.

The lyre actually originated among the early inhabitants of Mesopotamia and seems to have been their first stringed instrument. For the resonating cavity the Mesopotamians used a dried bull's skull, and the strings were taut dry cord. Historians believe that the "harp" the Hebrews hung in a tree during the Babylonian captivity and Homer's famous "harp" were actually lyres. The bull idolatry among early Cretans and Mycenaeans brought the lyre to prominence in these Greek cultures; in the West the Celts played lyres and etched them on the backs of their coins.

Like many early stringed instruments, the lyre has diminished in popularity in modern times. Today the instrument is still played in Ethiopia, the Sudan, and among fishermen of the Persian Gulf.

Flute, 3500 B.C.; Sumer and Egypt

Flutes existed in most early civilizations, and they have changed astonishingly little from those times. The Sumerian and Egyptian flutes were vertical instruments, about 1.5 feet long and 0.5 inch wide, easily blown because of the narrow air passage. Near the lower end were anywhere from two to six finger holes, which enabled the player to fashion a variety of musical sounds. Well-preserved specimens of Egyptian flutes have been found and tested; they produce the familiar pungent, tremulous sound characteristic of today's instrument. The tremolo in the Egyptian flute was caused by a slight deviation in the pitch occurring between the two tubes of the instrument, which created a beat — a feature rediscovered with organ pipes in Germany late in the 15th century.

Harp, 3000 B.C.; Sumer

The harp is the national symbol of Ireland, and its romantic charms were first enjoyed by the Celts in the 7th century A.D. The remains of several Celtic harps have been unearthed from the buried ship *Sutton Hoo* near Suffolk, England. The harp's mesmerizing sound did much to spread its popularity. One Celtic legend proclaimed that there were but three things necessary for a happy home — a virtuous wife, a chair cushion, and a harp.

For years the harp was thought to have originated in Ireland. But the recent discovery of three harps found in primitive burial chambers at an archeological dig at Ur in Sumer push the instrument's origin back to 3000 B.C. The Ur harps, whose shapes are thought to have been copied from a hunter's bow, were curved instruments with twelve to fifteen strings that apparently did not sound all that different from later Celtic versions. For reasons that have yet to be satisfactorily explained, the harp seems to have been one of the few instruments, if not the only one, played almost exclusively by women. This was the case in ancient Sumer and Egypt; later in Ireland, China, and India; and is even true today, where most harps are primarily orchestra instruments.

Clarinet, Pre-2700 B.C.; Egypt

A foot-long clarinet, made of cane and possessing a single reed, appeared in Egypt some time between the birth of the flute, in 3500 B.C., and the arrival of the double clarinet, eight hundred

A painting of a harp from a tomb at Thebes

years later. The first Westerner to realize the possibilities of the clarinet in modern compositions was the German musician Johann Christoph Denner, in the 16th century. He made the instrument of wood, gave it a single reed, and doubled its length. With Denner's improvements, and the later addition of several notes, forming what is known as the classical clarinet, the sound of the instrument was compared to the human voice. Clarinets acquired a tremendous following wherever they were played.

Lute, 2500 B.C.; Babylon

The lute is perhaps the most legendary of all stringed instruments. The earliest pictorial evidence of the instrument is a mural dating from 2500 B.C., depicting a Babylonian shepherd strumming a skin-bellied lute with a rounded back that appears to be made from a turtle shell.

Though the Greeks never cared much for the lute, the Romans loved the instrument's plucky sounds and spread its popularity. In time, the members of the lute family — which includes the **sitar, violin, fiddle, guitar,** and **ukulele** — became the most widely distributed stringed instruments in the world.

Our word "lute" comes from the Arabic *al'ud*, meaning "the wood." The instrument was a major source of music in Arab culture for more than a thousand years.

The lute's basic structure has not changed. The sound chamber is covered with strings, and a player moves his fingers up and down the neck, shortening and tautening the strings to produce various pitches. An 18th-century German musician sardonically noted that "when a lute player is eighty years old, he has spent sixty years tuning his instrument."

Bowed instruments such as the **viola** and **cello** are descendants of the lute, and the practice of *bowing* originated about the 8th century A.D. in the Islamic civilization.

Oboe, 1500 B.C.; Egypt

As is true of many wind instruments, the first oboe was played in Egypt. Called *mat,* the Egyptian name for pipes, the oboe resembled the flute. The instrument, made of cane, was about 2 feet long was blown in pairs, with one instrument playing a drone and the other carrying the melody. A later Greek version was the double-reed oboe, called an *aulos,* which was highly praised for its pungent sound, created by two divergent narrow pipes activated by one large reed.

Trumpet, Pre–1350 B.C.; Egypt

Early man fashioned trumpets from hollowing out bamboo cane, or using a narrow eucalyptus branch whose pithy center had been eaten by termites. The first metal trumpets, made of silver, were found in the tomb of the Egyptian king Tutankhamen, who died about 1350 B.C., after ruling during the New Kingdom era. The Greek trumpet called a *salpinx,* popular in the 5th century B.C., was a magnificently crafted instrument assembled from thirteen fitted sections of carved ivory. The ancient Romans had both straight and J-shaped trumpets, and they also seem to have made the first tuba.

Organ, 3rd Century B.C.; Alexandria

The earliest record of a keyboard instrument capable of producing a sustained sound from a set of pipes comes from the Greek engineer Ctesibius of Alexandria, who invented a single-manual, slider-chest organ with one keyboard and one pipe to each note. Organs are thought to have existed prior to the 3rd century B.C., but the evidence is so circumstantial that it seems safe to assume that Ctesibius' instrument was the progenitor of the versions that later were popular in early Roman Catholic churches.

Ctesibius' instrument was ingenious for its utilization of air. A piston pump supplied air through an ordinary clack valve to a reservoir that, in turn, communicated directly with the wind chest. The bottomless cylindrical reservoir sat in a large drum-shaped container partly filled with water. As air filled the reservoir, air also would escape from the periphery of the lower half. The method allowed air pressure to be maintained in the reservoir, and

A steam organ

led Ctesibius logically to name his instrument *hydraulis.* Models of this kind became very popular in Greece and eventually assumed the Greek name *organon,* from which our modern word derives.

Organ development during the early Middle Ages remains obscure, since few records and no intact instruments remain. But by the 8th century organs had become a regular addition to Catholic church services. Their use reached a peak in the 10th century with the completion of the famous instrument at the cathedral in Winchester, England. Its powerful sounds prompted the monk Wulfstan to remark that "the music of the pipes is heard throughout the town and the flying fame thereof is gone out over the whole country."

The **chromatic keyboard,** consisting of twelve keys per octave, was responsible for the organ's becoming an artistic, virtuoso instrument in the 13th century. An elegant example of this instrument was the cathedral organ at Halberstadt, Germany, which boasted three chromatic keyboards, with keys much wider than those of modern organs. Key size did not become standardized until late in the 15th century, and the colors of keys — white for naturals, black for sharps — did not become a regular feature for another hundred years. By this time, the organ had evolved to a stage where it contained all the pertinent components of the modern instrument.

Bagpipes, 1st Century A.D.; Asia

At one time bagpipes were thought to have been elaborate combinations of simple enclosed reed instruments. Which, of course, they are not. The first bagpipes were, however, strange instruments. The bag was the entire hide of a sheep or goat, with the chanter, the pipe with finger holes, fitted into a wooden plug in the animal's neck. The drones emerged from other plugs in the forelegs. A blowpipe filled the bag with air, and the player's arm over the bag provided pressure to make the pipes release their piercing sound. The chanter contained seven holes in front and thumbhole in the rear. In overall appearance, the finished product was not all that dissimilar to the animal whose body was the bag. Late in the 1st century bagpipes were introduced to Rome, where they were a great curiosity and an immediate success.

By the addition of horns, bagpipers were made to resemble a goat, whose body often served as the bag.

Clavichord, 1385; France

The clavichord was a distant relative of the piano, and it seems that the instrument originated late in the 14th century.

A stringed keyboard instrument called an *eschiquier* was known to have existed in the royal court of France in 1385. Though not much is known about construction of the instrument, it was described as "resembling the organ but sounding by means of strings." If it was a clavichord, as most music historians think, then the strings were struck by blades of metal that had to remain in contact with them as long as they were to sound. In a harpsichord, on the other hand, the strings are plucked; in the piano, the strings are struck by small hammers that immediately rebound from them. The harpsichord and clavichord were described and illustrated in the first half of the 15th century by Henri Arnaut of Zwolle, personal physician of Philip the Good, duke of Burgundy, and later physician and astrologer to King Charles VII and King Louis XI of France. Considering what is known about the origins of the harpsichord, it seems highly probable that the *eschiquier* was the first clavichord, the earliest stringed instrument with keys that could be pushed down by the fingers.

The **piano,** originally called *gravicembalo col piano e forte* (literally "harpsichord with soft and loud") was invented in Florence by Bartolommeo Cristofori, who referred to it as a "harpsichord with hammers," but the instrument did not come into general use until the 18th century.

Modern Orchestra, 16th Century; Italy

The Italian composer Giovanni Gabrieli, organist at St. Mark's Church in Venice in the late 16th century, is considered the father of the modern orchestra. He was the first composer to specify certain instruments for particular portions of a musical composition, a practice begun in his early works, such as the 1597 *Sacrae Symphoniae*. Though we may find it hard to believe today, espe-

The special effects of, say, an isolated trumpet blast, a drum roll, or the sweeping wave of strings, were unknown in early orchestras, when all instruments played together throughout a composition. Women then, as today, played the harp.

cially since a wide variety of musical instruments was in use by the late 16th century, before Gabrieli's clever innovation groups of musicians gathering to perform a work used whatever instruments were available and familiar to them, usually playing them *in tutti,* meaning "everyone together."

Gabrieli's contemporary, composer Claudio Monteverdi, adopted the practice of **orchestration,** carrying it to superlative effects in the 1607 performance in Mantova, Italy, of his opera *La Favola d'Orfeo.* The ground-breaking orchestration called for forty musicians, playing trumpets, trombones, flutes, cornets, strings, and keyboards. They played in solos, in various combinations, and *in tutti,* marking the first time a composer had heightened dramatic moments in a composition by the calculated addition and subtraction of instruments. The effect was said to be "stunning." By the middle of the 18th century the symphony orchestra already had assumed the appearance of a modern orchestra, though it was smaller in size.

21

Theater: Comedy to Kabuki

Musical Theater, 10,000 B.C., France

Before Greek tragedy, before Roman comedy, before satire and mime, there was musical theater.

Early man, using instruments fashioned from the environment, celebrated with music harvests, births, deaths, victories over his enemies, and successful hunts. What is thought to be the oldest document of musical theater, a Stone Age cave painting dating to 10,000 B.C., depicts a man wearing a buffalo mask, manipulating what appears to be a stringed instrument, and dancing wildly in the wake of a herd of reindeer. Not exactly Broadway fare, but by historians who determine these things, the cave painting, discovered in Ariège, France, marks the roots of the family tree of musical theater.

Growth continued with the Greeks. Their earliest theater incorporated music, mostly sung by a chorus, but sparingly. At drama festivals poets wrote their own music, but it too was more a background effect, against which a tragedy or comedy was highlighted. After the fall of Athens, in 404 B.C., Greek dramatists initiated a repertory system and a class of professional musicians to play at theatrical events. Greek mime, and later Roman pantomime, did much to increase the role of music in theater.

Then, in the 2nd and 3rd centuries A.D., musical theater suffered a major blow from the Christian Church. Theater in any form was deemed sacrilegious and sinful. By the 6th century the church had suppressed all forms of theater. A small flame was left burning in the form of the Mass.

When the organ entered church services some time between the 7th and 8th centuries, a new form of musical theater emerged, in the form of liturgical musical dramas. These slowly evolved during the Middle Ages in Europe into the equally religious mystery and miracle plays, which were performed in the vernacular instead of in Latin and had a strong musical element.

When Catherine de Médicis married King Henri II of France in 1533, she brought from Italy a taste for entertainment in which music and dance were prominent. She helped establish the court ballet, which became still another new source of musical theater, and a precursor of French opera. By the middle of the 17th century dance had split off and crystallized into ballet, singing theater into opera, and for two centuries musical theater became largely synonymous with opera.

The light opera, or operetta, of the 19th century, gave way to 20th-century America's unique version of musical comedy, exemplified by such shows as *Annie, Get Your Gun, South Pacific, The King and I*, and *Funny Girl*. The form reached its heyday between the 1930s and 1960s.

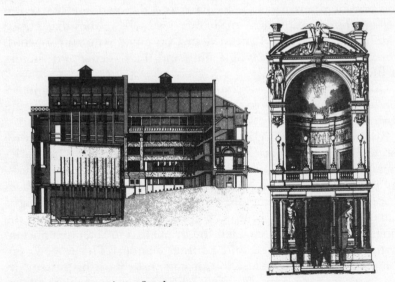

Details of construction of a theater

Drama, 6th Century B.C.; Greece

Greek theater — or at least that form of theater we have come to know as tragedy — was rooted in a ritualistic dance, accompanied by a hymn, called the dithyramb, performed in honor of Dionysus, the god of sex, the arts, and intoxication. Not surprisingly, during these "springfests," which celebrated with great emotion the ending of winter and the earth's return to fertility, the atmosphere was chaotic and the dancers drunk.

The dithyramb was born among the Dorians of Sicyon in the Peloponnesus. A speaker, probably in the role of a priest, introduced the ritual, and then maintained frequent dialogue with the dancing and singing chorus. At this point in drama's development, no two individuals on stage engaged in dramatic exchange. By the end of the 7th century B.C., performances of these bacchanalian dances had spread to Corinth, where they gained literary prominence, and soon afterward to Thebes and the islands of Paros and Naxos.

When, a hundred years later, the dithyramb was brought to Attica by the itinerant lyric poet Thespis, it underwent a drastic transformation to pure drama. Dispensing with disorderly dances and brawling performers, Thespis wrote, directed, and starred in well-organized productions of literary texts — tragedies that pulsed with human emotions of anger, desire, hurt, and sympathy — which were accompanied by a single flute and the dancing and singing of fifty men or boys.

Our word "tragedy" — from the Greek *tragos* for "goat" and *odē* for "song"—harks back to the village dithyrambs, in which singing performers donned goatskins and pranced about like animals.

By the 5th century, classical drama had reached its peak, with the writings of Sophocles, Aeschylus, and Euripides. The stories they told in their tragedies were well known to their audiences, but it was the manner in which the playwrights unfolded the tales that evoked in the viewers the emotions of fear and pity. **Dialogue** had come into use the century before; now, interspersed with the songs of the chorus, it enabled the dramatists to retell the ancient myths in a sophisticated and realistic manner. The tragedy encompassed three elements: the protagonist's flaw, his pursuit by the angry gods, and his downfall, which sometimes took the form of catastrophe for his community as well as himself. An example is Sophocles' **Oedipus Tyrannos (Oedipus the King),** in which Oedipus, king of Thebes, unknowingly marries his own mother, thus offending the gods, and meets his downfall when he discovers what he has done.

Mime, 6th Century B.C.; Greece

In ancient Greece, mime was to tragedy what in the American theater of the 1930s and 1940s a bawdy burlesque review was to serious Broadway drama. Though the classical playwrights scorned mime, issued harangues against its coarseness and frivolity, they did not hesitate to borrow some innovative mime techniques for their tragedies.

Today we tend to use the terms "mime" and "pantomime" interchangeably. But their origins and forms are quite distinct. Mime originated in the Dorian centers of the Peloponnesus, particularly Sparta, about 600 B.C. It was a form of comedy, mostly silent, in which an actor engaged in farcical behavior, depicting the travails of daily life, occasionally improvising words to heighten his comic effect.

Pantomime, on the other hand, was a later invention. It began with the Romans, and it drew for its action on mythology and history, satirizing both.

In early Greek mime, which had its roots in farcical village plays called *phlyakes,* players dressed in tights or short chitons with grotesquely padded rears and exaggerated phalluses. Each donned the traditional tragic actor's mask, which featured an oversized mouth that echoed and amplified the words, and whether acting out a husband and wife's bedroom problems, or the proper treatment of aberrant children, the player merely, to use modern jargon, camped it up.

Comedy arose in theater through mime. And the word itself derives from the Greek *komazein,* meaning "to wander around villages," suggesting that early comedy performers, because of their bawdy antics, had been forbidden to perform in cities.

Satire, or the satirical play, on the other hand, was a special form of comedy, characterized by intelligence and sharp, sardonic wit. It reached a height with the Greek dramatist Aristophanes, but really emerged as a special form of theater under the Romans.

Though the Greeks and Romans argued heatedly over the point, the Roman rhetorician Quintilian proclaimed that "satire is wholly our own," and acknowledged the founding father of satirical verse to have been Lucilius, who wrote acerbic poems in hexameter on political themes.

If the origin of satire is part Greek, part Roman, so too, coincidentally, are our modern forms of the word itself. Our noun "satire" comes from the Latin *satura*, meaning "melody," the *satura* having been a short poetic verse. As the *satura* evolved gradually into the form of a satirical play, the Romans sought a word to characterize this new art form. They could not merely call it a "satirical play"; the noun *satura* in Latin had no verbal or adjectival form, so of course, they couldn't talk of "satirizing" a subject. To solve the syntactical shortcoming, they chose the Greek word *satyros*, meaning "satyr," and its derivatives. Hence, while our English noun "satire" is Roman, our verb "to satirize" and our adjective "satiric" are Greek in origin.

Pantomime, 1st Century A.D.; Italy

Mime eventually traveled from Greece to Italy and became a popular form of entertainment in every city it reached. Like its Greek antecedent, Roman mime, or *mimus*, in its early days was a wild pastiche of crude stage performances that included mostly improvised farcical scenes, acrobatics, and juggling, all acted out by common people, instead of nobility or aristocracy, who could occasionally be found taking part in more serious dramas.

Women appeared frequently in Roman mime productions, and tales involving sex-role reversals were a favorite with audiences. Mime was refined somewhat during the time of the Caesars, acquiring a slightly literary bent, but the art retained its aura of licentiousness to such a point that stage performers frequently touted the pleasures of adultery.

Where mime involved some dialogue, Roman pantomime involved masked dancers noted for silently posturing their stories through emphatic gestures and rhythmic body movements. The stories for the most part were drawn from mythology and legend.

Two star performers of the day were Bathyllus and his sidekick, Pylades. They initiated rapid mask changes, which enabled the two men to play the numerous characters in their shows, all accompanied by a large male chorus and a small orchestra. Bathyllus, Pylades, and several other comic celebrities of the day not only received the adulation of the masses, but were welcomed into the homes of the affluent and were patronized by emperors.

Roman pantomime, in fact, became so widely popular, and its performers so renowned, that the inferior art form for many years drove the more literary writers off the stage — and into unemployment — since everyone preferred to be entertained by the hilarious comedies. Today, historians regard only two 1st-century pantomime writers, Lucan and Statius, as of literary merit.

Kabuki, 16th Century; Japan

Kabuki is an energetic, eclectic form of theater, blending music, song, dance, mime, and spectacular staging and costuming. It is distinctly Japanese. The word itself, written with three characters, says it all: *ka* signifying "song"; *bu*, "dance"; and *ki*, "skill."

Kabuki originated as a new form of theater in the 16th century, owing to the efforts of an enterprising young woman, a former priestess named Okuni, bent on spreading Buddhist doctrine. Personally staging her tasteful song-and-dance representations of Buddhist prayer, she began to attract the attention of audiences in her home town. Sagacious, ambitious, and certainly an early liberated woman, Okuni immediately recognized the possibility of gaining a larger following through heightened theatrics on a grand scale. She assembled a troupe of women, many with song-and-dance experience, and commenced to teach them her staging.

Kabuki's mainstay then as now was imaginative pantomime dancing, peppered with song, spoken dialogue, and audience participation. Okuni began a tradition whose long history also was characterized by the notoriety that Kabuki performers brought to the sensual meaning of dance.

In traditional Kabuki, actors and audience engaged in constant interchanges. Actors frequently departed from their dialogue to address spectators, who in turn responded with phrases or by clapping their hands according to a prescribed rhythm. They also were uninhibited about shouting out the name of their favorite actor during a performance.

Kabuki productions then had no prescribed length. The longer ones ran from morning till evening. There was always hubbub in the aisles, since some spectators came only for a single act, others for half a day, and still others stayed the entire day but periodically left the theater to take walks or to conduct personal business. At mealtime, food was served to the audience.

Much of the grist for Kabuki themes initially came from Buddhist teachings; later, from contemporary events and the vicissitudes of the seasons. All native Japanese customs were upheld and manners honored. Much along the lines of experimental theater in the Western world today, Kabuki performances of the 17th century often found actors dancing in the aisles, beseeching audience members to join in the theatrical celebration. When audience participation in Western theatrical productions began in the 1960s, many critics immediately pointed out that the practice touted as new by contemporary writers and directors actually was four hundred years old.

Circus, 1st Century B.C.; Rome

The first circus, like its 20th-century counterpart, boasted several death-defying acts. The only difference was that those early events were designed not so much to defy death as to guarantee it. The circus then offered thrills and spills, with the latter often involving the spilling of animal as well as human blood.

The **Circus Maximus** of Rome was where it began. Originating in the 1st century B.C. during the reign of Julius Caesar, its entertainment ran from brutal man-fights-beast-to-the-death encounters to spectacular horse-racing and charioteering, which also was likely to end in the death of a horse or rider. The arena, as was true of later Roman circuses, was modeled on the Greek hippodromes, in which chariot races and athletic games were staged.

Many Roman circuses seated up to 150,000 spectators, placed on three sides of the main course. The course itself, using the Circus Maximus as a standard, was 2000 feet long by 600 feet wide. This became known as the "arena," from the Latin for "sand" or "beach," and its area was divided lengthwise and slanted, not only for better viewing, but to provide ample room for the start of a race. As in modern races, the horses and chariots lined up at the common starting point, but in stalls instead of behind a gate. A sharp semicircular turn at the far end of the course sent the contestants speeding past the spectators for the race's climactic finish.

A tame day at a Roman circus

Charioteers often were slaves racing to win their freedom. Understandably, they drove their horses, which ran in teams of two, four, or up to eight animals, unmercifully hard, each man obsessed with victory. Serious accidents were commonplace, and the drivers, who wore helmets and wrapped lengths of reins around their bodies for stability, carried knives to cut themselves free if a spill occurred.

In many respects Circus Maximus events were not dissimilar to stadium events today. Competing charioteers wore bright individual colors — the precursor of jockey silks. Betting was encouraged, and during the races vendors, wine merchants, and cooks hustled their goods, prostitutes solicited openly, and pickpockets lifted on the sly.

The circus event that was in vogue depended on who was emperor at the time. Julius Caesar favored aggressive horse-racing; his successor, Augustus, had a macabre predilection for watching giant muscular men slay beasts. During his reign, from 27 B.C. to A.D. 14, more than 3500 lions, tigers, and other jungle cats perished in the arena, taking with them hundreds of gladiators. Under Nero, in the 1st century A.D., the most popular circus event became the notorious lion-versus-Christian spectacle. The savage practice, using Christians and, later, slaves, finally was outlawed in A.D. 326 by Constantine.

Although the Christian torture was staged at the Circus Neronis, most of the Romans' taste for bizarre spectacles was satisfied in amphitheaters, of which the largest was the **Colosseum.** The capacity of this great stadium, completed in A.D. 79, was between 45,000 and 50,000, all paying customers who came to view various forms of gladiatorial combat. In one season, 2000 gladiators and 230 wild animals were killed. Gladiatorial combat and the killing of jungle animals continued in the Colosseum until A.D. 523.

Modern Circus, 1768; England

The start of the modern circus, featuring daring human stunts and an assortment of caged and leashed exotic animals, is credited to Philip Astley, an Englishman and equestrian. Beginning with only the single skill of trick horseback riding, Astley introduced a tradition that grew quickly and still thrives today.

Astley started on a small scale. Prodding his mount to gallop in a full circle while he balanced on the horse's back, kept in place by centripetal force, he performed this "daring feat" for the first time in front of an audience in 1768. After adding several new balancing tricks, Astley took his gymnastic horse show to Paris in 1772, beginning the tradition of the **traveling circus troupe.**

Circuses quickly arose in England and France while the previously popular country fairs fell precipitously into decline. Fair performers like jugglers, aerial acrobats, tightrope walkers, gymnasts, and strongmen, faced with unemployment, joined the new circuses in teeming numbers to keep their acts alive.

Variety became the spice of European circus troupes. The French government, eager to offer its citizens circus entertainment, granted Astley and his band of performers the concession to perform in the largest amphitheater in Paris, but national jealousies between England and France forced Astley to withdraw from his own horse-show spectacular. He leased his circus to a Venetian entrepreneur, Antonio Franconi, who in no time became the best known of early circus masters. Franconi, along with his two sons, Laurent and Henri, actually is credited with founding the French circus and reputedly setting the diameter of the circus ring at 42 feet, still the standard size among international troupes.

Astley, meanwhile, kept on, undaunted. He was responsible for establishing eighteen permanent circuses during his lifetime, in locations as far from home as Belgrade and Vienna. His hard-

Daredevil horseback-riding, long the circus's predominant feat, was later accompanied by an abundance of death-defying acts.

working assistant, Charles Hughes, himself a performing horse-man, capitalized on Catherine the Great's love for horses and brought the circus to Russia for the first time in 1793. The empress, thoroughly impressed with daredevil feats performed on horseback, allowed Hughes to stage a private performance of his troupe the same year at the royal palace at St. Petersburg.

The same year saw the circus make its debut in America, first before cheering audiences in New York, then in Philadelphia, both spectacles under the direction of John Bill Ricketts. The circus's enduring nemesis — fire — first made its marauding mark here and abroad just a few years later. Astley's amphitheater in England burned to the ground, and Ricketts lost both his New York and Philadelphia circuses to blazes.

Ballet, 1581; France

Early in the fall of the year 1581, the sister of French queen Louise was to marry the duke de Joyeuse. Desiring the occasion to be remembered as the most lavish social event of that or any other year, the king's mother, Catherine de Médicis, who had left her native Italy earlier as the bride of the duke who eventually became Henri II, commissioned her favorite court musician and dance master, Baltazarini di Belgioioso, to arrange the entertainment. Belgioioso, known in France as Beaujoyeux, did not disappoint the queen mother. He devised the *Ballet comique de la Reine,* staged in the Salle Bourbon of the Louvre Palace on October 15, 1581. For most dance historians this pinpoints the birth of ballet.

The grand spectacle of pantomime and poetry, song and dance, lasted a numbing six hours, and only vaguely resembled anything we would today call ballet. In the absence of a formal stage, the performers cavorted on the floor of the great hall, and the audience perched in galleries along the walls. And although the title contained the word *comique,* the production was deathly serious, concerning Odysseus' escape from the enchantress Circe, until, in the end, the Greek gods defeat her and the people pay tribute to a far greater queen — the then-reigning, then-present Queen Louise of France.

Catherine was greatly pleased with the choreographed spectacle and distributed illustrated accounts of it throughout Europe. As for Beaujoyeux, his work was not entirely original; he had bor-

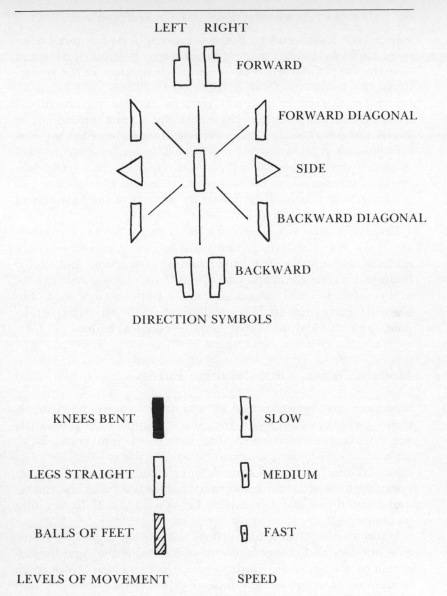

LEFT   RIGHT

FORWARD

FORWARD DIAGONAL

SIDE

BACKWARD DIAGONAL

BACKWARD

DIRECTION SYMBOLS

KNEES BENT   SLOW

LEGS STRAIGHT   MEDIUM

BALLS OF FEET   FAST

LEVELS OF MOVEMENT   SPEED

Until this century dances were passed on by tradition. The first dance notation was formulated in 1928 by choreographer Rudolf von Laban and became known as Labanotation. Variously shaped symbols *(top)* indicate direction; symbol size and shading *(bottom)* convey leg and foot positions and speed. Today several systems are employed, along with the video-taping of performances from one or more directions.

rowed from Italian and French court dance of past centuries; but in its use of extended choreographed steps, as opposed to earlier free motions, it marked a pioneering achievement in the history of dance.

Beaujoyeux's extensive notes paint a detailed picture of the thinking that went into his magnum opus. All the movement, he wrote, was based on the "geometrical arrangement of many persons dancing together under a diverse harmony of instruments." A knowledge of geometry, in fact, was required of all choreographers of the day, since they strove to reflect in the dancers' patterns the perfections of the planetary paths and the harmony of metaphysical ideas.

Because at this early stage of ballet dancers wore long, cumbersome costumes that greatly limited their movements, there were none of the now-familiar leaps, partner elevations, and on-toe footwork. These elements, which epitomize classical ballet, were first codified in 1820 in choreographer Carlo Blasis's book, *Elementary Treatise Upon the Theory and Practice of the Art of Dancing*. Its publication marked the formal birth of **classical ballet.**

Modern Dance, 19th Century; Europe

Modern dance, characterized by angular, "natural" body movements and irregular tempos, roared into prominence in the early years of the present century. The style had begun gradually almost fifty years before, as a protest against the existing forms of theatrical dancing, and as a means of elevating dance to a contemporary style of art every bit as valid and significant as the emerging atonal music and the earlier Impressionist and later Cubist painting.

Many of the freshest innovations initially came from Europe, from dancers and choreographers who felt that the rigid formalization of movement in classical ballet had dragged dance to an all-time nadir in artistic development. Just as they shunned classical ballet's excessive rigidity, they eschewed interpretive dance's excessive freedom, which they felt conveyed a single dancer's personal feelings but lacked the means for communicating to an audience universal sentiments and ideas. Something new, something totally modern was needed.

One pioneering leader in modern dance was a Frenchman,

François Delsarte. His contributions, ironically, did not at first involve dancers, but singers and actors. Delsarte decried the artificial mannerisms that had come to dominate virtually all kinds of performances on the Parisian stage. Naturalism had become extinct, and to revive it Delsarte worked out a system of facial expressions and body language whereby a performer's movements and glances could naturally express the meanings behind his or her spoken or sung words. As his repertoire of glances and gestures was adopted by increasing numbers of singers and actors, it also caught favor with choreographers and dancers.

Where Delsarte made his initial impact on actors and singers, so too did his Swiss contemporary, Emile Jaques-Dalcroze, have a profound influence first on musicians and only later on dancers. Jaques-Dalcroze devised a system of eurythmics, the representation of musical rhythms in strict body movements. He believed that any musician could improve his sense of rhythm if trained to respond to music through body movement. Many musicians of the day flocked to Jaques-Dalcroze's classes and swore by his techniques, and soon his formal exercises evolved into forms that were undertaken by dancers.

In the United States, Isadora Duncan explored an entirely different tack, harking back to Greek dance and ideals. Along the fluid lines of Greek sculpture she based her movements, which she proclaimed as "good, true, and beautiful," and what emerged through her own person was a sleek, natural body, clothed in loose robes, with bare feet, limning the swaying of trees and the ebb and flow of the ocean tide. The Romantic music of Beethoven, Schubert, and Chopin influenced Duncan's dance ideas, and music figured in her scheme in an integral way.

22

Art: Painting to Porcelain

Painting, 30,000 Years Ago; France and Spain

Up until about 30,000 years ago, man had done little esthetically to change his living environment, for bare survival was his predominant concern. By this time the male-female division of labor had become a standard practice, with men hunting game over the countryside and women gathering food close to the campsite and caring for the young.

What is most remarkable about this period, however, is the beginning of art in the form of painting. On the walls of caves at Lascaux, France, and Altamira, Spain, areas straddling the Pyrenees, superb paintings of bison, reindeer, ibexes, and other animals still exist, portrayed in vivid details.

The Altamira cave, near Santander, was the first to be found, discovered by chance in 1869, when a little girl playing in the area wandered into the cave's main atrium, not far from the entrance.

On the walls, about 7 feet above the ground, are life-size paintings of twenty bison, a few other animals, and occasional figures of men hunting. Some of the gigantic animals are depicted with lowered horns in the act of charging, others are reclining on the ground — all painted in vibrant red and brown ocher (made from iron oxide) and outlined in coal-black. The images are realistic, and the painters were skilled enough to convey through blurred brush strokes the motion of tails flailing the air.

The Altamira paintings date to the end of the Paleolithic era,

Tracing of a reindeer at Lascaux; 27.6 inches long from its muzzle to the tip of its stubby tail. It is one of many deer that adorn a chamber of the 30,000-year-old cave, located midway between the "Hall of the Bulls" and the "Hall of Cats." The procession of chambers constitutes history's first art gallery.

about 15,000 years ago, but the artwork at the Lascaux grotto, near Montignac, appears to be about 15,000 years older. Running through a series of caves, the paintings have an architectural layout, with the main atrium decorated with wall frescoes and ceiling murals that impart a monumental effect.

Bulls are the principal subjects in the main atrium. Three gigantic forms, each measuring 16 feet, are outlined in black but not painted in, a practice the Lascaux painters preferred. When they did use uniform coloring, mainly on smaller figures, they employed a sophisticated "blowing" technique, spraying pulverized pigment from a reed or hollow bone. Brushes apparently were green twigs with finely frayed ends.

Other rooms contain paintings of horses and deer in red ocher outlined in black, five reindeer swimming across a river, a study of jungle cats in what is called the Hall of Cats, and a stampede of immense bulls. In the innermost portion of the tunnel is a wounded bison lying on the ground in front of a dying hunter — the first "story" in the history of painting.

Even though the paintings at Lascaux are some 15,000 years older than those at Altamira, they are as skillfully executed. From artifacts found on the site it appears that the people of that period did not live in these caves, but entered them only to execute the paintings and perhaps to perform religious rituals.

Paint, 30,000 Years Ago

The first paints, used in the murals in the caves at Lascaux, France, and Altamira, Spain, were made from naturally occurring iron oxides. For thousands of years these substances were the artist's palette. Then about 6000 B.C. early Asiatic people began to discover the artistic possibilities of organic pigments made from gum arabic (from the acacia tree), egg white, gelatin, and beeswax, which enabled them to mix **varnishes** and **enamels,** and also to fashion the first colored **crayons** by using clay as a binder.

The Egyptians greatly extended the range of the artist's palette about 3000 B.C. They introduced a variety of new hues made from the different colored soils in the region, and about a thousand years later they began using such dyes as indigo and madder to make vivid blue and red varnishes. They also were the first people to use paint not only for decorative purposes, but as a protective coating to seal their wooden ships.

Lacquer, the finish given to certain metallic and wood objects by colored and frequently opaque varnishes, originated in China during the Chou Dynasty, which began about 1122 B.C. According to a Ming manuscript, from about the 15th century A.D., lacquer was first employed for writing on bamboo slips, then for decorating and sealing kitchen utensils; the exteriors of bowls, plates, and ceremonial vessels were usually black lacquer and the interiors a brilliant red.

The Chinese, in fact, went crazy with lacquer during the middle of the Chou Dynasty about 600 B.C. Gold and silver lacquer came into vogue and, along with the more traditional red and black, adorned carriages, harnesses, and weapons. At the height of the varnishing frenzy, entire buildings, inside and outside, glistened with lacquer finishes. It became the practice during the Earlier Han Dynasty, beginning in 206 B.C., to lacquer ornately all musical instruments.

The Chinese got their lacquer from the natural substance of a tree, the sap from *Rhus vernicifera.* Through distillation and filtering, impurities were stripped away, along with excess water, leaving a clear saplike paste. The Chinese waited until a tree was at least ten years old before tapping its sap with lateral incisions made in the bark. The slowly oozing sap was collected in buckets from

June to September. Branches too small to be "bled" were cut off and soaked to yield their sap, which produced a special quality lacquer called *seshime*. Sapping killed the tree, which was then used for carpentry.

By the Middle Ages paint-making was a sophisticated business, and each artist or manufacturer kept secret his own formulas. The price of paints varied greatly, depending on such costly additives as egg whites and rare gums.

White lead paint came into common use in the 17th century, but only about a hundred years later, with the increased availability of pigments, did houses, buildings, and bridges routinely receive coats of paint. The most significant discoveries that made paint a wide-scale commercial business came in the 18th century, when linseed oil from the flax plant and man-made zinc-oxide pigment were first used. Not surprisingly, with the sudden availability of relatively inexpensive paint, people began to coat everything in sight. Unpainted wood was regarded as a sign of poverty — or, worse, bad taste.

Wacky with Lacquer. In early days, Chinese, discoverers of lacquer, went wild with the lustrous finish, and coated everything in sight with red. black, gold, and silver lacquers.

Tapestry, 1500 B.C.; Egypt

Tapestry weaving in all likelihood evolved independently in many ancient civilizations, but the earliest extant example is some Egyptian linen tapestry made between 1483 and 1411 B.C.

The three fragments found in the tomb of Thutmose IV were in relatively good condition, due in part to the dry Egyptian climate. Two cloths bear cartouches of Egyptian pharaohs; the third contains a series of hieroglyphics. Tapestry weaving among the Egyptians clearly was not confined to wall ornaments and foot rugs, for an elaborate robe and glove woven by tapestry techniques were discovered in the tomb of Tutankhamen, dating to about 1350 B.C.

Some of the most magnificent of early tapestries are believed to have been those of the ancient Babylonians and Assyrians, who are thought to have taught the art to the Egyptians. But none of their work has survived.

Earthenware, 7000 B.C.; Near East

The first kind of pottery, earthenware, dates back about 9000 years and still is made in modern societies as well as underdeveloped nations. Earthenware pots then as now ranged in color from buff to dark red and from gray to black.

The earliest evidence of earthenware — a collection of various-sized, crudely shaped pots — was discovered at excavations of a Neolithic settlement at Catlhuyuk on the Anatolian Plateau in Turkey in the early 1960s. Somewhat more sophisticated hand-made pottery, fired by kiln and burnished, came into use about five hundred years later. By 3000 B.C. the inhabitants of Ur in Mesopotamia were spinning clay pots on horizontal wheels, and then hand-decorating them.

A more richly ornamented pottery still was the Susa pattern, originating about the same time in Shushan, in what is now southwest Iran. Bowls, goblets, and vases featured hand-painted scenes of running dogs and waterfowl in flight, all in vibrant reds and blues set against a background of creamy buff.

Stoneware, 1400 B.C.; China

Stoneware, a hardier form of pottery, arose in China at least as early as the Shang Dynasty. Like earthenware, its colors ranged from light brown to red and from gray to black, but the Chinese also discovered a way to give it a whitish coating, which became a favorite shade.

The Chinese apparently had a creative monopoly on stoneware for many centuries. It is not found in early Western cultures and did not appear in neighboring Korea until the beginning of the Silla Dynasty, about 57 B.C. Even more surprising is its late debut in Japan during the Kamakura period in the 13th century A.D.

Stoneware found its way into Europe in the 16th century via Germany, and soon became more popular than other kinds of pottery. For a number of years the British received their stoneware from China, along with shipments of imported tea. It became the custom for the shipper to send with each chest of tea a red stoneware pot kilned at I-hing in Kiangsu Province. Looking for a sturdy form of pottery for mass production, British potters at the end of the 17th century formulated a salt-glazed white stoneware, which in the next century was refined to near-perfection by **Josiah Wedgwood.** He also introduced a black stoneware called basalt, named for the volcanic rock that gives it its color. Pleased with stoneware's durability and attractiveness, the English continued to experiment with it and soon produced **ironstone ware.**

Porcelain, 7th Century A.D.; China

Porcelain, too, originated in China, and even today the Chinese produce some of the finest-quality porcelain in the world.

The first porcelain was a crude substance introduced some time during the T'ang Dynasty, between A.D. 618 and 907, and prized for its translucency. It reached the West in a more refined form in the 13th century, brought back by spice merchants traveling to the Far East. The chief ingredients were a white china clay called kaolin, and petuntse, a feldspathic rock that was ground into a fine powder and spun into the clay. The concoction was fired at temperatures of about 1450 degrees centigrade. The clay solidified, giving the pottery its shape, and the petuntse crystallized to form a glassy coating, lending the ware its translucent quality.

The French and British cherished their porcelain from China. Potters, meanwhile, sought doggedly to duplicate its shimmering glaze, but without a sophisticated knowledge of chemistry they were unable to break the Chinese formula; they could only experiment in hopes of producing the desired sheen. Eventually, the only translucent substance known in Europe, glass, was combined with clay. Liquid glass, however, interfered with the hardening of the clay base material and resulted in irregularly shaped objects. Soon potters turned to ground solid glass and produced a reasonable facsimile they called soft, or artificial, porcelain.

The Italians made many unsuccessful attempts to duplicate both the strength and sheen of Chinese porcelain. The accomplishment finally fell to the Germans in the 17th century. Working in Saxony, Count Ehrenfried Walter von Tschirnhaus, a mathematician and physicist, and Johann Friedrich Böttger, a chemist, substituted ground feldspar for ground glass and perfectly duplicated the Chinese formula. Soft porcelain quickly lost favor.

Experimentation continued, however. In the following century, the British potter Josiah Spode added pulverized bone ash — calcium phosphate obtained from roasted cattle bones — to ground feldspar and produced an elegant new kind of pottery. Called **bone china,** or English porcelain, it was easier to produce than Chinese porcelain and not as prone to chipping. Its sheen was an attractive ivory-white. Bone china quickly became fashionable in England and the United States; Chinese porcelain retained its popularity throughout most of Europe.

Jewelry, 3500 B.C.; Sumer

Early men and women may have worn trinkets of wood and bone, but true jewelry — fashioned from gold and silver and studded with precious and semiprecious stones — did not appear until about 3500 B.C., among the ruling classes in Sumer. Jewelry's history, in fact, is primarily a testimony to the affluence of its wearers, since in early days jewelry was a sign of social rank and could be worn only by priests and royalty. Subjects sometimes were allowed to don decorative talismans, but only to avert evil spirits.

The earliest jewelry of which there is any record was used by the Sumerians, and the first known woman in history to be elaborately festooned with jeweled finery was the Sumerian queen Pu-abi. She was buried in the 3rd millennium B.C. at Ur, now called Tell al-Muqayyar, and a glance at the assorted trinkets that adorned her body reveals the Sumerians' love of jewelry and their skill at fashioning it.

Her upper body was covered with a robe woven of gold and silver and studded with lapis lazuli. On her right arm hung three long willow-leaf pendants of gold with lapis lazuli, three amulets shaped like fish, and a gold bracelet showing the figures of two seated gazelles.

Three crowns rested on the queen's head, each smaller than its outermost neighbor and fastened by a gold band. The first crown, covering her forehead, was an intricate array of interlocking rings; the second and third were even more complex, woven of gold-braided ivy and willow leaves. Attached to the outer crown were gold flowers on drooping stems with blue and white petals. From her ears hung gold semitubular earrings.

Around her neck dangled three strings of semiprecious stones, and every finger bore several ornate rings. Large quantities of other jewels, such as wrist and arm bracelets and pectoral braids, which had belonged to funeral attendants, dignitaries, and even to the horses that pulled the funeral train, were placed in her crypt.

Though all later cultures developed their own jewelry, the lavish designs of the Sumerians left little to be discovered anew; in fact, most technical processes were known to them, from **welding** to **filigree** to **stone cutting.**

Carpets, 3000 B.C.; Egypt

The earliest floor coverings were probably crude mats made from strands of dry stalks and tendrils, which in time were replaced by plaited basketwork matting. These were kinds of carpets, but the exact origins of carpet weaving have not been determined. The Egyptians of the 3rd millennium B.C. wove carpets of linen, ornamented by sewn-on brightly colored pieces of woollen cloth. Their influence spread throughout the Middle East, then to Mongolia and China, where the Chinese by 1000 B.C. had perfected a knotted-silk-pile carpet backed by wool or cotton.

Oriental carpets originated in Central and Western Asia. They were laid initially over beaten-earth floors and only later used in temples and mosques. Their elaborate patterns, for which they are renowned today, began when they were introduced into royal palaces some time before the 8th century B.C..

Mosaic Floors, 1600 B.C.; Greece

Water-worn pebbles made up the first mosaic floors, found in ruins on the island of Crete and also on the Greek mainland. Later the Greeks began to form their mosaic floors in exquisite designs and by the 6th century B.C. had refined the technique, using marble, serpentine, alabaster, granite, and virtually any stone suitable for polishing. Their mosaic art spread through Asia Minor and into Sicily as well. Eventually even timber floors that had been used only for functional purposes came under the influence of mosaics and were transformed into decorative **parquet** designs.

The art of mosaics literally started on the ground and only centuries later moved upward to wall murals in marble and enamel.

Stained Glass, Pre—5th Century A.D.; Europe

The art of making stained glass sprang from earlier developments in both mosaics and enameling. The idea of composing monumental images from many separate pieces of colored glass was borrowed directly from the practice of mosaics, and the technique of binding the pieces with metal strips, then treating the strips themselves as an integral part of the design, came from the art of cloisonné enameling.

Mosaics and cloisonné enameling both were early Greek arts, originating in the 17th and 18th centuries B.C., respectively. Glass, too, was known to the Greeks; indeed, it was the vitreous glaze employed in enameling. Yet with the groundwork laid, it took many centuries for all the separate ingredients to be combined to form stained glass, and the exact date when these elements finally coalesced is uncertain.

Stained glass probably evolved over many years. Latin writers of the 5th century A.D., such as St. Jerome, Prudentius, and Lactantius, all commented on the existence of magnificent stained glass works in several early basilicas of their day, and a renowned bishop and writer of the era, Apollinaris Sidonius, described the colorfully glazed windows in a church in Lyon, France.

For 700 years stained glass windows were merely individual panels, depicting religious scenes. The narrative window was a popular innovation.

By the 7th century, stained glass windows certainly were a familiar sight to churchgoers. Their multicolored images depicting biblical scenes adorned England's Cathedral of York and the Abbey of Monkwearmouth, near Sunderland, and fragments of the abbey's windows have been found on its former site.

The first detailed record of stained glass windows is a sort of how-to crafts handbook, *Schedula diversarum artium,* written about 1125 by the monk Theophilus, who also practiced as a goldsmith under the name Rugerus of Helmarshausen. From this point on we know that designers were continually striving for more diverse and brilliant colors. Stained glass windows up to this time had been single panels depicting well-known scenes, such as the Virgin and the Child or Christ on the Cross. But the greatest innovation, arising in the 12th century, was a feature found in today's stained glass windows: the **narrative window;** that is, a series of closely spaced panels that tell a religious story.

Narrative windows made their first appearance between 1140 and 1144 at the Abbey of Saint-Denis near Paris, and soon their stunning larger-than-life presentations of the life of Christ and the saints attracted parishioners in droves. Through a new art form the church had found a way of beautifying its cathedrals, conveying a religious message, and at the same time increasing its Sunday fold. The latter fact was not overlooked and probably played a significant role in the sudden proliferation of stained glass narratives throughout Europe.

23

Medicine: Hospitals to Hypnosis

Medicine, Pre–3000 B.C.; Babylonia

"If the doctor, in opening an abscess, shall kill the patient, his hands shall be cut off."

That severe punishment for malpractice, which summarily put an end to a doctor's career, is found carved on a stone pillar dating to 3000 B.C. It is part of the Code of Hammurabi, which, along with dozens of cuneiform tablets of the period, constitutes the first written medical practices in history. If the patient was a slave, no retribution was meted out to the treating physician, but he was required to replace the slave with one of his own.

Medicine was a fascination of the Babylonians. When a professional physician was unavailable to treat a patient — usually with herbal medicines and a practice of divination in which the liver of a sacrificed animal was consulted to foretell the course of a disease — the sick person was laid in the street so that anyone passing could offer medical advice, making, in a sense, every Babylonian an amateur physician.

The Egyptians of that era were more discriminating, recognizing only licensed physicians. The first doctor of medicine to receive a degree, about 3000 B.C., was Imhotep, grand vizier to Egypt's King Zoser. Egyptian papyrus scrolls, discovered in the 19th century, reveal that Imhotep and his successors relied heavily on spells and incantations for treating disease, but also employed a variety of surgical procedures, such as blood-letting (to reduce fevers and

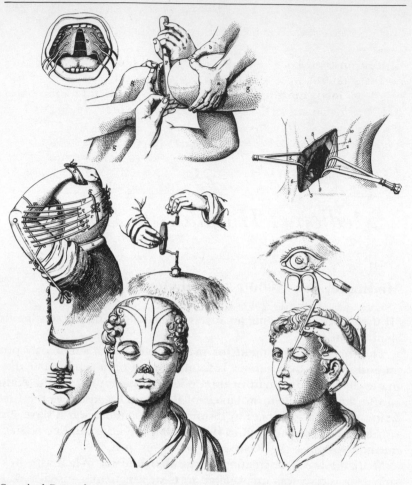

Surgical Procedures. Trephining, making a hole in the skull to release evil spirits that caused madness *(center)*, may have been practiced 10,000 years ago. Several skulls that have been unearthed contain what appear to be deliberate punctures.

to release evil spirits in cases of madness), as well as a storehouse of herbal medicines.

The origin of **modern medicine** dates to the early 4th century B.C., when the Greek physician Hippocrates established the foundations of medical diagnosis based on experience and observation.

Since classical times he has been regarded as "the father of medicine."

Born on the island of Cos, himself the son of a physician, Hippocrates taught in a medical school there and traveled and lectured on medicine throughout the Greek mainland. The *Hippocratic Collection,* a series of treatises on medical treatment and research, was written in part by Hippocrates and was still being used as a textbook in medical schools as late as the 19th century.

Because he believed that every illness or disease stemmed from a natural cause, Hippocrates scorned the notion that a person's taking sick was retribution from the gods. His caveat to physicians in treating any ailment was: "Life is short, and art long; opportunity fleeting; experiment dangerous, and judgment difficult."

In deduction, Hippocrates was nonpareil. He had no thermometers or stethoscopes to help him diagnose illness, but his own powers of logic and observation gave him an uncanny efficiency in finding the cause of an illness and foretelling its course.

Although the Hippocratic Oath probably was not written by Hippocrates but only named for him, it has provided a blueprint for medical ethics for more than 2000 years, and may be regarded as an authentic legacy of Hippocrates' principles. After Hippocrates, medicine progressed first through the biological research of Aristotle, then, in the 2nd century A.D., through anatomical studies of the Greek physician Galen of Pergamum, who practiced in Rome and laid the foundations for **experimental physiology.**

The teachings of Hippocrates, Aristotle, and Galen dominated throughout the Middle Ages and into the Renaissance. It was not until the 16th century that physicians began to dissect and rigorously examine human cadavers, revolutionizing medical teaching and making accurate surgery possible. This turning point is marked by a series of books known collectively as *De Humani Corporis Fabrica,* by the Belgian physician Andreas Vesalius; it usually is taken as the origin of **modern surgery.**

Embalming, 3000 B.C.; Egypt

Embalming originated with the ancient Egyptians, who went to elaborate lengths to preserve the bodies of their dead.

The earliest Egyptian method, dating to about 3000 B.C., called for wrapping the dead in cloth and burying them in charcoal and sand in the dry regions beyond the reach of the Nile. But by the dawn of the New Kingdom, embalming had become an exquisite art, and morticians strove painstakingly to give the dead as lifelike an appearance as possible.

The most elaborate methods of embalming the royal dead included extensive surgical procedures. The brain, intestines, heart, and other organs deemed vital to the Egyptians were excised from the body, washed in palm wine, and placed in fancy vases filled with herbs. Myrrh and other aromatic resins, as well as specially manufactured perfumes, then were poured into the body cavity and the incisions stitched closed. The body was packed in niter (saltpeter), an astringent, for more than two months, then removed, washed in wine, wrapped tightly in cotton bandages, dipped in a gummy substance (which may have been an antibacterial agent), put in an ornate coffin, and finally lowered into a sepulcher.

Modern embalming, in which the arteries are injected with a preservative, was initiated in the 1600s by the English physiologist and discoverer of the circulatory system, William Harvey. But the practice did not become widespread for another hundred years.

Perhaps a landmark corpse in the craft of embalming was that of Mrs. Martin Van Butchell, whose will specified that on her death, which took place in 1775, her husband had control of her fortune only as long as her body remained aboveground. Mausoleums were little known at the time, so the husband paid the Scottish anatomist William Hunter to embalm his dead wife; then he dressed her in fashionable attire and put her on display in the family parlor. Daily visiting hours were held for those who wished to view the corpse inside a glass-lidded coffin.

Undertaking quickly became a thriving business in England and the United States. Families were encouraged to soften the loss of loved ones through embalming. Some embalmers, to drum up new business, took their prize corpses on tour, exhibiting embalmed bodies in the windows of barbershops, in public halls, and at country fairs so that rural folk could get a glimpse of the latest in funeral treatment. And the public was duly impressed.

The technique of modern embalming has changed little over the last two hundred years. Blood is drained from the veins and replaced by a fluid, usually a preservative like Formalin (a solution of formaldehyde, methanol, and water). Another formaldehyde-based fluid, laced with alcohols, emulsifiers, and coloring agents, keeps the body from shriveling and turning a shade of liver-gray.

Arterial embalming is a temporary technique, and in cases where bodies are kept on display for long periods of time — such as Lenin's corpse in Moscow's Red Square — the procedure must be periodically renewed.

Pharmacopoeia, 2100 B.C.; Sumer

The first pharmacopoeia, or drug catalogue, originated near the end of the 3rd millennium B.C., when an unknown Sumerian physician began recording medical prescriptions he used to treat diseases. Preserved in cuneiform script on a single clay tablet, measuring 3.75-by-6.25 inches, are more than a dozen medications from animal, vegetable, and mineral sources. This oldest medical handbook known to man lay buried in the ruins of Nippur for more than 4000 years, until it was excavated by an American expedition in the early part of this century.

What did people take thousands of years ago for fevers, colds, sore throats, and more serious illnesses?

According to the ancient document, the favorite minerals were sodium chloride (salt) as an antiseptic and potassium nitrate as an astringent; the Sumerian physician seems to have obtained the latter from the nitrogenous waste products in sewage drains through which urine flowed. Among the most popular animal ingredients, made into thick salves and watery filtrates, were pulverized snakeskins, turtle shells, and dried milk.

The majority of Sumerian medicines were derived from the plant kingdom. The leaves of cassia, myrtle, asafetida, and thyme were dried, crushed, and added to salves; the barks of willow, pear, and fir trees were boiled to make potions. Salves were concocted from pulverized ingredients, mixed with *kushumma* wine and cedar oil, and smeared over an ailing limb. Filtrates were more complicated to make and show that the Sumerians had at least an elementary knowledge of distillation and crystallization.

The first pharmacopeia is disappointing in one regard: it fails to list the specific ailments that were treated with each medication. Sumerologists believe that this was the result of professional jealousy on the part of the physician compiling the catalogue (indicating that each doctor had his secret remedies), or the fact that medicines were regarded as interchangeable, since the Sumerians made no use of experimentation and verification.

Six hundred years earlier the Chinese had begun to record occasionally their own use of plant and mineral drugs. The Chinese emperor Shen Nung wrote what may well be the first scientific paper, in 2735 B.C., describing the antifever capabilities of an herbal substance known as *ch'ang shan,* which since has been found to contain antimalarial alkaloids.

About the same time, Egyptian physicians were treating constipation with a mixture of ground senna pods and castor oil, and also prescribing the chewing of caraway seeds and peppermint leaves to combat indigestion. To numb a person in great pain, Egyptian doctors resorted to ethyl alcohol, an effective stupefying agent.

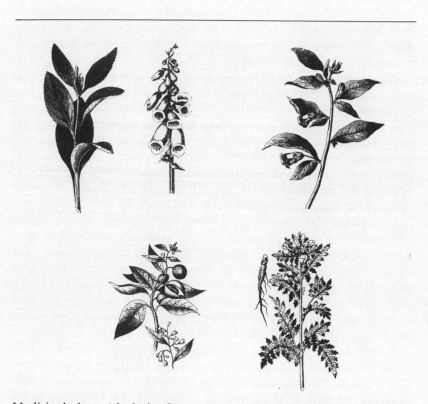

Medicinal plants (clockwise from upper right): Belladonna, lousewort, nutmeg, and purple foxglove (leaves and flowers), from which is derived the heart medication digitalis

The 16th century witnessed major discoveries in chemistry and correspondingly great innovations in pharmacology. The first **modern pharmacopoeia,** listing hundreds of drugs and medicinal chemicals, with explicit directions for preparing them, appeared in Nürnberg, Germany, in 1546. Drugs that had previously varied greatly in concentrations, and even in constituents, suddenly were stringently defined by text, which quickly spawned versions in Switzerland, Italy, and England. The *London Pharmacopoeia,* published in 1618, was available to doctors as well as to laymen who could afford it, and thus became the first national drug catalogue.

The Origins of Modern Drugs

Digitalis, 1785

A myocardial stimulant that comes from the leaf of the foxglove plant. Still used as a preventive of cardiac arrest, digitalis was introduced into medicine by William Withering of England.

Morphine, 1805

An alkaloid of opium, which is the dried latex of unripe poppy blossoms. The drug is employed as a narcotic analgesic, but its recent unsavory use by junkies has become more prominent than its medical use. Morphine was identified by the German pharmacologist Friedrich Sertürner in 1805, and first used in medicine in 1821, named by Sertürner after Morpheus, the Greek god of sleep.

Nitroglycerin, 1846

Although it won fame as an explosive agent, the compound also became widely used as a vasodilator for easing the cardiac disorder angina pectoris. This followed its initial application as an explosive in 1846 by Ascanio Sobrero of Italy.

Cocaine, 1859

Originally used as an anesthetic, this powdery substance, which also can be liquefied and injected, was separated from the Peruvian coca leaves in 1859 by Dr. Niemann and put into a formula a year later by Dr. Friedrich Wöhler. As a local anesthetic, its use dates to 1884.

Saccharin, 1879

An artificial sweetener, widely used as a sugar substitute, it was initially introduced for the benefit of diabetic patients.

Amphetamine, 1887

It did not come into general use until 1927, when its ability to elevate blood pressure, dilate bronchial passages, and stimulate the central nervous system was discovered. The first marketed amphetamine, in 1932, was Benzedrex, an inhalant which contained the active agent Benzedrine. Used by cold sufferers to open clogged nasal passages, Benzedrex and a later variety of amphetamines achieved popularity because they also helped the user to fight fatigue and increase alertness. Regular heavy use results in hallucinations and delusions, as well as depression.

Aspirin, 1893

The common name for acetylsalicylic acid, a carbon-based by-product often made from coal tar. The first antiuretic, it was introduced by Hermann Dresser, a German, who also noted its benefits as a painkiller and a fever reducer. Marketed in 1899 by the German company Farbenfabriken Bayer A.G., aspirin quickly became the world's largest-selling nonprescription drug. It was first available as a loose powder in individual doses in small envelopes, then as capsules. Aspirin tablets were introduced by Bayer in 1915.

Adrenalin, 1901

A hormone that constricts blood vessels, adrenalin is secreted by the medulla of the adrenal glands. Also a sympathomimetic, adrenalin was isolated by Jokichi Takamine. Its molecular weight was determined by Thomas B. Aldrich, and it was synthesized for the first time in 1904 by Friedrich Stolz.

Phenobarbital, 1903

A hypnotic, a potent sedative, and an anticonvulsant, it also relieves high blood pressure. Injections in the usual dosage of 50 to 100 mg cause drowsiness and muscular relaxation for several hours. Because it is a barbiturate, its hazards include addiction. Barbituric acid, from which all barbiturates are derived, was first synthesized in 1864 by the German chemist Adolph von Baeyer, who won a Nobel Prize in 1905. Other popular early barbiturates were Veronal, Seconal, Nembutal, Amytal, and Lumital.

Novocain, 1905

A trade name for procaine hydrochloride, introduced by Alfred Einhorn as a local anesthetic and as a substitution for cocaine, it has nonaddictive qualities but low potency.

Insulin, 1921

Used extensively in the treatment of diabetes, it was isolated from the mammalian pancreas by Sir Frederick Banting and Dr. Charles H. Best of Canada but was not synthesized until 1964.

Progesterone, 1929

A female steroid hormone secreted by the ovary, it was isolated by G. Corner and W. Allen. It occurs naturally to prepare the uterus for pregnancy following ovulation, and its related compounds are used with estrogen in oral contraceptives.

Testosterone, 1929

Identified by C. Moore, T. Gallagher, and F. Koch as an androgenic, or masculine hormone, testosterone is related to anabolic, or muscle-building, steroids, used by athletes. Its original purpose was to treat anemia victims.

Sulfa Drugs, 1935

The first of these forerunners of penicillin was sulfanilamide. Its prevention of the growth of bacteria soon led to more than 6000 derivatives — all known for their potent antibacterial effects.

Penicillin, 1940

Among the first of the so-called miracle drugs of the 20th century, it was discovered in 1928 by Sir Alexander Fleming. Its history is discussed later in this chapter.

Streptomycin, 1944

A sulfate important in treating tuberculosis, it was discovered by Selman A. Waksman, an American microbiologist, who won a Nobel Prize in 1952.

Cortisone, 1939

An agent first used, as an injection, in 1949 in the treatment of rheumatoid arthritis. The steroid hormone, derived from adrenocortical extracts, was identified and named ten years earlier. Its use was under suspicion until the Japanese research team of Kira and Morotomi coupled it with Vitamin E in 1967 and eliminated many of its serious side effects.

Oral contraceptives, 1955

"The pill," as this birth control device is commonly called, is made of synthetic hormones to prevent ovulation. The first reported studies of the contraceptive were made in 1955 in Puerto Rico.

Interferon, 1957

A natural body substance and a controversial drug of late for its reputed cancer-conquering qualities. It was first used to inhibit the spread of viruses.

Librium, 1960

A tranquilizer. This is a brand name for chlordiazepoxide. Developed by a Polish-American scientist, Leo Sternback, it quickly became more popular than its 1950 predecessors, Miltown and Equanil. It is effective in treating anxiety, tension, convulsions, and neuromuscular and cardiovascular disorders.

Valium, 1963

A tranquilizer. This is a brand name for diazepam. Developed for Roche Laboratory by Leo Sternback, discoverer of Librium. It fast became the single most widely used tranquilizer in the world.

Propanolol, 1968

A cardiovascular medication that affects the rate and rhythm of the heart and can be useful in the treatment of angina pectoris and hypertension.

Soap, 600 B.C.; Phoenicia

Soap as a cleansing agent for the body was first prepared by the Phoenicians in 600 B.C.; it was made from blending goat's fat with wood ash. Inveterate traders who sailed the Mediterranean, the Phoenicians introduced soap to the Greeks and the Romans, and, according to the Roman writer Pliny the Elder, sold it as a medication, possibly as a laxative, to the Gauls.

The Romans, with their exquisite baths and fountains, greeted

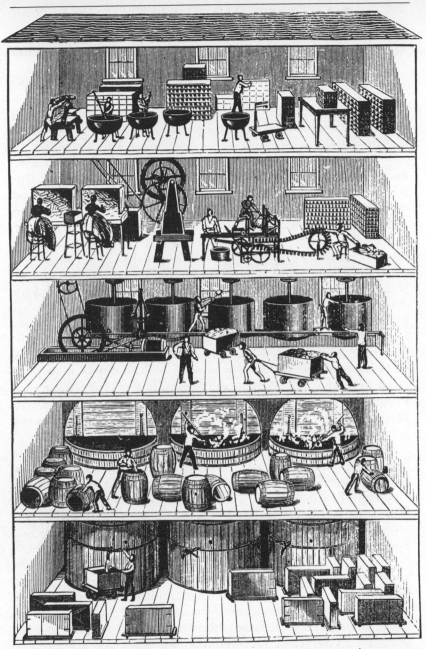

Early factory production of soap, a commodity that for centuries was regarded as a mystery, a novelty, and an insult to give as a gift

soap eagerly. The word derives from the soapwort plant, whose sap was an early cleansing agent, and whose ash was mixed with animal fats to make soap.

Today we don't think of soap as a medicine, but that's precisely how it was regarded by the 2nd-century Greek physician Galen. He saw its medicinal value in cleansing wounds in particular, and the body in general, and heartily recommended it to all Greeks and Romans.

The Phoenicians probably made soap by boiling goat fat in water and gradually adding plant ashes rich in potassium carbonate. They stirred in ashes until the water evaporated and the mixture hardened. What the Phoenicians did not know was that as the mixture was brewing, the neutral fats split, allowing the fatty acids to react chemically with the alkali carbonates of the plant ash to form the finished product. Today this process is called saponification.

Soap was not welcomed by all countries. During the Middle Ages, when a Celtic method for making soap spread throughout much of Europe, many people feared that bathing the whole body too frequently — more than once a month or, in some regions, more than once a year — could be dangerous to one's health, if not fatal. Even after the production of soap had become a flourishing business in Marseille, Genoa, and Venice in the 11th century, and in England in the 12th century (London became the soap capital of the world two hundred years later), the Central Europeans emphatically resisted use of the product.

When the duchess of Jülich in Germany was presented with a box of soap in 1549, she was highly insulted and, in a furor, evicted the gift-bearer. Even as late as 1672, when a German nobleman visiting Italy sent a parcel of Venetian soaps home to Lady von Schleinitz, he was forced to enclose instructions on how to use the mysterious product, and to stress that it was being sent only as a novelty.

By the 19th century sentiments had changed. Throughout France and England the tax on soap was so high for a time after the Napoleonic Wars that people secretly manufactured their own soap in the darkness of night. The German chemist Baron Justus von Liebig went so far as to issue a statement that the wealth of a nation, and its degree of civilization, could be judged according to the quantity of soap it consumed.

In modern times manufacturers have developed synthetic detergents for industrial cleansing and for washing fabrics. Initially they were based on the synthetic chemical ABS (alkyl benzenesulfonic acid), and for a number of years more than half of all detergents that went into washing machines worldwide had an ABS base. But in the late 1960s and early 1970s, ABS detergents, which are nonbiodegradable and thus present a hazard to the environment, were replaced by biodegradable products, ones that reverted to the environment from which they came, such as linear alkyl sulfonates, whose ingredients return to their natural form.

Hospital, 500 B.C.; India

As institutions for treating the sick and infirm, hospitals are relatively new, especially when compared with the origins of drugs and of the field of medicine itself, which date to about 3000 B.C. In the intervening centuries the sick were treated in their homes by physicians and faith healers, a practice that began to fade once hospitals were established.

The first hospitals of which there are records were set up in India about 500 B.C., and a few decades later, in the form of small clinics, in the region that is now Sri Lanka. Stressing cleanliness, proper nutrition, and the gentle treatment of patients by physicians' assistants, the equivalent of today's nurses, the first hospitals were in principle like their modern versions. One emperor of India, Asoka, to demonstrate humanitarian concern for his subjects, built eighteen hospitals during his reign in the 3rd century B.C.

About a hundred years earlier the Greeks had made a momentous medical discovery, establishing the basis for **public health.**

Plagued with a wave of malaria, Greek physicians, eschewing the age-old belief that pestilence was a punishment from the gods, sought a natural cause for the disease. In the middle of the 5th century B.C., they established a link between malaria and stagnant swamps, and some time afterward Hippocrates wrote a book, *Airs, Waters, and Places* — generally taken as the origin of public health — which represented the first systematic attempt to associate a variety of human diseases with environmental causes. The tome remained the theoretical basis for understanding epidemic disease until the new sciences of bacteriology and immunology emerged in the 19th century, and it served to encourage the spread of hospitals.

For the Greeks, and later for the Romans, temples took on the dual responsibilities of houses of worship and hospitals, a practice that became even more firmly established with the arrival of Christianity. The Christian emperor Constantine in A.D. 335 ordered that hospitals for the lame, the chronically ill, and the homeless be built in Rome, Constantinople, Ephesus, and in six other cities in the Roman Empire. Care for sick bodies became a church concern second only to care for sick souls.

Hospitals during the Middle Ages were run largely by monks, in wings of monasteries called *infirmitoria*. Each *infirmitorium* contained a pharmacy and a garden rich in medicinal plants. Combining spiritual and bodily healing, monks primarily treated members of their own orders, but they also opened their hospitals to pilgrims and other travelers in need of medical attention. With the Crusades, which began in 1096, *infirmitoria* opened their doors to wounded warriors who fought to liberate the Holy Land (Palestine) from the Saracens, followers of Islam.

The **modern hospital** originated in the 19th century, following the recognition of germs and the use of antiseptics by Louis Pasteur and Joseph Lister, and the transformation of nursing into a dignified profession by the pioneering efforts of Florence Nightingale.

The first hospital built in the Americas, established by the conquistador Cortez in Mexico City in 1524, is still standing today. Within the boundaries of what is now the United States, the first hospital was constructed on Manhattan Island in 1663.

Antibiotics, 500 B.C.; China

The moldy curd of soy beans appears to have been the first crude antibiotic; it was used by the Chinese about 500 B.C. for treating carbuncles, boils, and related infections. Almost as old, and existing in several civilizations, was the use of moldy bread and cobwebs in the treatment of festering wounds.

Curiously, though doctors for the next 2000 years sought a class of drugs to combat bacterial infections, not a single researcher thought to investigate scientifically the medical folklore surrounding molds. The first modern antibiotic, penicillin, discovered by the Scottish bacteriologist Sir Alexander Fleming in 1928, was a serendipitous find.

Fleming had been a medical officer in military hospitals in England during World War I. He realized the serious need for a bactericidal agent for treating infected wounds, and after the war he returned to St. Mary's Hospital in London to solve the problem. In 1928, while researching into *Staphylococcus aureus,* a bacterium responsible for abscesses and a wide range of other infections, he took a few days' vacation, leaving his glass culture dishes unsupervised. On returning he noticed that the lid of one dish had slipped off and the culture had become contaminated with mold from the atmosphere.

Fleming was about to discard the culture, but curiosity prompted him to examine it first. In the area where the mold was growing, the staphylococcus cells had died. He immediately realized the significance of this find and determined that the mold, a strain of the fungus *Penicillium,* was secreting a substance that destroyed bacteria. Although he failed to isolate the substance — that remained to be done ten years later by Ernst B. Chain and Sir Howard W. Florey in England — he named it penicillin. In 1945, Chain, Florey, and Fleming shared the Nobel Prize in medicine for the discovery of penicillin.

Britain, preoccupied in 1938 with worries of war, waived its right for eventual mass production of penicillin. The United States assumed responsibility, and after two years of additional research to purify and stabilize the substance, was credited with ushering in the era of modern medicine referred to as the "golden age of chemotherapy," symbolized by the development of penicillin.

Inoculation, 17th Century; Turkey

For many centuries smallpox was one of the most dreaded and disfiguring diseases in Europe. Each epidemic killed thousands of victims and left even more permanently scarred from the disease's blisters, which could completely obliterate facial features. The resultant pockmarks were hideous and a scourge the victim bore throughout life.

Some immunity was possible. The Chinese had discovered that smallpox resistance could be induced if the scabs that flaked off one victim were pulverized and blown up the nostrils of someone who had not contracted the disease. But it was a risky procedure, for sometimes the person, instead of developing immunity to smallpox, came down with a virulent case of the disease.

An equally dangerous immunization practice arose in the 17th century in Turkey, and also in Greece. Pus from the blisters of sufferers was scratched with a needle into the skin of a healthy person, producing, it was hoped, only a mild attack of the disease. Lady Mary Wortley Montagu learned about the practice when she lived with her husband, the English ambassador to Turkey, in Constantinople (now Istanbul). On returning to England in 1721, she had her son inoculated in a public demonstration for physicians. Effective and easy to perform, the practice of inoculation spread throughout Europe during the 18th century, even though an inoculated person risked contracting the disease.

The idea of a smallpox vaccine — and hence the modern practice of vaccination — originated with an English country doctor, Edward Jenner, in 1796.

Jenner was familiar with the folk belief that farmers who caught cowpox from cattle were safe from smallpox. If this was true, thought Jenner, the medical implications were profound; since cowpox was a very mild disease, it might be used to immunize humans from the dreaded smallpox.

For twenty years Jenner cautiously researched the possibilities. In the summer of 1796 he finally tested his theory by inoculating an eight-year-old farmboy with cowpox. The boy soon developed the mild rash characteristic of the disease, and when it cleared up Jenner confidently inoculated him with smallpox. The boy showed no signs of the disease, clearly indicating that he had been immunized.

Jenner named his procedure "vaccination," from the Latin word for cowpox, *vaccinia,* and its use spread rapidly throughout the world.

In 1877 the French chemist Louis Pasteur, and his countryman, Jules-François Joubert, found that anthrax bacteria, when injected into healthy animals, actually kept them from contracting the very disease the bacteria represented.

All our current immunization programs against the myriad of childhood and tropical diseases — including the Salk polio vaccine (1952), the Sabin oral polio vaccine (1961), and the Enders measles vaccine (1962), which virtually eliminated these illnesses in many parts of the world — stem from Jenner's discovery, which is considered one of the greatest medical breakthroughs in the history of medicine.

Hypnosis, 18th Century; France

The ways to alter human consciousness are so numerous — through herbal drugs, hyperventilation, meditation, to name a few — that it is impossible to determine when man discovered the extraordinary mentation of hypnosis. Accounts of various forms of trance-like behavior appeared in the writings of early Egyptian healers and, later, in the teachings of the Greeks. The word "hypnosis," derived from the Greek *hypnos,* meaning "sleep," was coined in the 1840s by a Scottish surgeon, James Braid.

The "discovery" of hypnosis in Europe usually is attributed to Franz Anton Mesmer, an Austrian physician working in France in the late 1700s. About the time of the American Revolution, Mesmer observed that ailing people often were benefited by magnets passed over their bodies. To learn more of this mysterious healing phenomenon, he held séances. The participants sat around an open tub from which magnetized bars protruded. Occasionally, reported Mesmer, a person entered a convulsive fit, or "crisis," then lapsed into apparent sleep, only to awaken either cured or considerably improved.

Soon Mesmer dispensed with the magnets and focused his treatment on soothingly touching the person, or on touching water that the patient then drank. He became convinced that his touch "magnetized" water; and from his seemingly miraculous cures, he concluded that he was blessed with "animal magnetism," a kind of "fluid" that he could store and transfer to the sick to heal them.

Mesmer's treatment was probably a blend of hypnosis and faith healing, and his alleged cures, if genuine, were most likely a result of hypnotic suggestion, a patient's desire to be healed, or the phenomenon used by many religious healers today, which psychologists refer to as "hysterical suppression of symptoms" — often short-lived relief.

A protégé of Mesmer's, the nobleman Chastenet de Puysegur, carried the charismatic approach even further, "magnetizing" a tree on his estate. Ailing peasants purportedly obtained comfort merely by touching the tree. De Puysegur abandoned the "mesmeric crisis" philosophy in 1780, after discovering that a person could be "mesmerized" simply by soft, monotonal talk. The practice of hypnosis has changed little since de Puysegur adopted this tack in the 18th century.

Psychiatry, 1792; Paris

The Babylonians were probably the first people to practice a formal kind of psychiatry; they prescribed opium and olive oil as a cure for madness, thought to be provoked by demonic possession. In more severe cases of lunacy, they may have practiced trephining (or trepanning), a primitive and brutal kind of brain surgery in which a hole was made in the skull to vent evil spirits. It put an end to madness, but often put an end to the patient as well.

Trephining is one those practices that seems to have been rediscovered several times in the history of medicine. A 12th-century Italian physician employed it to treat all sorts of psychiatric problems. He fitted onto a patient's head a contraption that held a large screw, which, turned by a crank, bore into the skull. The unanesthetized patient was usually tied down, or held immobile, by several assistants.

Trephining in a simpler form, in which a metal spike was driven by hammer blows into the skull, is discussed in the writings of early Greek and Roman healers, and many fossil skulls of prehistoric man reveal punctures that suggest the practice was employed tens of thousands of years ago.

Brain anatomy, particularly the arrangement of the brain's ventricles or fluid-filled cavities, was known to the ancient Greeks and contributed to a view of mental health that began with Plato and Aristotle and was periodically elaborated on well into the Middle Ages. The theory held that nutrients, absorbed through the intestines, passed to the liver, where a fluid called *natural spirit* was formed. This flowed to the heart, where it became *vital spirit,* which pulsed toward blood vessels at the base of the brain. Here it mixed with air entering through the nose. The final product was a perfect distillation, called *animal spirit,* which was stored in the ventricles. This spirit was the essence of life, the source of all intellect, and, when contaminated by illness, the seat of all madness. Not surprisingly, for centuries all attempts to treat mental illness involved some form of surgery to vent or purify this mental liquid.

Psychiatry took a turn, though not for the better, in the year 1400, when the first asylum was opened by two German Dominican priests in Valencia, Spain. Institutionalized patients were still shackled and copiously bled and purged to rid them of evil spirits, and the Dominicans broadened the definition of mental illness to include practitioners of witchcraft and the sexually promiscuous.

The "father of modern psychiatry," Johann Wier, a Belgian physician who practiced during the 16th century, was among the first to condemn belief in witchcraft as superstition. A more humane asylum, the Bethlehem Royal Hospital — called Bedlam — opened in England during the same century. There, the new practice of electric current therapy was employed on patients.

Modern psychiatry's origins, despite the ascription to Wier, is usually credited to the appointment in 1792 of Philippe Pinel as physician-in-chief at the Bicêtre hospital for the insane in Paris. Pinel removed the inhumane chains that hobbled mental patients and recognized emotional causes for psychiatric disturbances.

The origins of **modern psychosurgery** can be traced to a research report delivered by two neurologists at a conference in London in 1935.

Drs. C. Jacobsen and J. Fulton reported on an experiment in which they rendered a violent chimpanzee docile by surgical removal of part of the frontal lobes of the cerebral hemispheres. A Portuguese neurologist, Antonio Egas Moniz, rose after the talk and asked: "If frontal lobe removal prevents the development of experimental neuroses in animals, and eliminates frustrated behavior, why would it not be feasible to relieve anxiety states in man by surgical means?"

Within a year Moniz and a surgeon, Almeida Lima, had performed several such operations. Hearing of their success, two American doctors, Walter Freeman and James Watts, adopted the procedure in the late 1940s. A surgical instrument called a "precision leucotome," a blunt knife, was inserted into small holes made in the temples at the side of the skull. The blade was then swept up and down to cut the nerve fibers that run between the frontal lobes and the limbic system, or emotion center of the brain. Violent patients were calmed, but usually at the cost of chunks of memory and gross alterations in their personalities — so much that they became "different people."

The dapper, charismatic Freeman, in his eagerness to bring the relief of lobotomy to the largest number of sufferers from mental anguish, introduced this "blind" surgical procedure to the United States in an even simpler form. The patient was merely stunned by an electric shock to the head, and a sharp metal icepick was hammered up through the thin bone directly above the eye, then twisted from side to side to cut through the frontal lobes. The main complaint Freeman heard was that the patients got black eyes.

Freeman was a showman, touring the country, performing operations in front of lecture halls of students and on closed-circuit television, often without sterile precautions. Each side of the brain could be "done in a couple of minutes," he boasted, and "an enterprising neurologist [could] lobotomize ten to fifteen patients in a morning." One day in 1951, in Spencer, West Virginia, he operated on twenty-five women in a single workday.

Though Freeman's critics deplored the lobotomized patient's dullness — "It does disturb me to see the number of zombies that these operations turn out," wrote one fellow physician — Freeman himself argued that "lobotomized patients make good American citizens . . . the operation has potential for controlling society's misfits — schizophrenics, homosexuals, radicals . . ." By the mid-1950s more than 19,000 Americans alone, including prisoners and children, had been lobotomized. Finally, a storm of protests in the latter part of the decade virtually halted Freeman's procedure.

Psychiatry today can be viewed as a multidisciplinary field that includes Freudian psychoanalysis, several popular forms of psychotherapy, and the biochemical treatment of such ailments as manic-depressive psychosis and schizophrenia with a wide variety of new psychopharmacological drugs.

Modern Food Preservation, 1810; France

Early man battled the elements to keep a steady supply of food at hand. Whether he had to cope with a short growing season or survive periods of scarcity, there always were times when he needed the assurance that he could preserve his food to meet his nutritional needs. When he began trekking from his native habitat, taking to sea or going on military expeditions, food preservation became essential, and he devised methods like fermenting and pickling vegetables and fruits in brine, and smoking and curing meats and fish.

For centuries these methods sufficed. Then in 1795, with a burgeoning population in Europe and militarism at an all-time high, the French government sought better means. It offered a large stipend to anyone who could develop a transportable means of preservation that would enable food to reach soldiers in the field. Nicolas Appert, a chef from the town of Châlons-sur-Marne, who also happened to be a confectioner and distiller, became bent on devising a solution. In the years following the French Revolution, Appert toiled away in the face of spreading pestilence and starvation. Fourteen years later, he announced his system in the treatise *The Art of Preserving All Kinds of Animal and Vegetable Substances for Several Years.*

Its premise was that decomposition could be prevented if such foods as soups, jams, stews, and fruits were sealed in airtight jars and bottles. The exclusion of air staved off spoilage. Appert accomplished this by immersing the jars with their contents in boiling water for several hours. They were stoppered with corks, then sealed with wax, and, when sampled several months later, retained the flavor of fresh food — much to the amazement of the government panel, which awarded Appert a prize of 12,000 francs in 1810.

Appert's seemingly simple formula for preservation was a baffler, however, since the connection between microorganisms and putrefaction would not be revealed for another half-century with the investigations into fermentation and bacteria by another Frenchman, Louis Pasteur.

With the prize money Appert established the world's first bottlery, the House of Appert, which remained in operation until 1933. At the time Appert was demonstrating his process, an English merchant, Peter Durand, pioneered one of the real hallmarks of modern society — the **tin can.** Durand took out a patent in 1810 for preserving food in "tinplate" containers and three years later was supplying meat to the Royal Navy under a government contract.

Although introduced in 1819 to the United States — today its chief manufacturer — the tin can was virtually ignored until the Civil War, forty-two years later. Mass production began in 1895, and the symbol of prepackaged convenience foods was on its way to changing modern society.

Anesthetics, 1842; United States

In 1842 a rural Georgia physician, Crawford W. Long, excised a small cyst from the neck of a youth, James Venable, who was under the influence of **ether.** It marked the first successful use of anesthesia in surgery and prompted doctors to experiment with various other gases. Two years later, Long's wife became the first woman to deliver under ether, at the birth of their second child.

The term "anesthesia," from the Greek for "lack of feeling," was coined in 1846 in Boston, after the initial demonstration of the safe and effective use of ether on a male patient during major surgery.

Until anesthetic gases came into use, physicians had attempted to alleviate pain with a variety of processes that often inflicted more suffering than they relieved. To extract a tooth or amputate a leg, surgeons often resorted to such crude sedatives as mild asphyxiation, alcoholic intoxication, freezing the part of the body undergoing surgery, and having the patient inhale fumes from burning narcotic plants, a dangerous practice called stupefaction.

The anesthetic effects of a gas were first noted by the British physician Sir Humphry Davy, in the late 18th century. A great believer in sniffing and tasting unknown chemicals, Davy discovered that the gas called nitrous oxide, a compound of nitrogen and oxygen, possessed some unusual qualities. Inhaling it at first produced in Davy a soaring euphoria, which soon passed into uncontrollable paroxysms of laughter and sobbing, until he was rendered unconscious by the substance he unhesitantly called "laughing gas." Shortly afterward, carbon dioxide was found to stupefy animals, but it and nitrous oxide were used only intermittently on humans for several years.

Crawford Long was one of several American physicians who, between 1842 and 1846, proved the safety and effectiveness of anesthesia. His main pioneering colleagues were a Connecticut dentist, Horace Wells, who in 1844 extracted a tooth while his patient was under nitrous oxide, and an orthodontist, William Morton, who in 1846 at Boston's Massachusetts General Hospital anesthesized a patient with diethyl ether and removed a tumor from his jaw. A few months later, in England, Dr. John Snow, foreseeing the burgeoning field of anesthetics, devoted himself to experimenting with new gases and soon introduced **chloroform** as a numbing agent for women experiencing difficult childbirth.

Anesthesia revolutionized surgery. Physicians suddenly had more time to examine the patients on the operating table and detect malignancies and the spread of disease. Because an anesthetized patient was insensitive to pain, procedures were no longer hurried, and doctors began to associate certain diseases with pathological changes in organs and remove them surgically.

Physicians who viewed anesthesia as a panacea for all operating room procedures were frighteningly jarred, however, when patients undergoing chloroforming suddenly died during surgery. Awareness of dosage, and to a large extent the introduction of local anesthetics for minor surgery, lessened these fears. The use of "locals" stemmed from the discovery in 1884 that cocaine, when applied to the eye, produced an insensitivity to pain almost equal to that caused by gaseous anesthetics.

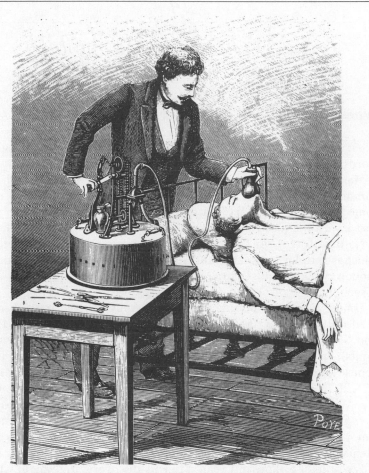

The fatal anesthetizing of patients was an early pitfall before physicians mastered the science of measured dosage of anesthesia.

24

Land: Wheels to Automobiles

Wheel, Pre–3500 B.C.; Sumer

What came first, the potter's wheel or the wagon wheel? In other words, the horizontal wheel or the vertical wheel?

Many archeologists believe that the potter's wheel, used for spinning earthenware, was already in use by 4000 B.C. and that some Sumerian visionary, watching a potter plying his trade, was struck with the idea for a brilliant new use for the horizontal wheel.

Natural forces, in fact, suggest that horizontal rotary motion, which is simpler to execute and sustain, did predate vertical rotary motion, which requires finer balancing of weights and forces and a keener sense of how to overcome friction.

Unlike other inventions, the wheel seems to have been discovered only once, by the Sumerians, approximately between 4000 and 3500 B.C., in the Tigris-Euphrates Valley. It was a frequent symbol in early Sumerian pictogram script, and actual wheeled vehicles, crude carts and wagons, were unearthed at royal tombs at Kish, Sura, and Ur, where they had been buried about 3000 B.C. When the wagon wheel arrived, it revolutionized transportation and greatly lightened man's burden, for Sumerian farmers suddenly had a new means of transporting their crops to city residents.

For at least a thousand years after its discovery, the wagon wheel remained a solid three-piece disc. The tripartite wheel, as it is called, consisted of three planks of wood carved as segments of a circle and clamped together by transverse struts with an opening in the center to accommodate an axle. The axle was constructed independently and extended several inches beyond the wheel's hub. But whether or not the wheel revolved freely or turned with the axle is unknown. The first great transportation invention spread rapidly, and by 2000 B.C. wagons with solid wheels were being pulled by man and beast in China, Syria, the British Isles, Scandinavia, Sardinia, and the Balkans.

The *spoke wheel* also seems to have originated among the people of the Tigris-Euphrates Valley, between 2000 to 1500 B.C. Lighter in weight, it facilitated more rapid transportation and, also discovered only once, it spread quickly to Syria, Egypt, and the eastern Mediterranean, all but replacing the lumbering solid wheel.

Of ancient wheels that have survived, two common types have wooden rims studded with copper nails, and wooden rims fitted with strips of bronze, which apparently served as the first tires.

Tunnel, 3000 B.C.; Egypt

The first man-made tunnels large enough for people to pass through freely were dug by the Egyptians — not for the purpose of transportation from one part of the city to another, but as ritual chambers for secretly burying their dead. As the design of burial tunnels became more structurally elaborate, and the Egyptian engineers became more skilled in tunnel technology, they began building tunnels that allowed metals to be mined from the countryside and water to be transported to arid land.

Appropriating the Egyptians' skills, other societies recognized the benefits of tunnels in warfare. Historians, for example, believe that the walls of Jericho almost certainly toppled because Joshua's army dug a tunnel underneath them and lighted a fire that burned the walls' wooden supports. The extensive tunnels built by the Romans, especially those which bored through mountains, were precursors of our modern subway systems.

In the middle of the 19th century, the rapid development of railroads and subways provoked a renaissance in tunnel engineering that continues unabated today. However, the most ambitious such venture ever undertaken, a tunnel beneath the English Channel to connect Great Britain with the continent, has been abandoned several times. Not because of insufficient technology,

Illustration of the Thames Tunnel in London, construction and completion

but because of continually rising costs, which now seem to have made the project forever a tunneler's dream.

Bridge, 700 B.C.; Babylon

Trees, felled by nature, that by chance connected opposite sides of a stream served as bridges in prehistoric times. Copying these natural constructions, early man learned to span rivers and streams by chopping down trees whose length, in a single unbroken stretch, conveniently became bridges. But the first true bridge, constructed from arrangements of logs and fastened together with twine, was laid about 700 B.C. across the Euphrates River at Babylon and lasted for many decades.

Bridge over the Susquehanna River, at Havre de Grace

Indian tribes in South and Central America constructed crude but successful suspension bridges about 2000 years ago. But the most successful of early bridge builders were the Romans, gifted in architectural design and adept at engineering. In 50 B.C., they linked the banks of the Rhine with a 1378-foot wooden bridge, completed within ten days after Julius Caesar ordered its construction.

Modern bridges originated in the 19th century. One early example was the suspension bridge built over Niagara Falls in 1855 by John Roebling, in its day considered the latest wonder of the world. Its present-day equivalent, the world's longest suspension span and a true architectural marvel, is the Verrazano Bridge, spanning the Narrows of New York Harbor and connecting Brooklyn and Staten Island.

Roads, Pre–300 B.C.; Rome

The earliest roads were simply animal paths followed by man as he emerged from the cradles of civilization, expanding his horizons. Although all of the early societies had roads — either natural pathways or clear stretches they made by felling trees and leveling the land — the first true road-builders were the Romans. With their meticulous nature and sophisticated engineering skills, they turned road-building into a science, creating a staggering 53,000 miles of paved roadways fanning out over their empire.

The Romans built twenty-nine major roads (most for military purposes) leading radially from Rome, the first and most famous the *Via Appia* (Appian Way). It was begun in 312 B.C. and ran 350 miles from the outskirts of Rome to Brundisium. Scientifically engineered, the Appian Way was 35 feet wide and built with two center lines paved with flint gravel laid over a foundation of stone. The main portion of road, a sort of fast lane, was separated from two outer one-way lanes by high stone curbs, or dividers.

The engineering ideas initiated by the Roman road-builders have survived to the present day. Modern roads still employ four Roman features: multilayered paving, slightly curved edges to allow rainfall run-off, elevation above the ground, and adjacent ditches to handle water spillage. In fact, Roman ideas dominated road-building throughout the Western world until the 18th century, when the French brought a new dimension to the art: the water-resistant surface. Blacktopping, or tarmac-surfaced roads, became the vogue with the introduction in this century of the rubber automobile tire.

The first fully paved trans-American highway, connecting New York to San Francisco, was the famous Lincoln Highway, begun in 1913 and completed in 1927.

Traffic Engineering, A.D. 100; Rome

With thousands of miles of paved roads, it is only natural that the Romans were the first people to develop the art of traffic engineering. Although they did not have street lights, they had practically everything else: stop signs, one-way streets, two-lane highways, and even alternate-side-of-the-street parking. And when daytime traffic in downtown Rome became a nightmare, with mounted horses, chariots, hand-pulled carts, and donkey-drawn wagons all vying for road space, the Roman Senate instituted the first traffic bans, allowing certain vehicles access to certain streets at particular times of the day. Personal hand-pulled carts, for example, were banned on downtown streets during the daylight hours in the 1st century A.D.

The **modern highway** is not an American invention, as many may believe, but of Italian design. This century's paved, high-speed thoroughfares, a real boon to motorized traffic, first appeared in the Italian automotive center of Milan, where two-lane *autostradas* were developed by the industry as an enticement to people to buy cars. After all, what fun would it be to own an expensive, fast, easily maneuverable sports car unless there were wide, smoothly paved, uncongested roads to race over?

The **freeway,** however, is an American invention of the current century. Italian roads, because of the country's mountainous topography, contained many zigzag hairpin turns, with four lanes suddenly merging into two that tightly hugged a mountainside, with a sharp precipice on the opposite side dropping to the sea. The freeway, on the other hand, called for elementary traffic logic: no sharp curves, clearly divided opposing lanes, no turns into the path of oncoming traffic, marked lanes of 12-foot standard width, and absolutely no roadside development or advertising — though the last restriction is routinely violated today.

The Pennsylvania Turnpike, constructed between 1937 and 1940, featuring a four-lane divided highway with overpasses, underpasses, and access limited to interchanges, served as the prototype for today's superhighways.

Bus, 1830; England

The first bus, an austere eighteen-seat, six-wheeled, steam-driven stagecoach, was invented in 1830 by Sir Goldsworthy Gurney of England. He personally drove the inaugural trip from London to Bath, a distance of 80 miles. So successful was the maiden run that in less than a year the first scheduled bus service was in operation between Gloucester and Cheltenham, transporting passengers on three of Gurney's steam coaches.

Like all early buses, Gurney's invention was primarily a modified truck — a top-heavy body mounted on a motorized truck chassis. This practical but ungraceful hybrid is still found today in the body lines of most school buses, which are set over reinforced truck chassis.

Copying the British design and refining it, Germany introduced in 1895 an eight-passenger omnibus powered by a small single-cylinder combustion engine. It was a considerable improvement in speed and handling, but still far from ideal. Buses at that time were large lumbering vehicles, puttering along almost breathlessly on a straight, smooth road, and never attempted a sharp, winding path (for fear of toppling over) or a steep hill (because of the inevitability of stalling).

The most advanced bus of that era came from the auto shop of Gottlieb Daimler, inventor of the **carburetor** (which made possible the first high-speed gasoline engine) and one of the founding fathers of the automobile age. Having spent more than two decades perfecting automobiles, in 1903 Daimler introduced a four-cylinder, eight-horsepower engine geared by four-speed transmission. Within two years German buses were effortlessly negotiating winding routes and mountainous roads, and also pulling trailers carrying passengers, a European practice that was discontinued only in 1962.

The first transcontinental bus service in the United States — from New York to Los Angeles — began in 1928.

Railroad, 1830; England

If "railroad" is interpreted in the modern sense of the word, its origins are found in England in the early 19th century. The actual inauguration of the railroad age took place with the public opening of the Liverpool and Manchester Railway on September 15, 1830, when a majestic procession of eight brand-new steam-powered locomotives left Liverpool, drawing trains that carried six hundred invited guests.

Ironically, that jubilant day was marred by the first railroad fatality. One train had stopped at Parkside to take on additional water. The former leader of the House of Commons of the British Parliament, the Honorable William Huskisson, was standing near the tracks, discussing with the duke of Wellington the tremendous future for railroads. Amidst the excitement of the day, Huskisson failed to notice another of the ceremonial locomotives approaching on the tracks behind him. In front of throngs of spectators, he was struck and killed.

In another sense of the word, railroads originated as early as the 16th century, under the name "wagonways," where both in England and on the continent they were used to ferry men and ore from mines.

One such wagonway drove into mines at Leberthal, Alsace, in France, in 1550, and a slightly larger version, which traversed wooden tracks and was guided by an iron pin running in a narrow gap between the rails, served a mine at Basel, Switzerland, in 1556. The evolution of wagonways over the next two centuries, along with the creative genius and technological foresight of several men, ushered in the modern railroad age.

One man among all others deservedly is known as the founder of the railroad. The self-taught British inventor and engineer George Stephenson developed the steam-blast engine in 1814 and thus made the **steam locomotive** practicable.

Born at Wylam, Northumberland, the son of a mechanic, Stephenson began working in the mines, operating the wagonways of his day. With little formal education, but a real instinct for repairing clocks, watches, and almost any kind of machine, Stephenson set out to improve the wagonways. After a string of successes with steam engines, he was hired in 1822 as company engineer for the newly proposed Stockton and Darlington Railway, designed primarily for freight and able to travel up to 12 miles per hour. His great personal success came five years later with the Liverpool and Manchester Railway, which zipped along at a then-amazing speed of 30 miles an hour and triggered the rapid development of rail systems in Europe and the United States.

*

The first public railway in the United States, the **Baltimore and Ohio Railroad,** began operations on May 24, 1830 (four months prior to Stephenson's maiden run), but it handled primarily freight on its 13-mile run between Baltimore and Ellicott's Mills (now Ellicott City), Maryland, and carried only a small number of passengers at nine cents a ride. However, where Stephenson's train was powered by steam engines, the Baltimore and Ohio cars were drawn by horses.

Nineteenth-century America began its love affair with steam-powered trains on January 15, 1831, with the inauguration of the

Early elevated railroad in New York.

South Carolina Railroad, out of Charleston. Ironically, the first American train fatality also occurred on the first true train. On June 17 of that year an engineer accidentally fell on the boiler safety valve of a South Carolina Railroad locomotive, causing the boiler to explode, which killed him instantly.

Perhaps the most famous of all railways, the **Orient Express,** began luxury service from Paris to Istanbul on October 3, 1833. It raised train travel to a pinnacle that few other lines could even attempt to equal.

Bicycle, 1839; Scotland

The bicycle is the most efficient means of converting human energy into propulsion, and in the health-conscious second half of the 20th century, its popularity has experienced a revival, almost 150 years after the bicycle's invention by a Scot, Kirkpatrick MacMillan.

   MacMillan, a blacksmith from Dumfrieshire, Scotland, completed his first workable bicycle in the summer of 1839, after four years of arduous experimentation. Others had tried but failed. A Frenchman, Jean Theson, was granted a patent in 1645 for a four-wheeled cycle, on which a "rider" propelled himself by walking the vehicle rather than pedaling it; and a pedaling bicycle prototype was demonstrated in Paris in 1779, built by François Blanchard, but it proved so unwieldy that no one could ride it.

Early bikes were called "boneshakers," because their metal-rimmed tires transmitted every bump and jolt from the road.

MacMillan's bicycle was perfectly balanced, with wheels rimmed with iron. The highly steerable front wheel, which stood about 30 inches high, and a pedal-driven rear wheel, about 10 inches taller, made MacMillan's bicycle maneuverable at brisk speeds.

MacMillan's large vehicle soon passed from vogue, and not until 1861, when two Frenchmen, Pierre Michaux and his son, Ernest, built a machine whose front wheel bore two turning cranks, or sprockets, was the modern bicycle here to stay. The new machine immediately won enthusiasts, even though its rigid iron and wood frame caused it to be dubbed the "boneshaker." A year after the first model, Pierre and Ernest Michaux made 142 machines, which they called velocipedes. By 1865, they were turning out four hundred a year.

The earliest American bicycles were related to the Michaux design, since the mechanic, Pierre Lallement, immigrated to the United States in 1866 and took out the first U.S. patent with James Carroll of Ansonia, Connecticut. The bicycle, more than any earlier invention, emancipated large numbers of ordinary people, particularly women, from lifetimes spent mainly within walking distance of their homes.

In a short time two more innovations were made that have left the bicycle largely unchanged to this day. In 1876, Archibald Sharp, a London inventor, introduced the **spoked tension wheel,** whose light weight and high strength opened up broad areas of design freedom, and permitted an extraordinary variety of bicycles to be produced. Finally, in 1888, John Dunlop guaranteed all future cyclists a smooth ride by introducing the air-filled or **pneumatic tire.**

Motorcycle, 1869; France

With the steam engine and the bicycle already household words by the 1860s, it was inevitable that someone would wed these inventions to produce the first steam-powered motorcycle. In fact, several inventors in several countries did just that in the final years of the decade. But since the most workable design originated in France, the motorcycle generally is taken to be that country's brainchild. Twenty years later gasoline-powered motorcycles made the scene, employing engine principles that are still used today.

In a relatively short period of time powerful cylinders, gearshifts, and twist-grip controls responsible for acceleration and braking allowed early motorcycle technology to outdistance that of the automobile. But comfort, and the status of owning a car, quickly prevailed, relegating the motorcycle to a minor sporting role in society.

Motorcycles, however, went through a renaissance of sorts in the late 1970s. With the unexpected worldwide gasoline shortages, their main economic feature, high mileage, ushered them onto American highways in unprecedented numbers. Many of the models, however, were actually **mopeds,** the modern-day hybrid of a motorcycle and a bicycle, and a device that surely would have delighted the early pioneers of bikes.

Automobile, 1885; Germany

The origin of the automobile is cluttered with the names and inventions of dozens of men in at least half a dozen countries who made small and large contributions to automobile technology, stretching back to the late 17th century.

The French physicist Denis Papin invented the **pressure cooker** (which he called the "steam digester") in 1690, and pondering his brainchild he proposed that a road vehicle could conceivably be constructed on similar steam power principles.

It remained only a dream, though. The first man to go for a ride in a steam-driven contraption of his own ingenious design was Nicolas Cugnot, who in 1769, along a Paris street, attained a speed of 2.5 miles per hour, only — at the height of his success — to smash into a tree, producing the first auto accident.

Most historians recognize two Germans, Karl Benz and Gottlieb Daimler, as the major pioneers of the gasoline engine automobile, and thus the fathers of the modern car. The first practical car to make a successful test run was the three-wheeled vehicle built by Benz, a mechanical engineer, at his factory in 1885. Resembling a giant perambulator, the car made four circuits around the factory on a cinder path, cheered on by Benz's wife and his employees, before one of the chains snapped and the car came to a standstill.

That same year, during a public display of his improved vehicle, Benz had his first automobile accident when, caught up in the excitement of his car's speed, he forgot to steer it, and the car collided with a brick wall.

Daimler's test run came a few months after Benz's laps around his factory, and he managed to make an accident-free run. Although inventors before them had eventually abandoned attempts to produce a workable automobile, both Benz and Daimler forged ahead, independently. In fact, their two companies merged in 1926 to manufacture **Mercedes-Benz** cars. Oddly, Daimler and Benz never met.

They were bitter rivals, though, arguing throughout their later life as to who actually invented the automobile. In retrospect, Daimler seems to have visualized the automobile as a kind of motorized horse carriage, where Benz, the more imaginative of the two, saw the car as an entirely new kind of transportation vehicle. Yet it was Daimler's engine that finally made the automobile a reality. When all the contributions are considered, historians award the honor of inventing the automobile to both men jointly.

During the late 1890s many of the great manufacturing names in automobile history became established throughout Europe. The French and Italians concentrated on speed and sleekness; the Germans focused on making their cars rugged and reliable. But a newcomer, the United States, trained its auto-making efforts on transportation and conveniences for the masses. In America there still were great distances to be covered where the railroads and highways did not yet extend. Numerous automobile factories sprang up within ten years after the first American model, a one-cylinder car built in 1893 by the brothers Charles E. and J. Frank Duryea. Of them, modern descendants are Oldsmobile (by Ransom Eli Olds), Chevrolet (by Louis Chevrolet), and Chrysler (by Walter Chrysler).

Most renowned of all, of course, was Henry Ford, who introduced the assembly line to heavy industry and mass-produced automobiles for the first time, driving down their cost dramatically and making them an affordable mode of transportation to a nation, and a world, eager for wheels. By 1918 the number of cars registered in the United States exceeded 5 million. In the entire history of technology, no industry, except perhaps computers, has ever grown so fast. (See *Computer*, page 366.)

25

Sea: Sailboats to Submarines

Ships, Pre–5000 B.C.

The origin of ships and boats has never been satisfactorily proven by historians. They do, however, concur that man first employed a flotation device before 6000 B.C. to help him cross small bodies of water, such as rivers and streams. His method consisted first of riding astride a floating log, then of riding on logs bound together with hemp to form rafts.

Man's first boats seem to have been crude **canoes,** made from hollowed-out logs. Such canoes, in fact, remain in use among many primitive tribes today. Then, some time before 5000 B.C., man learned that he could greatly lighten the weight of his canoe, and hence substantially increase its speed, by constructing a frame from pliant tree branches and draping the structure with stitched animal hide. Instead of hide, the North American Indians used long unbroken strips of birch bark, a practice some modern-day Indians still employ.

Man's first means of propulsion in water was hand-paddling, which was later supplanted by the use of canoe paddles or oars.

But what about real boats and ships?

From drawings unearthed in Egypt dating to at least 5000 B.C. historians deduce that the first sizable boats were constructed along the Nile River by the earliest inhabitants of that region, where there would not be a great civilization for another thousand years. The

One variety of man's earliest boat, the canoe

Nile boats assumed a crescent shape when the bunched reeds of which they were built were bent upward to form the bow and stern. This style of boat, which persisted for many centuries, was in fact dictated by the fact that the region lacked trees large enough to turn into either large dugouts or plank boats.

To the east, across the Red Sea, early shipbuilders, who had begun with dugout canoes, later turned to building wooden boats with slanted sides fastened to bow and stern supports; this design — the flat-keeled boat, with square corners at the ends — kept out water while increasing the vessel's carrying capacity.

The Egyptians, now more confident of their navigational skills, began venturing farther into the Mediterranean about 3000 B.C. Though they could sail only downwind, most of the time wind from the Nile Valley flows north and they were able to sail upstream. On the return trip from the Mediterranean, to navigate against the wind, Egyptian sailors learned to tilt their sails at a 90-degree angle into the wind; the voyage was negotiated by "tacking," or turning into and across the wind, a technique common to even novice sailors today.

The Egyptians discovered **sailing.** Their earliest sailboats were made of reeds, with the mast a bipod of two spars fitted together at the top to make a triangular frame to which a sail was attached. The sail usually was square and made of papyrus or cotton, laced at the head to a long, heavy horizontal spar called a yard. (The bipod mast gave way to a pole mast about 2000 B.C.) Fragments of these sails and ships survive and are on display in several museums.

An alternative source of power often was provided by a crew of strong oarsmen, who took turns steering the ship with a large oar, or two or three oars in parallel, slung over the side of the boat near the stern, called the quarter.

By 2000 B.C., the Egyptians, the Greeks, and several coastal societies had taken to the water for fishing and trading, and ships became imaginatively diverse. Merchant ships were strikingly different from warships, which the Egyptians had already developed, and which were the progenitors of the later Viking ships that terrorized the coasts of Europe.

The magnificent multimasted sailing ship originated in ancient China and was introduced to the West by the adventurer Marco Polo. The **galleon,** a sleek ship with slim hull, was the longest-lasting of sailing designs, dating from the New World. Following the galleon came the **clipper,** the fastest, most flawlessly tooled and romantic of all sailing vessels. Clad with more diaphanous canvas than any other sailing ship, with emphasis on speed, it was developed in the early 19th century in the United States, but was rendered obsolete by the advent of steamships, as well as of the transcontinental railroads.

The warship originated in Egypt in 3000 B.C., boasting both oars and sails as well as elevated decks fore and aft for archers and spearmen. One of the earliest missions involved the dispatch of forty ships to the Phoenician port of Byblos to plunder cedar wood from the famous cedar forests of Lebanon to build more warships. (Pictured above is a Phoenician vessel.)

Lighthouse, 4th Century B.C.; Greece

To warn ships of shallow waters and jutting peninsulas, fires were lit high on coastal bluffs and kept burning throughout the night. They served as forerunners of lighthouses and are mentioned in the *Iliad* and the *Odyssey*.

The first real lighthouse constructed as a permanent alert system was erected by the Alexandrians, who built their famed tower of Pharos 350 feet high. The stone edifice was not unlike modern lighthouses, and a custodian kept the rooftop fire roaring during the night. As sea trade increased among Mediterranean countries, lighthouses soon became a common, and welcome, sight to sailors,

Early lighthouses were situated on the mainland *(left);* only as construction techniques became more sophisticated were lighthouses moved offshore.

and by A.D. 400 the Romans alone boasted of more than thirty stone lighthouses dotting the shores from the Black Sea to the Atlantic Ocean.

The early Greek lighthouses usually burned either wood for firelight or, occasionally, oil torches, similar to those used in Olympic competitions. The Greeks were skilled in the application of mirror reflections (though it would be several centuries before the principles of reflection were understood), and they used curved surfaces, with a fire situated at a critical central point, to broadcast a broad parallel beam of light over many miles of dark sea. Candles and oil lamps, mounted inside glass enclosures, became the major light sources during the 1st century A.D. Virtually all lighthouses up until this time, and for the next seven centuries, were coastal structures, with one side facing the sea and the other the mainland.

The **modern lighthouse** arrived in the 16th century. Not only were these new structures sturdier and more powerful in light amplification, but for the first time lighthouses were being constructed fully exposed to the open sea, often many miles from the shore.

Designer Henry Winstanley's 120-foot-high tower overlooking the treacherous Eddystone Reef off Plymouth, England, was one of the first modern beacons, completed in 1699. Anchored by twelve iron stanchions drilled deep into solid rock, the lighthouse was thought by Winstanley and his engineers to be indestructible, but it survived only four years. One night, in a fierce gale, when Winstanley was manning the lighthouse, battering waves tore the structure from its moorings, sweeping away without a trace both the lighthouse and its designer.

Submarine, 1620; England

The Dutch inventor Cornelis Drebbel made real the dreams of hundreds of visionaries before him, and set the stage for one of man's finest examples of marine technology, when he invented the submarine in 1620.

Many men had entertained the idea of building an underwater vessel. In ancient times, Herodotus, Aristotle, and Pliny the Elder all wrote eagerly about the possibilities of "diving bells" or similar submersibles for exploration and travel beneath the sea. A 13th-century French novel, *La Vrai Histoire d'Alexandre,* described a fictitious underwater expedition by Alexander the Great in a giant glass barrel. And the great Italian inventor Leonardo da Vinci toward the end of his life, believing that great floods would eventually sweep humanity with all its vanities and evils into oblivion, drew up plans for a vessel capable of underwater travel.

But Drebbel, using designs drawn in 1578 by the British mathematician and naval writer William Bourne, succeeded where the others either had failed or dared not venture. His first submarine had an outer watertight hull of greased leather stretched over a wooden frame, and oars that extended through the sides, providing a means of propulsion both on the surface and below it. One of the first passengers to test Drebbel's novel ship was King James I of England, who, with Drebbel, descended to a depth of 15 feet for several minutes. Elated by the experience, the king spoke of nothing else for several days, and soon submarines became the talk of London society and the serious concern of most naval scientists.

By 1727 fourteen patents for submarines had been granted in England alone. Among them was an ingenious design by an unknown inventor whose submarine was the precursor of modern ballast tanks. Goatskin bags were attached to the hull, each bag connected to an aperture in the bottom of the craft. When the vessel submerged, the bags would take on water and drag the ship downward; when it was to surface, a twisting rod would force water from the skins.

An American first seriously entertained the notion of the submarine as a weapon of war. David Bushnell, a student at Yale during the American Revolution, designed and built a one-man sub, the *Turtle,* to make underwater passes at British warships and, when alongside, to attach an explosive to their hulls.

The *Turtle*'s only venture, in New York Harbor, proved fruitless when its pilot, after a successful launching and proper courses, was unable to screw through the copper hull of the intended target, the H.M.S. *Eagle,* and plant the explosive. After repeated failures, the pilot, Ezra Lee, an army sergeant from Lyme, Connecticut, jettisoned the gunpowder, which exploded without harming the British ship.

In the decade following World War I, the United States began to invest in earnest in submarine development, and built its first long-range vessel, the *Argonaut,* in 1928. With a length of 381 feet and a 2710-ton displacement, the *Argonaut* was the largest non-nuclear submarine ever deployed by the U.S. Navy; it was armed with four forward torpedo tubes and a complement of sixty mines. This design was the forerunner of American Gato and Balao classes, which matched in ingenuity the German submarines and out-foxed the Japanese during World War II.

In 1955, the United States launched the first **nuclear-powered submarine,** the *Nautilus,* with an unlimited underwater range at a top speed of 20 knots. By 1971, the United States and the Soviet Union had a combined total of more than ninety nuclear-powered submarines and had an annual rate of production of four atomic submarines for the U.S. and twelve to fourteen for the Russians, who also boasted more than five hundred conventional, or diesel-powered, vessels.

Steamship, 1807; United States

Had the French government not withdrawn its financial support in 1801 from the American inventor Robert Fulton — when his submarine, the *Nautilus,* failed to sink a warship in a test run — the steamship might well have originated in France and not in the United States.

The American steamship *Gutenberg*

Fulton actually built his first steamship — a 66-foot craft with paddlewheels at the side and an eight-horsepower engine — in 1803 while he was still living in France, and tested it on the Seine River. When the hull proved to be too weak to support the engine, the undaunted inventor ordered an even more powerful engine to be built in England and shipped directly to the United States.

After returning to New York in 1806, Fulton turned the new engine into the first passenger and freight steamship to show commercial promise. The 150-foot-long *Clermont,* launched on the Hudson River in 1807, traveled at 5 knots an hour and was such an immediate success that Fulton built additional ships, including the first steam-powered warship, the *Demologos,* launched also at New York Harbor on October 29, 1814, and intended for use against the British during the final months of the 1812–1814 war.

Although Fulton gave the world the first look at the wood-hulled steamship, it was the restless energy and inventiveness of a Briton, Isambard Kingdom Brunel, that nearly a half-century later convinced the world of the vast superiority of **iron-hulled steam vessels,** and thus initiated the era of modern transatlantic travel.

Brunel, a prolific engineer, designed and built railroads, bridges, and tunnels. But his greatest achievements were in shipbuilding, where his grandiose schemes brought him two major successes. He built the first transatlantic steamship, the *Great Western,* a giant wooden-paddle vessel that at the time of its launching, in 1838, was the largest steamer in the world.

His second ship, the *Great Britain,* was more revolutionary in that it was the largest ship ever to be built of iron, and it was the first ocean liner to be powered not by paddlewheels but by a propeller. Launched with jubilant fanfare in 1845, the 3270-ton vessel made several transatlantic crossings; then in 1846 it ran aground off the coast of Ireland. Where a wooden-hulled ship would have broken up on the jagged rocks, the iron hull of the *Great Britain* was only dented, not even punctured. The accident convinced the traveling public and shipbuilders that iron-hulled ships were vessels of the future and here to stay.

26

Air: Balloons to Bombers

Balloon, 1783; France

Early visionaries were convinced that the best way to become airborne was to emulate the wing-flapping of birds. Had they instead concentrated their efforts on fixed-wing crafts, such as gliders, they might have been successful at becoming lighter than air almost a thousand years before the invention of the airplane.

Every component they needed to conquer the air — sheer fabrics, light woods, and strong cord, as well as skilled scientists — already existed. The missing — and absolutely indispensable — element, however, was the concept of air as a fluid, and of its behavior as its flows around a body, creating an uplift.

The concept of air as a gas, though, which originated in the middle of the 17th century, paved the way for man to take to the air a century later in hot-air balloons.

*

The **mercury barometer,** invented in 1643 by an Italian physicist and mathematician, Evangelista Torricelli, proved for the first time that air was a gas, one that not only had weight but also responded to changes in temperature and pressure in the manner of all gases. This fact was well established by the year 1783, when two brothers, Joseph and Jacques Montgolfier, scions of a paper manufacturer in the town of Annonay in southeast France, launched their first hot-air balloon. Though both brothers were responsible for technological innovations in paper-making, it is unclear how well versed they were in scientific ideas of the day.

Certainly they did not know that when air is heated its density decreases, making it lighter in weight. The Montgolfiers, intrigued by the observation that smoke from a fire always flows upward, seemed to think that a mysterious gas in smoke was responsible for the motion; thus, they believed that such smoke-producing materials as damp straw and leaves would make the best sort of fire to lift their balloons. This incorrect assumption lends credence to the tale that Joseph, witnessing his wife's petticoat billowing in the air as she dried it over a fire, was suddenly struck with the idea of making himself ascend in a balloon.

The brothers began experimenting in the 1770s. To bring smoke's mysterious property, which they called "levity," under control, they held a small silk bag above a fire until it filled with smoke, then released it and watched it rise to the ceiling. Increasing the size of their air bags, they finally built a giant balloon, which was released before an amazed public at Annonay on June 5, 1783.

The crude balloon was made of light fabric with a paper backing, fastened together by buttons. A fire, stoked to give maximum smoke, rapidly inflated the bag and majestically lifted it off its platform, carrying it to an altitude of 6000 feet. After ten minutes aloft, it gradually descended about half a mile away. When the news reached Paris, the Academy of Sciences at once invited the Montgolfiers to the capital and set up a spectacular demonstration to take place at Versailles in the presence of Louis XVI and Marie Antoinette.

Since the scientific thought of the day was that the upper atmosphere held unimaginable dangers for anyone who breathed its air, the passengers in the Montgolfiers' second balloon, royally decorated in blue and gold, were a duck, a cock, and a sheep. When the balloon, which had a diameter of 41 feet and attained an altitude of 1700 feet, descended gently in a forest 2 miles away, the animals were found to be alive and healthy, except that the sheep had kicked the cock, damaging one of its wings.

King Louis, greatly impressed with the experiment, but not quite convinced of the safety of the upper air, insisted that the first manned flight must carry prisoners whose lives were expendable. However, the king's historian, a young scientist named Jean-Françoise Pilâtre de Rozier, beseeched his royal highness to let him venture up in the first manned balloon. On that historic day of November 21, 1783, in a balloon with a diameter of 50 feet, Pilâtre de Rozier, accompanied by the trusting Marquis d'Arlandes,

Balloons supporting a network of telegraph wires

traveled for twenty-five minutes over 5 miles of the French countryside. Man's centuries-long dream of taking to the air had finally
been realized.

One woman's dream of free-flying was realized the next year,
on June 4, when singer Elizabeth Tible ascended in a Montgolfier
balloon over Lyon, France. Throughout the flight in the balloon,
christened *La Gustave* in honor of King Gustav of Sweden, who
was a spectator, she sang operatic arias, drank tea, and ate bis-
cuits. Depending on one's point of view, these achievements could
make Elizabeth Tible simultaneously the first woman to fly, the first
stewardess, and the first example of in-flight entertainment.

Hydrogen Balloon, 1783; France

The first major improvement over the hot-air balloon came only
ten days after the Montgolfier brothers' inaugural manned flight.
Physicist Jacques-Alexandre-César Charles, working with Anne-Jean
Robert and his brother Nicolas-Louis Robert, had decided only a
month before the Montgolfier flight to use the newly isolated,
lighter-than-air gas, hydrogen, for the flight of his balloon.

Charles's balloon was made of varnished silk and had a diameter of 15 feet. Filling it required the largest amount of hydrogen

ever produced at that time. Despite a driving rainstorm, the balloon, which of course required no fueling fire, was released before a large crowd at the meadow at the Champ de Mars, Paris. Due to the inclement weather, its maximum altitude was not recorded, but it finally descended out of an overcast sky about 15 miles from its launch site, near the small village of Gonesse. Local peasants, fearing this apparition from the thunder clouds, attacked the "monster" with scythes and pitchforks and completely demolished the balloon.

Charles himself eventually completed a two-hour manned flight, issuing in a century of navigable balloons and airships. Little about ballooning, except for discretionary controls of air valves, has changed since Charles's day. When a series of fatal accidents occurred, because of hydrogen's volatility, the hydrogen balloons were outlawed and replaced by nonflammable helium ones. Helium, though heavier than hydrogen, remains the standard fuel for balloon travel today, and probably will be the fuel of the great airships whose rebirth, it has been predicted, will counteract the rising costs of jet travel.

Parachute, 1797; France

Man's fascination with falling through space to a safe landing on the ground dates back at least to Leonardo da Vinci, who in 1515, while musing over the possibility of man's copying avian flight, sketched a parachute in the form of a cloth pyramid.

He wasn't the only person of his day to consider such an invention, either. Two novels of the period described men using parachutes: one, published in 1595, featured a man floating to earth from the top of a tower, his descent made safe by an unspecified fabric panel stretched over a wooden frame; the other, published in 1632, had its hero escape by leaping from a prison tower with a bed sheet held over his head, billowing like a parachute.

During the early 18th century, many inventors tested parachutes, and some were victims of their own failures. The earliest parachute to make a successful flight to earth was dropped in 1797 by André-Jacques Garnerin. Ascending from the Parc Monceau in Paris in a basket attached to an umbrellalike parachute dangling from a hot-air balloon, Garnerin attained an altitude of 3000 feet, then severed his suspension cord, and descended safely, much to the amazement of gathered onlookers.

Though Garnerin is credited with originating the first practicable parachute, Joseph Montgolfier, one of the inventors of the hot-air balloon, was reported to have dropped from the top of a tower in Avignon a sheep in a basket fastened to a 7-foot-diameter parachute. Both the basket and sheep supposedly landed unharmed.

The Du Pont chemical company in 1939 announced commercial production of a new synthetic fabric, nylon, thus introducing the first **nylon parachutes,** which were immediately used in war by wave after wave of paratroopers, who were able to make pinpoint landings behind enemy lines.

Airplane, 1903; United States

Orville and Wilbur Wright, brothers from Dayton, Ohio, are unequivocally acknowledged by all aeronautical historians as the inventors of the world's first practicable airplane. The long-held notion that the brothers were semiliterate bicycle mechanics who serendipitously stumbled on the secrets of flight is fanciful and slanderous in light of what we know today.

True, the Wrights possessed limited formal education, and they first tried careers in printing and publishing a newspaper, then in selling and repairing bicycles. But once they became interested in bird flight, in 1899, they began a serious and committed study of aviation that in a short time turned them into true experimental scientists.

Their systematic approach to aviation started with observations of the hanging flights of buzzards in air thermals and of smaller birds in controlled dives. They were wise enough to realize that the flapping of a bird's wings offered no clue as to how to build a lighter-than-air powered craft. Instead they focused on three critical movements: pitching, the up-and-down motion; rolling, the side-to-side motion; and yawing, or the tendency of a bird to move to the right or left. Cleverly, they also observed the tips of a bird's wings when it came out of a dive and regained its lateral balance against the wind: the wings warped. They incorporated a mechanical duplication of wing-warping into their experimental machines. It provided flexibility and was the forerunner of ailerons in modern aircraft.

The Wrights progressed methodically but quickly, testing their ideas first on a biplane kite, then on a series of gliders based on

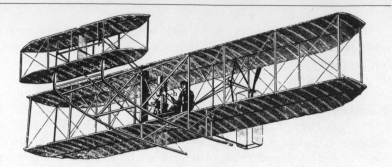

The Wright brothers' airplane, airborne, front view

the designs of the German aviation pioneer Otto Lilienthal, who later died in a crash of one of his own gliders. By the end of 1903 they had designed their own lightweight gasoline engine and a highly effective propeller and were ready, they believed, for the first sustained airplane flight in history.

Though rechristened the *Kitty Hawk,* the inaugural plane prosaically was called by the Wrights *Flyer I.* On December 14 the craft attempted to take off at Kill Devil Hill near Kitty Hawk, North Carolina, with Wilbur as pilot. Because of an error in judgment, the attempt failed. Instead, history was made three days later, when Orville guided the plane for a flight that lasted twelve seconds. That day the Wrights made three other flights; the longest was fifty-nine seconds. Almost five years passed before anyone else kept a controllable plane aloft for longer than a minute. By that time, Orville and Wilbur Wright had constructed a plane whose maneuverability and soundness of design kept them airborne for longer than an hour.

The press either paid little attention to the Wrights or cast doubt on their achievements with such headlines as FLYERS OR LIARS? Balloons had a future, but airplanes were merely dangerous toys, the papers speculated. It was not until Wilbur went to Europe in 1908 with a new plane and staged a spectacular public demonstration that the continent, and the United States, took respectful note.

The next year the U.S. Army submitted an order to the Wrights' factory for a military model plane. Orville became disenchanted with airplanes after they were introduced into aerial combat and commented that he almost regretted inventing the flying machine, after viewing the destruction wrought by it as a weapon. Wilbur died in 1912, but Orville lived until 1948, long enough to see his and his brother's invention usher in the era of commercial passenger transportation.

Bomber, 1911; Italy

Warfare from the air actually was attempted sixty years before the introduction of the first bomber airplane, and fifty-five years before the Wright brothers' maiden flight.

The year 1848 is often called "the Year of Revolutions" in Europe, because unrest swept the continent, precipitated by food shortages, economic recessions, and governmental repressions. The movement began in France, when an uprising of citizens drove out King Louis Philippe and brought in the Second Republic. The following year found the Austrians battling their enemies in Venice. On August 22, Austria launched a parade of unmanned balloons loaded with bombs that were sizzling with long time-delay fuses. The balloons were supposed to descend over Venice, and the bombs to explode on target, showering their incendiary payload over the city.

The science of ballooning and bombing being considerably inaccurate at the time, most of the bombs exploded in the air, en route to their destination. The idea, however, was recognized as legitimate and, soon picked up by several of the countries swept by revolution, was sometimes executed with a modicum of success.

When airships replaced balloons, it was only logical that they should become the new airborne weapons, raining down destruction from the sky. The time was now 1915, World War I had been going on for a year, and bombing from the air was fast becoming a science of precise trajectories and precision timing. On January 19, a large German zeppelin (named for its designer, Count Ferdinand von Zeppelin) dropped a bomb on the English countryside, marking the first time an airship had been used successfully in an attack. Encouraged by their accuracy, the Germans on May 31 unloaded the first destructive bomb from a zeppelin over London.

The airplane bomber itself got off to an inauspicious start in 1911. An Italian flyer, Captain Piazza, buzzing 500 feet over the Turkish army near Tripolitania in a Blériot monoplane, tossed a packet of explosives to the ground. Not having made proper allowances for the forward speed of the plane and the free-fall time of the explosives, Piazza missed his target. Three days later he flew over a battle site and successfully directed gunfire on the Turkish troops.

A French flier, Roland Garros, usually is given the distinction for creating the first true fighter plane, when in 1915 he mounted on his aircraft a machine gun that fired through a propeller outfitted with steel plates to deflect his own ill-timed bullets. Shortly afterwards, the Germans, having noted Garros's effectiveness against their own aircraft, devised the synchronized machine-gun mount, with a firing lever dependent on the rotation of the propeller.

The limited horsepower of early bombers in Italy, Germany, England, and the United States severely hampered their payload capacity. But when 2500-horsepower engines became commonplace during World War II, the modern bomber immediately earned a niche as the most devastating strike force in man's military arsenal. Boeing B-29 bombers dropped the first atomic bombs on Japanese cities in 1945, and their destructiveness brought about an end to the war.

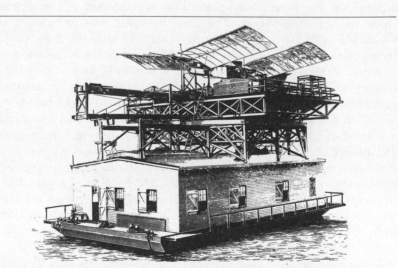

This early aircraft carrier, built by Samuel Langley in 1903, tried but failed to launch planes. However, the idea later came to fruition.

Jet Planes, 1942; Germany

The Germans, in 1939, developed the jet engine, a cigar-shaped propulsion machine that draws in air from the atmosphere, compresses it, heats it by combustion of a fuel, and ejects the resulting gases with sufficient force to produce a substantial thrust in the opposite direction. Three years later they incorporated that powerful engine into a military airplane design and came up with the **Messerschmitt-262** jet bomber as a desperate attempt to stave off defeat in World War II.

The Messerschmitt-262 carried bombs and four cannons and made propeller-driven planes obsolete by outflying them at speeds of up to 100 mph. In the later Korean conflict, the Russian MIG-15 fighter, a spin-off of captured German technology, ruled the skies at the outset, until the United Nations air force, which entered the fray with outdated American aircraft, matched the MIG with the U.S. **F-86 Sabre,** the first United States pure-bred jet. Today, jet warplanes are armed with conventional weapons as well as nuclear warheads, and rely on infra-red radar rather than pilots' eyesight for pinpointing their targets.

On the commercial side, the British **de Havilland Comet,** which began flying in 1949, was the first passenger jet transport. Regular transatlantic jet routes began in 1958, with the Comet 4 and the Boeing 707 as mainstays of early jet fleets. More than 50 percent of scheduled airline flights throughout the world were operating with jets by 1975, and the British-French **Concorde,** designed to fly at twice the speed of sound, went into service between New York, London, and Paris a year later as the first supersonic transport.

Helicopter, 1937; Germany

While most aviation pioneers sought speed and sleek fuselages for piercing the skies with smooth flight, one inventor's emphasis lay elsewhere. Igor Sikorsky, a Russian-born American aeronautical wizard, was convinced that the future of the airplane, and of air travel, was vertical flight.

Sikorsky wasn't the first to cherish the idea; the German firm of Focke-Achgelis actually flew a helicopter two years before Sikorsky's first model became airborne in 1939. But his ideas had been carefully mapped out: he had built a working toy helicopter at the age of twelve from a drawing of Leonardo da Vinci's, and his first craft, the Sikorsky VS-300, became the definitive design for all future helicopters. It was the first single-rotor helicopter, and the idea was embraced quickly and universally by helicopter manufacturers. The craft could be controlled gracefully when hovering, ascending, and landing vertically, in addition to flying backward and sideways.

Oddly, Sikorsky shelved plans for mass-producing helicopters during World War II to work on other aeronautical projects. But in 1945 he plunged immediately into refining his earlier designs and conceived both military and domestic craft, whose purposes included rescue and relief operations as well as low-flying combat missions.

Spacecraft, 1957; Soviet Union

Man has always harbored a lust for unshackling himself from the confines of gravity and soaring to heights forbidden even to winged creatures. The 2nd-century Greek writer Lucian of Samosata composed one such fantastic journey, a trek to the earth's nearest celestial neighbor, the moon. The advent of hot-air balloons, and later of airplanes, only whetted man's appetite for loftier travel — and convinced him that such fanciful dreams could soon become reality.

The space age officially began on October 4, 1957, when the Soviet Union launched the modest 185-pound Sputnik I, the first artificial **satellite** to orbit the earth. The following month, the Russians successfully launched the 1100-pound Sputnik II, which carried into space the first animal to orbit the globe, a female dog named Laika, who suffocated on the sixth day of the flight because of a failure in the internal temperature of the craft. But the ship itself orbited the earth for 162 days and burned up on re-entering the earth's atmosphere.

The United States, playing second fiddle to its superpower rival, orbited its first satellite, Explorer I, on January 31, 1958. It was a lightweight, 18-pound craft, carrying not animals but sensitive instruments to study the intense bands of energy in space known as the Van Allen radiation belts.

Within the next fifteen years man had gone to the moon, charted its surface, searched beneath its dry, dusty soil for signs of life (there were none, it seems), and begun probing more distant realms of the solar system.

One physicist, Werner von Braun, played a crucial role in this odyssey, especially in devising the bold scheme for the 1969 landing of three Americans on the moon.

His plan required a sophisticated new spaceship made up of three sections: a service module containing fuel, power, and life-support systems; a command module; and a lunar-landing vehicle. To boost the 40-ton mother ship into orbit, von Braun devised the most powerful rocket ever built, the giant Saturn V, over 360 feet long, weighing 3000 tons, and with its lift-off engines delivering an incredible 7.5-million pounds of thrust, burning more than 10 tons of fuel each second. Despite the monstrous complexity of all the systems in the booster and the three-part spacecraft, everything functioned perfectly, a testament to the ingenuity, dedication, and hard work of thousands of scientists and technicians.

During the 1970s the United States' space program took a different course, de-emphasizing manned flights and stressing instead unmanned ventures close to the surface of Mercury, Jupiter, and Saturn. In 1982, the Soviets succeeded in landing an exploration craft on the steamy, acidic surface of Venus, where it successfully transmitted to earth the first pictures of that planet's bubbling terrain.

The latest landmark in spacecraft design, the United States' **space shuttle** *Columbia,* probably will mark the true origins of commercial and passenger space travel. A sort of space bus, the shuttle holds the potential to open up space for industry, leisure travel, and for the permanent habitation of orbiting colonies, each housing — as is now being considered — 10,000 volunteer men, women, and children.

27

Technology: Flushing Toilets to Pneumatic Tires

Bathroom, 8000 B.C.; Scotland

Early man was quick to become aware of the toxicity of his own wastes, a source of contagion for plague and disease. He usually located near a water source that not only provided him with drink but also served as a means to remove excrement from his environment. The water source also served as a bathing facility — an imperative, since cleanliness was associated with social acceptance.

The earliest evidence of a bathroom was a series of latrinelike plumbing systems with crude drains found in excavations in the Orkney Islands, an archipelago northeast of Scotland, constituting the present-day county of Orkney, Scotland. The drains led from stone huts at least 10,000 years old.

Another six millennia passed before the late Minoan civilization, on Crete, developed a sophisticated water system made of terra-cotta pipes. The linkage drained waste from the royal palace, and the system also boasted a latrine with a reservoir that qualified as the first **flushing toilet.** Not until the 18th century was a similar device used in Europe.

The Minoan system, in fact, served as the model for modern plumbing, differing little except for steady water pressure and convenient hot and cold water controls. Only in the 19th century was the bathroom, long a separate structure, built in the home.

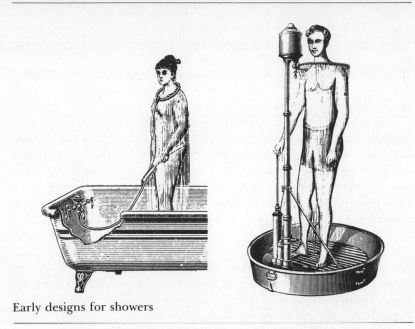

Early designs for showers

The first proponents of this construction were considered crude, because the thought of excreting waste and living under the same roof was repulsive to the upper classes.

Masonry, 4000 B.C.; Egypt

The **brick,** produced in a sun-dried form by the Egyptians at least 6000 years ago, was one of man's first major building materials. It is conceivable, archeologists believe, that the first bricks were made by accident, formed of mud deposited by the Nile River, or of silt; when the slosh hardened it cracked and formed solid cakes that then were shaped into rectangular blocks for constructing huts.

The Mesopotamians were first to sun-bake bricks intentionally. They used them to erect an arch at the major city of Ur about 4000 B.C. An extant plan for the arch (which itself has not survived) reveals that mortar other than mud was used for the first time: a pasty bituminous slime bound the bricks together.

For firing bricks at Ur a closed kiln was used. Potters discovered that controlling the heat during baking produced harder, more water-resistant bricks, and oven-burned bricks quickly replaced those baked in the sun. One of the earliest examples of monumental brickwork was the ziggurat at Ur, a temple tower in the form of a terraced pyramid. The original steps were of sun-baked brick, but in 1500 B.C. Mesopotamian craftsmen replaced them with the sturdier kilned bricks.

Bricks were instrumental in the rise of architecture. The Great Wall of China was built between 246 and 209 B.C. of both oven-burned and sun-dried bricks; the Pantheon in Rome was topped with a magnificent brick dome in A.D. 123, and Hadrian's Baths in the same city were built of bricks and terra-cotta pillars with brick floors sturdy enough to withstand the intense heat from subterranean fires.

The origin of **concrete** spelled the dawning of modern masonry.

Its invention by the Romans in ancient times was perhaps the most significant step in the history of masonry. Starting with **cement,** made from pozzuolana, a volcanic ash, the Romans soon discovered the hardier concrete, formed by mixing cement with water, lime, and stone fragments, and it enabled them to erect broad expanses of walls and to lay roadways that crisscrossed the empire.

With concrete the Romans also gained greater flexibility in forming their famous arches. Before, arches were limited in design and, handicapped by the stone's lack of tensile strength, often fell under their own weight. The Egyptians had successfully constructed dome-roofed temples, but only by placing support beams or columns close together, and the Greeks had averted collapse by using wooden columns covered with fine stone. These columns could withstand weight but not such natural disasters as wind, ice storms, and especially fire.

With bricks and concrete the Roman arch gained stability, because all the masonry work was under radial compression. In effect, the Romans' masonry allowed the arch to function as a barrel vault, which is seen in such roofed structures as the Temple of Venus in Rome. A "common keystone" was the point of intersection for several arches, forming a dome, as is still seen in the Pantheon's ceiling, which has a diameter of 142 feet, a span unequaled until the introduction of steel and reinforced-concrete construction in the 19th century.

Clocks, 3500 B.C.; Egypt

The earliest device constructed for indicating time is thought to be a vertical stick whose shadow gave a rough estimate of the sun's progression. It was used by the Egyptians about 3500 B.C. and was a crude forerunner of the more accurate sundial.

The **sundial** also originated in Egypt, at the start of the 8th century B.C., and was the first precision timekeeping device. It had a straight base inscribed with a scale of six time divisions and a crosspiece at one end. The crosspiece, when placed in an east-west position, cast shadows at various stages of the day which told the time.

An improvement on the Egyptian dial was the hemispherical sundial or hemicycle, devised about 300 B.C. by the Babylonian priest and astronomer Berosus. A cube was carved with a hemispherical opening, with a pointer, or gnomon, placed at the center of the space. The shadow cast by the path of the gnomon swept in a circular arc. Berosus, noting differences in elapsed time during the days of certain seasons, was the first to divide a sundial into twelve equal intervals, or hours. But discrepancies arose throughout the course of a year, because of the differences in a day's length. Still, Berosus' dial was the most accurate instrument of the time and remained in use for years.

*

Water clocks were devised in early Egyptian civilization as an ingenious means of measuring time at night or on days when clouds obscured the sun. The first ones, dating to about 1400 B.C., were bucket-shaped vessels from which water dripped through a tiny hole near the bottom. Changing levels on the scored inner surface of the water clock marked the passage of hourly intervals.

The Romans and Greeks improved the water clocks, or clepsydras, as they were called by the two peoples. The Roman model was a cylinder that received a steady flow of pure water from a reservoir. A float placed in the cylinder gave readings that minimized irregularities in telling time. Eventually the Romans added a wheel-and-ratchet mechanism for more exact readings. The shaft attached to the float had teeth, or gears, that engaged a cogwheel fastened to a pointer, which in turn swept over a dial. The Arabs and the Chinese further refined these dial clocks, which were popular in Europe through the 16th century and are used even today in some remote societies.

*

The **sand glass,** in which sand traveling from a glass vessel through a narrow passage into an identical second receptacle within a specific period of time, originated in Europe in the 1st century A.D. To begin the count of time, the vessel containing sand was lifted above its counterpart — empty at this stage — and then time began measuring itself, concluding an hour's duration when all the sand worked its way into the bottom half of the glass.

The first sand glasses usually ran off an hour's time and were quite bulky. Hour intervals, in fact, seemed for centuries to satisfy the time-telling needs of numerous societies. The first major change in sand-glass technology appears to have been prompted by the verbose and seemingly endless sermons that had become commonplace in Christian churches during the early Renaissance. In an effort to shorten these spiels, which could run on for two hours or more, the Catholic Church, pulling in its reins, requested technicians to construct sand glasses that measured time — and sermons — in bearable intervals of fifteen and thirty minutes.

Mechanical Clock, 1335; Italy

The first mechanical clock was also the first striking clock, invented in Italy in 1335 and placed in a monastery in Milan to sound an alarm and alert the sacristan to toll a bell that summoned the monks to vespers.

Clocks that chimed at hourly intervals soon spread rapidly throughout Europe, appearing predominantly in public places, adorning building and cathedral façades. The oldest extant English clock was hung at Salisbury Cathedral in 1386; the first French clock started ticking at Rouen in 1389. Perhaps the most prominent example of the mechanical clock during its formative years was one built for Wells Cathedral in England, now preserved in the Science Museum in London; it contained chimes that rang on the quarter-hour.

All early mechanical clocks were large and weight-propelled, and were usually constructed to fit cathedral towers. Looking at these clocks, one could not tell time in minutes, nor even hours, for they possessed neither hands nor dials. They were used only as ornamental timepieces for gonging at intervals, usually on the hour. As they became popular, they usurped the traditional place of the town crier.

Ornate lady's clock, with separate second hand and day-of-the-week dial; a man's pocket watch from Montgomery Ward & Company, Chicago; a Queen Anne grandfather's clock.

Watch, 1500; Germany

The invention of the mainspring, a flat coiled steel band, by Peter Henlein in Nürnberg, Germany, about 1500, marked the birth of one of our most valuable instruments — the watch. The word itself derives from the Old English *wæccen*, meaning "to keep vigil," as night watchmen did.

The mainspring, which was and is the heart of all watches (except, of course, computer-driven digital varieties of contemporary use), stole the timekeeping monopoly away from clocks, which were weight-driven and cumbersome, and for the first time made timepieces truly portable. Manufactured first in Nürnberg, then in Blois, France, mainspring watches were bulky in size, usually about 4 to 5 inches in diameter and 3 inches thick, and carried by hand or in a man's jacket pocket or a woman's handbag. The nobleman, not to be inconvenienced, designated a servant especially to carry a watch and trail behind his master, announcing the time whenever it was demanded.

Grandfather Clock, 1656; the Netherlands

Early inventors toyed for decades with the dilemma of constructing a consistent clock propelled by pendulum motion. The great physicist Galileo, who about 1582 noted that pendulums, then employed by physicians for taking a patient's pulse, presented a principle that might be applicable for keeping time, worked diligently to perfect such a clock.

Galileo's designs, however, never materialized. But a Dutch astronomer and physician, Christian Huygens, also had noted the promise of the pendulum, a weight dangling from a cord of predetermined length, sweeping in arcs of uniform distance. Huygens first successfully applied the pendulum to a clock about 1656, and this brilliant improvisation in timekeeping by itself almost revolutionized the clockmaking industry.

Clocks began to take on definite shape. Usually the face was encased in wood and hung on a wall, with the separate pendulum swinging to and fro in open air beneath the dial. Eventually the pendulum, which had been further refined in weight, shape, and material construction by an English clockmaker named William Clement in 1670, was itself enclosed; this called for even longer wooden casing with a glass front. Clement's design marked the origin of the grandfather clocks, which in the ensuing centuries could be found in homes throughout Europe and the United States.

Glass, 3000 B.C.; Mesopotamia

Man's mastery of fire made possible the discovery of glass, but thousands of years separated the two events, which is surprising, since heated sand and ash spontaneously fuse to form bits of glass. The kinds of sand and ash required were abundant, and we can only surmise that for many millennia early man marveled at the hard cloudy nodules he occasionally discovered while sifting through the remains of a fire, never realizing how they came into existence.

The Mesopotamians were the first people deliberately to fuse silica and alkali ash to make glass beads. For the next few hundred years pearl-sized transparent beads (many still exist) were the rage in jewelry among rulers and the wealthy classes. Beads were even tinted colors by doping molten glass with various compounds.

About 2000 B.C., craftsmen who heated silica-ash mixtures discovered that by increasing temperatures they could make the glass fluid enough to be poured into clay molds. While it was cooling, the glass could be shaped into an assortment of figures before it permanently hardened. As might be expected, this discovery produced a bonanza of glass trinkets, glass jewelry, glass-glazed pottery, and the first completely glass vessels, the origin of the **glass bottle.** However, these early bottles were not blown (a process the Babylonians would invent about 1200 B.C.), but were quickly and expertly sculpted while a mold of molten glass was cooling and hardening.

Ancient glass blowing and later Venetian crystal. The art of glass blowing originated among the Babylonians, was improved by the Romans into a true art form, and reached new heights in craftsmanship in 16th-century Venice.

Lock, 2000 B.C.; Near East

The lock was invented to prevent entry by intruders and to warrant safekeeping for goods that could not be given a standing guard at all hours of the day and night.

The first locks, pin tumblers dating back 4000 years, were in large wooden bolts that secured doors in the palace of Khorsabad near Nineveh.

The lock was simple in design; it was also adopted by the Egyptians. An assembly attached to the door was cut to allow the positioning of several wooden pins dropped into the slots, or holes, which gripped the bolt. Opening the lock required a special key; in this case it was a large wooden bar shaped like a toothbrush, which carried upright pegs that matched the pins and holes. When the key was put into the holes below the vertical pins and lifted, the pins moved free, allowing the bolt, with key still inside, to be slid back.

The pin-tumbler locks went unchanged for many centuries and became widespread, turning up in countries as far apart as Japan and Norway; they are still in use in parts of Egypt and India. In fact, a later derivation of the pin-tumbler principle, called the falling pin, became common during the Middle Ages and evolved into the modern Yale lock.

Metal locks were a Roman invention. Usually the Romans made locks of iron and keys of bronze. They were the first to introduce to the area around the keyhole the use of "wards" — projections inside the lock that restrain the key from being rotated unless the flat face of the key, called a bit, has slots on it to allow the projections to pass through the lock's inside. Wards helped locks become almost impenetrable by assuring that only the right key could open them, and great variations went into their designs to make locks secure. The Romans also were the first to make keys of different sizes, ending centuries of uniformity for locks. Some of their keys actually were so small, they were worn around the neck as trinkets or on the finger as rings.

*

Linus Yale, an American inventor, in 1848 parlayed the ancient pin tumbler into the lock that has become our contemporary standard, the **Yale lock.**

Twelve years later, Yale's son Linus Jr. improved the cylinder design, so that when a small flat key with a serrated edge was inserted into the tumblers, the pins in the cylinder were lifted to certain heights by the key's serrations and turned the cylinder. Usually the pins' heights were arranged in a combination of five different projections, making lock-picking all but impossible because of the countless variations they represent inside the cylinder.

The Yale lock remains in use in everything from school lockers to shop doors. But its supremacy has been challenged by lever locks, which are popular for protecting houses, and combination locks, whose tumblers are activated by the turning of a numbered dial on the face of the lock.

Windmill, A.D. 644; Iran

The windmill was one of man's early means of transferring the burden of work from muscle to machine. It originated not in Holland, the land now legendary in windmill history, but in eastern Persia, now Iran, near Afghanistan.

The first windmill, used to grind grain, is thought to have been constructed in A.D. 644 by a Persian millwright living in the town of Sistan. It would not be recognized today as a windmill, for it, and others constructed during that time, were horizontal rotating devices powered by sails. The sails were built below the millstones, and since the device had no gears, each sail drove a separate pair of stones. The Chinese soon adopted the windmill for their own purpose: to lift and evaporate sea water to gather salt.

Although the horizontal windmill wheel once was popular in the Crimea, Western European countries, and even the United States, today it is used occasionally only in Scandinavian countries to draw water.

It was replaced, of course, by the vertical wheel, an invention that was put to use by the Romans. Roman builders, learning of the windmill from the Arab world, constructed their own model in the form of an inverted vertical water wheel, relying on sails instead of the water wheel to drive millstones by a series of gears, an innovation the Persian mill lacked. A rotating post to which the mill was attached allowed the sails to catch wind squarely from any quadrant.

Windmills first appeared in France about 1180, and in England eleven years later, although the earliest extant illustration of a windmill in England was in the *Windmill Psalter,* published in Canterbury in 1260. From then until the early 19th century windmills were immensely popular throughout Europe. But their place was quickly usurped by steam power, and was then delivered the coup de grâce by the internal combustion engine and the spread of electric power after World War I. Lately, in an effort to develop a broad spectrum of energy resources and break away from a dependence on oil, people have turned again to windmills, which have regained a modicum of their early popularity.

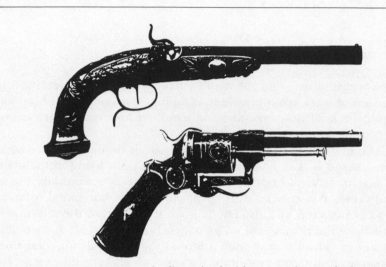

Antique Firearms. German dueling pistol with percussion caplock (top); French Lefaucheux six-shot double-action pocket revolver.

Gunpowder, 10th Century; China

Black gunpowder, the earliest explosive, was a mixture of saltpeter (potassium nitrate), sulfur, and charcoal. It's thought by some authorities to have been used first in China for propelling fireworks and then for military purposes, since 13th-century Chinese journals recount how it was placed in cut bamboo branches to launch stone "bullets."

Other authorities argue that the Chinese mixture was similar to real gunpowder only in its pyrotechnic qualities, and that true gunpowder was exclusively a European invention. Sir Roger Bacon, the English philosopher and scientist, in 1242 outlined a formula for an explosive powder that included saltpeter, charcoal, and sulfur, but did not elaborate on the possibility of using the substance as a propellant. Bacon's recipe, however, was virtually identical with modern gunpowder, varying only in its proportions.

The existence of black gunpowder certainly was the impetus behind the development of **firearms,** whose invention is often attributed to a 14th-century German monk, Berthold Schwarz. Firearms were in use throughout medieval Europe by the mid-14th century, and a record exists of a transaction for a shipment of guns and powder from Ghent, in Belgium, to England in 1314.

Black gunpowder came into peacetime use in the 17th century, when it was employed in mining for uncovering mineral veins. Its first application in civil engineering, for road-building and fracturing rock foundations, was in the construction of the Malpas Tunnel of the Canal du Midi in France in 1679.

Nitroglycerin, 1846; Italy

An explosive more lethal than gunpowder was nitroglycerin, discovered in 1846 by an Italian chemist, Ascanio Sobrero. It was, however, so risky to manufacture and dangerous to detonate that it remained for years a laboratory curiosity, until a father-son team, Immanuel and Alfred Nobel, demonstrated its commercial potential in 1860.

The Nobels built a small factory at Heleneborg, Sweden, in 1862, to make a mixture of nitroglycerin and gunpowder. But the plant's safety features were inadequate, considering the volatile nature of nitroglycerin, and two years later the factory exploded, killing several workers, among them a third Nobel, Alfred's younger brother, Emil Oskar. Saddened but determined to carry on, Alfred erected his next laboratory on a barge moored in the middle of a lake, and soon confidence in handling the explosive encouraged him to build two manufacturing plants on land — one at Krummel, Germany, the other near Stockholm, Sweden. He then came to the United States, seeking capital to finance his experiments, and while here was granted an American patent for nitroglycerin. But for reasons of finances and red tape he was unable to go public with nitroglycerin, and after he had been swindled by a number of crooked businessmen, he sold his American holdings in 1885 for $20,000.

Nobel, never unaware of the pervasive threat of destruction made possible by his many explosives (including dynamite), funneled a large amount of his royalties into a foundation that became the governing body and source of funds for the Nobel Prizes.

Dynamite, 1867; Sweden

The word "dynamite" comes from the Greek *dynamis*, meaning "power," and invention of the explosive belongs solely to Alfred Nobel, who pioneered its use in 1866.

Nobel, who experimented with many materials that could touch off an explosion, found that a porous siliceous earth, guhr, absorbed large quantities of nitroglycerin, making a product that was much safer to handle and more practical to use than his earlier mixture.

The formula called for 75 percent nitroglycerin and 25 percent guhr. But the mixture, which Nobel called Dynamite No. 1, was not as potent as he wished, because the guhr contributed nothing to the power of the explosive and actually detracted from its force by absorbing heat that otherwise would have intensified the blast. In its place Nobel substituted other natural active ingredients, such as wood pulp for an absorbent and a salt (sodium nitrate) for an oxidizing agent. These "dopes" enabled Nobel not only to improve the efficacy of dynamite, but to prepare the explosive in varying strengths, which he termed "straight dynamite." Forty percent straight dynamite, for example, consisted of a combination of 40 percent nitroglycerin and 60 percent dope. He patented his new invention in 1869.

Refrigeration, 1748; Scotland

The origin of the refrigerator begins with the discovery of the principles of artificial refrigeration in 1748 by Scottish scientist William Cullen at the University of Glasgow, and culminates in 1913 with production of the first commercial home refrigerator, the Domelre, which retailed for a whopping $900.

Prior to these developments, man had to rely on nature and in-genuity for cooling and preserving food. The ancient Greeks and Romans transported snow and ice from mountaintops into their homes. A great luxury then was a snow cellar: a hole dug in the ground, lined with logs, insulated with heavy layers of straw, and packed densely with snow. The compressed snow turned into a block of solid ice, which remained frozen for months, providing refrigeration for those who could afford it.

In dry, temperate climates, particularly in parts of India and Egypt, a natural phenomenon served as a source of cooling to produce ice. Around sundown water was placed in shallow clay trays on a bed of straw. Rapid evaporation from the water surface and from the damp sides of the tray (due to the dry air) combined with the nocturnal drop in temperature to freeze the water — even though the temperature of the environment never fell near the freezing point. Sometimes only a thin film of ice formed on the surface of the water in the tray, but under more favorable condi-tions of dryness and cooling the water froze into a solid piece of ice.

Artificial refrigeration was discovered when William Cullen, ex-perimenting with ethyl ether, evaporated it into a partial vacuum, heralding the dawn of vapor cooling. Several inventors improved on Cullen's method, and in 1834 Jacob Perkins patented a refrig-erator employing a compressor and a closed system containing a volatile liquid, though he never marketed the device. An Ameri-can physician, John Gorrie, built his own refrigerator to provide ice and cool air for his hospital in Apalachicola, Florida.

Between the two World Wars, Kelvinator, Frigidaire, and Gen-eral Electric made refrigerators a new household necessity.

Rubber Tires, 1845; England

At one time all rubber was natural, bled from beneath the bark of many tropical trees and shrubs and known to several civilizations. The American Indians discovered rubber at some early, undeter-mined date, and Christopher Columbus, on his second voyage to the New World in the mid-1490s, saw Indians in what is now Haiti playing a game with rubber balls.

Early Spaniards in the New World copied the Indians' method of bleeding "milk" from trees and conceived the ingenious idea

An early contraption for attaching tires to wheels

(though there is a belief that they copied this, too, from the Indians) of dripping the liquid over their coats, capes, hats, pants, and the soles of their shoes. They thus produced a type of rain-gear and hardy footwear that surpassed the ancient kind, made of animal hides soaked in oil.

But synthesizing rubber proved a complex task. The British scientist Michael Faraday assigned an empirical formula to rubber in 1826, but for the next hundred years chemists sought to synthesize the substance without success.

A major advance in terms of clothing was achieved in the early 19th century, when a Scottish chemist, Charles Macintosh, discovered that rubber dissolved in coal-tar naphtha. This permitted the manufacture of more clothlike waterproof overgarments, and was the origin of the **mackintosh.**

Charles Goodyear, the son of a Connecticut storekeeper, with no scientific training, stumbled on a discovery in 1839. After accidentally dropping a mixture of sulfur and rubber on the top of a stove, he quickly scraped it off and discovered the rubber had lost its stickiness and, on drying, resisted its former tendency to harden and become brittle. The process of adding sulfur to rubber became known as "vulcanization," after Vulcan, the Roman god of fire, and marked the beginning of the modern rubber industry.

Solid rubber tires first appeared on bicycles in London in 1845. A Scottish-born veterinarian and inventor, John Dunlop, developed the air-filled **pneumatic tire** in 1888, initially for bicycles, but it was quickly adopted by the newly emerging automobile industry. Roads then were terribly rough and bumpy, and the pneumatic tire did much to add to the appeal and comfort of early automobiles.

Typewriter, 1867; United States

"An Artificial Machine or Method of Impressing or Transcribing of Letters Singly or Progressively one after another, as in Writing, whereby all Writing whatever may be Engrossed in Paper or Parchment so Neat and Exact as not to be distinguished from Print."

That ambitious boast, made in 1714 by a British inventor, marked the earliest known attempt at building a typewriter. But the first true working model did not appear until 1867, when an American inventor, Christopher Latham Sholes, inspired by news of British and French progress on such a machine (particularly in producing Braille for the blind; see **Braille,** page 84), retired to his workshop and constructed a portable (albeit heavy) typewriter.

His second model, produced a year later, had improved to the point that its speed surpassed that of writing by hand. Sholes continued to perfect his machines, and in 1873 he signed a contract, with the E. Remington and Sons Company of Ilion, New York, to produce typewriters (THAT COULD PRINT ONLY IN UPPER CASE). The Remingtons, gunsmiths by trade, introduced their commercial model in 1874, naming it not after its inventor, Sholes, but after themselves.

Mark Twain was the first author to submit a typed manuscript, which he wrote on a Remington soon after the machines went on sale, for a costly $125. The shift-key typewriter, which introduced lower-case letters, appeared in 1878, and "visible writing," which let the writer see the printed line as it was typed (instead of having to lift the carriage to check a letter or word), originated the same year.

Always eager to improve the speed of typing, Sholes experimented with electrically operated typewriters, but that invention, in its first incarnation, sprang from the imaginative efforts of Thomas Edison in 1872. The machine was so crude as a typewriter that it was soon converted into a ticker-tape printer. The direct ancestor of the line of electric typewriters we use today appeared in 1920, the product of American inventor James Smathers.

28

Science: Metrics to Microscopes

Weights and Measures, 3000 B.C.; Near East

Following the domestication of plants and animals came a period of thriving agricultural growth and commerce. Tribes traded foods indigenous to their lands, and within tribes farmers bartered wares with members of other trades. Making a fair exchange with a bundle of wheat, a bag of grain, or even bunches of grapes required a system of standard weights. On the other hand, the rise of architecture in the form of temples and pyramids necessitated a system of measure.

The Egyptians and Babylonians appear to be the first peoples to establish standards of weights and measures.

To measure lengths, the Egyptians turned to parts of the human body. We know many of these measurements by terms later derived from Latin. A **cubit,** the most enduring early standard of measure, devised about 3000 B.C., was the length of a grown man's arm from the elbow to the tip of the outstretched middle finger — about 20.5 inches in modern units.

Just as 1 modern yard is subdivided into 3 feet, and the foot further divided into 12 inches, so too was the cubit broken into smaller measures, again using a body part, this time the finger. The cubit's basic subunit was a **digit,** which was the breadth, not the length, of a finger. Twenty-eight digits equaled 1 cubit.

The **palm,** not surprisingly, was another unit. One palm equaled 4 digits. (Measure it for yourself, by holding the four fingers of a hand against the other hand's palm.) A palm plus a digit totaled 5 digits, or a **hand.**

Palms were combined to make several larger units (such as the *t'ser* which consisted of 4 palms, or 16 digits), and a digit was elaborately subdivided, forming a system of measurement that became increasingly complex — but amazingly accurate. The dimensions of the Great Pyramid of Gizeh, built by thousands of workers with minimal architectural knowledge, boasts sides that vary no more than 0.05 percent from the mean length — that is, a deviation of only 4.5 inches over a span of 755 feet.

The ancient Greeks borrowed from Egyptian and Babylonian systems and made their own refinements; they too preferred terms related to the human body. For instance, they combined 16 fingers to arrive at 1 **foot,** and 24 fingers made an "Olympic cubit." The Romans copied from the Greeks, but subdivided the foot into 12 **inches.** They also used the **mile,** the **yard,** and, for weight, the **pound.**

A system of standard weights based on the human body was unfeasible, since there were too many natural variations to permit reliance on an average man. Instead, the Babylonians devised a system based on metal objects, or trinkets, of various sizes and shapes.

The earliest unit of weight was the **mina.** Minas often were shaped like ducks, and each of several unearthed at an archeological dig weigh roughly 640 grams. Also discovered there was a **swan,** weighing 30 minas. The Babylonians also used standard size "coins," from which the Hebrews adopted their unit of weight, the "shekel," about half an ounce, and also a silver coin, which weighed that amount and is mentioned frequently in the Bible.

Eventually, almost all of the ancient and medieval weights and measures would fall into disuse, to be replaced by the metric system.

Metric System, 1799; France

The French Revolution, which broke out in 1789, not only transformed the government of France, but overturned many of the country's previously sacrosanct institutions. With the fall of the Bastille on July 14 of that year, King Louis XVI had to give way to a constituent National Assembly, composed of commoners, which proceeded to make many changes. Prominent among them was the adoption, in June 1799, of the metric system.

The idea of a metric system was not new. It had been bandied about by scientists and statesmen since 1670, when Gabriel Mouton, vicar of St. Paul's Church in Lyon, proposed a sensible system in which weights and measures would be divided decimally. At the time a uniform standard was badly needed, since the welter of national systems severely handicapped European scientists who wanted to exchange ideas and collaborate on projects.

French scientists lobbied the National Assembly in April, 1790, and the French Academy of Sciences was ordered to devise a metric system for consideration. The academy members decided that the length of the meridian passing through Paris from the North Pole to the Equator should serve as a fixed distance, and that one ten-millionth of that distance should be called a **meter.** The new unit of weight, the **gram,** was to be related to the weight of a cubic meter of water. Subunits of one one-hundredth (centimeter) and one one-thousandth (millimeter) were also proposed, along with such superunits as a thousand meters (kilometer).

A group of twelve mathematicians and physicists met with the king, who scrutinized their proposal. But as the Revolution heated up, the king was arrested trying to flee the country, and his actual proclamation to begin work on measuring the meter was made from a jail cell. The assignment was undertaken by two astronomers, Jean-Baptiste Delambre and Pierre Méchain, who spent six years surveying the distance on the meridian from Barcelona, Spain, to Dunkirk in northern France. Meanwhile, other scientists used existing geodesic data to extend the full measure of the distance that would be subdivided into meters.

Although the work was completed by 1793, debate delayed its official acceptance until 1799, and its full implementation took still more time. The metric system was adopted under the motto "For all people, all the time," a sentiment in accord with the revolutionary tenor of the era.

Calendar: Julian, 46 B.C.; Gregorian, A.D. 1582

The ancient, or Julian, calendar, introduced by Roman statesman Julius Caesar, was based on calculations of the phases of the moon and seasonal movement of the sun made by the Greek astronomer Sosigenes of Alexandria. It served Western Europe for more than 1500 years, before being replaced by the Gregorian calendar.

The Julian version was dropped in 1582, when Pope Gregory XIII ordained that the day of October 5 should henceforth be numbered October 15. The Pope's decision was not an arbitrary one. A discrepancy had accumulated in all calendars since the year A.D. 4, when Augustinian monks ruled that every fourth year should contain 366 days, thus introducing the **leap day** and **leap year.** This addition was required because of the astronomical reality that the Earth takes 365.24219 days to make one full revolution of the sun, although, of course, it was not yet acknowledged that the Earth revolved around the sun. The accumulated fraction over four years adds up to an additional day, making the leap day necessary.

Italy, France, Portugal, and Spain switched immediately to the Gregorian calendar, but England and its colonies, including those in North America, did not adopt the version until 1752. Several countries began using the new style of mapping out a year in this century: China, 1912; Bulgaria, 1915; Turkey and the U.S.S.R., 1917; Romania and Yugoslavia, 1919; and Greece, 1923. By this time, all seven of these countries were lagging behind the rest of the world by thirteen days.

The origin of the word "calendar" is the medieval Latin *calendarium,* meaning "interest register," or "account book." It in turn is derived from the older word *calendae* (taken from Greek), the first day of the Roman month, the time at which all feasts, government events, and public market days for that particular month were posted in the public square.

The origin of the **day** is a natural consequence of the rising and setting of the sun, but the history of its measurement has several sources. Now days are clocked from midnight to midnight, but astronomers from about the 2nd century A.D. until as recently as 1925 measured days from noon to noon. Many primitive tribes, including the American Indians, reckoned days from dawn to dawn, hence the reference to a succession of days as the passage of so many "suns." The Italians opted for a more romantic system of counting, from sunset to sunset; the Teutons numbered midnights, grouping fourteen nights together, the origin of the term **fortnight.**

The origin of the **week** also has diverse sources. One early reckoning of time was to count moons (or months), but as civilization became more complex, shorter periods proved more convenient as measurements of time. For a long while, almost every group of people had its own system. West Africans used a four-day week; central Asians opted for a five-day week; the Assyrians adopted a week of six days, which usually corresponded to the intervals between market days, when merchants gathered in town squares to peddle their wares.

The Babylonians preferred to measure a month by its natural phase of twenty-eight days (more accurately, the moon's waxing and waning takes approximately twenty-nine and a half days). For convenience in business transactions — and also because of their religious belief in the sacredness of the number seven — they grouped the days into four seven-day weeks, the origin of our present system.

Our names for the days of the week and the months of the year come from two sources: celestial bodies and mythological gods and goddesses. Four of our weekdays — Tuesday, Wednesday, Thursday, and Friday — received their appellations from a mythological husband and wife and their two sons.

Personification of the days of the week *(left to right):* Venus, Thor, Mercury, Mars, Moon god, Sun god, and Saturn.

English	Latin	Anglo-Saxon	Origin
Sunday	Solis Dies (Sun's Day)	Sunnan Dæg (Sun's Day)	The Latin for "sun" is **solis.**
Monday	Lunae Dies (Moon's Day)	Monan Dæg (Moon's Day)	The Latin for "moon" is **luna.**
Tuesday	Martis Dies (Mars' Day)	Tiwes Dæg (Tiu's Day)	Tiu was one of the Anglo-Saxon spellings of Tyr, the Norse god of war, son of Odin and Frigg. His counterpart in Roman mythology was Mars.
Wednesday	Mercurii Dies (Mercury's Day)	Wodnes Dæg (Woden's Day)	Woden was the Anglo-Saxon form of Odin, the Norse god of war and victory, and husband of Frigg. In Roman mythology, Mercury, the messenger of the gods, often brought word of victory.
Thursday	Jovis Dies (Jove's Day)	Thueres Dæg (Thor's Day)	Thor was the Norse god of thunder. He was the eldest son of Odin and Frigg. The chief of the Roman gods, Jove (also called Jupiter), was sometimes referred to as the Thunderer.
Friday	Veneris Dies (Day of Venus)	Friges Dæg (Frigg's Day)	Frigg was the Norse goddess of love, wife of Odin, mother of Thor and Tyr. Her Roman counterpart was Venus.
Saturday	Saturni Dies (Saturn's Day)	Sæternes Dæg (Saturn's Day)	The Latin god Saturn was sometimes thought to be the father of Jove.

English	Latin	Origin
January	Januarius	Named after Janus, the two-faced Roman god of entryways. He presided over the "opening" of the New Year.
February	Februarius	Derived from the Latin festival of purification, called Februa, celebrated on February 15.
March	Martius	The month of Mars, the Roman god of war and protector of crops.
April	Aprilis	Named after the Latin for "to open," *aperire,* since it was the time of year when trees and flowers blossomed.
May	Maius	Named after the Latin term for "elders," *maiores,* since in ancient times this was the month set aside by the Romans to honor the elderly. The month possibly was named after an obscure goddess, Maia.
June	Junius	Named after the Latin word for "youngsters," *juniores,* since the month was reserved for honoring youth. It is also very possible that the month was designated for Juno, queen of the goddesses.
July	Julius	Named in honor of the famous Roman statesman and soldier, Caius Julius Caesar, who died on March 15, 44 B.C.
August	Augustus	Named after the second Caesar and first Roman emperor, Augustus Caesar.
September	*septem*	Latin for seven, since in ancient times this was the seventh month of the year.
October	*octo*	Latin for eight; originally the eighth month.
November	*novem*	Latin for nine; originally the ninth month.
December	*decem*	Latin for ten; originally the tenth month.

Capricorn the goat.

Leo the lion.

Pisces the fishes.

Aquarius the water carrier.

Sagittarius the archer.

Western astrology arose in Mesopotamia in 650 B.C., but horoscopes were seldom personal; they were concerned with predicting major wars, floods, plagues, and famines. Personal destiny horoscopes originated with the 4th century B.C. Greeks, who set down the houses and signs of the Zodiac. Considered a major science for centuries, and taught in all European universities, astrology fell from scientific credibility following the astronomical discoveries of Copernicus and Galileo.

Seismograph, A.D. 132; China

It seems only fitting that the seismograph, a device that registers the ground's trembling during an earthquake or explosion, should have been invented in China, a country long prone to major quakes.

The construction of the first devices, elaborate and ornate, was much better than their accuracy in predicting an impending quake or measuring the severity of an actual occurrence. But in principle they were the forerunners of all later mechanical seismographs that attempted to detect earth tremors.

The first seismograph was made in A.D. 132 by Chang Heng, a Chinese scholar and inventor. At the center of the device was a large cylinder that had arranged around its upper circumference eight carved ivory dragon heads, each with a ball in its mouth. The lower circumference was rimmed with eight carved frogs, their open mouths positioned directly beneath the dragon heads. In the event of earth tremors, or a full-scale quake, one or more balls fell from the dragons' mouths, where they were loosely held by rods, into the corresponding frogs' mouths. Each such contact emitted a popping sound.

Many similar devices were constructed in China and in other earthquake-prone regions. Some imitated Chang's seismograph in that they featured dropping balls; others detected tremors by spilling water from upper containers into lower ones, the quantity of spilled water representing a crude measure of the earth's disturbance.

Mechanical seismographs gave way to more accurate electrical **seismometers** in the 19th century. This time Italy, also a country with a history of severe quakes, marked the point of origin.

In 1855 an Italian inventor, Luigi Palmieri, built the first true seismometer. Several U-shaped tubes, similar to barometers, were placed at various points around a compass. An earth tremor caused the mercury to make an electrical contact with a switch that first stopped a ticking clock; this recorded the precise time of the quake. The electrical contact also turned on a recording drum on which the motion of a float on the surface of mercury was registered; this measured the relative intensity and the duration of ground disturbance.

The modern era in the science of seismography began in 1880, following a severe earthquake near Tokyo. Studying tremors in that region with the hope of one day making accurate predictions, three British scientists — Sir James Alfred Ewing, Thomas Gray, and John Milne — organized the Seismological Society of Japan. Under its guidance a number of modern detection devices were invented that served as the immediate forerunners of today's sophisticated earthquake-prediction equipment.

Microscope, 15th Century; Holland

The first simple microscopes, limited to magnification by single lenses, were built during the middle of the 15th century and used primarily to probe the world of insects: gossamer wings, bristly legs, and multifaceted eyes.

Because of the difficulty of making very pure glass at that time, microscope lenses greatly distorted images and surrounded them with halos in rainbow hues. In the next century, a Dutchman named Zacharias Janssen, not trained as a scientist, finally developed lenses to a high degree of refinement, earning himself the distinction of the "father of microscopy."

Anton van Leeuwenhoek was born in 1632 in Delft, the Netherlands, where he learned the drapery trade, and in his spare time experimented with grinding glass to make lenses. He produced microscopes of such efficiency that almost singlehandedly he established the field of microbiology. Gradually he convinced a largely skeptical scientific community that a major theory of the day, spontaneous generation — the belief that living organisms can originate from nonliving matter — was utter nonsense. Maggots were not born from rotten meat, nor fleas from sand, nor eels from the muddy banks of lakes and streams; these creatures reproduced from hatched eggs that had been laid by the female and fertilized by the male.

Much to his own surprise, Leeuwenhoek discovered that aphids reproduced by "virgin birth," the process of parthenogenesis, in which female eggs hatch without fertilization from males. Ambitious, always sliding new specimens under his superior lenses, Leeuwenhoek also is credited with giving the first accurate descriptions of red blood cells (to the amazement of physiologists of the day), of the bacteria that inhabit the human mouth and gut (to the horror of the populace), and of the shape and locomotion of human sperm (whose collection brought cries of immorality and murder).

The first practical **electron microscope,** a marvel of modern technology, was constructed in 1937 by two Canadian scientists, James Hillier and Albert Prebus, but its roots go back to France and the year 1924.

That year a French physicist, Louis de Broglie, startled the scientific world with the suggestion that matter, usually thought of as a solid and well-defined mass, could, under appropriate conditions, act like waves, evanescent and propagating through space like light. It was a dramatic, though not altogether unreasonable, variation on Einstein's earlier observation that waves of light could at times behave like a hailstorm of matter. Through a complex series of experiments, de Broglie's idea proved to be correct and won him international acclaim and the Nobel Prize in physics in 1929.

The concept also opened the way for an electron microscope. Ordinary optical microscopes illuminate specimens with light waves, and a microscope's resolving power, or the sharpness of its image, depends on the light's wavelength. Once scientists realized that matter (in this case, electrons) possesses wavelengths much shorter than visible light, they immediately saw the chance of building a microscope of immense resolving power, or magnification.

Progress was fast. In 1926 French scientists demonstrated that magnetic fields could act as lenses for electrons, focusing and aiming beams of matter. Five years later the first two-lens prototype of an electron microscope was developed, and in 1937 came the first practical model. At that time the best and most powerful optical microscope had a magnification of 2000; Hillier and Prebus's electron microscope magnified objects 7000 times. Today the best electron microscopes achieve magnifications of up to 2 million, exposing the once-hidden details of viruses, crystals, minerals, and even the intimate process of a sperm fertilizing an egg.

Thermometer, 16th Century; Italy

The ancient Greeks could have invented the thermometer, since they were well acquainted with the behavior of certain liquids and gases under conditions of changing temperature. In fact several scientists of the time attempted to measure quantitative differences between hot and cold. But success at the task came only late in the 16th century to the Italian astronomer Galileo.

Galileo's first thermometer was unlike the devices we use today. It was actually a thermoscope, which had no degree scale, and measured only gross changes in temperature. A large glass bulb with a long, narrow, open-mouthed neck rested inverted over a vessel of colored water or alcohol. When air was forced from the bulb, the liquid rose up a short distance into the neck. When the bulb's temperature changed, the air in it either expanded or contracted, changing the level of the liquid.

A contemporary of Galileo's, Sanctorius, in 1611 introduced the first scale for the thermoscope. He constructed the gauge's low point by noting the level at which liquid stood when the thermoscope was surrounded by melting snow; then he held a candle beneath it to mark the high point. From his observations he arrived at a scale with 110 equal parts, or degrees. Thus the thermo-"scope," a device to "see" changes in temperature, was converted into a thermo-"meter," one that measures those changes.

The readings on early thermometers were often inaccurate because of changes in barometric pressure, which could cause liquid levels to vary when the temperature did not. This problem of exposure to the atmosphere finally was solved in 1644, when Grand Duke Ferdinand II of Tuscany introduced the hermetically sealed thermometer. He further advanced the nascent science of thermometry by helping to found the Academia de Cimento in Florence in 1657, which served as a laboratory for experimentation in making accurate thermometers, many of which stayed in use for centuries and are museum pieces today. They did not use mercury, as modern models do (though members of the academy experimented with the liquid metal), but red wine instead, since it expanded faster when heated.

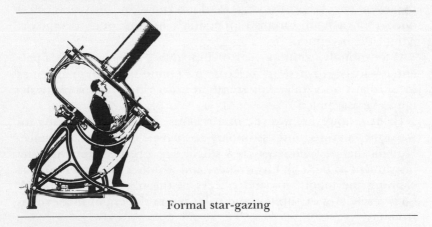

Formal star-gazing

Telescope, 1608; the Netherlands

To present the cloudy origins of the telescope in a nutshell: a Dutchman, Hans Lippershey, built a refracting telescope in 1608; a Scot, James Gregory, expounded the principle of the reflecting telescope in 1633; and the first one was built by Sir Isaac Newton in 1672. But the story is more complex than that.

Any instrument for viewing objects from afar is called a telescope, the name taken from the Greek *tele*, meaning "far," and *skopein,* "to see." Although the great Italian astronomer Galileo is often credited with inventing the telescope in 1609 (stealing the idea from Lippershey), the practice of telescopy, which requires merely simple magnifying lenses, dates back many centuries.

Glass was known to the ancient Egyptians, and it probably gave rise to the lenses that have been unearthed in Asia Minor and on Crete, dating from 2000 B.C. These lenses are very crude, but each produces magnification, and combinations of them could have produced a telescope. In addition, both the phenomena of light reflection and refraction (the bases for two major categories of telescopes) were expounded on by the Greek geometer Euclid in the 3rd century B.C.

Even when history tells us that astronomer Hans Lippershey of Middelburg in the Netherlands applied in 1608 for a patent for his telescope, it also dashes all hope for finding the true origin of the instrument by making it clear that Lippershey was summarily turned down because "many other persons had a knowledge of the invention." Who they were we don't know, and may never find out, so for many historians Lippershey's instrument marks the origin of the invention.

(Interestingly, within a year of Lippershey's rejection for a patent, telescopes turned up in Paris and London, and in many cities in Germany and Italy. Apparently it was an instrument just waiting to be assembled.)

Galileo, however, was the first scientist to point a telescope toward the heavens, and astronomy has never been the same since. He built his first telescope in a single day, greatly improving the instrument as built by Lippershey, and within a short time he was charting the mountains and craters of the moon, adding to the known satellites of Jupiter, and ushering in the era of modern astronomy.

Photography, 1826; France

Two Frenchmen, Joseph-Nicéphore Niepce and Louis-Jacques-Mandé Daguerre, helped launch the field of photography in the first half of the 19th century, Niepce with a crude film that captured the first fixed photographic image, and Daguerre by improving early cameras.

Niepce came to photography through his business interest in li-

The French invention of photograph, and the British discovery of celluloid, paved the way for Thomas Edison's "peep show" motion pictures.

thography, the process of copying drawings by hand onto stone, then imprinting them on paper. Employing the artistic skills of his son, Niepce established a thriving enterprise in the field, but when his son was conscripted into the French army, he was suddenly without a draftsman. Forced to turn to his own inventive powers, since he had no artistic talent, Niepce conceived a process that did away with a draftsman altogether — it used ambient light to capture a scene on film.

For film Niepce used glass coated with a kind of asphalt (bitumen of Judea), which becomes soluble in oil if exposed to sufficient light. His first photograph showed a barnyard as seen from the upper window of his country estate. So much time was needed for adequate exposure to capture the image that shadows of trees shifted as the sun advanced across the afternoon sky; the picture was severely blurred, but the door to a new industry had been opened.

Niepce's idea itself was not original. Several decades earlier scientists had discovered that certain salts of silver darkened when exposed to light. Thomas Wedgwood, a physicist and the son of the English potter Josiah Wedgwood, took the first photograph in 1802, when he smeared a thin layer of moist silver salts over a piece of paper and focused an image on the surface. The image took, but soon faded; Niepce, though, had found a way to fix images in time.

Daguerre was a successful landscape painter, who traced the outlines of a scene on canvas by using a "camera obscura" — a hollow box with a lens at one end, which projected an enlarged image on the opposite surface. Hearing of Niepce's discovery, Daguerre suggested in 1829 that they form a partnership, which lasted until Niepce's death, four years later. Daguerre then toiled to perfect the camera and its photographs, and by 1837 was producing remarkably clear and detailed pictures on silvered copper plates. He and Niepce's son eventually sold the rights to their invention to the French government, which guaranteed them royalties for life.

Cameras continued to improve, and a major breakthrough occurred when heavy photographic plates were replaced with flexible, lightweight celluloid film. Celluloid had been discovered by the English chemist Alexander Parkes in 1826 (it is, by the way, the origin of **plastics**), but it was not transformed into a commercial product until 1869, by an American inventor, John W. Hyatt. Thus, Niepce, Daguerre, Parkes, and Hyatt all had paved the way for one of the greatest entertainments of the 20th century, motion pictures. (See *Motion Pictures,* page 222.)

Holography, or three-dimensional photography, was the brainchild of Hungarian-born physicist Dennis Gabor. The process records an image, called a hologram, as a pattern of stripes and whorls that is unrecognizable but that, when illuminated by laser light, projects the information into a three-dimensional representation of the original object.

Gabor invented holography in 1948, and for it received the 1971 Nobel Prize in physics.

Gabor coined the word "holography" from the Greek *holos,* or "whole," and *graphein,* "to write or draw," because the process records — writes down, so to say — all the optical information of an object that later is required to render a faithful picture.

Computer, 1822; England

It is no mere coincidence that our word "calculus" stems from the Latin for "stone," for stones are believed to have been one of man's first calculating devices, aiding in the tasks of addition and sub-traction throughout primitive times. The practice of rearranging stones in columns, in fact, is thought to have given rise to the first true calculator, the **abacus,** which originated in China during the 6th century B.C. Its stonelike beads, shifted along vertical strings, enabled the Chinese and, about two hundred years later, several Mediterranean civilizations to perform basic arithmetical opera-tions with speed and accuracy, the test of any true computer.

The abacus had limited uses, though, and during the next twenty-four centuries, in which it served as the only major computational device, the science of calculations remained tedious drudgery, often greatly hampering scientific progress. This was particularly true in the field of astronomy, where stupendously large computations were required to determine the orbits and motions of the planets. Done entirely by hand, such calculations took mathematicians years to complete.

A major advance appeared in 1614, when John Napier, a Scots-man, published, three years before his death, his famous *Mirifici Logarithmorum Canonis Descriptio,* the origin of **logarithms.** Loga-rithm tables converted at a stroke the lengthy processes of long multiplication and division into the faster ones of addition and subtraction.

The first actual calculating machine for adding was built in 1642 by Blaise Pascal, the son of a French tax collector. A philosopher and mathematical prodigy, Pascal grew up observing his father engaged in hours of tedious calculations. Determined to lessen his father's burden (and possibly his own one day, since he contem-plated becoming a tax collector himself), at the age of nineteen Pascal constructed an automatic device that, by the turning of lit-tle wheels, added and subtracted. Accurate and speedy for its day, Pascal's calculator never caught on, though: clerks throughout France, whose livelihood derived from hand calculations, viewed the gadget as a job threat and refused to use it.

In 1671 the German mathematician Gottfried Wilhelm von Leibniz (coinventor with Sir Isaac Newton of the **calculus**) con-structed a "stepped wheel" device for multiplying by means of re-peated additions. "It is unworthy of excellent men to lose hours like slaves in the labor of calculations," said Leibniz, whose device enjoyed limited use among scientists.

Such mechanical contrivances, however, were no more than

clumsy calculators that could do only arithmetic. The first man to conceptualize and build a true computer was the English mathematician Charles Babbage. Incensed by the inaccuracies he found in the mathematical tables of the day, Babbage (father of the speedometer, the locomotive cow-catcher, and the first reliable life-expectancy tables) constructed in 1822 a system of cogs and gears called the "Difference Engine"; it could rapidly and accurately calculate long lists of functions. He managed to build only a simple model, though, because the craftsmen of the day were unable to machine the precise parts the engine required.

Further experimentation led Babbage to conceive of (though never to build) the even more complex "Analytical Engine," which had all the essentials of a modern computer: logic circuitry, memory, and data storage and retrieval. Most important of all, it was programmable.

Babbage's ally in his work, Augusta Ada Byron, countess of Lovelace and Lord Byron's only legitimate daughter, was history's first computer programmer. As physically beautiful as she was mathematically gifted, Ada described the first set of computer instructions to tell the machine to compute a series (known as Bernoulli numbers) generated by a complex mathematical equation.

She envisioned her program being written on **punch cards,** which had been invented in 1728 by a French weaver, Joseph-Marie Jacquard, for weaving patterns on looms. They operated simply by permitting (through a hole) or blocking (no hole) a passing needle. Thus they presaged the on-off language of present-day electronic computers. Babbage's computer was never built (it would have been as big as a football field and probably would have needed half a dozen steam locomotives to power it), but Ada poetically claimed that in theory "the Analytical Engine weaves algebraical patterns just as the Jacquard loom weaves flowers and leaves."

The first really commercial calculating machine was devised in 1885 by William Burroughs of St. Louis and was manufactured in Chicago and sold in substantial numbers. Another American, a young engineer named Herman Hollerith, persuaded the Census Bureau to try punch-card programming in compiling data for the 1890 census. Soon punch cards were widely used in office machinery, including that made by a small, little-known firm that absorbed Hollerith's company to become International Business Machines, which launched the modern computer age.

Computers then were immense. The first electronic digital computer in the United States, ENIAC, unveiled at the University of Pennsylvania, contained more than 100,000 vacuum tubes, resistors, capacitors, and switches, and occupied the space of a two-car garage. Despite its size, ENIAC (for Electronic Numerical Integrator and Calculator) was really a dunce; it repeatedly made mistakes and broke down, because its tubes kept burning out. Built to calculate artillery firing tables, the half-million-dollar computer could perform 5000 additions and subtractions per second. Today, almost any home computer, costing only a few hundred dollars, can outperform the first digital number cruncher.

29

Sports and Games: Baseball to Bullfighting

Sports, 6000 B.C.

Man conceived the ideas that led to sports only after self-preservation ceased to be his constant preoccupation. This occurred some time after the establishment of farms and the domestication of animals and was first observed in the cradles of civilization in Egypt, along the Nile River and in Mesopotamia, now part of Iraq.

Among the earliest avocations of the ancient Egyptians were a game of bowling strikingly similar to the modern version; an entertainment called "throwing sticks," which may have been like dominoes; and the first game known to involve a ball and players. Strangely enough, this last game was played only by girls.

The most significant single development in the history of sports certainly was the **ball.**

We know that wild apes and chimpanzees toss rocks, stones, and rounded fruits, so there may never have been a time in human evolution when some form of ball was not chased, batted, or thrown. The two earliest civilizations, the Egyptian and the Sumerian, were both familiar with the ball, which was either a sculpted piece of light wood or strips of leather sewn together and stuffed with hair, feathers, or cloth. Later the bladders of animals were inflated and covered with leather to minimize the risk of puncture.

The earliest references to rubber balls are from the Aztec Indians, and travelers to the New World around the end of the 15th century reported seeing Indians "bouncing balls." From these early diversions emerged a variety of modern sports and games centered on the chasing and capturing of a ball.

Bowling, 5200 B.C.; Egypt

The origin of this sport can be traced to items found in the tomb of an Egyptian child who was buried around 5200 B.C. The game was played by setting up nine vertical stone shafts as pins and rolling a round stone ball to topple them. The ball first had to roll under an archway constructed of three pieces of carved marble. A noisy game, and undoubtedly subject to frequent equipment changes because of breaking stones, it nonetheless remained the model for many games that followed.

A later Polynesian version, called *ula maike,* also played with stone balls and pins, introduced the modern lane distance of 60 feet.

In Italy about 2000 years ago, **bocci,** a game still widely played, began in the Alps. Similar to bowling, bocci called for the underhand tossing of stones at a fixed object.

The contemporary idea of bowling at wooden pins originated in Germany, not as a sport but as part of a religious ceremony. In fact Martin Luther, the leader of the Reformation, even posited arguments as to why nine pins was the ideal and only number to be used at the end of the lane.

Bowling at wooden pins in the United States likely arose either from the German custom or from that of early Dutch settlers, who set up what is known today as Bowling Green, at the tip of Manhattan Island in New York City, where the game was played until 1840.

The origin of the tenth pin that now characterizes Western bowling apparently rests with a law prohibiting the game of ninepins because so much betting was associated with it. A tenth pin was added in 1845 to thwart the legal ban.

Gambling, 3500 B.C.; Egypt

Games of chance date back at least to ancient Egypt, where paintings in tombs and on pottery have provided archeologists with copious evidence for the existence of the first gambling **casinos.**

Fencing originated in Egypt in 1190 B.C., under the reign of Ramses III. Sword points were covered, and fencers wore masks tied to their wigs, as well as large bibs, ear pads, and narrow protective shields strapped to their left arms. The picture shows a 19th-century gymnasium.

One popular game of the time was **astragali,** similar to modern dice. An astragalus was an uneven, four-sided polished bone from the ankle of a sheep or dog, with each face assigned a different value. It was tossed and scores were tallied, but unless further written records are discovered, the rules of the game will remain obscure.

Equally popular was the early gambling festivity of "throwing sticks," similar to dominoes. The sticks were made of wood or ivory, about 3 inches long, square or elliptical in cross-section, and marked in various stylized ways. Similar sticks have been found in such disparate locations as ancient Britain, Greece, and Rome and in habitats of the Mayas in North America. The rules for the oldest form of throwing sticks, the Egyptian game, are unknown.

Dice, 3500 B.C.; Egypt

The ancient Egyptian game of astragali seems to mark the first unequivocal use of dice for gambling. But the origin of dice themselves reaches back some 40,000 years to magical rites of primitive man, who used dice to divine the future in a casting practice known as sortilege.

Among the fossil remains of early *Homo sapiens,* archeologists have found dice shaped from the anklebones of sheep and dogs, and slightly later in history dice appear in many geometrical shapes and made from almost every hard material. The early inhabitants of North America, the South Sea Islands, and the Arctic, for example, sculpted dice from plum and peach pits, buffalo and caribou bones, deer horns, stones, walnut shells, and beaver and woodchuck teeth. Since these dice, too, were probably used in religious rites, it is doubtful that they were desecrated by gambling.

After the Egyptians liberated dice for fun and games, the Greeks and Romans fashioned exquisite dice from onyx, agate, alabaster, marble, and amber.

As for the origin of cheating with **loaded dice,** it appears to be as old as the objects themselves. Many of the Egyptians' game dice are unmistakably loaded, and even some of the older religious dice used to augur the future of an individual or tribe are weighted to favor one side over the others. The first written account of dice practices is a 2000-year-old Sanskrit epic, the *Mahabharata.*

Skiing, 3000 B.C.; Norway

Skiing's origin clearly establishes it as one of man's oldest outdoor sporting activities. Skis discovered in bogs in Sweden and Finland are believed to be between 4000 and 5000 years old, and a rock carving in a Norwegian cave of two men on skis dates to about 2000 B.C.

Skiing at this time was only partly recreational; most skis were used by those traversing snow drifts and by hunters pursuing game. Snow skiing spread into other parts of Europe with the Vikings' 10th- and 11th-century conquests.

Until the mid-1800s skiers were connected only tenuously to their skis by toe straps, which greatly hampered jumping and fast turns because they limited a skier's control over his skis. In 1860, Sondre Nordheim from Telemark, Norway, introduced willow bindings around the heel from each side of the toe strap to fasten boots to skis. The arrival of stable bindings revolutionized skiing and marked the birth of modern skiing as a popular sport. Another of Nordheim's innovations that was soon standardized was skis with sides curving inward. With this design he introduced the christiania turn, a balletic move in which the body swings from a crouch to change direction or stop, and the telemark, in which the skier shifts his weight forward on the ski that will be outside the turn.

The Trysil Shooting and Skiing Club, founded in 1861, is the oldest of its kind and the precursor of today's chic ski clubs.

The earliest downhill race was contested at Montana, Switzerland, in 1911, but not until the Winter Olympics became a reality in 1924 was skiing considered a major sport. The International Ski Federation was founded on February 2, 1924, seven days after skiing was inaugurated into the Winter Games.

The first American exposure to skis began in the 1860s, when California races were staged on downhill courses with the competitors outfitted in skis 12 feet long and the older leather toe straps.

Wrestling Roman and American styles. Sumo wrestling *(lower left)* first became a sport in Japan around A.D. 710; opponents often weighed more than 400 pounds and fought in a 15-foot circle. Banned by the shoguns for more than four centuries during the Middle Ages, it eventually regained its place of honor in Japanese sport.

Wrestling, 3000 B.C.; Near East

The sport of wrestling, and other weaponless contests such as boxing, reaches back to the prehistoric truism "Only the strong survive." For wrestling almost certainly stemmed from rituals designed to enable one to acquire skills essential for establishing and maintaining leadership in a communal group. The aim, of course, was to overcome a foe in personal combat. But by employing sports instead of duels to the death, killing or disabling members of the group was avoided while at the same time the participants became skillful during their contests.

The earliest evidence of grappling as a recognized sport comes from the belt wrestling bouts of ancient Egypt and Mesopotamia. Cylinder seals and a copper statuette depicting this sport have been recovered and traced to about 3000 B.C., and a Sumerian literary work of that period, *The Gilgamesh Epic*, describes a wrestling match between the protagonists, Gilgamesh and Enkidu. Illustrations of belt wrestling holds and throws in vividly realistic poses have been found in Egyptian tombs at Beni Hasan dating from about 2500 B.C.

Wrestling received its greatest early impetus, however, from the Greeks. They put the sport on a pedestal, making the focal point of a young man's social life his membership in a palestra, a training place for wrestlers. Greek literary works are rich in descriptions of the sport's rigors, but wrestling was such an ordinary activity, and everyone understood it so well, that no chroniclers of ancient Greek history felt compelled to describe its actual holds and techniques, even though it was a major sport in more than a hundred cities over a period of 1200 years. All that is known from scenes etched on Greek vases and painted in murals is that loose wrestling was stylish and that contestants faced each other naked, like other athletes of the day.

Checkers, 2000 B.C.; Egypt

Checkers, older than the prominent board game of chess, was first played during the 2nd millennium B.C. by Egyptian aristocrats. With little change, it was adopted later by the Greeks, then by the Romans, but when the game reached China it became a distinctly different endeavor. The earliest book on checkers was a 1547 instructional pamphlet by Antonio Torquemada of Valencia, Spain. Known in England as draughts, checkers today is universally recognized.

The earliest international match was staged between the United States and Great Britain in 1905, and won by the Scottish Masters, 73–34, with 284 draws. In subsequent matches the U.S. won two, in 1927 and again in 1973. The longest unbeaten championship reign was that of the American Melvin Pomeroy, whose international record was unblemished from 1914 until his death, in 1933.

Football; Ancient Egypt

The earliest evidence of a game that featured two opposing teams kicking, tossing, and aggressively advancing a ball in opposite directions is found in an ancient Egyptian fertility rite, but little is known about the rules of this 5000-year-old ceremony. Other written records suggest that football was played in China about 300 B.C., and that the industrious Chinese later developed the spherical leather ball, which they stuffed densely with animal and human hair to achieve light weight.

A relative of this fray also is found in Greece, where it was known as *harpaston* and was alleged to have captured the fancy of all athletically inclined young men. The Romans adopted the game after their 2nd-century conquest of Greece and altered relatively few of the rules in popularizing their version, which even included a similar name, *harpastum*. Football then was a fierce battle that began when the ball was tossed into the air between two bands of charging players, who pushed, shoved, and did whatever was necessary to gain possession of the ball and advance it beyond what today would be considered the opponent's goal line.

The rugged Britons were quick to copy the Roman sport during the islands' occupation, but at least one historian wrote that the legions were late in bringing the game to Britain, since the Irish had kicked a stuffed ball about fifty years prior to the Romans' arrival.

By the 19th century, running with the ball, instead of merely kicking it, became an accepted practice. This allegedly arose when a youth caught a kicked ball and, instead of setting it down or taking a free kick, tucked it under his arm and sped goalward. This gross violation of the kicking rule was strongly condemned, and eventually British football branched into two distinct forms, soccer and rugby, the latter calling for running with the ball, the former frowning on it. The first governing body for clubs favoring the kicking game was the Long Football Association, founded in 1863; the opposing faction formed the Rugby Football Union in 1871.

From rugby came the American game of football.

American Football, 1869

Brought to the New World by early British colonists, football underwent many changes over a period of two hundred years. Not until the middle of the 19th century was a single style adopted, when it was taken up by many colleges and universities.

Two instances are cited as the origin of American football, one with somewhat more legitimacy than the other. The first, a game played between New Jersey's Rutgers and Princeton universities, was held in 1869, and followed the so-called 1867 Princeton Rules, which specified twenty-five players to a side. The Rutgers-Princeton clash, however, was actually soccer-style football, which to many authorities damages its claim as forerunner of the modern game.

The second more valid claim as the initiator of American football belongs to Harvard University. Disdaining the British version of the game, which prohibited handling the ball, Harvard in 1869 established the "Boston game," which featured running with the football. Harvard declined to join the Intercollegiate Football Association, because that outfit favored the British game, and instead contracted to play McGill University of Montreal, Quebec, which also preferred the rugbylike handling of the ball.

The first game played under the Harvard Rules took place in Cambridge, Massachusetts, in May 1874. A little more than two years later, a new body, acting on Harvard's precedent in revolutionizing the rulebook, was initiated as the second Intercollegiate Football Association, with a charter membership of five colleges. In November 1875, Harvard challenged Yale to the first game played under the Concessionary Rules, and thus began America's most hallowed football rivalry. Harvard won the game, largely because it was played, at the Crimsons' request, with fifteen men on each side instead of the eleven-man teams preferred by Yale.

*

The game continued to look like rugby until Walter Camp began a series of innovations in 1880.

Relying less on brawn and endurance, Camp emphasized strategy and quickness. He introduced a definite line of scrimmage from which play began, thus replacing the movable scrummage of rugby; he first suggested the position of quarterback — the trigger role for offensive maneuvers; and he pared down teams on the field from fifteen players to a side to eleven — seven forwards in the "line," a quarterback, two halfbacks, and a fullback.

When the sport became so vicious that eighteen players were killed in 1905, editorials demanded that football be outlawed in America. Only direct intervention from President Theodore Roosevelt saved the game. Roosevelt, an avid football fan, summoned athletic representatives from Harvard, Yale, and Princeton to the White House for an emergency session that not only commuted the game's death sentence but ultimately made football a safer and fairer sport.

Horse-racing originated in Assyria in 1500 B.C. The chariot race in Homer's *Iliad* was long regarded as the origin of the sport, but modern discoveries of clay tablets show that Assyrian kings maintained elaborate stables and professional trainers centuries before the Trojan War, the subject of Homer's classic. Seen here is a 19th-century English race.

Track and Field Sports, 2000 B.C.; Near East

The Egyptians held track and field events, as organized and formal sports, hundreds of years before the Christian era, and the early Irish, as far back as 1829 B.C., had begun their Lugnasad or Tailteann Games, which were predominantly track and field spectacles.

The Greeks, however, with their fetish of physical fitness, brought track and field into prominence. They put the sports on the agenda of almost all religious feasts, until finally track and field assumed their own identity in the Olympic Games, which began in 776 B.C. The early Olympics continued uninterrupted for more than a millennium, before the Roman emperor Theodosius stopped them in A.D. 393.

Early Olympic track and field events differed little from modern variations. The earliest known contest was the **stade,** a run of about 200 yards, first won by a professional cook and amateur athlete, Coroebus, a citizen of Elis. The tradition that only amateur athletes could compete in the Olympic Games started with the Greek rules. Records for distance in field events began during the Olympiad of 656 B.C., when a long-jumper named Chionis leaped 23 feet 1.5 inches, and a discus thrower named Protesilaus made a toss of 152 feet.

The Greeks, chauvinistic in athletics as well as society, ran male-only games, but eventually gave women their own contests, the Heraea Games, staged, like the Olympics, every four years with events similar to those of male competitors. The founder was Hippodamia, who around 600 B.C. organized the first of the Heraea to celebrate her marriage to Pelops. One popular contest was the 165-yard dash.

When Theodosius outlawed the games in the 4th century A.D., track and field ceased to exist on a formal basis for hundreds of years. The sports were not reinstated until the later Middle Ages, when the English became interested in athletic competition in the courts of the Norman conquerors.

Boxing, 1520 B.C.; Greece

The "manly art" practiced with gloves had its beginning in early Greece. A Greek mural, dating to about 1520 B.C. and depicting

In early Greek games the word "gymnastics" also embraced such activities as boxing, wrestling, and fencing. The first Olympic Games took place in July of 776 B.C., and this also marked the first time the term "Olympic Games" was used.

fighters wearing gloves, was discovered on the island of Thera. The early Greek fighers received no pay, only the glory of victory. They typically wore thongs of soft leather bound about the fists and often two thirds of the way up their forearms for additional protection.

First introduced into the Olympic Games in 688 B.C., fist fighting had no weight divisions; size, strength, and skill were the only qualifications for early pugilists. In the games forty years later, boxing combined with wrestling to form a new sport called *pancratium,* or complete contest, which experienced a brief vogue, then declined in popularity.

Some time during the 4th century B.C., tough, coarse leather was substituted, and the gloves themselves became weapons. The brutal practice of using them culminated during the peak of the Roman Empire with the introduction of a hand glove called the *ces-*

tus, which was studded with iron or brass nuggets. Wealthy men trained their slaves as boxers and forced *cestus*-wearing men to bludgeon one another to death in the Roman arenas. This perversion of the sport apparently delighted those who thronged to the arenas to witness such savagery. The ascendancy of Christianity and the concurrent decline of the Roman Empire put an end to pugilism as entertainment for centuries.

The sport's re-emergence in England was followed by the development of a strict code of prizefighting rules, drawn up on August 16, 1743, by the champion boxer Jack Broughton, whose reign spanned twenty-one years, until 1750. More than a hundred years later, the British added other restrictions to the sport with the Marquis of Queensberry Rules, adopted in 1867. Named for the eighth marquis of Queensberry, John Sholto Douglas, the codified rules gave boxing credibility, but its recognition as a professional sport in England was not established until after 1900. In a sordid irony, boxing was legalized following the ring death of Billy Smith (Murray Livingstone was his real name) at a fight in Covent Garden, London, on April 24, 1901.

Swimming

Swimming was scorned in Europe during the Middle Ages, because outdoor bathing was mistakenly cited as a cause of spreading the epidemics and plagues that periodically gripped the continent. Only in the latter portion of the 19th century did swimming return to popularity, and aquatic competition was restored for the first time in hundreds of years. When the modern Olympic Games began in Athens in 1896, swimming was on the agenda, and in 1904 diving events were added. Eight years later, women's swimming and diving became part of the competition.

Breaststroke, 1696; France

Early recreational swimming and lifesaving techniques stem largely from the breaststroke, thought to be the precursor of all other swimming strokes. Ideal for treading rough water, the breaststroke was described in a 1696 book by M. Thevenot, *The Art of Swimming,* as a wide lateral pull of the arms combined with a symmetrical action of the legs. The Frenchman compared the stroke to the movement of a frog. The breaststroke now is termed the "orthodox breaststroke" to avoid confusion with the butterfly breaststroke, or butterfly.

Butterfly, 1926; Germany

The butterfly breaststroke was a variation first introduced by a German, Eric Rademacher. An American, Henry Meyer, refined and popularized the stroke in the United States in 1933, arguing that the butterfly conformed to rules of the breaststroke as then written, and that it should be allowed in competitions. An international swimming dispute ensued, climaxing in 1953 with recognition of the butterfly as a legitimate stroke. Next to the crawl, the butterfly has emerged as the fastest competitive stroke. It originally was used with a frog kick, but later butterfly swimmers preferred a more vertical kick, along with both pulling and recovering both arms simultaneously to increase their speed.

Backstroke, 1912; United States

The backstroke in its present form was known as the back crawl and was revolutionized from an inverted breaststroke by U.S. Olympian Harry Hebner in 1912. A 1903 edition of *Swimming* by Archibald Sinclair and William Henry closely linked the backstroke to the trudgen. Henry described the backstroke in such a way that it seemed closer to the inverted breaststroke than to its present form: it combined arm action simultaneous with a frog kick as a swimmer lay on his back.

Hebner's innovation featured alternating arm pulls, like the crawl stroke. The first time he used this stroke, he was almost disqualified for swimming improperly in a race. His Olympic victory was preserved when American officials successfully argued that the rules required only that a swimmer remain on his back over the course of a race. Rivals recognized the superiority of Hebner's action and discarded the old backstroke, and in the ensuing half-century little change has been made in the stroke.

Crawl, 1893; Australia

The crawl probably originated with South Pacific natives as a means to keep from being swamped or submerged by powerful waves. Known also as the freestyle, it eventually became the fastest and most widely used stroke in swimming.

It was practiced early by natives in the Solomon Islands and then copied by two Australian brothers, Syd and Charles Cavill, who introduced the stroke to Europe in 1902 and to America a year later. The Cavills are thought to have learned the stroke in Australia from Harry Wickham, who began using it about 1893 and was described by one coach as "crawling through the water."

Because of the nationality of the Cavills, the stroke was originally known as the Australian crawl. It differed from the trudgen in leg action: it called for a fluttering kick, and the older stroke used a wider scissor kick, which created drag. When the crawl reached the United States, swimmers sped up the kicking motion to four kicks per stroke over the Cavills' two. The four-beat leg thrash, as the motion came to be called, was immediately deemed effective and was refined to one comparatively wide and three very narrow scissors motions — known as the four-beat trudgen crawl or the four-beat single-rhythm crawl.

The modern six-beat kick was first demonstrated successfully in 1917 by two women, Charlotte Boyle and Claire Galligan, both of New York's Women's Swimming Association. A year later, they had lowered records in long races of 800 yards and a mile by using the stroke, and shortly afterward the six-beat kick crawl was embraced universally as a recognized racing stroke.

The sport of archery originated in Italy in A.D. 300 as contests among the Genoese during the Roman reign. The bow and arrow were invented much earlier, about 48,000 years ago, with the emergence of Neanderthal man.

Bullfighting, A.D. 415; Spain

The earliest origins of bullfighting are found prior to the Punic Wars, when Iberian people realized the belligerent nature of the rowdy cattle that roamed their forests. They soon figured a way to harness the cattle and provoke them to stampede through opposing armies, and in 228 B.C., when the Carthaginian general Hamilcar Barca, father of Hannibal, drove his army into Ilici and blockaded the city, the embattled residents rounded up a large herd of cantankerous cattle, hitched them to wagons loaded with cords of kindling wood, then lighted them and incited the animals to charge at the invaders. The Iberians succeeded in destroying the enemy, and Hamilcar was killed during the battle.

Within a short time the Iberians had transformed their use of the cattle into a ritual to prove their manhood: they would deal a death blow to the horned bulls with an ax or lance. They also introduced at this time the cape for eluding the repeated thrusts of the beasts.

Bullfighting from horseback was introduced to Spain by the conquering Muslims from Africa, who would usually take the lance from their vassals, the natives, and demand that they prance on foot to tease the bulls into a frenzy in order to allow the mounted Muslim masters to move into better position for the kill.

By the 18th century bullfighting had evolved almost to the point where it stands today. Matadors were the actual bullfighters, who also wielded the cape; banderilleros were the assistants on foot who implanted darts to enrage the bull, and picadors were mounted assistants with pike poles or lances. The largest *plaza de toros* ("place of the bulls") in Mexico City opened in 1945 with a capacity of 50,000 spectators. Spain has more than four hundred *plazas de toros,* ranging in size from a few hundred seats to the tiered stadia of Madrid and Barcelona.

Chess, 2nd Century A.D.; Russia

It was long thought that the game originated in Persia, because the people of that nation were foremost among early players of chess. Recently, however, the discovery in the Soviet Union of two ivory chessmen dating to the 2nd century A.D. pre-empts the Persian claim, which would have placed the beginnings of chess around A.D. 590. The game is known to have reached Britain in 1255, and France some time later. The Internationale Fédération des Echecs (International Chess Federation) was established in 1924.

The Soviet Union, which has produced the last two world chess champions, boasts more than 7 million registered chess players.

Tennis, 1496; France

The modern outdoor sport of tennis is thought to have evolved from an indoor spectacle called *jeu de paume* ("palm game"), popular with French royalty in the late 15th century. It was originally a game played only by kings and their closest associates, and seventeen royal courts still survive in France and England; one, the Royal Tennis Court at Hampton Court Palace, was a favorite of King Henry VIII and was rebuilt under King Charles II in 1660.

As an outdoor activity, "field tennis" was first mentioned in the English tabloid *Sporting Magazine* on September 29, 1793. The game was also known then as "lawn racquets" and "pelota."

The first book of rules for tennis was published in 1873 by Major Walter Wingfield of Nantclwyd in north Wales, who is credited as the father of the modern game. His guide led to his taking out a patent on the game the next year. Among Wingfield's rules was an hourglass-shaped playing surface that he borrowed from badminton.

The americanization of tennis began in 1874, when a New Yorker, Mary Outerbridge, watched British soldiers playing the game at a garrison in Bermuda and returned to her home on Staten Island with two racquets and a set of balls. They were quickly expropriated by her brother, director of the Staten Island Cricket and Baseball Club, and put to use. Tennis courts sprang up rapidly in New York, New Orleans, Boston, Newport, Rhode Island, Plainfield in New Jersey, and Philadelphia.

The English, meanwhile, gave the game a formal home at the All-England Croquet Club, which in 1875 set aside one of its lawns at Wimbledon for tennis — and thus the hallmark of the game came to be.

Lottery, 1530; Florence

Games of chance in which prizes or cash are distributed among a winning group of people were popular in biblical times and are frequently mentioned in Scripture. In the Old Testament, for instance, Moses is instructed by God to take a census of the Israeli population and divide the land among the people by lot. And throughout Roman history, as well, there are numerous examples of lotteries: Emperors Augustus and Nero both distributed slaves and property by lottery during feasts and holidays.

The real precursor of modern lottery and state lotto games, however, is the public lottery held in Florence, Italy, in 1530. La Lotto de Firenze was the first sweepstakes to pay its winners with cash, and the custom spread quickly to other Italian cities. Once governments realized that the practice was an excellent source for raising revenue and unifying their populations, lotteries were enthusiastically promoted throughout Europe. The first national lottery emerged when the kingdoms of Italy became unified in 1861. Regular drawings, staged weekly, provided the government with new income. Again, the Italian version spread rapidly, leading to such contemporary games as lotto, bingo, keno, and policy, also known as the numbers game.

America's first dealings with lottery arrived with the dawn of the Revolution in 1776, when the nascent nation, desperately in need of funds for its army, established a lottery. Its attraction, however, for the strongly religious colonists, who looked on gambling as a sin, was minimal, and the national lottery was abandoned. The game was tried regionally, with smaller drawings, and thrived in college towns, where it accounted for "voluntary taxes" that eventually helped build such schools as Yale, Harvard, Dartmouth, Columbia (formerly King's College), William and Mary, and Brown.

Privately staged lotteries soon became popular in America, allowing merchants to sell goods and property for more money than could be garnered at public sale. In 1832 a Boston newspaper reported that the number of popular lotteries in the New England states alone totaled 420 in one year. Today many states depend on lotteries as a means of raising revenues without raising taxes. Often, some of the money is used for institutions of education.

Lacrosse, Pre–1492; North America

Lacrosse is the oldest team sport in North America, the oldest organized game, and also one of the few games indigenous to the continent. Lacrosse originated without foreign influences, such as those attributed to the beginnings of "American" baseball and football.

Under one of its earliest names, "baggataway," lacrosse was played in upper New York State and lower Ontario by the Six Nations of the Iroquois long before Columbus sailed into the New World. The sport was brutal and at times deadly. Among some tribes as many as a thousand players took part on each side, with goals miles apart, and a game might last for three days.

The spilling of blood was frequent and even encouraged. Strategy called for each player to disable as many opponents as possible with his stick, and only after this was accomplished could he focus his sights on scoring a goal. So rough and tumble was the game that the Cherokees named it "little brother of war" and considered its rigors excellent preparation for combat.

The origin of surfing can be documented only from the time the British explorer Captain James Cook first witnessed Polynesians riding waves on slats of wood in 1771. Surfing was regarded as "most perilous and extraordinary . . . altogether astonishing, and scarcely to be credited."

Lacrosse was included in the Olympic Games in 1908, then put on the roster of the 1928 and 1948 games as an exhibition sport. Of three world tournaments, the United States twice has won the championship; Canada, once. This is fitting, since the two countries were the first territories where the game was played.

Soccer, 1530; Italy

Because its simplified rules give rise to many imitations, soccer's roots often are disputed. A game with many similarities called *"tsu-chu"* was played in China during the 3rd and 4th centuries B.C., but the most striking early example of a soccerlike game is depicted in a print from Edinburgh, Scotland, dated 1672. Some two hundred years later, with the formation of the Football Association in England on October 26, 1863, soccer became standardized.

An earlier, Italian version, played in Florence about 1530, boasted twenty-six players to a side and strategy much like modern soccer's. The fact that its rules were clearly codified in a 1580 manual, *Discorsa Calcio*, adds credibility to the Italians' claim of originating the game, regarded today as the world's most popular sport. Its universal championship, the World Cup, contested every four years, is the most aggressively pursued prize in sports.

The world's oldest soccer club is the Sheffield Football Club of England, formed October 24, 1857; it was instrumental in helping refine the rule stipulating eleven players to a side, which went into effect in 1870.

Basketball, 16th Century; Mexico

The origin of this major American sport is still heatedly disputed. Many claim the game is exclusively American, invented by James Naismith on December 1, 1891, at the International Young Men's Christian Association Training School, now Springfield College, in Springfield, Massachusetts, where Naismith served as a physical education instructor.

Other authorities object strenuously and argue that the game can be traced to the 16th-century Aztecs of Mexico. They relate basketball to an Aztec game called *"ollamalitzli";* the object was to land a solid rubber ball through a fixed stone ring high on one side of a stadium. The player who accomplished this feat was awarded a prize that would make even today's most fanatic sports fans blush: the clothing of all spectators present. The captain of the opposing team forfeited even more — often his head, by decapitation.

An earlier game that also might have been a forerunner of basketball was *pok-ta-pok*, played in the 10th century B.C. by a Mexican tribe, the Olmecs. As in *ollamalitzli*, players had to pass a round object through a fixed ring.

Naismith, however, probably knew of neither of these predecessors when he hung two peach baskets (with their bottoms intact) at opposite ends of an overhead gymnasium track and chose teams of nine men each. He had designed the modest new exercise in the hope of relieving student boredom in his classes, and basketball did just that. Along with calisthenics and marching, the newfangled game proved to be so popular that students eagerly awaited class. During Christmas break of that school year, all eighteen of Naismith's students spread word of the game to friends and relatives, and the professor was besieged with requests for rules, which he hurriedly published in the campus paper, *The Triangle,* on January 15, 1892.

Naismith had gleaned many of the ground rules for his game from such sports as football, soccer, hockey, and other assorted outdoor activities, and his basic principles remain in force in basketball today. Among them were the rules that the ball must be handled, not kicked, and never carried. The game might have been called "boxball" today if Naismith had carried out his original plan to use boxes as goals.

In the early days of the game, participants were not limited in number, and it was common to find a hundred players on the court during a single game. By 1897, rules established that five players should appear for each team. Glass backboards were introduced in 1908, to the chagrin of overzealous spectators who used to sit behind a goal and reach out and deflect the ball to favor their team. The first semblance of the modern net basket was introduced by Lew Allen of Hartford, Connecticut, in 1892, when he suggested a cylindrical basket of heavy woven wire. The following year the Narragansett Machinery Company of Providence, Rhode Island, marketed an iron rim with a hammock-style basket akin to the nets used today. Open-bottomed nets, which considerably accelerated the game's pace, did not appear until 1912.

Ice Hockey, 1850; Canada

Pictorial evidence suggests that an early version of the game was played on the frozen canals of the Netherlands in the 17th century, but the game's real roots probably are to be found in Canada, where British soldiers were stationed during the 1850s and 1860s.

The Redcoats were acquainted with field hockey and equipped with ice skates, and they found a natural arena in the frozen lakes near their base. (Whether or not American Indians had fashioned iron skates and preceded the British and the Dutch in ice hockey is only speculative.)

Canadians soon proved avid hockey players. Rules like those for the modern game probably were first employed at Kingston, Ontario, in 1855. Before these refinements the game was ill organized, and sides varied from fifteen to twenty players. Though several Canadian cities zealously proclaim themselves as the cradle of hockey, the first recorded use of a puck instead of a ball is credited to Kingston in 1860.

Hockey superseded lacrosse as Canada's national pastime by the turn of the present century. The trophy symbolic of hockey supremacy, named after Frederick Arthur Stanley, Lord Stanley of Preston, governor general of Canada from 1888 to 1893, was donated, to be given annually to the top Canadian team, then determined by play-off. The sterling silver Stanley Cup was first awarded in 1894; its winner was the Montreal Amateur Athletic Association. For about the next twenty-five years hockey was strictly amateur, but with the birth of the National Hockey League in 1917, winning the cup became a professional achievement.

Baseball, 18th Century; England

Pinpointing baseball's origin has long baffled historians. There seems little doubt that the game came to America from England, where it was played as a children's diversion called "rounders" and is pictured in a 1744 woodcut as "base-ball."

But rounders differed strikingly from the version of the game introduced to America in the 1840s by Alexander Cartwright. The former called for a fielder to put out a runner heading for a base by hitting him with the ball, precluding use of the hardball, which was a hallmark of Cartwright's game. Cartwright recognized the need for tagging a runner in some way — either by touching him with the ball or with the hand holding the ball. The introduction of Cartwright's hardball, initially a miniature cricket ball, coincided with the formation of the first baseball organization, the Knickerbocker Baseball Club of New York in 1845, which helped popularize the sport that was to become America's national pastime.

Uncovering the game's British origin proved difficult because of men like A. G. Spalding, a sporting goods magnate, who formed the Spalding Commission in order to refute the "preposterous idea" that any foreign nation could have contributed in the slightest way to the great American invention of baseball. Defying all British claims by this spirit of nationalism, the Spalding Commission reported in the official 1908 *Baseball Guide* that the game was exclusively American, from its modern rules to diamond dimensions to even its name, which could be traced to Abner Doubleday, who had organized the first game on a field at Cooperstown, New York, in 1839. Only thirty years later, when a historian from the New York Public Library, Robert W. Henderson, issued his own scholarly study of the game's roots, was the English bid legitimated.

Corroborative evidence for the British case were the woodcut and the name applied to it ("base-ball"), and a novel by Jane Austen, written in 1798 and entitled *Northanger Abbey*, in which the heroine as a child is described as preferring to books "cricket, baseball, riding on horseback, and running about the country." The book containing the "base-ball" woodcut, *A Little Pretty Pocket-Book*, was published twice in America before the end of the 18th century, and there is evidence that soldiers in the Continental Army at Valley Forge may have played the game first as British subjects before joining the colonial cause.

Two other Americans have vied over the years with Doubleday for the distinction of "the father of baseball." Both of them — Cartwright and Harry Wight — certainly helped foster the game; Cartwright by drafting rule modifications in 1845 and Wight as a professional player and later manager of professional teams in Boston and Cincinnati.

Doubleday also promoted the game zealously, primarily during his cadet days at West Point. Doubleday's claim as baseball's originator has been disputed by witnesses who said that what he really played was the British version of the game. Cartwright usually is credited with Americanizing the game, although the Baseball Hall of Fame is located in Cooperstown, where Doubleday played his first exhibition.

References
Index

References

In a work such as this, which is indebted to so many journals, magazines, newspapers, trade books, and encyclopedias, it would be impractical to cite a reference for each and every fact. What would better serve a reader interested in any particular topic discussed in this book, I felt, is a list of the sources that I used in writing each chapter. That material is provided here, along with comments, when appropriate, as to a particular source's accessibility (or lack of it) to the nontechnical reader, as well as its comprehensiveness in treating a subject, and the extent to which it incorporates photos and illustrations. Because it is common to use a recognized dictionary as a standard for word usage, I felt it was also necessary to have a standard "fact bible," a source whose information I could assume was correct when other sources, be they books or articles, disagreed about information on a particular discovery, invention, or the like. Several months into research on this book, I decided that the new *Encyclopaedia Britannica III,* scholarly and exhaustively comprehensive work that it is, would serve excellently as just such a bible. Not that it is infallible, of course, but on the whole it is probably more accurate than many other reference works. Thus it was the final arbiter on all otherwise unresolvable disputes.

1 Creation: Stars to Shining Sea
  This chapter, beginning with the creation of the universe 14.5 billion years ago and ending with the birth of the solar system,

was compiled from a number of sources, the principal ones being:

The First Three Minutes: A Modern View of the Origin of the Universe, by Steven Weinberg, 1976, Basic Books. Weinberg, a Nobel laureate, devotes his highly readable book to a detailed account of what happened in the first 180 seconds after the Big Bang, the chaotic time when elementary particles came into existence and when matter fought antimatter for dominance.

Beginning at the same point, but carrying his account through the formation of stars, our sun and solar system, and into the origin and evolution of life on earth, is Robert Jastrow, in *Until the Sun Dies,* 1977, Norton. This is an excellent, easily accessible account of the origins of many things mentioned in the first four chapters of the present book.

Man and Cosmos, edited by J. Cornell and E. N. Haynes, 1975, Norton, gives a thorough history of the solar system, sun, moon, planets, and the evolution of Earth's atmosphere.

A more detailed technical account of the formation of stars and planets is *Protostars and Planets, Studies of Star Formation and the Origin of the Solar System,* edited by Tom Gehrels, 1978, University of Arizona Press.

The origins of oceans, which I touch on only briefly, is found in depth in *Origin of Continents and Oceans,* by Alfred Wegener, 1966, Dover.

2   Sea Life: Sponges to Sharks, and
3   Land Life: Millipedes to Monkeys

An excellent source, and one I relied on heavily, is *Life on Earth,* by David Attenborough, Little, Brown, 1977, Boston, a companion to the highly acclaimed thirteen-part BBC television series. Piling fascinating detail on the latest scientific fact, Attenborough covers the entire history of nature, from the emergence of tiny one-cell organisms in the primeval slime more than 3000 million years ago to apelike but upright man, "equally well adapted to life in the rain forest of New Guinea and the glass canyons of a modern metropolis." Highly recommended.

A more detailed, but still easily readable, account of the chemical origins of life is *The Origins of Life,* by Cyril Ponnamperuma, 1972, Dutton. The author, a professor of chemistry at the University of Maryland and former director of the program in Chemical Evolution at the Exobiology Division of NASA, is universally regarded as a leading authority on the earth's "primordial soup" and how it created and nurtured the formation of life.

A thoroughly readable account of evolution, though comprehended best by those with a background in biology, is "Evolution," the entire September 1978 issue of *Scientific American,* which also served as a major reference for this book.

Two highly technical subjects, the origins of genes and eukaryotes, are from: "The Origin of Genetic Information," by M. Eigen, W. Gardiner, P. Schuster, R. Winkler-Oswatitsch, *Scientific American,* April 1980; and "Origins and Evolution of Eukaryotic Intracellular Organells," papers from a conference Jan. 1980, Jerome F. Frederick, editor, New York Academy of Sciences, N.Y., 1981, vol. 361. The former presents a rigorous account of the laws governing natural selection of molecules and the formation of the earliest RNA and DNA genes, along with the proteins that produced the first error-correcting and -detecting codes that led to higher stages of evolution. The latter gives a technical account of the formation of cells with nuclei, which made possible the emergence of plants, animals, and man.

The selection on birds was enriched greatly by Attenborough's discussion on the origin of feathers and flying, as well as *The Complete Birds of the World,* by Michael Walters, 1980, T.F.H. Publications.

Readers interested in an alternative view of the origins of life can find it in *Life Itself: Its Origin and Nature,* by Nobel laureate Francis Crick, 1981, Simon & Schuster. Crick maintains that primitive bacteria did not originate on the earth's surface, but, through a process called "directed panspermia," were sent here in an unmanned rocket from another stellar system and deposited in the primeval oceans. From there it was a simple matter for these bacteria to feed on the primitive soup, and for all life as we know it to evolve. A similar theory, recently proposed by the British astronomer Fred Hoyle, suggests that the first bacteria rained to earth from passing (and melting) interstellar comets. Controversial as both theories are, they have many proponents and certainly make for interesting reading. Due to space limitations, neither theory is treated in this book.

Evidence from fossil records on the dates of origin of mammals, rodents, rabbits and hares (lagomorphs), and birds is from the *Encyclopaedia Britannica III,* where each species is treated separately (and alphabetically) in the appropriate volume.

4   Human Life: Primates to Pundits

The material on the origin and evolution of man and the human brain has been assembled from several excellent books, the major ones being: *The Dragons of Eden,* by Carl Sagan, 1977, Random House; *Origins,* by Richard Leakey and Roger Lewin, 1977, Dutton; and *Lucy: The Beginnings of Humankind,* by Donald C. Johanson and Maitland A. Edey, 1980, Simon & Schuster.

Lucy is the name given to the skeleton of a four-foot-tall prehuman female who walked the African plains on two legs nearly 4 million years ago. The oldest and most complete specimen of a two-legged human ancestor (40 percent of her bones were found), Lucy revealed that bipedalism — long considered a human characteristic — was fully evolved 2 million years before the earliest known specimens of *Homo,* the first true humans, appeared. Because Lucy's brain was still ape-sized, she seriously challenges the old notions that brain enlargement preceded bipedalism or that the two evolved in tandem. Although the date of Lucy's bones has recently been questioned (she may have died 500,000 years later than her discoverers first thought), her existence has opened for debate the issues of bipedalism and brain development, and this book's discussions of those subjects derives from Johanson and Edey's work, as well as from the review of their book in the *New York Times Book Review,* "About to Be Human," by Boyce Rensberger, Feb. 22, 1981.

Material on human behavior and gestures, and on primitive man's social interactions, is from three sources: *The Social Contract,* by Robert Ardrey, 1970, Atheneum; *The Hunting Hypothesis,* by Robert Ardrey, 1976, Atheneum; *The Naked Ape,* by Desmond Morris, 1970, McGraw-Hill; and *Gestures: Their Origins and Distribution,* by Desmond Morris, Peter Collett, Peter Marsh, and Marie O'Shaughnessy, 1979, Stein & Day.

The section "Continuous Sex" is from *The Sex Contract: The Evolution of Human Behavior,* by Helen E. Fisher, 1982, William Morrow. The author, an anthropologist at the New School for Social Research in New York City, notes that male-female bonding is rare among nonhuman primates and that it could have come about only as the result of an enormously increased female sexual capacity. The book's sexual hypothesis is controversial, since it attempts to establish that the "sex contract" occurred between 8 and 4 million years ago — a period for which there is still no fossil record — but the balance of the book's treatment of evolution is solid, and the volume is more fun than most anthropology works.

An excellent overview article on the origins of the five characteristics that separate man from other hominoids — a large neocortex, bipedality, unique jaw and molar formation, material culture, and unique sexual and reproductive behavior — is "The Origin of Man," by C. Owen Lovejoy, *Science,* vol. 211, no. 4480, Jan. 23, 1981.

Information on the Incas, Aztecs, and Mayas is from *History's Timeline: A 40,000-Year Chronology of Civilization,* by Jean Cooke, Ann Kramer, and Theodore Rowland-Entwistle, 1981, Crescent Books. It is an excellent general source for anyone interested in a bird's-eye view of history.

The chromosome discussion relating man, gorilla, and chimpanzee is from "The Origin of Man: A Chromosomal Pictorial Legacy," by Jorge J. Yunis and Om Prakash, *Science,* vol. 215, March 19, 1982.

The section on human culture is from "The Origins of Culture," by John H. Douglas, *Science News,* April 14, 1979.

References to the evolution of tools is from "Ethiopian Stone Tools Are World's Oldest," Roger Lewin, *Science,* vol. 211, Feb. 20, 1981.

5 Language: Sanskrit to Surnames

Material on the origins of language, as well as the roots of specific ones — Greek, Latin, English, French, Italian, Spanish, Yiddish, and German — has been assembled from the following: *Origins of the English Language,* by Joseph Williams, 1975, Free Press; *The Story of Language,* Mario Pei, 1966, New American Library; *The Treasure of Our Tongue,* Lincoln Barnett, 1967, New American Library; and the *Encyclopaedia Britannica III*'s section on language, vol. 10. Each of these sources gives a comprehensive picture of how and why language originated and of its spread throughout the world.

The chart on the branching of Indo-European languages is adapted from *Webster's New World Dictionary of the American Language,* Second College Edition, 1970, World; the book's introduction gives an excellent summary of the development of language. The chart on the evolution of romance languages is adapted from the *Encyclopaedia Britannica III*'s section on language, vol. 10.

The origins of state and city names is primarily from Pei; the material on first names and surnames is also from Pei, as well as

The Name Game, by Christopher P. Anderson, 1977, Simon & Schuster; *Origin of English Surnames,* by P. H. Reaney, 1976, Routledge & Kegan Paul, England; *Family Names: How Our Surnames Came to America,* by J. N. Hook, 1982, Macmillan.

The section "Ethnic Slurs" is from the *Dictionary of Slang and Unconventional English,* 7th edition, edited by Eric Partridge, 1976, Macmillan; and the delightful *Native Tongues,* by Charles Berlitz, 1982, Grossett & Dunlap. This is a treasure trove of language trivia and is strongly recommended.

The origins of various words and phrases used throughout the text are from any of the above, plus *Word Origins,* by Cecil Hunt, 1962, Philosophical Library; and *Phrase and Word Origins,* by Alfred H. Holt, 1961, Dover, both highly recommended for anyone interested in quick references to word and phrase origins.

6   Writing: Scribble to Shorthand

Information on the origin of the written word is primarily from three sources: *History Begins at Sumer,* by Samuel Noah Kramer, 1981, University of Pennsylvania Press. Curator emeritus of the university museum and one of the world's leading Sumerologists, Kramer presents thirty-nine essays that are "firsts" in the history of man's civilization in many of the major fields of human endeavor. Kramer's book covers the contributions of the Sumerians; information on Egyptian contributions is from *Native Tongues,* by Charles Berlitz, 1982, Grosset & Dunlap, and *The Roots of Civilization,* by Alexander Marshack, 1972, McGraw-Hill.

The origin of the alphabet is from Pei and Barnett and *History's Timeline,* both referred to above.

The information on paper, pens, ink, and shorthand is from the *Encyclopaedia Britannica III,* the volumes covering those particular subjects; as well as from *Ancient History,* by Michael Cheilik, 1969, Harper & Row; *The Guinness Illustrated Encyclopedia of Facts,* compiled by Norris McWhirter, 1981, Bantam; and *Printing Inks,* by J. I. McDuffy, Chemical Technology Review Series, vol. 139, Noyes, 1980. The section on Braille is from *Scientists and Inventors,* by Anthony Feldman and Peter Ford, 1979, Facts on File Publications.

7   **Beverages: Tea to Tab,**
8   **Fruits: Apples to Oranges,**
9   **Cereal: Corn to Croissants, and**
10 **Spices: Sugar to Salt**

These four chapters were among the most fun to research, because I love to eat and because there were so many interesting and amusing anecdotes surrounding the discovery of each food and beverage. These chapters were also the most frustrating to research, because space limitations meant I had to exclude many popular foods and their colorful histories. For example, I had intended to write a chapter on vegetables, another on nuts, another on cheeses, and another on spices; the origins of these foods are copiously documented. However, after much reading and deliberation, and after recognizing that this book could contain at most four chapters on foods (before it became a book on the origins of foods), I chose four general categories: beverages (which gave me a broad spectrum of drinks), fruits (because they had some of the most colorful discovery stories), cereals (because they were so important to early civilizations), and spices (also because of their historical role).

Many individual facts in these four chapters came from a number of sources, among them: *The Appetites of Man*, by Sally DeVore and Thelma White, 1978, Anchor; "Chocolate's Oh-So Sweet Seductions," by Jack Denton Scott, *Reader's Digest*, May 1981, and *The First of Everything*, by Dennis Sanders, 1981, Delacorte. However, three references were paramount to my research. A word about each of these.

The Joys of Wine by Clifton Fadiman and Sam Aaron, 1975, Abrams, is a must for the connoisseur as well as the neophyte. It is a sumptuous collection of wines, plus a huge encyclopedia on the subject, full of fascinating lore, of which I've taken just a few drops.

The World Encyclopedia of Food, by L. Patrick Coyle, Jr., 1982, Facts on File Publications. A hefty, fascinating volume whose 4000 entries cover every conceivable foodstuff and beverage, describing their history, folklore, means of cultivation or preparation, use in ethnic fare or in classic cuisine. Some things that I did not have room to digest: potatoes and pasta; ethnic specialties like haggis, matzoh, scones, and marzipan; delicacies ranging from fried locusts and magpie en casserole to caviar and truffles — plus every type of cheese, herb, nut, berry, fish, and pastry. A fun, informative book enhanced by at least 200 beautiful color plates, line drawings, and photographs.

Food, by Waverly Root, 1980, Simon & Schuster; also lushly illustrated. Root, who died in November 1982, devoted his writing career to food after his three-volume work, *The Food of France,* was published to much acclaim in 1958. This last work of his is a cornucopia of fascinating facts, amusing anecdotes, and the origins and esthetics of food from ancient times to the present, including references to food in literature and art. Written in a witty, personable style, Root's book, together with Coyle's, certainly must cover every food and beverage ever known to man. Both books made for fascinating browsing and are highly recommended.

11   Books: Dictionary to Dickens, and
12   Printing: Pulitzer to Popeye

Information on the origins of dictionaries and references to Samuel Johnson and Nathaniel Bailey are from the introduction to *Webster's New World Dictionary of the English Language,* Second College Edition, 1970, World. Though most of us tend to use the dictionary only for the correct spelling and meaning of words, usually the opening several pages, particularly in the *Webster's,* are a treasure house of information on the history and development of language and dictionaries.

The origin of dictionaries is from a dictionary, and the origin of encyclopedias is from an encyclopedia, the *Britannica III*'s vol. 6.

Most of the information on the origin of the novel is from two sources: *Introduction to English Literature,* by Jorge Luis Borges, 1974, University of Kentucky Press, and a beautifully written, highly entertaining volume, *The Novel,* by Richard Freedman, 1975, Newsweek Books.

The history of printing and the printing press is assembled from several sources, each highly comprehensive and detailed: *Printing Presses: History and Development from the Fifteenth Century to Modern Times,* by James Moran, 1973, University of California Press; *Printing and Publishing in Medieval China,* by Dennis Twitchett, 1981, Sandstone; *Printing: Its Birth and Growth,* by William Jaggard, a 1979 reprint of a 1908 edition, Longwood Press; and *History of Printing in America,* by Isaiah Thomas, edited by Marcus A. McCorison, 1975, American Antiquarian Society.

The information on the origins of newspapers and magazines is primarily from three sources: *Magazines in the Twentieth Century,* 2nd edition, by Theodore Peterson, 1964, University of Illinois Press; *Newspapers: An International History,* by Anthony Smith, 1979, Thames Hudson; and *Newspapers,* Leo E. Fisher, 1981, Holiday. The dates of first publication by various magazines and newspapers, as well as the table on cartoons, are mostly from the *Encyclopaedia Britannica* volumes on newspapers (vol. 13), magazines (vol. 11), and comics (vol. 4).

13 Education: Sumerians to Jesuits

From the dawn of civilization some 6000 years ago, historians recognize the origins of twenty-six civilizations, of which I have listed only the seven that still survive. The entire list can be found in *The Guinness Illustrated Encyclopedia of Facts,* by Norris McWhirter.

The detailed information on the nature and operations of one of civilization's first schools is from an informative and amusing essay in *History Begins at Sumer,* by Samuel Noah Kramer. Kramer, a leading Sumerologist, has personally translated hundreds of Sumerian cuneiform tablets, and his essay draws many entertaining parallels between school life then (in Sumer in 2500 B.C.) and now, from which I've only been able to extract a few details.

Most of the material in "Educational Innovations" is used with the permission of the sociologist D. Stuart Conger, from his comprehensive monograph "Social Inventions," 1974, Saskatchewan NewStart, Prince Albert, Canada. The monograph is available for under $5.00 from Mr. Conger at: Employment and Immigration Canada, Ottawa, Hull, K1A OJ9, Canada. Any alterations and updating in the material are the result of my own research.

14 Government and Organizations: Crowns to Corporations

The origin of kingship is from *History Begins at Sumer,* and the origins of government innovations are from D. Stuart Conger's monograph, both cited in the notes on Chapter 13.

Information on advertising is from: *History and Development of Advertising,* by Frank S. Presbrey, 1968, Greenwood, a reprint of a 1929 edition; and *Advertising in America,* by Stanley M. Ulanoff, 1977, Hastings.

The origins of paper money and coins is from: *History of Money in Ancient Countries from Earliest Times to the Present,* by Alexander

Del Mar, a 1969 reprint of an 1885 edition, B. Franklin; and *History of Money and Prices from the Thirteenth Century to the Beginning of the Twentieth Century,* by J. Schoenhof, 1977, Gordon Press. Information on the appearance of images on coins and bills is from *How Do They Do That?* by Caroline Sutton, 1981, Morrow.

Material on the origins of insurance is from: *Lloyd's of London: An Illustrated History,* by Raymond Flower and Michael W. Jones, 1974, Hastings; *Lloyd's of London,* Anthony Brown, 1974, Stein & Day; and the *Encyclopaedia Britannica III,* vol. 9, on insurance.

An interesting book on the birth of economic ideas and innovations, on which I've only briefly touched, is *Origins of Economic Ideas,* by Guy Routh, 1977, Random House.

15   Religion: Bible to Buddhism

Of the world's many religions, space has permitted me to cover only eight of the most ancient and widely practiced; the information is derived from *Religion,* by Myrtle Langley, 1981, Cook, a clearly written, copiously illustrated volume that gives countless interesting facts on the world's religions; and *The Guinness Illustrated Encyclopedia of Facts,* compiled by Norris McWhirter, which gives brief descriptions of the major religions.

16   Man's Best Friends: Afghan to Abyssinian, and
17   More Friends: Bunnies to Broncos

Animal lover that I am, I found it particularly difficult to keep these two chapters to moderate lengths. I was not helped by the tempting assortment of many excellent books on animals and pets. I list here, by animal, those references I relied upon.

Cat: The International Encyclopedia of Cats, edited by G. N. Henderson and D. J. Coffey, 1973, McGraw-Hill, contains everything you may wish to know about cats, with over 700 alphabetical entries on breeds, as well as articles on the role of the cat throughout history, and 160 illustrations and color photographs. *The Encyclopedia of the Cat,* by A. Sayer, is a beautifully illustrated book. It covers all aspects of keeping and understanding cats, as well as detailed sections on their evolution, biology, behavior, and psychology. *The Cat Catalogue,* edited by Judy Fireman, 1976, Workman Publications, is also a lavishly illustrated book, full of legends, trivia, and lore on the world's many breeds. *The Observer's Book of Cats,* by Grace Pond, 1978, Frederick Warne, London: Pond, well known as an international cat judge and as organizer of the National Cat Club

Show, presents in her small volume (153 pages) a store of fascinating information, from the history of the domestic cat in Egyptian times to the scientific breeding of modern species.

Dog: Encyclopedia of Dog Breeds, by E. Hart, 1980, T.F.H. Publications, includes everything you may ever wish to know about dogs, from their origins and evolution through training and breeding modern species. *Dogs of the World,* by Ivan Swedrup, 1969, Arco: Swedrup, a member of the Swedish Kennel Club, presents a comprehensive picture of the 115 dogs recognized by the American Kennel Club, as well as the major dog species from around the world.

Horse: The Encyclopedia of the Horse, edited by Wlwyn Hartley Edwards, Octopus, is graced with some 400 color illustrations, and features text on over 150 horse and pony breeds throughout the world, as well as a glossary of more than 500 equestrian terms.

Others: The New Larousse Encyclopedia of Animal Life, edited by Maurice Burton, Bonanza Books: this beautifully illustrated volume contains 800 color photographs and covers practically every animal from amoeba to zebra. *The Observer's Book of Pets,* by Tina Hearne, 1978, Frederick Warne, London, covers most of the common pets, giving in brief their origins and information on breeding, health and feeding. One particularly interesting feature is a list of plants that are poisonous to animals. Equally as comprehensive as all the above is *Encyclopedia of Animals,* edited by David Stephen and Tom McCormack, 1979, St. Martin's Press.

18 Communications: Smoke Signals to Stereo

Information on the origins of stereo and hi-fi is from "A Hundred Years of Stereo: Fifty of Hi-Fi," by Barry Fox, *New Scientist,* Dec. 24, 1981, pp. 908–912. Information on FM radio is from "Recalling the Genius Who Devised FM Radio," by Hans Fantel, *New York Times,* Dec. 27, 1981.

Information on the origins of motion pictures is from: *The Film Encyclopedia,* by Ephraim Katz, 1979, Crowell. In addition to its comprehensive listing of actors, films, directors, and awards, it has several excellent sections on the history and development of film technology. *Cinema,* by Kenneth W. Leish, 1974, Newsweek Books, is a lucidly written, wonderfully illustrated volume that presents a comprehensive history of cinema, as well as several excellent tables on Academy Award winners, top-grossing motion pictures, and awards for best foreign films.

The early development of telegraphy, Morse code, the telephone, and television is assembled from several sources: *Scientists and Inventors*, by Anthony Feldman and Peter Ford. This is an excellent book for the general reader interested in the development of technological inventions. As a history of breakthroughs and discoveries, the book presents information in the form of individual biographies on each great inventor from Empedocles to Einstein, laid out in chronological order.

Two additional sources from which I selectively borrowed facts and an occasional anecdote are: *Ascent of Man*, by Jacob Bronowski, 1973, Little, Brown, a companion to the excellent television series featuring the author; and *The Dictionary of Discoveries*, by Isaac A. Langnas, 1968, Greenwood.

19 Music: Renaissance to Rock, and
20 Instruments: Oboe to Bagpipes

Ever since the first *Grove's Dictionary of Music and Musicians* attained completion in 4 volumes (1890), through the appearance of the 5th edition in 9 volumes (1954), it has been held in high esteem throughout the English-speaking world. Now, however, all but 3 percent of that 5th edition has been replaced by *The New Grove Dictionary*, in 20 volumes and 18 million words, by Macmillan Publishers Ltd, of England (not to be confused with the Macmillan Publishing Co., Inc., in this country). This work was invaluable in researching the two chapters on music in this book. My treatment of the origin and evolution of musical notation, for example, is a 1-page condensation of 100 pages in Grove, whose 150 graphics on the subject are an education in themselves. So too are the divisions dealing with the origins and development of musical instruments.

Despite the comprehensiveness of *Grove*, I also borrowed from three smaller, more compact sources: *History of Music*, by Hugh M. Miller, 1973, Harper & Row; *Music*, by Frederic V. Grunfeld, 1974, Newsweek Books; and my brief comments on Handel and Bach, Mozart and Haydn, are from a book that for more than a decade has been a favorite of mine, *The Lives of Great Composers*, by Harold Schonberg, 1970, Norton.

For those interested in purchasing *The New Grove Dictionary*, it costs $1900 (plus $25 for shipping), or may be paid on an installment plan of payments of $190 per month for 10 months, with 2 volumes delivered for each settlement. Much as I'd love to own it, I used a library's copy.

21 Theater: Comedy to Kabuki

The sections on the origin of musical comedy, drama, mime, and comedy are constructed from information in three sources: *Ancient Greek Literature and Society,* by Charles R. Beye, 1975, Anchor; *Theater,* by Jacques Burdick, 1974, Newsweek Books, and *Encyclopedia of American Theater,* by Edwin Bronner, 1980, A. S. Barnes.

The section on dance is mainly from *Dance,* by Jack Anderson, 1974, Newsweek Books. The Newsweek Books listed throughout these notes and references are part of the magazine's "World of Culture" series and cover a wide range of subjects from mythology to cinema. A list of the books and their cost is available from Newsweek Books, 444 Madison Avenue, New York, N.Y. 10022. They all are highly recommended.

Material on the origin of the circus from ancient times to the present is from three sources: *Circus: From Rome to Ringling,* by Marian Murray, 1956, Greenwood; *Circus in America,* by Charles P. Fox and Tom Parkinson, 1969, Country Beautiful; and *Circus: Its Origin and Growth Prior to 1835,* by Isaac J. Greenwood, a 1970 reprint of an 1898 edition, B. Franklin.

22 Art: Painting to Porcelain

The material on the origins of painting and paint came from two sources: *Painting,* Terisio Pignatti, 1974, Newsweek Books, and "The Archeology of Lascaux Cave," by Arlette Leroi-Gourham, *Scientific American,* June 1982. The article details the cave paintings at Lascaux, France, presenting floor and wall plans, and the author speculates on the various reasons for the existence of the art, from purely esthetic purposes to religious and fertility rituals. The paper also gives a fascinating account of the chemical composition of early paint, and the various techniques the cave dwellers used to apply it to walls and ceilings.

Information on the origins of jewelry came from two sources: *Jewelry Through 7000 Years,* British Museum Publication Series, 1977, Barron; and *History of Jewels and Jewelry,* by Ingrid Kuntzsch, 1981, St. Martin's Press.

Material on early pottery and ceramics is from: *Pottery in Ancient Times,* by Rivka Gonen, 1974, Lerner Publications; and *Pottery and Early Commerce: Characterization and Trade in Roman and Later Ceramics,* edited by D. P. Peacock, 1977, Academic Press.

The section on glass is from the *Encyclopaedia Britannica III,* vol. 17, on stained glass, and from "Glass: Brilliant Offspring from the

3,000 Year Marriage of Form and Technology," by Alfred Meyer, *Science 81,* May 1981.

23 Medicine: Hospitals to Hypnosis

A fascinating subject, since it deals with the health and well-being of humans, medicine, as practiced in primitive times through the early Greek and Roman periods into the Middle Ages, is comprehensively covered in several references. One of the best I found is *History of Medicine,* 2 volumes, by Henry A. Segerist, Oxford University Press. Volume 1 covers all aspects of primitive and archaic drugs and surgical procedures; volume 2 deals with the more sophisticated ministrations of the early Greeks, Hindus, and Persian physicians, soothsayers, and folk healers. Each volume contains sections on herbal medicines of the time.

More detailed material on the first drug catalogue can be found in the essay "Medicine: The First Pharmacopoeia," in *History Begins at Sumer,* by Samuel Noah Kramer. Translating the cuneiform diary of an anonymous Sumerian physician who lived toward the end of the third millennium B.C., Kramer presents the animal, plant, and vegetable remedies that at least one early physician prescribed for the sick.

The table on the origins of drugs is compiled from four sources: *Drugs from A to Z: A Dictionary,* 2nd edition, by Richard R. Lingeman, 1974, McGraw-Hill; *Drugs and Foods from Little-Known Plants,* by Siri V. Altschal, 1973, Harvard University Press; *Drugs in America: A Social History, 1800–1980,* by H. Wayne Morgan, 1981, Syracuse University Press; and *The Guinness Illustrated Encyclopedia of Facts,* compiled by Norris McWhirter.

Material on the origins of soap and hospitals is from the *Encyclopaedia Britannica III*'s volumes on those two subjects, 16 and 8. Material on antibiotics and inoculations is largely from *Scientists and Inventors,* by Anthony Feldman and Peter Ford. This book presents historical biographies on the discoverers of antibiotics and the practice of inoculation, Sir Alexander Fleming, and the 18th-century physician Edward Jenner.

The origin of hypnosis can be found in *Supersenses,* by Charles Panati, 1974, Quadrangle; *Hypnosis; Theory, Practice and Application,* by Raphael H. Rhodes, 1960, Citadel Press; and *Hypnosis: A Journey Into the Mind,* by Anita Anderson-Evangelista, 1980, Arco.

An excellent book on the origins of psychiatry and the early theories of the mind is *Mechanics of the Mind,* by Colin Blakemore,

1977, Cambridge University Press. Dr. Blakemore also presents the evolution of theories on sleep, memory, and sensation, plus a critical analysis of the abuses of early psychosurgery. This latter topic is richly elaborated on in *Lobotomy: Resort to the Knife,* by David Shutts, 1982, Van Nostrand. Shutts focuses on a central figure in the early development of lobotomies, the dapper and charismatic American surgeon Walter Freeman. Information and quotations on Freeman are from Shutts's book, which makes for enlightening and horrifying reading.

Information on modern techniques of food preservation is largely from *Scientists and Inventors,* by Anthony Feldman and Peter Ford.

24 Land: Wheels to Automobiles,
25 Sea: Sailboats to Submarines, and
26 Air: Balloons to Bombers

These three chapters cover the broad spectrum of transportation through the ages and have been compiled from many articles and specialized encyclopedias on each mode of transportation. The vehicles are presented here in alphabetical order.

Airplanes: "The Origins of the First Powered, Man-Carrying Airplane," by F. E. C. Culick, *Scientific American,* July 1979; *The International Encyclopedia of Aviation,* edited by D. Mondey, Outlet. This lavishly illustrated book, containing over 1200 black-and-white and color photographs, is an invaluable reference work for anyone interested in all aspects of civil, military, and space aviation from the earliest planes to jets of the future. Two equally impressive books, focusing on the men and the companies behind the birth of the world's most notable aircraft, are *World's Greatest Airplanes: The Heinkel IIE 111 to the Concorde,* and *World's Greatest Airplanes: The Wright Flyer to the Piper Cub,* both by Richard Trombley and published in 1981 by Lerner Publications.

Airplanes in military service is from *Vehicles at War,* by Dennis Bishop and Chris Ellis, 1979, A. S. Barnes, which is a comprehensive history of the vehicles of mechanized warfare from the earliest suggestion for the use of traction engines in the Crimea to the missile carriers of the Cold War.

Bicycles: A treatise on the design and construction of the vehicles, *Bicycles and Tricycles,* by Archibald Sharp, Massachusetts Institute of Technology Press, is a 1977 reprint of a superb 1896 work. The treatise, first published in London by Sharp, an instructor in engineering design at the Central Technical College in

South Kensington, was the only book of its kind until 1975, when the MIT Press published *Bicycling Science: Ergonomics and Mechanics,* by Frank Rowland Whitt and David Gordon Wilson, a work that reviews later design developments in bicycling by means of modern engineering principles. Both volumes are highly recommended for bike enthusiasts, as is a recent article, "Pedal Pushing," by David Holzman, in *Technology Illustrated* Aug.–Sept. 1982, which presents an excellent overview of the origin and evolution of bicycles.

Cars: A large number of books exist on the origin and development of cars, and though I've borrowed facts here and there from several references, these were the three principal works: *The Complete Encyclopedia of Motor Cars, 1885 to the Present,* edited by G. N. Georgans, 1973, Dutton; and *World of Cars,* by the editors of *Automobile Quarterly,* a lushly illustrated volume covering some 200 of the world's most beautiful cars; and *Scientists and Inventors,* by Anthony Feldman and Peter Ford.

Railroads: Principal sources for this section were: *America's Railroads,* by Don Ball, Jr., 1980, Norton. It presents a sweeping look at the American railroad system's transition from steam to diesel engines, with a treasury of information about the engines used during the 1940s and 1950s, covering the history, lore, and personalities of such lines as the Santa Fe, Illinois Central, and Union Pacific. *A Treasury of Railroad Folklore,* by B. A. Botkin and A. F. Harlow, boasts that it is the largest collection of railroad lore in print, covering the men, machines, robbers, gamblers, hobos, and empire builders of the famous lines, and it certainly goes a long way toward living up to that claim. A good history of railroads in the United States is *American Heritage History of Railroads in America,* by Oliver Jensen, 1975, American Heritage. Copiously illustrated with historical photographs, authentic paintings of the period, and sketches and cartoons, the book contains stories of the ingenious men who built the transportation system that opened the American West.

Ships: This section was compiled primarily from three sources: *Sailing Ships: The Story of Their Development from the Earliest Times to the Present Day,* by E. K. Chatterton, 1977, Gordon Press; *Sailing Ship: Great Ships Before the Age of Steam,* by C. B. Colby, 1970, Coward; *Sailing Ship: Six Thousand Years of History,* by Romola Anderson and R. C. Anderson, Arno.

The three chapters on transportation origins were also greatly enriched from facts gleaned from these other works: *Let's Discover*

Series, edited by Patricia Daniels, vol. 12, *Land;* vol. 13, *Ships and Boats,* and vol. 14, *Flying; The International Encyclopedia of Transportation,* edited by D. Mondey, which, as its name implies, tells you everything you ever wanted to know about all modes of transportation; and *History of Roads* by Geoffrey Hindley, 1972, Citadel Press.

27   Technology: Flushing Toilets to Pneumatic Tires, and

28   Science: Metrics to Microscopes

An excellent general reference on the early scientific and technological developments and their effects on society is *Ascent of Man,* by Jacob Bronowski. Other general references I used, which cover a broad range of developments and inventions, are: *Technology in America: A History of Individuals and Ideas,* edited by Carroll W. Pursell, Jr., 1981, MIT Press; *Technology in the Ancient World,* by Henry Hodges, 1970, Knopf; *Technology in the Western Civilization,* 2 volumes, edited by Melvin Kranzberg and Carroll W. Pursell, Jr., vol. 1: "The Emergence of Modern Industrial Society: Earliest Times to 1900"; vol. 2: "Technology in the Twentieth Century," 1967, Oxford University Press; and *Technology of Man, A Visual History,* by Carlo M. Cipolla and Derek Birdsall, 1980, Holt, Rinehart & Winston.

Some sections are derived from specialized sources. The material on the origins of clocks is from *The History of Clocks and Watches,* by Eric Bruton, 1980, Rizzoli International; as well as from the *Encyclopaedia Britannica*'s volumes on timekeeping (18) and clocks (4). Explosives is from two works of that title: *Explosives,* by Gail K. Haines, 1976, Morrow; and *Explosives: Their History and Manufacture,* 3 volumes, by Arthur Marshall, 1980, Gordon Press. Glass is from "Glass: Brilliant Offspring from the 3,000 Year Marriage of Form and Technology," by Alfred Meyer, *Science 81,* May 1981.

An excellent overview article on the appearance of machines throughout the ages is "The Mechanization of Mankind," by Peter Marsh, *New Scientist,* February 12, 1981.

Information on the origins of microscopes and telescopes is primarily from: *Microscope Past and Present,* by S. Bradbury, 1969, Pergamon; *Telescope,* by Louis Bell, 1981, Dover; and *History of the Telescope,* by Henry C. King, 1979, Dover.

Material on photography is from: *Photography: The Early Years,* by George Gilbert, 1981, Harper & Row; and *Photography: A Handbook of History, Materials and Processes,* by Charles Swedlund, 1974, Holt, Rinehart & Winston.

Information on the origins of the computer and calculating devices is from three recent articles: *Time* magazine's cover story, "Machine of the Year: A New World Dawns," January 3, 1983; "Can Ada Run the Pentagon?" in *Newsweek,* January 10, 1983 (Ada being Augusta Ada Byron, Lord Byron's daughter, and confidante of Charles Babbage); and "The Digit," *Science Digest,* March 1982.

29   Sports and Games: Baseball to Bullfighting

This chapter could easily have been a large book in its own right. Indeed, there are so many books devoted to the history of various sports and games that it was difficult to narrow them down to the few from which information in this chapter was assembled. After much searching and perusing, I found my principal references to be: *Sport in Greece and Rome,* by H. A. Harris, edited by H. H. Scullard, 1972, Cornell University Press; *Sport in Classic Times,* by Alfred J. Butler, 1975, W. Kaufman; *Sports in America,* by James A. Michener, 1977, Fawcett; and *History of Sport and Physical Education to 1900,* Earle F. Zeigler, 1973, Stipes.

Two particularly fun books, chock full of sports firsts and trivia, are: *Sports Firsts,* by Patrick Clark, 1981, Facts on File Publications; and *Sports Roots: How Nicknames, Namesakes, Trophies, Competitions and Expressions Came to Be in the World of Sports,* by Harvey Frommer, 1979, Atheneum.

The section on baseball is from: *The Official Encyclopedia of Baseball,* 11th revised edition, by Hy Turkin and S. C. Thompson, revision by Peter Palmer, 1979, A. S. Barnes; and *Baseball: The Early Years,* by Harold Seymour, 1960, Oxford University Press.

Brief synopses on the origins of most major sports are also found in the *Guinness Book of World Records,* compiled by Norris McWhirter.

A superb sports series is the Sports Illustrated Books on virtually every major and minor sport from badminton to volleyball. The volumes are published by either Lippincott or Harper & Row.

Two excellent reference books on games, a topic I've only briefly touched on, are *History of Board Games,* by Robert McCornville, 1974, Creative Publications; and *History of Board Games Other Than Chess,* by J. H. Murry, a 1978 reprint of a 1952 edition, Hacker.

The information selected from many of the above sources was checked for confirmation against the appropriate volume for each sport in the *Encyclopaedia Britannica III*. This seemed prudent, since there was greater variation in facts, dates, attributions of origins, and the like in the area of sports and games than in almost any other topic I had the pleasure of researching.

END OF THE VOLUME.

FOR THE BEST IN PAPERBACKS, LOOK FOR THE

In every corner of the world, on every subject under the sun, Penguin represents quality and variety—the very best in publishing today.

For complete information about books available from Penguin—including Puffins, Penguin Classics, and Arkana—and how to order them, write to us at the appropriate address below. Please note that for copyright reasons the selection of books varies from country to country.

In the United Kingdom: Please write to *Dept. JC, Penguin Books Ltd, FREEPOST, West Drayton, Middlesex UB7 0BR.*

If you have any difficulty in obtaining a title,.please send your order with the correct money, plus ten percent for postage and packaging, to *P.O. Box No. 11, West Drayton, Middlesex UB7 0BR*

In the United States: Please write to *Consumer Sales, Penguin USA, P.O. Box 999, Dept. 17109, Bergenfield, New Jersey 07621-0120.* VISA and MasterCard holders call 1-800-253-6476 to order all Penguin titles

In Canada: Please write to *Penguin Books Canada Ltd, 10 Alcorn Avenue, Suite 300, Toronto, Ontario M4V 3B2*

In Australia: Please write to *Penguin Books Australia Ltd, P.O. Box 257, Ringwood, Victoria 3134*

In New Zealand: Please write to *Penguin Books (NZ) Ltd, Private Bag 102902, North Shore Mail Centre, Auckland 10*

In India: Please write to *Penguin Books India Pvt Ltd, 706 Eros Apartments, 56 Nehru Place, New Delhi 110 019*

In the Netherlands: Please write to *Penguin Books Netherlands bv, Postbus 3507, NL-1001 AH Amsterdam*

In Germany: Please write to *Penguin Books Deutschland GmbH, Metzlerstrasse 26, 60594 Frankfurt am Main*

In Spain: Please write to *Penguin Books S. A., Bravo Murillo 19, 1° B, 28015 Madrid*

In Italy: Please write to *Penguin Italia s.r.l., Via Felice Casati 20, I-20124 Milano*

In France: Please write to *Penguin France S. A., 17 rue Lejeune, F–31000 Toulouse*

In Japan: Please write to *Penguin Books Japan, Ishikiribashi Building, 2–5–4, Suido, Bunkyo-ku, Tokyo 112*

In Greece: Please write to *Penguin Hellas Ltd, Dimocritou 3, GR–106 71 Athens*

In South Africa: Please write to *Longman Penguin Southern Africa (Pty) Ltd, Private Bag X08, Bertsham 2013*